UTSA DT LIBRARY RENEWALS 458-2440

DATE DUE

GAYLORD			PRINTED IN U.S.A.

Planning Power

Planning Power

Town planning and social control in colonial Africa

Ambe J. Njoh

London and New York

First published 2007
by UCL Press

The name of University College London (UCL) is a registered trademark used by
UCL Press with the consent of the owner

UCL Press is an imprint of the Taylor & Francis Group, an informa business

Taylor & Francis
2 Park Square, Milton Park, Abingdon, Oxon OX14 4RN, UK

Published in the USA
by Routledge-Cavendish
270 Madison Ave, New York, NY 10016

© 2007 Ambe J. Njoh

Typeset in Times by
HWA Text and Data Management, Tunbridge Wells
Printed and bound in Great Britain by
Biddles Ltd, King's Lynn

British Library Cataloguing in Publication Data
A catalogue record for this book is available from the British Library

Library of Congress Cataloging in Publication Data
Njoh, Ambe J.
Planning power : social control and planning in colonial Africa / by Ambe J. Njoh.
    p.   cm.
1. City planning–Africa–History. 2. Regional planning–Africa–History.
3. Colonies–Africa–Administration. 4. Social control–Africa. 5. Power (Social
sciences)–Africa. 6. Colonial cities–Africa. I. Title.
HT169.A3N47 2007
307.1'216096–dc22
2006025218

ISBN10: 1–84472–160–4 (hbk)
ISBN10: 0–203–96486–1 (ebk)

ISBN13: 978–1–84472–160–3 (hbk)
ISBN13: 978–0–203–96486–6 (ebk)

To a teacher, mentor and friend,
Michael Mattingly

Contents

Preface

There is certainly no shortage of works dedicated to highlighting the distinction between British and French colonial ideology and practice. Although consensus on the nature and magnitude of the distinction is rare, there is a considerable level of agreement that the two European colonial powers differed considerably on the following three related dimensions:

- colonial administrative philosophies;
- rationales for the colonial project; and
- racial ideologies.

Colonial administrative philosophies

A lot has been written on the European colonial era in Africa. However, more often than not, the focus is on how the colonial administrative strategy of one European power differed from the rest. Resulting from efforts in this connection is a significant degree of consensus that the British were inclined to adopt the 'indirect rule' strategy while the French favoured 'direct rule'. A more rigorous analysis of the administrative practices of the British, French and other European colonial powers reveal that none of them had monopoly over any specific administrative strategy. Thus, the French employed the 'indirect rule' strategy whenever it was convenient or necessary to do so. Similarly, the British adopted the 'direct rule' strategy whenever the occasion was apropos. Thus, the difference in the colonial administrative styles of these two colonial powers, for example, is often exaggerated.

Rationale for colonization

Another aspect of the colonial project that is often amplified relates to the objectives of the different colonial powers. In this regard, the British colonial enterprise is said to have been motivated by economic reasons, while the French were driven into colonialism by a desire to bolster their country's prestige at home, throughout Europe and globally. Ronald E. Robinson (1964: vii) succinctly captures this perceived difference in the following words:

The liberal Anglo-Saxons painted the map red in pursuit of trade and philanthropy, and the nationalistic French painted it blue, not for good economic reasons, but to pump up their prestige as a great nation.

Robinson concedes that this may be an oversimplification of the objectives of the colonial projects of the two European colonial powers. However, he contends that given the state of their economies during the Victorian age, the need for colonies was commercially great for Britain but not for France. To be sure, while France's economy was self-sufficient, with very limited, if any, foreign trade, and little appetite for foreign imports, the British society and industries had developed a voracious appetite for food and raw materials from abroad. This explains the fact that colonial commerce constituted a large portion of Britain's economic interest but a very insignificant part of France's. However, to contend, based on these differences, that Britain's desire for colonies was driven by economic interest, while France's was not, constitutes an oversimplification. It is equally a brave simplification to attribute exclusively to France the desire to use colonies as tools for ameliorating the prestige of metropolitan countries. Yet, this is exactly the impression one gets from the following statement by Robinson (1964: ix).

French imperialism by the end of the nineteenth century was driven by nothing more complicated than a passion for national honour and cultural extraversion.

It is foolhardy to talk of the goals and objectives of the colonial projects of different colonial powers in absolute terms. Rather, these goals and objectives can be more accurately discussed in terms of gradations or a continuum. Thus, the French may rank higher on this continuum than the British with respect to employing colonialism as a tool for attaining the goal of national honour; and lower than Britain when it comes to using colonies to attain economic goals.

Racial ideologies

It is widely believed that the French colonial project was rooted in a sense of cultural superiority while that of the British was grounded in a sense of racial superiority. Thus, while the British emphasized race, the French considered culture to be the distinguishing mark of European superiority. In theory this had two implications. On the one hand, the British could never accept a non-Caucasian as an equal since race is a permanent and inalterable attribute. On the other hand, the French were prepared to accept non-Caucasians as equals as long as they could embrace French culture.

Theory and reality

It would appear that the differences characteristic of British and French colonialism highlighted above are confined to theory. This assertion holds particularly true in the context of town and country planning. Planning councils or committees in, for instance, British colonial Kenya were just as exclusive of native Africans as were cognate bodies in French colonial Madagascar. Also, it is hard to miss the fact that French colonial towns such as Brazzaville, Congo and Conakry, Guinea were just as racially segregated as British colonial towns such as Freetown, Sierra Leone and Lagos, Nigeria despite the theoretical differences in the racial ideologies of French and British colonial authorities. Furthermore, French colonial Abidjan had as much of an economic objective as did British colonial Lagos. Port cities such as these were designed mainly to facilitate the evacuation of raw materials from the colonial territories for onward transmission to the metropolis. This renders hollow any theory that attributes economics, trade and commerce as objectives of the colonial enterprise exclusively to Britain.

What accounts for this apparent inconsistency between theory and reality? Analysts have largely ignored this important question. With a few exceptions (e.g., Njoh, 2004; Freund, 2001; Goerg, 1998), researchers are yet to conduct meaningful comparative studies of the urban planning policies of different colonial powers in Africa. Far more absent from the literature are studies focalizing on the impact of racial ideology on spatial structures in colonized areas. The question is at the heart of the discussion in this book. The book marshals evidence from the planning policy field throughout colonial Africa to demonstrate that the French and British colonial authorities throughout sub-Saharan Africa employed identical strategies to attain equally identical goals of the colonial enterprise. Thus, theoretical differences made no difference to the practice and outcome of colonialism.

The planning policy field, particularly the built environment, constitutes an ideal context for examining questions relating to the strategies that were employed to attain the multi-faceted and complex objectives of the colonial enterprise in Africa. This is because the built environment in colonial Africa constitutes an embodiment and reflection of the colonizers' interests. Yet, the literature is replete with gaps on how colonial town and country planning legislation was employed to facilitate the realization of these interests. Similarly, questions regarding how colonial authorities employed spatial policies in efforts to accomplish broader goals of the colonial enterprise are yet to be adequately addressed.

A central objective of this book is to contribute to efforts aimed at addressing these and cognate questions. What types of programmes and projects were conceived, formulated and implemented in the town and country planning policy field by French and British colonial authorities in Africa? Which specific pieces of planning legislation programmes and projects were used to accomplish which particular goals of the colonial enterprise? How did these strategies differ from one colonial territory to another and from one locale to another within the same territory?

It is hoped that uncovering answers to these questions will help promote understanding of:

- the origins, nature and extent of formal town and country planning in sub-Saharan Africa; and
- the nature as well as the political, social and economic goals of colonial town and country planning in the region.

The stated goal of colonial town and country planning was to accomplish the laudable objectives of ensuring sound architectural standards, protecting public health and promoting the efficiency and effectiveness of the built environment. A more critical look reveals that despite their avowed intentions, colonial authorities employed urban planning policies and projects as tools to facilitate the accomplishment of broader goals of the colonial enterprise, including but not limited to:

- self-preservation;
- cultural assimilation;
- political domination;
- social control;
- territorial conquest; and
- the perpetuation and consolidation of colonial rule.

This book summons a preponderance of evidence to show how urban and regional planning legislation was employed to facilitate attainment of these goals. The book focuses particularly on the town and country planning activities of British and French colonial authorities. The importance of interrogating the French and British experiences hinges on two factors. The first is the fact that France and Britain controlled most of Africa during the colonial era. The second relates to the need to explore the impact on town and country planning policy, of the difference between Britain's 'indirect rule' and France's 'direct rule' administrative strategies. I demonstrate that despite rhetoric to the contrary, both colonial powers employed town and country planning legislation, projects and schemes to accomplish many, sometimes disparate, objectives of colonialism and imperialism. A few procedural differences notwithstanding, French and British colonial planners shared common political, philosophical and ideological goals.

Acknowledgements

The seeds for this project were sown in 2002/03 whilst I was on sabbatical and serving as a Fulbright Fellow at the Université de Niamey, Niger. In fact, I had proposed the project as part of my application for the Fulbright Fellowship application. I therefore wish to heartily thank the Fulbright Organization for favourably reviewing my proposal and consequently funding the project. I collected most of the data on French colonial urban planning in Africa during my sojourn in Niger, and would like to acknowledge my debt of gratitude to the courteous and exceedingly helpful staff of the Franco-Nigerien Cultural Centre and Library, and the equally gracious staff of the library of the Faculty of Political and Economic Sciences of the Université de Niamey. I wish to sincerely thank Mrs Kadidia Konto, who served as the Fulbright Program Coordinator at the Cultural Service of the United States Embassy in Niamey.

Authors of scholarly works are invariably indebted to a multitude of researchers who have done previous work on the subject with which they are concerned. This is more so in the case of a project such as this one that depends largely on secondary sources. I am certainly not capable of adequately thanking the multitude of previous researchers whose works have been instrumental in informing and stimulating me in the course of completing this project. However, I hope that my reference notes suffice to acknowledge my enormous debt to them.

Many thanks to my students, whose thought-provoking questions over the years have been incredibly helpful in refocusing my attention to questions I might otherwise be inclined to ignore. I would also like to thank my colleagues at the University of South Florida, especially Bill Heller, Darryl Paulson, Earl Conteh-Morgan, John Daly, David Carr, Ray Arsenault, Jay Sokolovsky, and Winston Bridges, for their constant encouragement.

Finally, it is with great delight that I dedicate this book to a teacher, mentor and friend, Michael Mattingly of the Development Planning Unit, University College London, UK.

Ambe J. Njoh,
The University of South Florida

1 Power and the built environment in colonial Africa

The built environment received much attention during the heydays of colonialism in Africa. For colonial authorities, each opportunity to influence spatial form and function was seen as an occasion not only to solidify their grip and control over the colonized but also to reaffirm preconceived notions of European supremacy and power. Colonial authorities had ample opportunity to influence the structure and purpose of the built environment in Africa. For one thing, colonial Africa boasted vast areas of unsettled terrain. For another thing, colonial powers controlled valuable resources, and were therefore able to manipulate the built environment to suit their own goals. As Kim Dovey (1999: 1) suggests, 'place creation is determined by those in control of resources'. There was certainly no question regarding who controlled the resources. Quite early in the colonial epoch, colonial powers had crafted and implemented perfidious plans that ensured them uninhibited access to, and control over, all economic resources in Africa.

Increasing attention is being paid to the fact that the built environment in colonial settings was designed and programmed to accomplish certain goals – particularly those relating to profit, prestige and political power – of the colonial powers (see e.g. Abu-Lughod, 1980; AlSayyad, 1992; Çelik, 1997; Coquery-Vidrovitch, 1993; Njoh, 2004; Wright, 1991; Yeoh, 2003). Thus, as the authority system that governed it, the built environment in colonial Africa was essentially political. It manifested to a lesser degree silhouettes of struggles between the colonizer and the colonized. To a greater extent, it reflected the multiple interests of the colonial powers.

Theoretical framework

Before delving further into the notion of 'state power', it is necessary to examine the concepts of power, ideology and social control that are central themes in this book. These three concepts are inextricably interconnected in the discourse on spatial policies and structures as instruments of domination (see e.g. Foucault, 1982; Yeoh, 2003; Elleh, 2002; Lefebvre, 1974; AlSayyad, 1992; Çelik, 1997). Although the concepts are central to social enquiry, they are yet to assume universally accepted

1

meanings (Oliga, 1996; Mannheim, 1985; Knights and Willmott, 1985; Lukes, 1974; Mannheim, 1950). My aim in this segment is not to undertake an exhaustive review of the literature on these widely discussed concepts. Rather, my objective is a modest one – namely, to provide a theoretical backdrop against which French and English town planning schemes in colonial Africa will be examined later in this book.

Power

Power is the ability to influence the outcome or results of events (Dovey, 1999; Mannheim, 1985; Oliga, 1996; Shively, 2001; Therborn, 1980). Karl Mannheim's (1985) characterization of the concept of power is particularly insightful. Mannheim breaks power into a number of categories. One of these categories, institutionalized power, is of particular interest in efforts to appreciate planning, an institutional activity, as a tool of power and social control in colonial Africa. Mannheim notes that, 'the most advanced form of institutionalized control is the law as interpreted and enforced by courts and police power' (Mannheim, 1985: 50). Therborn (1980) has also proposed a useful analytical framework for understanding power as an important force in society. Therborn's framework suggests that power may assume three main forms, namely 'subjectivist', 'economic', and 'dialectical materialist' (Oliga, 1996: 70). From a subjectivist's perspective, the focus is on the 'subject' or entity, be it an individual or group, exercising power. Of primary importance in this case is the question of 'who has power?'. The focus from an economic perspective is on the quantity of power as a capacity to attain desired ends (Oliga, 1996). Thus, the question to be addressed from this perspective has to do with 'how much power' does a given entity possess over another. It also has to do with 'how much power' a given entity possesses to complete a specified task.

Marxian structuralists, such as Althusser (e.g. 1971), Poulantzas (e.g. 1973) and Therborn (1980), view power as the ability of any given class to realize its objectives in society. Underlying this definition is the assumption that the privileged class almost always possesses the ability to realize its desired objectives. This perspective raises questions about the focus on interpersonal relations, particularly because such a focus tends to ignore the impersonal, structural basis of domination and exploitation, which are commonplace in society in general, and colonized territories in particular.

Scholars in the 'dialectical materialist' camp, particularly Marxists, focus on capitalism as a mode of production. The aim in this case is, more often than not, to illuminate its 'social contradictions', 'historical reproduction', and 'evolution' (Oliga, 1996: 70). Thus, the questions of interest relate to the type of society in question, the role of the state (including all entities acting on its behalf) in society, and the impact of state power on society. Oliga (1996) has done a fine job summarizing Therborn's conceptualization scheme. His summary, which incorporates the views of Robson and Cooper (1989), suggests that power may assume one of the following four forms: (1) 'a conflictual zero-sum, negative view: power over whom', (2) 'a harmonious, synergistic, positive view: power to accomplish a common goal', (3) 'a conflictual, negative, and essentially critical view: oppressive and exploitative power' or (4) 'the analytic relations of power', which considers knowledge as an important source of power (Oliga, 1996: 70). It is the connection between knowledge and power that constitutes the focus of one of Michel Foucault's best-known works, *Power/ Knowledge* (Foucault, 1980a). However, it is important to note that Foucault never equated knowledge with power, as did earlier writers such as Francis Bacon in his well-known maxim, 'knowledge is power'. This notwithstanding, it is knowledge in the Foucaultian sense of 'savoir', as we will show, that was employed as a dominant source of power by French and English architects, planners, and other authorities in colonial Africa. We therefore posit that European knowledge on how to organize space in a manner designed to facilitate the functioning of human settlements and improve living conditions constituted an important source of power in colonial Africa. Here, it is safe to say that knowledge and power enjoyed a reciprocal relationship in which they enhanced each other (cf. Yeoh, 2003). The genre of reciprocal entrainment between planning knowledge and administrative or disciplinary power hypothesized here is central to Foucault's discourse on the power–knowledge nexus (Allen, 1999: 70).

Ideology

The concept of ideology is commonly associated with Marxism. However, while most of the significant statements on this concept are rooted in Marxian thought, the concept predates Marxism (Mannheim, 1985). Given the long history of the concept, one would think that it has succeeded in taking on a universally accepted meaning. It has not. Karl Mannheim (1985) makes a similar observation but contends that the many meanings of the term can be subsumed by two distinct conceptual categories – the particular and the total.

> The particular conception of ideology is implied when the term denotes that we are sceptical of the ideas and representation advanced by our opponent.
>
> (Mannheim, 1985: 56)

This is particularly evident in situations wherein questions exist in relation to the ulterior motives of an authority's ideas or proposals. Such questionable plans, Mannheim (1985: 55) contends, are often meant to camouflage the intentions of those involved or the real nature of situations whose recognition may be at variance with the interests of authorities. The disguises employed usually differ from one situation to another, but generally tend to range from outright fabrications to half-truths. Ideology of the 'total order' is relatively more inclusive.

Control

To understand the notion of, and need to, control in the context of colonialism, it is necessary to first appreciate the main goals and objectives of the colonial enterprise. This is particularly because 'every control action entails a set of objectives, goals or values' (Oliga, 1996: 125). Some of the best-known goals and objectives of this enterprise include territorial conquest, the economic development of the metropolitan countries, incorporation of the colonized territories into the global capitalist system, acculturation and assimilation of the colonized peoples, and broadcasting of Europe's real or perceived grandeur and superiority. Tucked in the shadows of these grand goals was the objective of ensuring the maintenance and functioning of colonial governments in the conquered territories. It is arguably within this context that instruments of control found their most immediate utility. In this respect, control was required to sustain the system of colonial governance in place.

The success of colonial authorities in this regard can be better understood by re-examining the notion of ideology, particularly in terms of what Althusser (1971) and Therborn (1980) call the 'subjection-qualification' dialectic (Oliga, 1996). On the one hand, subjection alludes to the individual's (or subject's) 'subjugation to a particular force or social order that favors or disfavors certain values and beliefs' (Oliga, 1996: 172). On the other hand, qualification has to do with training subjects to carry out activities necessary for the system's survival. Prominent in this regard, is the role of participating in the social change process. In practical terms, subjects are formally trained or informally socialized to appreciate: (1) 'what exists and what does not exists', (2) the difference between 'good' and 'bad', 'right' and 'wrong', 'just' and 'unjust', and (3) what is possible (Oliga, 1996: 173). This three-mode interpellation make up what Oliga (1996) calls the 'is-ought-can' trio and constitutes part of a rather elaborate and meticulous process to structure the subject's view of the social world, and shape his desires, preferences, values, hopes, ambitions, and fears. Resulting from this process is a situation in which subjects, that is, the ruled, unquestioningly accept the rulers' ideologies as dominant. According to Oliga (1996: 173), 'this means subjecting the ruled to a social order that is in the interest of the ruling class; the ruled thus become qualified to obey'.

An important rationale for obedience is predicated upon, or results from, a fear of the consequences of acting otherwise or disobeying. In this case, the consequences, usually in the form of fines, punishment or other penalties, for non-compliance are clearly stated by the ruler. Thus, when the subjects obey, it is not out of a sense of 'inevitability', 'deference', or 'resignation', but out of a fear of the consequences of disobeying. In modern societies, the state is the sole agent endowed with the power to fine, punish or otherwise sanction violators of government rules, regulations and/or laws.

Such power as the state (including the colonial state) and/or its representative may wield from time to time is generally referred to as 'authority' or 'legitimated power'. Authority or legitimated power in this case is defined as power based on a general agreement that: (1) a person or group has the right to issue certain sorts of commands and (2) those commands should be obeyed (Shively, 2001: 139). Perhaps the most succinct and insightful statement to date on the question of 'power' (on the part of the state or other powerful entities) and 'obedience' (on the part of the citizenry or other less powerful or powerless entities) was made by Jean Jacques Rousseau (1712–1778) when he opined that the pinnacle of the relationship between the powerful and the powerless is attained when the former has successfully transformed his strength into a right and obedience into a duty (cited in Gerth and Mills, 1964: 195).

In practice, and with the exception, to some extent, of the advanced democratic polities, the state and its agents constitute the powerful while the citizens are the powerless. It is therefore hardly any wonder that governments in non-democratic polities consider the range of activities over which they can exercise authority as limitless. Colonial governments in Africa were particularly notorious in this regard. These governments perceived authority as a cost-effective kind of power. As is commonly the case with states throughout the world, the state in colonial Africa employed a number of strategies, including the threat of punishment, coercion, persuasion, or in rare instances, the construction of incentives, to effectively back its authority in all spheres.

Backing authority with the threat of punishment on the part of the state or government entails making the citizenry aware of the fact that violators of any law, rule or regulation will be punished accordingly. In some cases, compliance is sought by persuasion, such as through programmes designed to teach the citizenry about the importance of doing what the government wants them to do. British and French colonial authorities are well-known for coaxing and persuading members of the indigenous population to adhere to Euro-centric standards of hygiene as part of indefatigable colonial efforts to create healthy environments especially for Europeans based in colonial Africa. The fact that diseases, especially those in tropical Africa, were communicable dictated a need for colonial sanitation and public health officials to extend health campaigns to the non-European or so-called 'native areas', including 'native reservations'. Success in this connection hinged tightly on the ability of these officials to convince members of the indigenous population to observe proper, and quite often Euro-centric, rules of hygiene. This entailed simply educating them on the need to diminish the spread of communicable diseases.

Occasionally, colonial officials deemed it necessary to back their authority with the 'construction of incentives', which entailed making the alternative to the desired behaviour so unattractive that the 'natives' had no choice but to indulge in the desired behaviour. This strategy was commonly used in efforts designed to discourage members of the native population from re-locating to urban centres. Here, the colonial state employed strategies ranging from those requiring 'natives' to obtain written authorization to settle in towns (e.g. the infamous pass laws of southern and east Africa), to refusal to extend utility services to non-European settlements. In contemporary terms, consanguine policies are used, for instance, in the US, for the purpose of managing growth. In this case, the local state may refuse to extend utility services to areas outside the city limits as a means of promoting more intense land use, and/or 'in-filling' within the built-up areas. In this case, the local state's decision against extending necessary services beyond the city limit serves to make the option of developing such areas an unattractive choice to developers.

The extent to which any one of these strategies can succeed in achieving the desired ends depends on several factors. At a more general level, Shively (2001) contends that the ability of any form of power to attain its intended objective(s) depends on factors such as money, affection, physical strength, legal status (e.g. a police officer's power to control traffic), the possession of important information, a winning smile, strong allies, determination, and desperation. Four of these factors, namely money, strong allies, determination and knowledge (or possession of important information), constituted incontestably viable sources of power for colonial governments. After all, what was colonialism without guaranteed and uninhibited access to a seemingly limitless pool of resources in the colony?

Colonial authorities in Africa possessed and exercised other forms of power. For instance, they exercised what may best be characterized as 'naked power' as opposed to 'legitimated power'. As hinted at already, the latter is typically associated with governments in democratic polities, while the former constitutes what victors of a war are wont to exercise over captured territories. Colonial territories were, for all practical purposes, captured territories and the colonialists treated them as such. Over time, even in territories captured through war, the victors would succeed in transforming 'naked power' into 'legitimated power'.

In the case of colonial governments in Africa, this was seldom the case as most were never successful in transforming the power they wielded over citizens or the so-called natives into 'legitimated authority'. For this to have taken place, the colonialists needed to have first and foremost clothed colonial government power with elements of 'justice', 'morality', 'religion', and other cultural values. These values, as Gerth and Mills (1964: 195) note, are necessary to define acceptable 'ends' and 'means', including the responsibilities of those who wield power in the process.

Power and the built environment

A number of works, including books (e.g. Abu-Lughod, 1980; AlSayyad, 1992; Dovey, 1999; King, 1990; Rabinow, 1989) and articles (e.g. Cooper, 2000; Faubion (on Foucault), 2000), have analysed the built environment as a source or tool of power. I find Kim Dovey's (1999) discourse on the articulation or mediation of power in 'built form' particularly illuminating in appreciating how colonial authorities employed physical and spatial policies as a source and tool of power in Africa.

In everyday life, power is often construed as having to do with control 'over' others. Thus, power can be sub-divided into two categories, namely 'power to' and 'power over'. These two sub-categories are essentially synonymous with power as capacity, and power as a relationship between individuals, agents or groups (Dovey,

1999). Although 'power over' is generally more obvious in everyday life, it is the 'power to', as Dovey (1999) contends that is more primary. Thus, for example, Ralph Miliband (1969) is talking of the 'power of the state to' make citizens do as the state wants, rather than the power of the state 'over' citizens as in the case of an 'oppressor's' 'power over' the 'oppressed', when he asserts that more and more people in capitalist societies are living under the shadow of the state. Miliband was talking of advanced capitalist states, where oppression is unlikely although not non-existent. To be sure, there are instances in which the state everywhere may elect to use any one of many forms of power. Dovey (1999) identifies five specific forms of 'power over', including force, coercion, seduction, manipulation, and segregation, that are relevant to the built environment.

Force entails making an individual or group comply with another's will without any choice of acting otherwise. Foucault's notion of the 'Great Confinement', exemplifies the use of force in the built environment. As Markus (1993: 95) narrates it, Michel Foucault used the phrase, 'great confinement', in reference to what he described as a

'phenomenon of European dimensions' which was born with the 1656 decree setting up the landmark Hôpital Général in Paris.

What Foucault was alluding to, was a system designed to collect and confine, within a specific space delineated with walls, fences or similar barriers, those considered to be a real or potential threat to social order. Structures for enforced spatial confinement, including asylums, prisons, orphanages and sanatoriums were plentiful in eighteenth-century Europe and constitute manifestations of the use of force in built form. In colonial Africa, the application of force involving the manipulation of elements of the built environment included the use of visible objects such as fences enclosing the residential areas of Europeans, or those circumscribing or 'enframing' workers' camps, and military barracks.

Coercion is a latent kind of force as it only threatens the use of force but does not quite use it. The threats are used to secure compliance. Its power is derived from implied sanctions. Coercion finds expression in the built environment in several ways, including the use of armed or unarmed uniformed guards of honour, public monuments and exaggerated scale. These conspicuous structures coerce through 'domination' or 'intimidation'. The construction of gigantic monuments and buildings of exaggerated scale such as chapels, government official and residential facilities and so on by colonial powers or their agents in Africa achieved the goal of 'domination' and 'intimidation' in two ways: by ostentatiously displaying Europe's resourcefulness and technological might; and by overwhelming and belittling the African with sheer size. Or as Kim Dovey (1999: 10) puts it,

spatial domination through exaggerated scale or dominant location can belittle the human subject as it signifies the power necessary to its production.

Coercion also occurs in the built environment through surveillance. Colonial authorities in Africa typically situated their offices and residential districts on elevated sites overlooking the low-lying residential quarters of the colonized. Here, coercion manifested itself in built form through surveillance to the extent that such a spatial arrangement placed the colonized under the constant gaze of the colonizer.

Seduction is a potent and complex form of 'power over'. This form of power was commonly used in colonial Africa. Colonial authorities, in their bid to achieve the imperial and capitalist goal of expanding markets for European goods, particularly building and cognate materials, proceeded with unprecedented alacrity to develop a plethora of propaganda campaign strategies. The aim of these strategies was to promote pseudo-European middle-class standards of environmental design. These campaigns included disparaging qualification and disdainful treatment of traditional construction practices and materials while extolling European equivalents. The strategies, which succeeded in irreversibly changing the housing consumption taste and habits of Africans, constitute a classic case of 'power over' gaining expression through seduction.

Manipulation 'is a form of coercion which operates primarily by keeping the subject ignorant' (Dovey, 1999: 11). An example of this form of coercion, itself a form of 'power over', found expression in the built environment of colonial Africa through policies that provided housing for Africans working as domestic servants in Servant Quarters in 'White-Only' residential districts at a time when racial spatial segregation was considered the only 'prophylaxis' against malaria. In this case, manipulation as a form of power was used 'over' two groups of Africans: the ones confined to 'Native' districts who actually believed that they posed a viable threat to the health of Europeans, and those working in domestic capacities in 'European' districts, who erroneously believed they were favoured by Europeans. Manipulation as a form of 'power over' worked in this case to ensure that the European enjoyed round-the-clock domestic services from the 'native' domestic servants. At the same time, it ensured that those whose services were not needed remained at a distance safe enough to guarantee the European the uninterrupted serenity he treasured.

Segregation is also a form of 'power over'. In the built environment, it constitutes the construction of boundaries and/or pathways, which may separate space by the status, gender, race, culture, class, age or other attributes of the occupants. It is usually designed to create privileged enclaves of access. Segregation, particularly racial residential segregation, was the most commonly used form of 'power over' in colonial Africa. A close second in this regard was segregation along the lines of socio-economic status. Both forms of segregation left indelible marks on the built environment in Africa.

Focus of the book

As stated earlier, this book examines the town and country planning projects that were conceived and implemented by two European powers, Britain and France, during the colonial era in Africa. Students of the European colonial experience in Africa tend to emphasize the differences, while paying hardly any attention to the similarities, characteristic of the colonial administrative and economic strategies and objectives of these two imperial powers. On the one hand, the British had a penchant for implementing colonial development policies through indigenous institutions under the rubric of what came to be known as the 'indirect rule' strategy. This strategy was effective not only in ensuring the efficient and effective attainment of colonial development objectives and goals but also the preservation, growth and development of indigenous institutions in the colonial territories. As a result, contemporary formal institutions in the erstwhile British colonies are likely to embody a fusion of British and indigenous administrative principles and practices.

On the other hand, the French had a penchant for centralizing colonial administrative authority. Under the banner of what is often characterized as the 'direct rule' strategy, the French colonial authorities oversaw the implementation of most colonial development policies directly from Paris.

Later on during the colonial era, especially after France regrouped its sub-Saharan African colonial territories into federations (1895 for the Federation of French West Africa (FWA) and 1908 for the federation of French Equatorial Africa (FEA)), some decision-making authority was delegated to federal governors in Dakar (for FWA) and Brazzaville (for FEA). The French colonial administrative strategy not only concentrated decision-making authority in the centre, but also actively sought to discourage local or indigenous initiatives and institutions. This, combined with efforts designed to attain the French colonial goal of civilizing and assimilating the 'natives', effectively supplanted the indigenous institutions with French varieties.

It would appear that the difference between the two seemingly opposite strategies has been overplayed. To be sure, the British colonial authorities are also on record for employing strategies that possess elements of centralization or 'direct rule'. For example, where well-established indigenous institutions were non-existent, they created theirs. The appointment of 'warrant chiefs', as the British colonial authorities did in Nigeria in instances where a paramount indigenous or traditional chieftaincy or kingdom was non-existent (as was the case in Tiv society), is illustrative. Similarly, the French colonial authorities are on record for implementing the 'indirect rule' administrative strategy (e.g. Gallienni in Madagascar). Perhaps most important of all is the fact that the goals of the two colonial powers – that is, exploiting the colonial territories for the benefit of the colonial master nation – were identical.

This notwithstanding, some works have suggested that contemporary development in the erstwhile colonial states is a function of the colonial public administration strategy to which they were subjected. Prominent amongst these works is Ali Mazrui's (1983) 'Francophone Nations and English-Speaking States'. Based on qualitative data, Mazrui found that while the French strategy of administrative centralization and cultural assimilation helped to forge a sense of nationhood – implying the 'concentration of sovereignty at the center' – in Francophone African countries, the

British helped to establish a sense of statehood – which 'implies substantial cultural homogeneity' – in Anglophone ones (1983: 25). This finding led him to the following conclusion. First, former French colonies are more developed as 'nations' than erstwhile English colonies. This suggests, for instance, that national unity is more likely in countries with a history of French colonialism than in those that experienced English colonialism. Second, countries that experienced English colonialism are more developed as 'states' than their counterparts who were subjected to French colonization. By implication, therefore, the former English colonies are more capable of handling matters relating to public or government administration than countries with a history of French colonialism.

In a more recent study, I employed quantitative data to establish a link between 'colonial heritage and development' (Njoh, 2000). The findings of this study suggest that countries, which experienced 'indirect rule' – that is erstwhile British colonies – are more 'developed' than their counterparts who experienced 'direct rule' – that is former French colonies. Within the framework of the study, the development construct was operationalized in terms of the Human Development Index (HDI). The HDI is increasingly gaining acceptance as a valuable indicator of the development construct, particularly because unlike more orthodox indicators such as Gross National Product (GNP) and Gross Domestic Product (GDP), it takes into account social dimensions of development. However, the indicator leaves something to be desired, especially because of its inability to account for non-quantifiable or qualitative aspects of development.

As mentioned earlier, the differences between French and British colonial rule in Africa has traditionally been exaggerated. This book deviates from the norm by focusing on the similarities characteristic of the two systems. Particularly, it seeks to show that the two colonial authorities were bent on gaining political and social control over the colonial subjects by all means necessary. The use of 'direct' and/or 'indirect' rule must therefore be seen in this context. That is to say, the expediency of any one of the two strategies was judged based on the extent to which it helped the colonial authorities accomplish the covert goal of dominating and controlling the colonial subjects as well as exploiting the colonial territories.

Few policy instruments guaranteed colonial authorities as much success in this connection as those available under the general rubric of physical and spatial planning. This is despite the fact that colonial planners, like their counterparts elsewhere, professed to be apolitical experts concerned uniquely with technical and aesthetic matters of the built environment. As shown in the chapters that follow, these so-called apolitical and technical experts proved rather adept at employing their talents and skills to complement efforts designed to attain larger goals of the colonial enterprise. This was as true in the British as in the French colonies. Earlier in the brief European colonial era, three important goals of the colonial enterprise had surfaced and rapidly moved to the top of each colonial power's agenda. The first was to defend the newly conquered territories from rival European powers. The second was related to assuaging nationalistic resistance within the conquered territories or colonies. The third was to assert the superiority and dominance of the colonial power in particular and Europe in general, over Africa.

It is difficult to overstate the role of colonial architects, urban planners and civil engineers in efforts to accomplish each of these goals. At a more generic level I hasten to draw attention to the careful selection of sites for forts, and the design and construction of these forts for purposes of military defence. A number of these forts pre-dated the official commencement of the European colonial era in Africa. For instance, French involvement in military and related construction projects in Gorée (in present-day Senegal) dates as far back as the seventeenth century. Colonial planners and engineers were also at the forefront of efforts to design and implement massive public works projects such as the construction of roads, streets, bridges, sanitation and related facilities, dams and so on. These facilities were necessary to broadcast the authority and power of the colonial state over the colonial subjects. The roads and streets were particularly important as they facilitated the movement of forces of law and order and that of the colonial military in the event of civil unrest or political upheavals. Finally, colonial architects, engineers and planners were not only instrumental but they were also indispensable in designing and erecting the monumental structures that served as the home of the colonial governments and symbols of European superiority. To appreciate the political importance of these structures is to understand how Europeans consolidated and perpetuated colonial power and rule in Africa.

Colonial authorities had moved rather early during the colonial era to craft a series of town and country planning legislation designed to control all aspects of urban life in colonial Africa. The need to ensure effective control necessitated the reinforcement of the powers of the police, sanitation inspectors, and mayors. This reinforcement constituted an expansion of the state apparatus or the exercise of a form of power akin to what Foucault (1982) has characterized as 'pastoral power'. Pastoral power in the Foucaultian sense focuses on salvation, particularly with respect to reforming people's health or habits and the use of 'individualizing techniques' (Yeoh, 2003). In noting similar dynamics within the colonial urban environment of Singapore, Brenda Yeoh argued that the British colonial authorities created and charged several institutions with the task of urban governance. Yeoh further observed that

> although each institution had its own 'field operation', they shared the use of common disciplinary forms to mould the colonized body and the space it inhabited so as to facilitate social order and economic advancement, the twin imperatives which supplied the rationale for action and which came to dominate colonial policy.
>
> (Yeoh, 2003: 11)

This implies an important but largely ignored function of urban and regional planning policy – a tool for consolidating socio-economic and political power. This book marshals a plethora of evidence to show how French and British colonial authorities used planning legislation to accomplish not only the goal of consolidating power but also other important objectives of the colonial enterprise in Africa.

Organization of the book

The book contains twelve chapters. This introductory chapter undertakes a theoretical analysis of the relationship between 'power and the built environment' in colonial Africa. Chapter 2 is dedicated to an examination of French colonial planning ideology, principles and practices in sub-Saharan Africa. Of particular interest are the ideas and thoughts that provided the foundation for planning policies and projects in French colonies in the region. With respect to urban development projects, the chapter draws attention to the fact that French involvement in such projects pre-dated, by more than two centuries, her colonial adventures in the region. Furthermore, the chapter examines French colonial government efforts to control land, land use activities and all transactions related to land in the colonies.

Chapter 3 focuses on 'spatial policies and economic ventures in British colonial Africa'. The underlying premise of the chapter is that unless British economic activities in colonial sub-Saharan Africa are adequately understood, efforts to fully appreciate the structure of colonial and contemporary spatial structures in erstwhile British colonies are unlikely to be fruitful. This is because economic motives were more central to the British colonial project than to that of any other colonial power.

Chapter 4 focalizes on town planning politics and practice in British colonial West Africa. Of interest are the planning activities of colonial officials in Gambia, Ghana, Sierra Leone and Nigeria. Chapter 5 concentrates on 'French West Africa' (Afrique Occidentale Française), including Benin, Burkina Faso, Côte d'Ivoire, Guinea, Niger and Senegal. Chapter 6 examines colonial urban planning activities in 'French Equatorial Africa' (Afrique Equatorial Française), including Central African Republic, Chad, People's Republic of Congo and Gabon. The chapter also examines planning politics and practice in colonial Madagascar, which was never a part of any of the French colonial federations.

Chapter 7 focuses on the former German West African colonies, which became League of Nations mandated territories following the outcome of World War I. The territories, which were held in trust by the French and British colonial powers from 1919 to 1960, include British Southern Cameroons, French Cameroun and Togo. Chapter 8 examines town and country planning in British Southern Africa, including South Africa, Zambia and Zimbabwe. Chapter 9 is concerned with planning ideology and practice in British East Africa, including Kenya and Tanzania.

Chapter 10 concentrates on 'mining, plantation agriculture and company towns' in colonial Africa. Chapter 11 focuses on an obviously important but often ignored aspect of planning, namely the protection of public health. Town planning and public health emerged in response to a common problem – the health consequences of the industrial revolution. When the European colonial era began in Africa, European town planners wasted no time in transplanting town planning schemes that were already in use in Europe to the colonies. This chapter describes some of the major planning schemes that were designed to accomplish health objectives. The focus is particularly on projects with obvious spatial implications.

It is clear that colonial authorities were very active in the urban and regional planning arenas of their colonial territories. Testimony to this resides mainly in the many planning and related policies they conceived, formulated and implemented in Africa prior to the end of the colonial era. Also, a number of large and costly urban and regional development projects such as roads and urban infrastructure attest to the interests of colonial authorities in this arena. While evidence attesting to these efforts abounds, one important question is yet to be adequately addressed. Why were colonial powers interested in town and country planning in Africa? This question, which is at the heart of this book, is revisited in the final chapter, Chapter 12. Essentially, therefore, the chapter seeks to uncover the rationale and *raison d'être* for colonial town and country planning policies and projects in colonial Africa. The chapter begins by comparing and contrasting French and British physical and spatial planning policies in the region. Then, it culls examples from the previous chapters to demonstrate that both colonial powers employed physical and spatial planning policies, including those with the professed objective of protecting public health, as tools of power, social control and domination in colonial Africa.

Target audience

The primary audience for this work includes researchers, and advanced undergraduate and graduate students in the following areas: history of urban and regional planning in Africa, history of the built environment, land use policy and administration, development geography, sociology of development, development planning, multicultural studies and the European colonial experience in Africa. The book can be used as a primary or secondary text for courses in the named fields. Particularly, the book can serve as a text in courses designed to promote understanding of the implications of colonial history as well as urban and regional planning policies and projects for development in the developing world. In this respect, students and instructors will find utility in the country-specific case studies presented and discussed in the book. Similarly, courses in public works and infrastructure development will find the experience of European colonial authorities in this field very informative. The book can also serve as a valuable source of reference for researchers and consultants interested in the relationship between the built environment and socio-economic development in sub-Saharan Africa. Social critiques, and international political economists, political scientists and cultural anthropologists will equally find some grist for their mills in this book.

2 French colonial planning ideology and practice

Introduction

There is a dearth of knowledge in the relevant English literature on French colonial urban planning activities in sub-Saharan Africa. It follows that English-speaking planners and researchers know very little about the indisputably rich experience of French colonial urban planners in the region. To be sure, French colonial urban planning authorities established the foundation for almost all major cities in the erstwhile French colonies of sub-Saharan Africa. The main objective of this chapter is to examine the nature, extent and *raison d'être* of French colonial urban planning activities in the colonial territories of said region.

Initially, I characterize the region in question in terms of its political organization during and following the colonial era. In the process, I draw attention to the state of urbanization in the region prior to the French colonial époque. Then, I examine French colonial urban and regional planning policies, legislation and projects in the region. This exercise will seek to, amongst other things, demonstrate that most major cities in the erstwhile French colonies owe their existence to French colonial urban planning efforts. Also of interest in the chapter are French colonial government efforts to attain the goal of controlling land and all transactions involving land throughout the colonies. Special interest is paid to the instruments, techniques and procedures that were brought into play to achieve this goal.

French presence in pre-colonial sub-Saharan Africa

The presence of the French in Africa south of the Sahara began long before the European colonial era in the region. Most of the human settlement development activities during this period were limited to the establishment of outposts, or comptoirs along the West African coast. The first of these outposts was established in Saint-Louis in present-day Senegal as far back as 1659. The outposts included units designed to house French and other European traders as well as their commercial activities. Some of the commercial activities in the outposts, especially those that were located in the area occupied by present-day Senegal, were related to the highly lucrative slave trade of the time. The outposts grew correspondingly with the growth of these and other commercial activities such as trading in tropical products (e.g. spices, ivory, elephant tusks, rubber). French traders were generally concerned with the possibility of being attacked by members of the native population and/or other adversaries. This concern led to the decision by French authorities to locate their outposts in areas such as islands and peninsulas that were naturally protected from possible attack. Additional measures including the installation of military posts and physical fortification were taken to further protect these settlements. The settlements typically comprised buildings constructed of local materials, particularly earth. The spatial distribution of the buildings did not follow any preconceived geometric order. Thus, apart from the presence of Europeans and the relatively higher densities of the outposts, they were not dramatically different from the settlements of the indigenous population. It is also noteworthy that until later in the eighteenth century the outposts were never under the administrative jurisdiction of any particular member, or appointee, of the French government. Rather, employees or representatives of commercial firms with interests in the region controlled the outposts and activities therein.

With the passage of time, the number of outposts as well as the population within them increased significantly. This increase attracted the attention of French authorities back home. The authorities were perturbed by the absence of administrative authority as well as what they considered a lack of moral rectitude and spatial order. Accordingly, as the French grew increasingly interested in territorial acquisition in sub-Saharan Africa in the eighteenth century, they began contemplating appropriate measures to bring administrative, moral, and spatial order to the outposts. Measures to introduce spatial order to the outposts initially included the drawing up of urban physical development plans. The plans prescribed a gridiron pattern of streets, with emphasis on perpendicularity and the orderly alignment of buildings along, and at specified uniform distances from, the streets. For a long time, these plans constituted simply an expression of the wishes of French authorities, particularly because problems of resource constraints permitted them to do little more than construct units designed to serve as military posts. The problem of resource scarcity also rendered the task of taking charge of the economic and administrative affairs of the outposts difficult at best. In the meantime, the authorities were preoccupied with developing sub-division plans/regulations as well as instruments capable of guaranteeing them full and uninhibited control over land in the outposts. By the end of the eighteenth century, the French had neither implemented any of their spatial schemes, nor enacted any coherent land policy in the region.

With the decline and subsequent demise of the slave trade at the beginning of the nineteenth century, the French had to look for other lucrative commercial avenues. Thus, interest was shifted to plantation agriculture, which at the time showed great potential. This led to the development or active encouragement of plantations for groundnuts (in Senegal) and palm oil and related products (further down along the coast). With the passage of time, the idea of amassing overseas territories as colonies began gaining momentum in relevant circles in France. By the middle of the nineteenth century the French bourgeoisie, which had become very thirsty for not only new markets but also new products, encouraged the French government to acquire colonial territories abroad. The idea of colonial expansion was not greeted positively in all quarters in France. Opponents of the idea included leaders of financial institutions and those with intimate connections to such institutions, who had preferred seeing France concentrate its limited resources on domestic investments. They contended that colonial expansion would result in the French state spreading scarce resources rather too thinly. Proponents of colonial expansion, including geographers (under the banner of the Geography Association or Société de Géographie), politicians, businesspeople, and the military, made a forceful case arguing that the acquisition of colonial territories would strengthen France intellectually, economically and militarily. In 1893 these proponents formed an association, the French Colonial Union (l'Union Coloniale Française). The main aim of the association was to convince the French populace that colonial expansion bore the potential of strengthening France especially economically and militarily. Accordingly, they set up a propaganda machinery designed to sway public opinion in their favour. An important element in this machinery was a newspaper, *La Quinzaine coloniale*, which preoccupied itself with selling the colonial ideology. A common thread that ran through the discourse on French colonialism was that it was designed to 'civilize and modernize' the primitive world.

By the beginning of the twentieth century the French citizenry and politicians had been sold on the idea of French colonial expansion. Accordingly, the plan to penetrate, with the goal of acquiring colonial territories in Africa, was adopted in 1879 by the Ministry of the Colonies. The ministry devised a plan to establish a commercial link between Algeria and Senegal as a means of unifying the two colonies and facilitate further penetration into the African hinterland. This plan was later abandoned and in its stead a plan to construct a railway linking the two main rivers in the region, River Senegal and River Niger, was crafted. This plan was anything but novel as René Caillé had proposed an identical plan as far back as 1828. Faidherbe, who went a step further by sending a team to conduct reconnaissance studies of the region in 1865, is credited with initial efforts to resuscitate Caillé's plan. The railway was seen as a necessary component in the colonial objective of amassing natural resources from colonial territories for transmission to the metropolitan country.

Soon after the French National Assembly endorsed the colonial plan, French colonial authorities embarked on strategies to acquire colonial territories in Africa south of the Sahara. The prior presence of French traders in Senegal made this territory an obvious guinea pig for France's colonial adventure in the region. However, the acquisition of Senegal as a colonial territory did not come to pass without resistance from the native population. France eventually conquered the territory and assumed effective control over it as a colony in 1854. Thus, French efforts to acquire colonial territories included a strong military component. This was necessary to subdue populations in areas that resisted or opposed French colonialism. Eventually through forceful and peaceful means, the French succeeded in signing treaties that enabled them to assume total control of territories in the region.

In 1895, the French colonial government regrouped all territories under its control in West Africa into a federation, named the French West Africa (FWA) (la Fédération de l'Afrique Occidentale Française (l'AOF)). This federation encompassed eight countries, including Guinea, Mauritania, Senegal, Côte d'Ivoire, French Sudan (present-day Mali), Niger, Dahomey (present-day Benin), and Upper Volta (present-day Burkina Faso). Dakar, Senegal was designated as the capital of the federation of FWA. In 1908, the government took an identical action which culminated in the regrouping of its colonies in the central African region into the federation of French Equatorial Africa (FEA) (la Fédération de l'Afrique Equatoriale Française (l'AEF)). The federation of French Equatorial Africa (FEA) was relatively smaller and included only four colonies as follows: Chad, Ubangi-Shari (present-day Central African Republic), Middle Congo (Moyen Congo) (present-day People's Republic of Congo) and Gabon. The capital of the federation of FEA was Brazzaville. Two colonies, namely Cameroon and Togo, which were German colonies until the end of World War I, became Trust Territories of the League of Nations (forerunner to the UN) and were placed under the control of French colonial authorities. It is noteworthy that although these two colonies were never officially made part of any of the federations, for most practical purposes Cameroon was treated as part of FEA, and Togo was perceived as part of FWA. A common thread running through the named countries is the fact that they were under French control in one form or another especially between the end of World War I and the earlier part of the 1960s, when they gained political independence.

The urban experience

The urban phenomenon is of recent vintage in the former French colonies. Of course, it is incontestable that the sub-Saharan region lays claim to an urban tradition that pre-dates the arrival of European colonialists. Examples of large human settlements in the region include, but are not limited to the city-state of the Kingdom of Benin (in present-day Nigeria), commercial cities such as Mombassa in Kenya and Zanzibar in Tanzania, on the coast of the Indian Ocean. At least one ancient human settlement of considerable size, namely Timbuctu (or Tombouctou) was located in present-day Mali, which is a former French colony. However, I hasten to note that Timbuctu had declined and became insignificant by the time French colonial authorities arrived in the region (i.e. towards the end of the nineteenth century). Thus, it is safe to assert that colonial urban planners laid the foundation for the major cities in the former French colonies.

Urbanization at any significant level did not begin in these countries until towards the end of the colonial era (Venard, 1986). Hardly any human settlement in these countries boasted an urban population higher than 10 per cent in 1950. Five years later in 1955, fewer than 100 towns had populations of more than 10,000. Amongst these,

Dakar and Leopoldville (present-day Kinshasa) had more than 200,000 inhabitants. Three cities, namely Brazzaville, Abidjan and Douala, had populations of 100,000 to 200,000. Six cities, namely Lomé, Bamako, Bangui, Yaoundé, and Libreville, had populations of between 50,000 and 100,000. A good many capital cities of the countries under consideration had less than 50,000 inhabitants. Cities in this category include Conakry, Ouagadougou, Cotonou and Niamey. We note that Nouakchott, the capital of Mauritania was not yet established at that time (1955).

French colonial urban planning policy

As noted above, the French had been present in sub-Saharan Africa in one capacity or another prior to deciding to colonize territories in the region in the later part of the nineteenth century. Gorée Island in present-day Senegal served as the entry point of the French into the sub-Saharan region. The first Europeans to occupy this island were the Portuguese. Upon the departure of the Portuguese, the island fell into the hands of the Dutch and later came under French control in the seventeenth century. French urban planning activities began soon after their arrival on the island. It was, however, not until 1842 that systematic efforts were made to realign housing units and other structures on the island. An essential goal of the realignment exercise was to provide access roads, and hence facilitate the movement of people, goods and services on the island. Great care was taken to ensure that the street network conformed to a classical gridiron pattern, with the streets intersecting perpendicularly. I hasten to note that the island was only one of a number of trading outposts occupied by mostly European traders at the time.

The demise of the slave trade resulted in the decline of some of these trading outposts. Some of the outposts did, however, survive but assumed new functions, particularly as important ports through which plantation products and other raw materials from the hinterland were shipped to the metropolitan countries. Prominent amongst the cities that developed to play this new role within the French colonies were Saint-Louis and Rufisque in present-day Senegal, and Porto-Novo in present-day Benin. With the passage of time, the population of French citizens in a number of coastal settlements increased significantly. In some cases, the increasing French population in the region resulted in the creation anew of cities designed for Europeans by French planners. Noteworthy in this connection is the city of Dakar, which was conveniently established on the peninsula across from Gorée Island, an important transit and holding point for slaves that were bound for the Americas. It is necessary to understand that Gorée Island also served as a French settlement during the pre-colonial era. The Portuguese were the first Europeans to live on the island as far back as the fifteenth century. Thereafter, the Dutch, the English and the French successively occupied the island. Despite its relatively small size, the island experienced physical and socio-economic development similar to the other outposts that were occupied by the French in particular and Europeans in general. Some of the most noticeable developments undertaken by the French on the island took place in the mid-1700s, especially after the French governor of the island had acquired the necessary rights of occupation. These rights were formalized after intense protestations from the natives in 1765.

A number of other outposts existed in the region. The most prominent outposts in this regard include Grand Bassam (in present-day Côte d'Ivoire), Ouidah (Judah) and Hogbodou (later renamed Porto-Novo) in what later became Dahomey (present-day Benin), and Libreville in present-day Gabon. In 1824, the French, after intense negotiations with the local chiefs, secured rights over Grand Bassam. This was immediately followed by the construction of a large wooden military barracks. The French wanted to establish their presence in this area as a means of discouraging the British and other Europeans from effectuating treaties involving land and other resources with the local chiefs. The French were, however, not interested in permanently living in Grand Bassam. This was particularly because malaria-carrying mosquitoes and outbreaks of yellow fever were commonplace in the area. By the mid-1800s many European lives had been lost to malaria and yellow fever in West Africa. As a result, the region was dubbed 'the Whiteman's grave'. The outpost in Ouidah (also called Judah) was established towards the end of the seventeenth century. The French, English and Portuguese occupied the outposts simultaneously. Each group constructed a fort of its own. Towards the end of the eighteenth century Portuguese and Brazilian negotiators set up a station in a nearby village called Hogbodou, which they later named Porto-Novo. This was the headquarters of local kingdom prior to the arrival of Europeans. By 1820, the population of this town stood at between 7,000 and 10,000 (Venard, 1986). The slave trade played a crucial role in the town's growth and development. However, after the demise of this trade, it regained its prominence – this time as an important palm oil market. By the mid-1800s, Porto-Novo counted amongst its residents a significant number of French people. Further away from Porto-Novo, and in what was later to become Gabon, yet another outpost was established in the mid-nineteenth century. In this outpost, a village named Libreville (i.e. Freetown in English) was established in 1849 to harbour freed slaves. Housing units and a piece of land for cultivation were assigned to each freed slave. As time went by, there was a need to meet the basic needs and protect the health of the European inhabitants of the outpost. One of the efforts designed to respond to this need was the construction of a hospital. Nearby, at the Fort of Aumalé, the Catholic Mission constructed a church with stones as the principal walling materials in 1863. This was the first permanent building – and for a long time, the most conspicuous evidence of European presence – in the area. As time went on, the town was divided into three zones as follows: the village of freed slaves, the industrial district, which was located at the foot of the plateau, and the administrative district as well as the European residential area, where stone buildings were commonplace. By 1886, the town boasted several important facilities, including a hospital, a military barracks, a chapel, officers' residential quarters, a number of shops, several permanent buildings and a park surrounded by mango trees. These facilities made this town stand in sharp contrast with the surrounding areas inhabited by members of the indigenous population. Outbreaks of contagious and other diseases were commonplace at the time. This led authorities to construct a hospital designed mainly to isolate those diagnosed with contagious diseases. The hospital was located on a nearby estuary. In a way, Libreville might have served as a testing ground for some of the urban spatial and socio-economic development schemes that the French were later to implement with fortitude in the territories they controlled during the colonial era.

By the beginning of the twentieth century, French colonial urban planning principles had crystallized at least in theory. In practice, the lack of funds rendered their implementation impossible. Cities in the French sub-Saharan African colonies thus developed mostly according to the desires of businessmen who were able and willing to make the necessary investments. These entrepreneurs paid hardly any attention to the urban development legislation in force. During World War I, funds for infrastructure development in the colonies were drastically curtailed.

However, with the departure to the warfront of many Africans (particularly those resident in the urban areas), the colonial authorities saw an opportunity to reinforce urban development control measures. This era marked the advent of 'native residential areas' (*quartiers indigènes*) in some of the colonial territories. The end of World War I witnessed a number of other changes. African soldiers had just returned from the warfront in Europe and other places. The colonial authorities worked fervently on measures designed to reintegrate the returning soldiers into the population. The soldiers had risen in status – they belonged to the middle class (*classes moyennes*) within the French colonial system – and therefore deserved living space in the urban areas. Schemes designed not only to resettle the returning soldiers in the cities but also to improve the social, economic and physical conditions of the cities, especially for the European population, were initiated.

The implementation of these schemes was intensified in the late 1800s. The creation of France's two sub-Saharan federations (French West Africa, with its capital in Dakar, Senegal and French Equatorial Africa with Brazzaville as its capital) was accompanied by a wave of such schemes. Each territory within the federations had an administrative headquarters. Most urban and economic planning efforts were concentrated on the capitals of the federations and on the territorial headquarters, in that order. In French West Africa, the more developed of the two federations, most of the investment in public infrastructure and city building was concentrated largely on Senegal and to a lesser, but significant, extent on the coastal regions, particularly Guinea and Côte d'Ivoire in which the colonial establishment was making significant gains from plantation agriculture and forestry exploitation. The hinterland territories, such as Mali and Upper Volta (present-day Burkina Faso), served as a reservoir for the manpower that was needed in the booming economies of the coastal areas.

In the federation of French Equatorial Africa, which was considerably less populated and less significant than the federation of French West Africa, almost all investments in infrastructure development went to Brazzaville, the capital. The economic activities of the federation centred on the exploitation of forest products.

The creation of urban centres

French colonial authorities were inclined to promoting urbanization in the politico-administrative centres of the conquered territories. These centres were almost always located on the coast. A number of hinterland areas, which were considered to be of economic importance, were encouraged to grow but only as far as they assumed a secondary or tertiary position *vis-à-vis* the politico-administrative centres. This led to the development of a hierarchical urban system that was often concentrated on the politico-administrative capital. Earlier in the colonial era the systems were concentrated first on the regional capitals and then on areas of economic importance.

It is therefore little wonder that the coastal areas of the region remain relatively more developed than their counterparts in the hinterland areas. If the contrast between coastal and hinterland cities is not as sharp in the former federation of French Equatorial Africa (FEA), it is because the French paid little more than passing attention to the development of the region, which was relatively less resourceful and far less populated than the federation of French West Africa. Investments in infrastructure in Brazzaville, the capital of FEA, were therefore relatively meagre.

At the end of World War I, urban planning was accorded a new and more significant place in the French colonies. Under the pretext of hygiene, policies designed to compartmentalize land use activities (e.g. commercial from residential) were enacted. Also, racial residential segregation measures were put into place. Thus, European residential areas were geographically separated from areas inhabited by members of the local population or the 'natives' (*la ville européenne et la ville indigène*).

Thus, three features of French colonial spatial planning are worthy of note. The first is the practice of racial residential segregation, particularly the partitioning of human settlements into two distinct zones wherein the one was for Europeans and the other for members of the local population or the natives. The second is the segregation and compartmentalization of land use activities. This typically resulted in strict spatial separation of functions (administrative, commercial, industrial and residential). In this latter regard, the French were very interested in creating human settlements that conformed to the principles of urban design that were in vogue in France at the time. This objective dovetailed neatly into the 'civilizing mission' (*mission civilisatrice*) of French colonialism.

The third peculiar attribute of French colonial urban planning practice has to do with the selection of sites for the location of administrative centres, which invariably became urban centres. The site of choice was usually a well-ventilated elevated area – a plateau, which permitted an uninhibited view of the surrounding region. The sites occupied by the cities of Yaoundé, Abidjan, Brazzaville and Bamako are illustrative.

Within the framework of French colonial development, urbanization was crucial, not only because it promised to facilitate the attainment of this goal but also because urban centres were considered a propellant of economic development. Accordingly, the French colonial administrators encouraged the growth and proliferation of strategically located urban centres in the colonial territories. In some areas there were pre-existing large or emerging human settlements that were located in locales deemed non-strategic. In such cases, the French colonial authorities moved quickly to discourage their growth in favour of those they deemed critical to their colonial development objective.

Efforts in this regard often began with the creation of an administrative district and/or military base. By conferring the status of administrative centre on any locale, the colonial state influenced in no small way the social, economic and spatial growth of that locale. The cases of Dakar and Brazzaville, which served as the capitals of French West Africa and French Equatorial Africa respectively, are illustrative. Also, Yaoundé, the capital of present-day Cameroon, would have been a lot less developed without the decision in 1946 to transfer the colonial government's administrative functions there from Douala. Similarly, Ouagadougou, the capital of Burkina Faso, would be far less developed were it not for the 1947 decision that transferred the territory's administrative capital there from Bobo-Dioulasso. Similarly, Pointe Noire's growth was accelerated by the decision to transform it into the administrative capital of Middle Congo. Conversely, a number of prominent cities experienced a significant decline in population and status by decisions to dispossess them of their status as administrative centres. Two examples, namely the relocation of administrative activities from Saint-Louis to Dakar in Senegal, and the transfer of the capital of Niger from Zinder to Niamey in 1924, come to mind here.

Concomitant with the establishment of administrative functions was the creation in these centres of facilities such as schools, colleges, hospitals, prisons, and religious institutions. These activities required in the first instance, a labour force to construct the large buildings and other facilities necessary for their functioning, and in the second instance, a pool of full-time workers. This essentially explains how these administrative centres became and continue to be the place of choice for inhabitants of rural areas seeking to ameliorate their economic status.

A significant feature of administrative centres is their location. These centres were often located on the highest elevation (e.g. Abidjan, Yaoundé, Brazzaville, and Bamako). This was usually designed to provide the French colonial establishment an unimpeded view of the 'native settlements', which were usually in low-lying areas. Immediately outside the administrative district was positioned the commercial zone. In many cases, this was often tied to a seaport or a railway station. The aim was to facilitate the movement first of goods from the colonial territories to the metropolitan country, and second of goods and services from the administrative centres to other regions within the colonies. The European residential areas were usually located in isolated areas, far-removed from other activity centres. In order to attract qualified personnel to the colonies, the housing units in these areas were usually very large and set on vast aerated parcels of land (no more than five units per hectare). No effort was spared to equip the units with amenities that were standard in French housing at the time.

Urban development policies and projects

As noted earlier, France's involvement in town planning and spatial development policymaking in sub-Saharan Africa predates her colonial adventures in the region. As Table 2.1 shows, one of the French government's early urban design projects was executed as far back as the 1700s in Gorée Island in present-day Senegal. A number of similar projects were initiated in the late-1800s when France colonized most of the territories. The table identifies and briefly describes the specific urban development projects initiated by France prior to, and earlier in, the colonial era 1700s–1800s. Until very late during the said era, the control of urban development was left in the hands of the territorial governments. The activities of these governments in the urban development arena were confined to the enactment of legislation focusing on aspects of building construction relating to hygiene, safety, security and aesthetics. In 1945, the Secretary of State for the colonies moved to control urban development activities in the French Overseas Territories (Territoires d'outre-mer). In this regard, the jurisdiction of the French Law of 1943 originally designed to regulate urban development activities in France was broadened to cover similar activities in the colonies. In June 1945, a text stipulating the structure and procedure of this new ordinance in the colonial territories was crafted. This text, which was basically a slightly modified version of the 1943 Law, required the territories to draw up comprehensive urban development plans. Up until 1956, these plans had to be reviewed by the central committee on urban planning and housing and approved by the Minister of Urban Planning and Housing, all based in the colonial master nation. The committee, which went under the name National Committee on Town Planning and Housing in the Colonies (Le Comité National de l'Urbanisme et de l'Habitation aux Colonies) (hereafter, the National Committee), was responsible for all matters relating to town planning and housing in the colonial territories. By the late 1950s, the law requiring urban plans had been adopted in many cities throughout the two federations. As noted by Venard (1986: 23) at least twenty-three towns in the federation of French West Africa and six towns in the federation of French Equatorial Africa had adopted the law by that time. The twenty-three towns which had adopted the law in French West Africa included: Cape Verde, Dakar, Rufisque and Thies, Kaolack and Saint-Louis in Senegal; Bamako, Segou and Gao in French Sudan (present-day Mali); Niamey in Niger; Ouagadougou and Bobo-Dioulasso in Upper Volta (present-day, Burkina Faso); Conakry, Kankan, Kindia, Labé and Dalaba in Guinea; Abidjan, Sassandra, Bouake and Man in Côte d'Ivoire; and Cotonou and Porto-Novo in Dahomey (present-day Benin). The six towns in French Equatorial Africa that had the law in force included: Port Gentil in Gabon; Brazzaville and Pointe Noire in Middle Congo (present-day People's Republic of Congo); Bangui in Ubangui-Shari (present-day Central African Republic); and Fort Lamy and Fort Archambault in Chad. Four towns in the former German colonies, which became League of Nations' mandated territories of the French, had also adopted the law. These towns included: Yaoundé, Douala and Dschang in French Cameroun (part of present-day Republic of Cameroon); and Lomé in Togo.

Table 2.1 Urban development projects realized by colonial authorities in the former French colonies of sub-Saharan Africa before and during the 1800s

---

MALI
Bamako
1890: Plan of 'Liberty Village'. Purpose: develop facilities to accommodate freed slaves. The project comprised four large squares, each of which had 24 small round buildings (internal diameter = 5m). The squares were separated by wide streets lined with banana trees and cassava plants. Funds for the project were from the colonial budget and implementation was placed under the charge of the governor of the colony.
1894: Foundation plan for an administrative centre in the colonial territory of the French Sudan. Project was designed by the topographic wing of the French Army Engineering Corps (service topographique du génie militaire) and financed by the colonial budget.

SENEGAL
Gorée
1700s: Urban redesign project. Gorée Island served as a holding place for slaves during the infamous Trans-Atlantic Slave Trade. The island's structures comprised mostly buildings for slave dealers, a church and a health post. With funds from the colonial budget, the project was designed by the French Army Engineering Corps (génie militaire). The governor in charge of the colony was responsible for implementation.

St Louis
1828: First St Louis Island building restoration and spatial redesign project. Structures on the island were suffering from physical and functional obsolesce after the English left in 1817. The French undertook refurbishing works soon after taking over the island. Project was designed by the topographic wing of the French Army Engineering Corps (service topographique du génie militaire) and financed by the colonial budget. The Conseil du gouvernement et administration was responsible for implementing the project.
1837: St Louis Island Extension project. Aim: to create a New Town named, St Philip, across the river. The plan was quite modern for its time as it was designed based on French spatial planning principles of the time. The plan allowed for lots of 20 × 20m and 20 × 40m, separated by streets, some of which were 8m and others 10m wide. However, it was neither site-specific (it did not take the site into account) nor sensitive to its socio-cultural environment (it ignored African culture and spatial planning principles). With funds from the colonial budget, the project was designed by the French Army Engineering Corps (génie militaire). The governor in charge of the colony was responsible for implementation.
1843: St Louis extension project. Aim: to ease population tension on the Old Town. With funds from the colonial budget, the plan was drawn by the French Army Engineering Corps (génie militaire). The governor in charge of the colony was responsible for implementation.
1880: Design and construction of a military camp. Purpose: to house the families of French military personnel stationed in the colony. Funds were from the colonial budget. Drawing of the plan and construction of the camp was by the French Army Engineering Corps (génie militaire).

Dakar
1862: Re-alignment plan. Aim: to put in place a spatial structure with a view to future expansion. The plan for the project was drawn by M. Pinet-Laprade. Funds were from the colony's budget and the governor of the territory (gouverneur du Sénégal) was responsible for implementation.
Thies:
1885: Subdivision and realignment plan. Purpose: to promote spatial order and residential development. The plan was designed by the Topographic Division of the French Public Works Department. The governor of the colony was responsible for implementing the project, which was funded from the colonial government budget.

Source: Based on data contained in Sinou *et al.* (1989).

The responsibility for drawing these plans was placed under the charge of teams of architects and town planners based in the metropolitan country, while local public works departments under the technical direction of metropolitan-based civil and public works engineers were responsible for implementing the plans. Most of the plans were presented to the National Committee between 1946 and 1950. However, by the time most of the countries became independent in the 1960s, the actual implementation of the plans had not even begun.

Urban housing

French colonial authorities played an important role in the urban housing delivery system in the colonies. Their involvement was not limited to the actual construction of housing for colonial officials and the regulation of building activities in the urban centres, but also included activities to promote the development of public housing units. Such housing, which constituted a critical aspect of the housing delivery system in France at the time, was novel in the territories. This development, it must be noted, belongs to the post-World War II era. Prior to that period, the financial resources of France permitted it to do no more than defray the cost of central colonial government administration, and that of maintaining troops in the colonial territories. Each colonial territory or colony was expected to cover its own budget, including the costs of government, providing urban and other necessary infrastructure. Governors of the colonial territories were placed in charge of marshalling the funds necessary to cover said costs. The main sources of revenue were import and export taxes. Also, colonial governments could request guaranteed loans or advances from the French Treasury. This latter option was short-lived, particularly because it had the negative reputation for encouraging indebtedness on the part of colonial governments. Since such loans or advances constituted an important source of revenue for the colonial governments, discontinuing them required the creation of alternative sources. Accordingly, following discussion of the matter in Brazzaville, the French Administration for Overseas Territories (l'Administration des territoires d'outre-mer) in 1946 created a new financing arrangement, which was placed under the charge of two institutional bodies:

- The Central Fund of French Overseas Territories (La Caisse Centrale de la France d'Outre-mer (CCFOM)); and
- Economic and Social Development Fund (Fonds d'Investissement et de Développement Economique et sScial (FIDES)), managed by CCFOM.

The purpose of the first of these two funds was to provide an avenue from which colonial territories could borrow funds needed for local and regional development initiatives. The second fund was designed to cover the cost of implementing urban infrastructure and other development plans.

In 1926, the French colonial administration established a Bureau of Low-Cost Housing (l'Office de l'Habitat Economique, OHE). The purpose of this institution was to help defray the cost of low-income housing for qualified families in French West Africa. However, by the outbreak of World War I, the OHE, whose activities had been limited to Dakar, had financed no more than a dozen or so housing units.

By 1948, authorities in France had registered their opposition to the production of public housing unless such housing was designed to house employees of the colonial establishment. This opposition was not directed at efforts designed to develop housing for colonial officials based in the colonies or other high level functionaries working for the colonial government. However, to reinforce the housing demand power of employed urban residents through long-term, low interest home loans, the colonial governments established housing credit institutions. There were two such well-known institutions, namely the housing authorities (or *sociétés immobilières*) and housing credit organizations (or *organismes de crédits*). The housing authorities were established as para-state institutions in the 1950s. The interest rate for loans through these institutions was fixed at a non-variable rate of 2.5 per cent for a term of twenty years. Two options, namely simple rent and rent-to-own, were available to qualified consumers. The following specific housing authorities were in existence by the end of the 1950s: the SICAP of Cape Verde, which was created in 1950; SIAEF for the French colonies of Equatorial Africa, created in 1949 and revamped in 1952; SIHCI of Côte d'Ivoire, which was created in 1951; SIM Madagascar, established in 1951; the SIG in Guinea, which was created in 1952; and SIC in Cameroon, which was also created in 1952.

These housing credit entities were responsible for constructing thousands of 'low-income' housing units in the colonies before the end of the colonial era. As intimated above, the French colonial establishment was also involved in the regulation of building activities. In this regard, it enacted legislation stipulating conditions for obtaining a building permit as well as the minimum standards that must be met by building units, especially in the urban areas. Such legislation was usually under the pretext of protecting the health, safety and security of the building's inhabitants as well as users of urban space. Under the same pretext, legislation designed to demolish all structures that threatened human health and safety were enacted. In this connection, a law that was enacted in France on 13 April 1850 to achieve this objective was introduced in Senegal in 1889. A decree of 14 April 1904 designed to protect public health established sanitation units in the colonial territories of French West Africa. Initially introduced in Senegal and later to all territories in the two federations, these units were endowed with powers to form committees that advised the colonial governors on matters relating to sanitation, hygiene and disease prevention.

Land tenure

Prior to the arrival of the French colonial authorities, the land tenure system of Africa was based on the communal ownership (Njoh, 2000; Meek, 1957, 1949). Under this system, the value of land was tied to its use. This value could not be converted to financial or market terms. To be sure, the sale or outright transfer of land was forbidden under this system. A local chief aptly summarized the philosophy underlying the African traditional land tenure system when he stated thus:

> I conceive that land belongs to a vast family of which many are dead, few are living and countless members are still unborn.
>
> (Quoted in Meek, 1949: title page)

Upon their arrival, the French colonial authorities immediately initiated actions to drastically alter the system. Efforts to purchase land from local chiefs at token prices and insisting on bills of sale attesting to such transactions constituted part of the activities in this connection. Such transactions fell outside the purview of laws in force at the time. In 1830, the French colonial administration decided in favour of controlling land-related transactions. In this regard, the French Civil Code was decreed applicable initially in Gorée, Dakar, Saint-Louis and Rufisque in Senegal. These were towns with a significant number of resident French people. The broadening of the jurisdiction of this code to cover said towns, permitted European settlers to legitimize their land entitlements and began a process that had the ultimate goal of commodifying land throughout the colonies. Outside the mentioned towns, the traditional land tenure system remained operational. This did not bode well with the French colonial establishment, which was bent on seizing control over all transactions in land throughout all French overseas territories. The efforts of these officials to supplant the African traditional land tenure system with French varieties were inspired by the success of the English to institute the Torrens Act in Australia. A good recapitulation of the thrust of the Torrens Act is contained in Ridell (1988). The Act recognized land rights as completely separate from human rights and instituted an official land register in which all transactions in land were entered. Earlier on in 1896, the Germans had instituted such a document under the name Grundbuch, concurrently with the passage of the Crown Lands Act in their African colonies (Njoh, 1998, 1995). Perhaps above all, the Napoleonic Doctrine of 1810 informed French colonial land reforms initiatives. The 'Napoleonic property doctrine' stressed individual, as opposed to corporate or communal, property rights.

In 1899, an important decree was enacted on 8 February and modified on 28 March. This decree established two distinct categories of land, communal and public lands, and instituted the land register in the French Congo. The decree was later modified and its scope broadened to cover the entire federation of French Equatorial Africa, on 12 December 1920. The land register was instituted in French West Africa by a decree of 24 July 1906. The decree was slightly modified and introduced in Cameroon on 21 July 1932 (Fisiy, 1992).

A notable aspect of the land reform measures introduced by French colonial authorities was the transformation of 'unoccupied and ownerless lands' (i.e. what was termed *terres vacantes et sans maître*) into property of the colonial state. A number of notable pieces of legislation dealing with state and public lands were enacted before the end of the colonial era. Examples of these include the decrees of

28 September 1928 and 15 November 1935 in French West Africa, the decree of 28 June 1939 in French Equatorial Africa, the decree of 1 September 1945 in Togo and the decree of 5 July 1921 in Cameroon.

This discussion cannot be deemed complete without mention of the French colonial government's decision in 1917 to operate two parallel systems of land tenure wherever this facilitated the attainment of colonial development objectives. As I observed elsewhere (Njoh, 2000), the one system – *l'indigénat* – governed what the French colonial authorities branded the 'natives' or *les indigènes*, while the other governed European residents as well as what the French labelled, *les assimilés*, that is, Western acculturated members of the indigenous population. The *indigénat* system was introduced in Cameroon by a decree of 4 October 1924. It is important to note that the distinction between the two systems is certainly one without a difference. That is despite the fact that in theory the indigénat system suggests some degree of sensitivity to the indigenous land tenure system.

As mentioned earlier, the French colonial establishment was bent on supplanting the indigenous land tenure system with French varieties. It was therefore inconceivable that it could take any steps designed to retain significant aspects of the indigenous system. It is, however, erroneous to assume that the French attained their ultimate goal of supplanting said system with ease. More often than not, success came only after several attempts, particularly with experimental schemes designed to determine the system most likely to guarantee the colonial state's grip on all land in the colonies while minimizing the probability of alienating the native population.

In most cases, land legislation or portions thereof, that were currently in force, or had been at one time or another, in France were simply transplanted verbatim to the colonies. Here, I hasten to draw attention to a French colonial government Land Law of 24 July 1921, officially known as la législation d'attente. Simply an extension of a law that had been employed several decades earlier in 1855 to introduce the transcription system in France, the law was later repealed on 17 June 1959 by Law No. 59-47 of that same year. It was also common practice for the French colonial government to transplant land use and related legislation from one colonial territory to other territories. For instance, the policy in French Equatorial Africa, Cameroon and Togo, to convert into colonial state property all land that was neither individually owned nor duly registered, was an upshot of a 1907 French West Africa Court of Appeal decision, which had ruled that all unregistered customary rights and interests in land were deemed null and void. It is, however, important to note that the law met with fierce resistance in the colonies and had to be rescinded in November 1935. The law that spoke to the issue of '*terres vacantes et sans maître*' mentioned earlier, was designed to replace said policy.

Colonial urban development, research and implementation

To ensure the successful execution of urban development projects, the French colonial authorities created a central agency in charge of designing, conducting feasibility studies and overseeing the implementation of such projects in the colonial territories. Created in 1949 and located in the colonial master nation, this agency was named le Bureau d'Etudes pour les Equipements d'Outre-mer (BCEOM). The creation of an agency such as BCEOM is only one manifestation of the preference for centralized administration on the part of French colonial authorities. However, the stated rationale for creating the agency had to do with the absence of the necessary expertise and technical support in the colonial territories. For about two years after its creation, BCEOM was involved mainly with drawing up of urban plans. As of 1951, it became involved with housing and related activities. To ensure efficiency and effectiveness in this arena, BCEOM created a housing committee (le comité de l'habitat). The committee was composed of representatives of all organizations and agencies, such as public works, economic affairs, and public health, with interest in the housing policy field. In practice, BCEOM was and continues to be involved in carrying out special and general studies, overseeing the implementation of technical or specialized projects, providing technical advice, and drawing up urban master plans. Furthermore, the agency conducted and continues to conduct research on the implications of urban planning for socio-economic development. In addition, the agency has worked and continues to work in collaboration with other agencies, such as the Centre for Tropical Wood (Centre du Bois Tropical) and the Laboratory for Bridges and Road (Laboratoire des Ponts et Chaussées) as well as agencies based in project beneficiary territories.

Emphasis on collaboration with entities based in the colonial territories was accentuated in the 1950s. In this respect, efforts were made to encourage the use of local talent and labour in the execution of all projects. One reason for this policy was to reduce the high cost involved in hiring skilled labour from Europe. Prominent amongst these efforts was the decision to establish a centre for training professionals in general administration and project implementation in Dakar. This did not result in a diminished role for BCEOM. Rather, the agency remained active and involved with urban projects in the territories in the capacity of overseer and technical advisor.

Urban planning and French colonial development objectives

Based on the foregoing account, the French were deeply involved in the town planning field in sub-Saharan Africa. As noted earlier, this involvement predated, and continued through, the French colonial era in the region. In fact, this involvement continues to this day as attested to by ongoing urban development projects in which French architectural and planning firms are playing leading roles. Jean-Louis Venard's work (1986), entitled *Interventions françaises dans le secteur urbain en Afrique noire francophone*, contains a detailed account of some of these projects, especially those in which the French government has/had a significant input. My concern in this chapter is however with the urban development projects in which the French colonial authorities were involved as opposed to contemporary ones. Given the enormous demands on the constrained colonial budget, one cannot help but ponder why urban planning and related projects were accorded such a priority place in the context of colonial administration. It is easy to appreciate the raison d'être of these projects once we understand the role that urban centres played in the calculus of colonial development. Almost always located on the coast or at major traffic nodes, these centres were crucial in facilitating the movement of natural resources from the colonial territories for onward transmission to the metropolitan country. Additionally, as hinted at earlier, activities such as urban development, which were designed to improve the standard of living in the colonies, were necessary as a strategy to attract qualified administrators to the so-called overseas territories. Perhaps above all, urban development projects, particularly because they were based on principles of spatial organization in vogue in the metropolitan country, were part of France's larger *mission civilisatrice* agenda. Based on this agenda, the French colonial authorities considered the task of civilizing what they saw as backward and primitive societies of 'the dark continent', a compelling one.

Discussion and conclusion

French colonial architects and urban planners proved rather adept at employing their talent and skills to complement efforts designed to attain broader goals of French colonialism in Africa. Initially, these goals entailed capturing and defending colonial territories from other European rivals, and then assuaging nationalistic resistance within the captured territories. The need to defend the territory partially explains the tendency to locate colonial government capitals on high altitudes which afforded an uninterrupted view of their surroundings. It also explains the apparent infatuation with the construction of forts during the early phase of the European conquest in areas such as Gorée and Rufisque (Senegal). The need to assuage nationalistic resistance was at the root of policies aimed at promoting the growth and development of colonial towns while neglecting traditional settlements. It also explains, at least in part, why two parallel systems of land tenure, the 'traditional' and the 'modern', were created in the French colonies. This system afforded an opportunity for the colonial authorities to placate members of the civil society, particularly those who were quick at adopting the French culture or what the French preferred to call *les évolués*. The extension of special benefits such as access to prime land, the provision of infrastructure and other necessary services in their neighbourhoods, helped to neutralize the politically active and threatening segment of the population. Furthermore, using zoning ordinances to confine members of this potentially volatile population in one specific location effectively placed them under the watchful eyes of colonial authorities.

French architects in colonial Africa were also aware of developments in thinking about the colonial enterprise as a whole. The final years of the French colonial era in Africa were marked by a general retreat from the more overtly domineering and assimilating strategies for which the French colonial enterprise was well-known. Accordingly, French colonial authorities had decided in favour of more subtle and persuasive strategies aimed at 'winning the hearts and minds' of the indigenous populace. Hence they designed schemes that employed planning as a tool of association and persuasion rather than one of overt domination and assimilation as was previously the case. Within the framework of this new orientation, French colonial urban planners began making efforts to incorporate the wishes and concerns of the indigenous population in the structures they produced. For instance, planners in the predominantly Muslim regions of sub-Saharan Africa included regulations requiring that dwelling units be enclosed within fences of at least 1.5 metres high (Sinou *et al.*, 1989). This policy constituted an important part of efforts to show some sensitivity to the Muslim culture that treasures privacy within people's living quarters. If nothing else, this requirement went a good way towards blurring the otherwise sharp contrast between the colonial structures and fenced compounds of members of the predominantly Muslim indigenous population. The practice of ensuring that colonial structures blended in with the surrounding environment had become widespread throughout French colonial Africa in the 1900s.

In Morocco, for instance, when French colonial architect Joseph Marrast designed Casablanca's courthouse in 1920, he incorporated many aspects of Moroccan indigenous/Islamic architecture (Elleh, 2002; Wright, 1991). Marrast's aim, as Wright (1991: 1) suggested, was to help quell the hostility of Moroccans toward European domination. In Marrast's own words (quoted in Wright, 1991: 1), 'little by little we conquer the hearts of the natives and win their affection, as is our duty as colonizers'.

Marrast's view that the hearts and minds of the members of the indigenous population could be won through architecture was neither novel nor unrealistic. Several years earlier, French colonial architects in Indochina had advanced identical arguments. These architects had contended that the incorporation of indigenous features in colonial designs would serve as a gesture of respect and tolerance for Indochinese culture (Cooper, 2000). The main purpose of this was to gain the gratitude and support of the indigenous population. Such support was a critical element in efforts on the part of colonial authorities to consolidate political power and ensure social control in the colonial territories.

Elements of physical planning such as architecture had finally made their mark as tools of political and social control in colonial Africa. Political leaders in the colonial master nations particularly appreciated this development. In France, political leaders of the time, such as Hubert Lyautey, who served under Gallienni when Madagascar first became a French colony, had publicly acknowledged the importance of architectural and spatial structures in the French empire building effort. Lyautey was one of the most ardent advocates of employing architecture and physical planning as tools to combat resistance in the colonies and winning political support at home (in France) (Wright, 1991).

French colonial authorities in Africa spared no effort in cladding urban planning within the institutional garbs necessary for making it a powerful tool of the colonial state. One way by which this feat was accomplished was by incorporating urban planning within an important colonial state institution, the Army Corps of Engineers.

Another strategy was to accord important planning decisions the power of law. In most cases, as noted above, laws already in force in the metropolitan country were transplanted verbatim to the colonies. Yet another strategy to institutionalize urban planning in colonial Africa was the formalization of previously informal activities with spatial implications. For example, colonial planning laws required registration in the colonial government land registry of activities such as the acquisition, alienation and/or transfer of land. Similarly, building permits were required for all construction works. These requirements, part of efforts to institutionalize planning, were without precedent in pre-colonial Africa.

French colonial powers in Africa were certainly not unique for striving to empower the colonial state by institutionalizing urban planning. The institutionalization of planning, or any government activity for that matter, is an established means for attaining the objective of power, defined as the ability to effect change in the environment (Hoch, 1984, 1994). A more glaring picture of the link between institutionalization and power can be seen through Marxist theoretical lenses. According to Marxist planning theorists, power is 'the exercise of political domination based on the exploitation of the working class by the capitalist class' (Fischler, 1995: 16). In the context of French colonial Africa, power entailed the domination of the colonized by the colonizers. This domination would have been less effective without institutionalization. Thus, as Fischler (1995: 17) states, 'when a capacity to be effective is institutionalized, the result is domination. And when domination is legitimate, it is called authority'. Institutionalization of colonial urban policy in Africa was also necessary to effectuate compliance or obedience.

Ideological objectives

While it is difficult to know with exactitude what French colonial town planners in Africa were thinking, it is possible to make some inference from the product of their actions. An analysis of these actions suggests the following as major ideological objectives of physical and spatial development projects in colonial Africa: formality; spatial order; bourgeoisification; Euro-centricity; and capitalism.

Formality

An important but largely ignored objective of French urban planners and architects in colonial Africa was to formalize land development activities, especially building construction, infrastructure provision and spatial organization that were informal until the onset of the colonial époque. Accordingly, rules were introduced governing representation in planning practice, the production and exchange of this representation (cf. Fischler, 1995), professional communication, the 'how much', 'when' and 'where' questions (as in rate, timing, and location) of land development activities, and procedural issues (e.g. the building application process; acquiring and transferring land rights). Formalization, perhaps above all, spelled new rules for interacting in space and introduced penalties for defaulters. This action, that is the formalization of previously informal processes, had several negative implications. To appreciate these implications, it is important to note that colonial planning documents were written in planning jargon supplemented with technically produced graphics that made little if any sense to the formally educated, let alone the illiterate members of the native population. Resulting from this was, amongst other problems, the fact that colonial planners' specialized language was incomprehensible to those they were professing to plan for. The problem in this situation is not as much one of comprehensibility as it is tantamount to the use of the planning ideology itself as an instrument of power and domination (Fischler, 1995; Edelman, 1964; Forester, 1989; Schön, 1983). Fischler's (1995: 18) assertion to the effect that 'power is inscribed in the professional culture of planners through practice and representation, that is, through the selective organization of attention and the construction of meaning' is particularly informative here.

Spatial order

Spatial order has always been an important objective of urban planning. French planners in colonial Africa, like their professional colleagues elsewhere, were interested in creating an idealized world in which the location of land use activities and traffic flows observed a well defined spatial order. This is not to say, as popular opinion may suggest, that spatial order was absent in pre-colonial Africa. Rather, it is important to note that the idealized spatial order introduced in Africa by French colonial authorities was/is Euro-centric. In consequence, indigenous spatial structures that pre-dated the colonial era were effectively supplanted by a European variety. Spatial order dictated a need for compartmentalizing land use activities in the colony. Here, the instrument of choice was the zoning ordinance, whose pretext transcended spatial order as it was used to achieve the objective of racial residential segregation. In this connection, French urban planners in colonial Africa produced urban design plans that ensured the physical separation of the European from the indigenous populations with the former occupying better areas richly furnished with modern amenities while members of the latter group were assigned the least desirable areas equipped with minimal modern amenities. This had several negative implications, prominent amongst which was the problem of inequality. This conspicuous problem was at once a consequence and a source of oppression. In *The Wretched of the Earth*, Fanon (1963) considers racially segregated urban areas as psychologically oppressive and amounting to a form of violence against members of the native population in colonial cities.

Bourgeoisification

An important ideological objective of French colonial urban planners was to replicate the idealized living conditions of the French middle class, or bourgeoisie, in Africa.

This objective was at the heart of urban development projects that sought to create clones of French housing units and neighbourhoods (e.g. the European Districts) in colonial Africa. To be sure, French colonial planners were not unique in this regard. Rather, it would appear bourgeoisification was the objective of many urban development schemes throughout colonial Africa. It is this phenomenon to which Mazrui (1986) alludes when he talks of how European middle-class men and women sought to fulfil some of the ambitious spatial and architectural dreams they could not fulfil in Europe by building monumental residential units surrounded by spacious gardens in Africa.

Euro-centricity

Euro-centricity, the view that what is good for Europeans is good for everyone, was yet another important ideological objective of colonial planning schemes in Africa. French colonial planners in the region vigorously pursued the ideological objective of universalizing European middle-class environmental standards. In this connection, conscious efforts were made through colonial government legislation (e.g. via specified standards in building codes) or seduction (a form of 'power over') to discourage the use of local materials in favour of European varieties. This caused several problems which can best be appreciated by re-examining the notion of ideology, particularly in terms of what Althusser (1971) and Therborn (1980) have called the 'subjection-qualification' dialectic (Oliga, 1996). On the one hand, subjection refers to the individual's (or subject's) 'subjugation to a particular force or social order that favors or disfavors certain values and beliefs' (Oliga, 1996: 172). In colonial Africa, the values and beliefs of the natives associated with the production of housing and spatial form were discounted in favour of those of the French in particular and Europeans in general. On the other hand, qualification has to do with training subjects to carry out activities necessary for the system's survival.

Capitalism

As stated earlier, French planners in colonial Africa were adept at employing their expertise and the power conferred on them by their profession to contribute towards attainment of the broader goals of the colonial enterprise. Prominent amongst these goals was the objective of integrating Africa into the global capitalist system. The formalization of previously informal processes such as those involved in the production of space was part of a larger scheme to attain this objective. French planners in colonial Africa were thus inspired by the ideology of urban planning laws and policies, and that the spatial structures they produced were capable of providing a model for capitalist economic development. Ideology was particularly a motivating factor in efforts on the part of colonial authorities in Africa to vigorously develop and implement land reform measures that succeeded in replacing the region's traditional land tenure system with a European variety. A critical ideological aim of initiatives in this connection was to transform land, a previously traditional factor of production, into a commodity, which can be transferred, exchanged and alienated with facility in the 'open market'. This transformation effectively individualized the ownership and control of land, thereby eliminating all claims thereto based on kinship or community.

Thus, colonial land reform efforts in Africa constituted an ideological buttress designed to perpetuate the historical legacy linking private property to the private ownership and control of the means of production – an important condition for the viability of capitalism (Njoh, 1998; Burgess, 1985).

3 British colonialism, economics and spatial structures

Introduction

Liberal and dependency characterizations of the state in colonial Africa tend to attribute excessive weight to colonial government officials. To be sure, an overwhelming majority of those who participated in the colonial policy implementation process in French colonies were directly employed by the metropolitan colonial state in France or a local colonial state in Africa. However, this was not the case in British colonial Africa, where private entities, particularly chartered companies, played a critical role in the colonial policy implementation process. Thus, to fully address questions relating to planning ideology and practice in colonial Africa, it is necessary to gain some appreciation of the activities of private entities. Prominent in this regard are those activities that were designed to promote the growth and development of commerce, plantation agriculture and mining. This chapter proposes to address the following specific questions. What was the nature and magnitude of the collaboration between private entities and the colonial state in economic development in British colonial Africa? How did the economic development initiatives of the colonial state and private entities affect the spatial structure of British colonies in Africa?

British colonial Africa is ideal for exploring these and cognate questions for at least two major reasons. First, as Robert Home (1997) noted, mercantile capitalism and the colonial state represented the Crown in British colonies more than elsewhere. Second, British colonies, more than other European colonies, witnessed unparalleled emphasis on mining, railways, iron and steel production and plantation agriculture, which created new urban landscapes through a mixture of public and private sector enterprises. Mahmood Mamdani (1996) provides a number of other reasons that make British colonial Africa ideally suitable for exploring the central question of this chapter: 'Britain was the first to marshal authoritarian possibilities in indigenous culture' (p. 286). Perhaps more importantly, British colonial authorities were the first to consider a cultural project – particularly the need to harness the moral, historical, and community impetus behind local custom to achieve broader colonial goals – as a key to realizing hegemonic domination in the colonies.

The state in British colonial Africa

There are three competing characterizations of the state in colonial Africa that must be reviewed at this juncture in the chapter in particular and this book in general, especially because of the centrality of the colonial state, its motives and capabilities. Characterizations of the nature of the colonial state in Africa have undergone three distinct transformations since the demise of the colonial era in most of Africa in the 1960s (Willis, 1995). Initially, colonial policymaking and outcomes were considered a function of the personal proclivities of colonial authorities 'on the ground' in the colonies. The 1970s witnessed the emergence of an alternative view of the colonial state in Africa, rooted in dependency theory. Dependency theorists consider colonial rule one of many episodes in efforts designed to marginalize Africa. Furthermore, dependency theorists perceive major policies of the colonial state as a reflection of the needs of the colonial power. Recently, Bruce Berman (e.g. 1984, 1997, 1998) and others (e.g. Berman and Lonsdale, 1992) have offered well-reasoned and sometimes persuasive critiques of these two major views. Berman and Lonsdale are especially critical of characterizations of the colonial state in Africa that are informed by dependency theory.

For instance, in his copious critique of Crawford Young's analysis of 'the African colonial state' (Young, 1994), Berman (1997: 563) charges that, 'Young's main thesis regarding the autonomy and irresistible power of the colonial state is, very simply, incorrect'. According to Berman, the colonial state in Africa possessed limited power, although colonial authorities wanted their African subjects to see the state as powerful, omniscient, omnipotent and in possession of irresistible force. The need to portray the colonial state in this light was especially magnified in the case of British colonial officials, who were desirous of conveying a bloated image of their power and authority to Africans. The truth, as Berman (1997: 563) noted, is that,

> Rather than imposing bureaucratic apparatuses of power, most colonial states were ramshackle operations, constantly short of money through their dependence on local sources of revenue, lacking in the most basic forms of expert knowledge, and possessing only the most limited resources of coercion.

While Berman's criticism is well-reasoned, I must say that it tends to exaggerate the colonial state's powerlessness. In fact, Berman appears to concede this point when he acknowledges the fact that the colonial state was armed and capable of wreaking havoc on what were usually unarmed local populations. I do, however, agree with Berman that there was usually the need for colonial officials to enlist the co-operation of members of the indigenous population. As Berman (1997: 563) puts it,

> To balance the conflicting demands of accumulation and legitimation and achieve a degree of law and order that outwardly appeared as unchallenged control, colonial states had to constantly negotiate a modus vivendi accommodation with their African subjects.

While this is true, we cannot lose sight of the fact that colonial authorities usually entered such negotiations from a position that was, by far, stronger than that of their colonial subjects. The mere fact that members of the African population were referred to as (colonial) 'subjects' is telling. Thus, the relationship between colonial officials and Africans was akin to a master–servant relationship.

It is true that colonial authorities, especially the British, as part of the indirect rule strategy, enlisted the participation of local elites and other indigenous entities in the colonial policy implementation process. However, this did not result in eroding the power of the colonial state. If anything, it served to bolster the colonial state's powers. Any theory of colonial power that fails to treat indigenous or other entities on the payroll of the colonial state as part of the colonial machinery is inherently contradictory. Thus, local or indigenous agents of the colonial state constituted part of the larger colonial apparatus. To better appreciate this assertion, it is important to understand colonialism for what it is. It is, as Fieldhouse (1981: 7) reminded us, 'exploitation by the foreign society and its agents who occupied the dependency to serve their own interests, not that of the subject people'. Throughout British colonial Africa, agents of imperial governments were comprised of a coterie of European expatriates working as colonial civil servants; or missionaries, teachers, doctors and small-scale entrepreneurs; or as managers of mines, railways, plantations, banks and trading companies that were owned and operated by private entities based in the colonial master nation. Except in the few settler colonies, such as South Africa and Zimbabwe, most of these individuals had no attachment to Africa, and strived to save as much as possible for their retirement in Europe. The private companies had one important objective, namely profit maximization. Realization of this objective required the collaboration of the colonial state. I discuss the specific nature of this collaboration in the urban and regional planning domain later. For now, I examine the ideological foundation of British colonial physical planning.

British colonial planning ideologies

Robert Home (1997) asserted that the overseas expansion project of which British colonial ventures in Africa constituted a part, contained three competing and co-existing ideologies. These ideologies, which Home discussed under the broad categories of 'state control', 'capitalist', and 'utopian' simultaneously influenced colonial structures in British colonies in Africa and elsewhere.

The ideology of state control

This ideology saw colonies as nothing more than an initiative by the British colonial power, or more accurately the Crown, through its agents. Agents of the Crown in this case were not limited to colonial authorities on the ground in the colonies. Rather, such agents included the local ruling elite and other indigenous institutions whose participation in the colonial administrative process was accorded officialdom through the colonial administration policy of 'indirect rule'. The local colonial state, including the colonial governors and ruling elites, articulated political authority in many forms, but particularly through spatial and physical planning. In this regard, they seized every opportunity to influence the spatial structure of villages, towns, or regions. The local colonial state also exercised enormous political power through the writing and promulgation of laws designed to regulate the timing and rate of growth of the built environment.

The capitalist ideology

This ideology had one main objective, namely the accumulation of wealth, within the framework of imperial and colonial development. The established sources of this wealth were trade (commerce), extraction (mining), and plantation (cash crop agriculture). The ideology is at the root of the intense collaboration that took place between the British colonial government/the colonial state and chartered companies such as the British South Africa Company. As noted above, an important objective of the chartered companies was profit maximization. In their efforts to attain this objective, chartered and other private companies pressured the local colonial state to relax municipal planning regulations. More often than not, the colonial state obliged. Thus, the colonial project was tantamount to a mixed venture in which the colonial state or the Crown collaborated with private capitalist interest to exploit colonial territories (Home, 1997). Essentially therefore, power was shared amongst these entities.

The utopian ideology

Seen as a utopian project, colonial town planning was designed to achieve a number of ideals. More importantly, colonial planning was viewed as 'an opportunity to experiment with forms of social organization (such as communal control of land) that were less achievable at home' (Home, 1997: 4). As a utopian project, planning in British colonial Africa strived to promote Euro-centric notions of property ownership and environmental design. The inability to implement plans that embodied or reflected pure Euro-centric ideals, was usually a function of financial and other resource constraints. However, every once in a while, it succumbed to local pressures for designs that embodied African traditional constructs of property ownership (e.g. land tenure) and spatial organization.

Why would the colonial state even bother to pay attention to local pressures? The scant number of colonial officials in British colonies, an important reason why Britain adopted the 'indirect rule' strategy, dictated the need to unveil innovative strategies to legitimize the colonial state's authority. It did not take long for authorities to determine that the destruction and/or transformation of African traditional practices or institutions seriously threatened control and legitimacy. As Berman (1984) noted, colonial authorities were especially fearful of the possible emergence of a class-conscious and combative African working class that was completely detached from the land. Accordingly, the colonial state proceeded to enact what could best be described as an ambiguous set of policies that at once promoted Euro-centric and indigenous African ideals in the areas of property ownership and spatial order.

Trade, extraction and plantation

Following on the heels of the Portuguese, who had been developing military outposts and forts along the West African coast as far back as the sixteenth century, the British constructed protective outposts in Accra and Sekondi in Ghana, in the seventeenth century. It was, however, not until after the signing of the Berlin Treaty of 1884/5 that imperial Britain proceeded to develop most of the cities that were later to constitute the nucleus of urbanization in its African colonies. In Nigeria alone, the British established five notable cities, namely Jos (1903), Maiduguri (1907), Enugu (1909), Port Harcourt (1912), and Kaduna (1913), immediately following the Berlin Treaty. While not all the early trading posts developed into large cities, and while some have not survived to this day, it is worth noting that the port cities and other British-initiated settlements, such as those mentioned above, served as major trading nodes in British colonial economies. Hodgkin (quoted in Gugler and Flanagan, 1978: 30) succinctly characterizes the role of these towns in the colonial economy in the following words:

> Their main function [was] to drain out of Africa its ground-nuts, palm-products, coffee, cocoa, cotton, minerals; and to pump into Africa European consumer goods – cloth, kerosene, bicycles, sewing-machines.

Thus, the cities were active in three respects. First, they directed trade towards the coast. Second, they steered trade toward the colonial metropolis in particular and the global economy in general. Finally, the cities served as warehouses for European goods penetrating the continent. Therefore, trade played a critical role in shaping the spatial structure of human settlements in British and other European colonies in Africa.

Patterns of urbanization during the colonial era in Africa tended to proceed largely along the lines traced by the flow of goods destined for overseas markets (Gugler and Flanagan, 1978). It is therefore hardly any wonder that the seaport cities, because of their role as trading posts or conduits for the transmission of goods from the colonies to the metropolis, developed in size and importance at rates that far exceeded those of their non-coastal counterparts.

Thus, any worthwhile effort to understand activities designed to shape the built environment in Africa during the colonial era must pay more than passing attention to the role of the colonial state and that of private, especially commercial, entities. Here, it is important to know that British colonial authorities in Africa did not begin crafting policies aimed specifically at shaping the built environment until later in the colonial epoch. Initially, these authorities were preoccupied with policies designed to advance British economic interest. Accordingly, they crafted and implemented schemes that sought to exploit and export natural resources from the colonies to the metropolitan countries.

Commerce and trade constituted important components of colonial economic development policies. However, British imperial authorities might have been a little slow in recognizing that infrastructure was and remains a sine qua non for success in these twin areas. In fact, there can be no commerce or trade unless the necessary infrastructure is in place. Lord Frederick Lugard, best known for his role as Governor of colonial Northern Nigeria and for advocating 'indirect rule' as a viable strategy for colonial policy administration in Africa, erroneously believed otherwise. He opined that trade would always go wherever the Union Jack went (Pedler, 1975). However, as it turned out, it was infrastructure, particularly the railway, and not the flag, which attracted trade. The following examples are illustrative. The Cape was largely an agrarian society, with 80 per cent of its White population employed on the land (Katzenellenbogen, 1975: 388). This was the case as late as 1854 when the region boasted only one railway line – a privately owned and operated line – that was at most 65 miles (about 104 km) long. However, the discovery in 1870 of diamonds at Kimberly triggered a flurry of railway-building initiatives by private entities and the government alike. Initially, with funds from the public treasury, the Cape government undertook to extend the lines from the Cape and from Port Elizabeth to Kimberly. Later, with the initiation of efforts to extract gold at the Witwatersrand from 1886, private entities began investing in the development of railway lines in the Transvaal.

In Nigeria, the opening of the Kano railway in 1911 was soon followed by an unprecedented increase in goods bound for Europe leaving the northwestern region of the country through the Lagos seaport. The local groundnut market, which saw the arrival of eighteen new purchasing firms, was the leading beneficiary in this regard. As for the groundnut-farming community in Kano and surrounding areas, it reacted to the opportunities presented by the new railway line by multiplying its productivity. In short, the advent of railways in Nigeria resulted in a dramatic increase in the economic productivity of remote areas.

More noteworthy for the purpose of the present discussion is the fact that, while it might not have been the intention of colonial authorities, the building of railways not only drastically altered the spatial structure, it also facilitated surface transportation in colonial Africa. The growth of commerce and trade led to the enactment of a number of policies with far-reaching implications for the spatial structure of colonial territories. For one thing, this growth accentuated the need for the colonial government to enact policies designed to reorganize commercial land use activities. For instance, in 1913, the British colonial authorities enacted a policy aimed at demarcating and auctioning trading sites to able and willing traders. The policy sought to ensure that non-indigenous traders were physically separated from their indigenous counterparts. In Nigeria, this policy effectively compartmentalized trading activities such that each local product – groundnuts, cotton, hides and so on – had its own specific site. Schemes such as this are forerunners to the plethora of formal zoning ordinances that were later to constitute conspicuous elements of physical planning in British colonial Africa. For another thing, the British colonial authorities devoted a disproportionately large portion of the resources for transportation infrastructure development to railway construction, particularly because of this transport mode's relative cost-effectiveness. This policy effectively discouraged the development of competing modes of transportation such as roads. In fact, some analysts (e.g. Pedler, 1975) suggest that rather than simply being a consequence of the development of railways, the discouragement of road building activities was actually a premeditated act on the part of planners in British colonies. In practice, this policy entailed deliberately leaving gaps in road networks. This means that most (interior) areas that were accessible by rail were inaccessible by road.

The growth of commerce and trade also accounts for a significant proportion of the increase in immigrant population that occurred in British colonial Africa. Particularly noteworthy in this regard is the growth of the population of immigrants from the Middle East and India. Irrespective of their nationality, members of this immigrant population were collectively referred to in West Africa as 'Syrians or Lebanese'. It is important to note that East and Southern Africa also witnessed an influx of a significant number of people of Asian origin during the colonial era.

Often starting off as poor traders, who made their living by buying and selling local and foreign goods, members of the Middle Eastern and Indian immigrant population, over time, prospered and rose to wield immense economic and political power in West Africa. The situation was similar in Southern and East Africa, where Asians soon saw their social status as superior to that of their native counterparts. This view was reinforced by the official policies of the colonial state. One manifestation of these policies was in the area of spatial planning, where the perceived superiority of Asians in East and Southern Africa was reflected in the town planning schemes of colonial governments. We discuss specific aspects of some of these schemes later in this book.

Sir Frederick Pedler (1975) does a fine job summarizing Britain's trading and other commercial activities in colonial Africa. Prior to, and earlier on in, the colonial era, Africa was seen as hardly more than a 'continent of outposts' (Pedler, 1975: 95). However, this view significantly changed in the 1880s when the British imperial government and private entrepreneurs recognized Africa's commercial importance. British colonial authorities set out to secure a number of vital trade routes as a means of facilitating the accomplishment of their commercial and economic goals in the region. Prior to that time Arabs and Swahili-speaking natives, supported by Indian capital, controlled most of the routes in North and East Africa, respectively. These trade routes had grown in popularity as a function of the slave trade. The British colonial era in the region, however, coincided with a period when Britain had embarked on a mission to abolish the trade in human cargo. A noteworthy by-product of British efforts in this regard is the decline that was suffered by a number of previously great human settlements. This was particularly the case with human settlements which owed their growth and development largely to the slave trade and related activities. Here, I draw attention to sizable ancient human settlements, some of them parts of city-states (e.g. Benin) and others parts of kingdoms (e.g. Ashanti) or simply trading posts (e.g. Elmina), which declined significantly in status once the British had succeeded in abolishing the slave trade in the region. The activities of the British colonial authorities in this connection culminated in the administrative separation in 1874 of their possessions on the Gold Coast and Lagos from those in Sierra Leone farther west on the West African Coast. This resulted in the creation of a new dependency, the Gold Coast Colony.

Colonial rule, economic life and spatial development stand out as predominant purposes of British imperialism in the nineteenth century. In this regard, and especially following the abolition of the slave trade, British imperial policy had two avowed aims, namely to transform African societies into: (1) communities capable of producing raw materials and trading freely, and (2) viable consumers of manufactured British products. With respect to the first objective Pedler (1975) makes the following observation regarding Britain's position on commerce in the Niger Delta region at the time: 'In the Niger Delta the Foreign Office was determined that trade should be open to all and should not be restricted by the old-established palm-oil merchants' (Pedler, 1975: 97). One outcome of the British imperial government's positive predisposition towards trade in the newly acquired territories was increased traffic in navigable rivers such as the River Niger. The increased traffic in turn resulted in the growth of the commercial sector and commensurate expansion of the built environment, especially in areas along navigable waterways.

While by the late 1870s there were at least four private British companies operating in the Niger Delta region, no such company operated on the east coast of Africa. However, Pedler (1975) notes that William Mackinnon, founder of the British and Indian Steam Navigation Company, had contemplated launching such an operation in the region at about that time. He was discouraged from doing so in 1877 by the British Foreign Office, which was not prepared to offer his business the necessary protection against foreign powers. The Foreign Office, however, later changed its position and effectively opened the way for British private investors to establish business in the region. In doing so, the British imperial government had hoped that a British investor would venture into, and subsequently occupy, inland territories such as Uganda, with royal charters. Mackinnon's British East Africa Company, which was chartered in 1888, was encouraged by this policy. The company, however, went bankrupt four years after it was chartered, although not before it had set up its own administration, which was endowed with powers to negotiate with the local chiefs.

The role of chartered and other private companies

Chartered companies played a dual role as colonial government administrators and entrepreneurs. In both capacities, chartered companies wielded enormous socio-economic and political power and played instrumental roles in shaping the built environment in colonial Africa. The case of the British South Africa Company (BSA Co.), whose founder, Cecil Rhodes, is one of the best-known figures in African colonial history, is illustrative. The company was chartered in 1889 and concomitant with this charter was its empowerment to negotiate with African chiefs. The charter also endowed the company with powers to acquire land from the local chiefs. The company had jurisdiction over the Rhodesias (i.e. Northern Rhodesia or present-day Zambia and Southern Rhodesia, now Zimbabwe). The BSA Co. was active in the Rhodesias for more than three decades. During this period, it rose to prominence as a player in British colonial politics. In fact, the BSA Co. functioned, for all practical purposes, as a colonial government. In this regard, it constructed public infrastructure, particularly railways. Although here it bears stressing that unlike a conventional government, the company was expecting to recover its expenditure out of commercial profits. Such recovery never occurred until the company gave up its governmental functions (Pedler, 1975).

The need to promote commerce and trade in the colonies was in line with the British liberal economic theory that was in vogue at the time. British liberal economic thinkers had advised the colonial authorities on the need to make colonial territories self-sustaining. The state, they contended, had no role 'in organizing production or in accumulating and investing capital, except in roads and harbors' (Flint, 1966: 141). This British colonial doctrine dictated that colonies live from their own resources, without depending on subsidies from the metropolitan power. This was in diametric opposition to the French colonial philosophy, which had adopted the policy of subsidizing, whenever necessary, colonial government revenues from the metropolitan government coffers.

The British imperial philosophy of cultivating self-sustaining colonies explains, at least in part, the dearth of planned or purposeful actions for development in territories that were under British control. The absence of such actions notwithstanding, British colonial rule had a profound effect on the economies and built environment of the territories it controlled in the region. British rule brought an end to internal tolls on the movement of goods, and facilitated the movement of people, goods and services through especially improved water-based facilities. As noted earlier, British colonial rule also contributed to the abolition of the slave trade. The demise of the slave trade resulted in, among other things, compelling members of the native population to re-channel their productive energies to more morally acceptable economic endeavours. This in turn resulted in intensifying the goods, savings and capital accumulation process.

This process ignited a new wave of urbanization as economically progressive Africans deemed it necessary to migrate to the urban centres. The migration of Africans to the towns or urban centres is something the British colonial authorities not only frowned on but also strived vigorously to discourage. Colonial authorities were bent on preserving the 'good life' of towns, complete with concomitant amenities, exclusively for Europeans in the colonies. The European population in the colonies had, until the late-1890s, been growing steadily in East and Southern Africa. In West

Table 3.1 Road density in colonial Africa, 1935–1963

Colony	1935	1950	1963
Basotoland	0.02	N/A	0.06
Bechuanaland	0.001	N/A	0.01
Gambia	0.004	0.09	0.12
Gold Coast	0.04	0.05	0.13
Kenya	0.03	0.05	0.08
Nigeria [a]	0.02	0.04	0.08
Northern Rhodesia	0.02	0.02	0.05
Nyasaland	0.06	0.07	0.11
Sierra Leone	0.03	0.04	0.09
Southern Rhodesia	0.04	0.06	0.19 [a]
Swaziland	0.11	N/A	0.13
Tanganyika	0.02	0.04	0.04
Uganda	0.03	0.06	0.08
British Empire Average	0.02	0.04	0.00
French Equatorial Africa [b]	0.007	0.007	0.03
French West Africa [c]	0.01	0.02	0.05
French Empire Average	0.009	0.014	0.04
Belgian Congo	0.02	0.04	0.07
Ruanda-Urundi	0.10	N/A	0.21 [d]
Angola	0.02	0.03	N/A
Mozambique	0.03	N/A	N/A
South Africa	0.11	0.23	0.27 [d]

a) Includes British Cameroons.
b) Includes Cameroon, Chad, Gabon, Moyen Congo, Ubangi-Shari (now Central African Republic), but not British Cameroons.
c) Includes Dahomey, Guinea, Ivory Coast, Mali, Mauritania, Niger, Senegal, Upper Volta.
d) Data from 1965.

Source: Herbst (2000)

Africa, this population had been growing only very gradually. One reason for this, and indeed a plausible explanation for the absence of a 'settled European population' in West Africa, has to do with the poor health conditions that were a notorious feature of the region. Pedler (1975: 99, citing Kingsley, 1897: 32) notes that in 1894 alone, more than half of the White people in the Gold Coast (now Ghana) died, while 'at Bonny, nine men out of eleven perished of yellow fever'.

Private entities and transport infrastructure development

Infrastructure development in British colonies was certainly not a monopoly of the colonial state as was the case in French colonies. Rather, private enterprises were involved in the development of railways, ports and harbours. For instance, as noted earlier, the British South Africa Company (BSA Co.) was responsible for constructing railways in Northern Rhodesia (now Zambia) and Southern Rhodesia (present-day Zimbabwe). Similarly, a private entity, the Niger Company, was responsible for constructing harbour facilities at Burutu in Nigeria. Also, a private enterprise, the Sierra Leone Development Company, is on record for building a railway and a port in colonial Sierra Leone.

The vessels and vehicles that used the transport infrastructure in British colonies were in a good many cases privately-owned as well. For example, private vessels were known to navigate the rivers Gambia, Volta, Niger and Benue. In addition, private companies such as Swanzy Co., were involved in the operation of ferries, which had become a common feature of inter-modal transportation combining roads and waterways in British colonies in Africa. Private enterprises proved more effective, in some cases, than colonial government transport departments. The case of Sierra Leone where the colonial Public Works Department (PWD) was replaced by the United Africa Company as the operator of the colony's ferries in 1931, is illustrative.

The activities of private enterprises would be of little or no significance in the context of the present discussion were it not for the vital role such enterprises played in the construction of physical space in colonial Africa. As implied earlier, these enterprises made their most indelible mark on the colonial landscape through their activities in mining, plantation agriculture and the concomitant workers' housing they developed. Recall that some of these enterprises not only enjoyed the same rights and privileges but also functioned as colonial governments. The case of the BSA Co. mentioned above is exemplary. The BSA Co. remained in its role as the sole administrative entity in Northern Rhodesia until 1924. That the BSA Co.'s administrative control over Northern Rhodesia came to an end in 1924 is only of academic importance. This is particularly because long after the end of its administrative responsibility over the colony, the BSA Co. continued to own and operate the mines in Northern Rhodesia, and with the many innovations in metallurgy realized in the early 1900s, the BSA Co. was able to build a vast copper industry in the colony. The successful record of the BSA Co. in mining is arguably at the root of the tremendous growth in the urban population experienced by Northern Rhodesia during the heydays of British colonialism in southern Africa.

The growth in mining triggered an increase in urban and peri-urban activities throughout the colony. In discussing this phenomenon, Pedler (1975: 103) states thus:

The mines created markets for all kinds of products. The growing urban populations had to be fed. Money went into such enterprises as workshops, repair outfits, electric-power plants, cement factories and water works. The Northern Rhodesian mining companies had to build and manage their own townships. They also created medical facilities. Development in turn attracted a multitude of people anxious to supply the growing demand for building materials, fuel, clothing and all manner of personal services.

In addition to the mining sector, other areas such as agriculture, particularly cash crop farming, also experienced tremendous growth. In West Africa, especially in Nigeria, as noted above, the groundnut industry experienced unprecedented growth. Here, the role of the British colonial government, which had developed an effective railway system linking Kano to the Nigerian coast, cannot be ignored. Additionally, the colonial government, through its agricultural extension services and research, had helped to foster growth in groundnut and other areas of agriculture, such as cotton and kola nut, which involved peasant as opposed to plantation farmers.

Growth of the cotton sector was promoted especially by the British Cotton Growing Association, which was established in 1902 and assumed the mission of educating Africans on proper techniques of cultivating cotton. Developments in peasant agricultural activities had a relatively less significant impact on the built environment in especially the urban areas, in comparison to plantation agriculture. Plantation agriculture involved British companies, which depended on the natives for labour. Elsewhere (Njoh, 2000: 41), I have observed that 'European plantation agriculture and related activities in the coastal areas ... triggered an unprecedented surge in the population of these areas' throughout colonial Africa. The growth resulted from the large influx of mostly single men migrating from the hinterlands to take up employment in the plantations and mines.

Transport infrastructure

Pre-colonial era

To place the colonial transport infrastructure development efforts in perspective, it is important to appreciate the quantity and quality of what had been accomplished in this domain prior to the colonial era. Activities in the area of road development were limited by many factors, the most prominent of which was the lack of sophisticated tools and equipment. Thus, people could only go as far, and only transport as much, as their natural energy could take.

To be sure, Africans had domesticated some animals to help address the growing need of moving people, goods and services over land prior to the colonial era. At the same time, a number of innovations, such as the construction of rafts and canoes capable of providing water-based transportation services, had been made. Thus, the transport infrastructure in Africa at the time consisted largely, but not exclusively, of tracks for pedestrian and animal traffic, and natural navigable waterways. Some evidence suggests that a number of the ancient empires and city-states of the region had done well to develop a system of well-aligned roads and streets, as opposed to meandering footpaths. For instance, one of the entries in a Dutch explorer's diary in

1602 made the following notation with respect to the ancient city of Benin (Njoh, 1999b; Tordoff, 1984):

> The town seemeth to be great; when you enter into it you go into the great broad street, not paved, which seems to be seven or eight times broader than Warmoes Street in Amsterdam; which goeth right out and never crooks …; it is thought that that street is a mile long [about four English miles]. … When you are in the great street aforesaid, you see many great streets on the sides thereof, which also go right forth.
>
> (Njoh, 1999b: 45)

The ancient Ashanti Empire, which later became part of the British Gold Coast Colony, is said to have constructed an extensive series of roads that converged on the capital, Kumasi (Herbst, 2000). Griffiths (1995: 182) provides further evidence of the existence of a relatively extensive network of roads and water-based transport systems pre-dating the arrival of Europeans in Africa in the following statement:

> To reach Timbuctoo Gordon Laing followed well-established Caravan Routes across the desert from Tripoli. René Caillé obtained passage on a boat, one of many sailing regularly up and down navigable inland Niger to Timbuctoo. Caillé returned to Europe via the very old Caravan route through Morocco.

This extensive series of roads, footpaths and waterways later served to facilitate the transportation of slaves during the infamous transatlantic slave trade.

The emphasis on road construction – albeit on a small scale and using very rudimentary tools commensurate with that era – that took place before any significant number of Europeans had arrived in Africa, was abruptly terminated during the colonial era. The colonial authorities were interested in penetrating the hinterland primarily to extract and transport raw materials to the seaports for onward transmission to the colonial master nations. As noted above, rail transportation presented itself as the optimal means of accomplishing this objective as well as that of militarily defending the colonial territory. For one thing, as implied earlier, the cost of developing rail transportation facilities was far less than that associated with developing road transportation infrastructure. For another thing, it was easier and cheaper to transport heavy and/or bulky goods by rail than by road.

Colonial transport infrastructure development efforts

Although some significant accomplishments had been made in the area of transportation infrastructure development technology by the onset of the European colonial era in Africa, most public works in the colonies depended on rudimentary and crude technology. Thus, there was little infrastructure development activity beyond the colonial administrative towns. This meant that movement from hinterland regions throughout the colonies was possible only through footpaths or navigable waterways, where such was available. The transportation of heavy goods such as minerals (except gold dust) and other bulky but valuable resources from the hinterland remained a nagging problem. The railway, which was technologically simple, labour intensive and placed relatively modest demands on financial resources, was considered indispensable in efforts addressed to dealing with the problem.

British colonial development policy underwent a dramatic change in the late-1890s and particularly in 1895, when Joseph Chamberlain assumed the post of Secretary of State. Chamberlain was best known for promoting what came to be widely known as 'scientific colonization'. He was adamant in his stance that the responsibility of developing British colonies, particularly in economic terms, rested squarely on the shoulders of the British government. Accordingly, he underscored the need for British citizens to dedicate some of their financial resources to development efforts in the colonies. Among Chamberlain's many accomplishments as Secretary of State were the reforms he initiated at the Colonial Office. Worthy of note in this regard was the creation of departments responsible for sectoral development in the colonies. These departments (e.g. the Agriculture Department) were endowed with powers to procure infrastructure-building equipment through Crown Agents (Pedler, 1975).

Arguably, Chamberlain's most notable achievement was in the medical area. The malarial and related research activities of Dr Ronald Ross, discussed in greater detail in Chapter 11, took place during Chamberlain's tenure as Secretary of State. Medical research of this genre, which took place at the London School of Tropical Medicine (established in 1889) and/or the Liverpool School of Tropical Medicine (created in 1898), resulted in the dramatic improvement of living conditions, especially for Europeans in the colonies. For instance, the development of methods and techniques to deal with mosquitoes and related problems resulted in a significant increase in the population of Europeans working and living permanently in the colonies. Research in the medical area was paralleled by equally momentous efforts in agriculture. Apart from the promotion of plantation agriculture, which involved the direct input of European firms, local farmers were encouraged to cultivate cotton, kola nuts, rubber, cocoa and oil palms. To provide the necessary scientific assistance in this regard, botanical gardens (along the lines of the Royal Botanical Gardens in the metropolitan country) were set up throughout the colonies.

The cost of these and cognate development projects was defrayed by funds from European firms operating in the colonies, tax revenues (from taxes imposed on Africans), grants and outright loans. Grants and loans guaranteed by the British government constituted the primary source of funds that were used to realize major capital improvement and infrastructure development projects such as railways, roads and seaports. For instance, funds for the Kenya–Uganda Railway, whose cost was in excess of 5.5 million British pounds, came in the form of an interest-free loan from the British imperial government. We note that this loan was later written off. Railways stand out as one the most prominent of the infrastructure development projects realized by British colonial authorities in Africa.

Water-based transportation

A significant portion of investments in transportation during the colonial era went to the development of seaports. Seaports were extremely important in efforts to evacuate and export natural resources from the colonial territories. This explains the fact that seaports constitute the terminuses for all the railways that were constructed during this period. Colonial efforts to develop railways and other transportation infrastructure made hardly any attempt to link the colonies. Rather, conscious efforts were made to discourage interaction amongst the colonies. This was particularly true when two colonial territories were under the colonial auspices of different colonial powers. It is noteworthy that the heydays of European colonialism in Africa coincided with a period when there was extreme rivalry, and severe animosity amongst European countries. Recall that the two World Wars occurred during this era.

That colonial authorities assigned a lot more weight to cost-saving than to regional integration is further proof that they were more interested in exploiting, and not in developing, the colonial territories. There are two known cases of a rare attempt to link territories under different European colonial powers. Both involved German colonial authorities. One case has to do with the German decision in 1916 to link the Tanga rail line in German East Africa (Tanganyika, now Tanzania) to the Mombassa rail line in British-controlled Kenya. The other relates to the decision earlier on, to extend the railway from the Cape (South Africa) into German South-West Africa (Namibia). However, it is important to note that these projects were propelled by military strategic reasons, and not reasons related to the socio-economic development of the colonies. In this case, the Germans were interested in averting the impending danger of being pushed out of the region, by especially South African forces under the command of General Smutts.

Railway building

In 1890, once the British and the Portuguese had agreed to demarcate and establish the boundaries of their territories in central Africa, they embarked fervently on building railways. If the British colonial authorities were particularly interested in constructing an extensive network of railways in the central and southern African region, it is because of the large amount of mineral-producing hinterland territories they controlled in the region. The British colonial authorities had lots of allies in the private sector whose interest in railway building was a function of their interest in the region's vast mineral wealth. This explains, at least in part, the large-scale involvement of private entities in colonial railway development schemes. The British Foreign Office moved to support a number of private entities, which acquired and operated several railway lines in the colonial territories in southern and central Africa.

The efforts of Cecil Rhodes in this regard are worth noting at this juncture. The British colonialist, Cecil Rhodes, was an eccentric Pan Africanist. He strongly believed in the notion of one Africa under the Union Jack and badly wanted to build a railway line from Cape Town to Cairo. Although his grand plan was never implemented, he did succeed in building or participated in one capacity or another in the development of several memorable railways in central and southern Africa. Rhodes was exceedingly ambitious and sought in many ways to dominate and control vast territories in the region. Accordingly, he sought to acquire as much territory as he possibly could for his British South Africa Company (BSA Co.). Although he succeeded in controlling only Northern Rhodesia (present-day Zambia) and Southern Rhodesia (now Zimbabwe) under the canopy of the BSA Co., he pressed for the extension of the Cape's railway through the Orange Free State to the Transvaal (Katzenellenbogen, 1975). At the same time, he vigorously sought permission and funds to construct railway lines throughout the two Rhodesias, which he had named after himself. In 1889, a charter was granted to the BSA Co. to construct a railway from the southern to the northern limits of the two Rhodesias.

Many railway-building projects other than those initiated by Rhodes and the BSA Co. were going on in central and southern Africa during the late-nineteenth century. The importance of railways for efforts that were designed to exploit what at the time were newly discovered mineral resources in that region cannot be overstated. As early as 1892, the Cape rail line, one of the earliest in the region, had been extended to the Rand.

In 1893, a railway company, the Bechuanaland Railway Company, was formed. The company oversaw the construction of a 106-mile railway line, the Mafeking Line, which was completed in 1894. This line was extended to Bulawayo in 1897 and was linked to Salisbury in 1902. Prior to that, in 1895, the Lourenço Marques line and the line from Durban were opened to traffic. Rhodes had agreed to build the line from Kimberly to Vryburg. However, the ink on the agreement giving Rhodes the authorization to build the Kimberly–Vryburg line was hardly dried when work began on a shorter line designed to link Fontesville, located on the Pungwe River in Northern Mozambique, to Salisbury in Southern Rhodesia (present-day Zimbabwe). This line, amongst other things, provided a shorter link to the coast for hinterland traffic.

The discovery of significant deposits of coal in Wankie and other areas around the Victoria Falls in the early to mid-1890s led to another flurry of railway building activities. Notable, in this regard, was the creation in 1894 of the Mashonaland Railway Company, whose immediate task was to provide railway access to what at the time were newly discovered coalfields. The company fulfilled its obligation and in 1905 extended the rail line serving the coalfields across the Zambezi River and beyond, as far as to Kalomo. A number of branch lines were later added to link the gold mines in the area to the main regional system.

The construction of the Kenya–Uganda railway, which was started in 1896 and reached Lake Victoria in 1902, cannot be considered an effort to establish a veritable interregional linkage because Uganda and Kenya were both British colonies. Apart from facilitating the evacuation of natural products from landlocked Uganda to the coast in Kenya, this railway also made it possible for the English to protect their colonial possessions from their rivals, the Germans, who controlled neighbouring Tanganyika (now Tanzania).

For the sake of comparison, the French controlled most of the colonial territories of West Africa under the rubric of what was at the time known as French West Africa. This explains the fact that railway lines link Senegal and Mali and Côte d'Ivoire and Burkina Faso (formerly Upper Volta). The important role played by these rail lines to link the hinterland territories to the coast cannot be exaggerated.

On their part, the Germans constructed two rail lines, one from the agriculture-rich Mount Kilimanjaro to the Port of Tanga, and the other from Dar es Salaam to Kigoma on Lake Tanganyika. These railway projects had an important military purpose, namely to facilitate the rapid movement of troops to defend the borders of Tanganyika were the English to decide to launch an attack from neighbouring Kenya or Uganda. The efforts by the British to build a railway from Kisumu (Port Florence) on Lake Victoria to Uganda were driven by military concerns as well (Njoh, 1999b). Thus, in colonial Africa, the railway was not only an 'instrument of occupation' (Mabogunje, 1981), but also a tool of exploitation and military defence.

Nigeria is where British colonial authorities developed one of the most elaborate railway systems in Africa. The system, which links all of Nigeria's three major regions, East, West and North, was initiated a decade following the Berlin Conference (1884/5), which sanctioned the partition of the continent. The project, which began in Lagos in 1895, reached Ibadan in 1900, was extended to Ilorin in 1908 and reached Kano in the northern part of the country in 1912. An east-bound link was added from Port Harcourt in 1913. This link was extended into the coalfields of Enugu in the eastern region in 1916, and in 1926, the link was connected to the western line at Kaduna. In 1929, the final link from Zaria through the cotton-producing areas of Kaura Namoda was completed.

British colonial road building efforts

We have already hinted at the fact that British colonial authorities were interested in minimizing the cost of, and maximizing profits from, colonization. Thus, they invested mostly in railways, which guaranteed them the highest returns on their investments. With respect to road projects, the need to minimize cost led them to build only those roads and streets that were absolutely necessary for colonial governance. In this connection, they 'essentially built the minimum number of roads necessary to rule given the Berlin rules', which recognized rule over the capital of any given colony as constituting effective control over that colony (Herbst, 2000: 167). In addition, British colonial authorities developed a few roads that were necessary to broadcast authority and especially to permit the movement of colonial administrators in a bid to bring the colonial state to the people. British colonial authorities, more than other colonial powers, had been quick to recognize the importance of their physical presence throughout the colonies as a critical element of control. This is essentially why they were well-known for locating colonial officials such as district officers in remote areas and taking tours involving colonial government officials. The tours, which were seen as an essential component of ruling, were necessary to 'learn what was happening' in the territory (Herbst, 2000: 87). These authorities were also quick to recognize that the objective of 'learning what was happening' could not be accomplished without roads. Accordingly, they proceeded to build a few roads linking some hinterland areas to the colonial government centres. Table 3.1 shows the extent of the road-building effort in each of the territories of colonial Africa for the years 1935, 1950 and 1963 (Herbst, 2000: 86).

Conclusion

Colonial authorities recognized rather early during the colonial era the importance of commerce, trade and transportation in achieving the related imperial objectives of exploiting and shipping abroad the natural resources from colonial territories. Accordingly, they embarked indefatigably on efforts to develop a network of dependable transportation infrastructure. The fact that colonial authorities concentrated their transportation infrastructure building efforts on railways is certainly not accidental. Rather, two important reasons account for this proclivity on the part of colonial authorities. First, railway construction is labour intensive. This gave the colonial authorities an opportunity to exploit what they saw as an otherwise wasted pool of labour power. The exploitation was by way of forced labour. The second has to do with the railway's versatility in serving the penetration function that was necessary in colonial efforts to reach remote areas of the colonies. Elsewhere (Njoh, 1999b: 215), I have summarized the main purpose of colonial transportation systems to include the following. These systems served to connect the colonial headquarters, which are mostly located on the coast to hinterland regions in order to: (1) facilitate the tapping of areas of exploitable minerals; (2) reach areas of potential agricultural export production; and (3) permit easy access by troops into the interior for political and military controls. If nothing else, this demonstrates the inextricably interconnected nature of trade, commerce and transportation, which constitutes important sources of colonial power.

4 Town planning in British colonial West Africa

Introduction

There is a tendency on the part of analysts to exaggerate the differences between British and French colonial policies in Africa. Conversely, little attention is paid to the similarities characterizing these two colonial powers. Yet, it is clear that both colonialists were identical in many respects. For instance, both strived to consolidate power in the colonial territories. However, it is important to note that while the British employed mostly economic or commercial strategies, the French depended largely on military means. This explains the intense involvement of military engineers in town planning projects in the territories under French colonial control. Military engineers played hardly any role in town planning projects in the British colonies. As Robert Home (1990: 23) has observed, those who were typically in charge of executing such projects included surveyors or engineers, who were members of the colonial civil service (e.g. McLean in Egypt), professional architects and town planners, who were hired as consultants to execute specific town planning and related tasks (e.g. Lancaster in India), and roving propagandists, who were occasionally assigned to canvass for the planning ideology (e.g. Geddes in India and Jerusalem). This chapter shows how the British colonial authorities employed non-military men with skills and talents in spatial and physical planning to consolidate power and effectuate socio-political control in British West Africa.

The colonial administrative entities referred to here as British West Africa included the Gambia (present-day Republic of Gambia), Sierra Leone, Nigeria and the Gold Coast (present-day Republic of Ghana). After World War I, this administrative grouping was expanded to include British Southern Cameroons and part of Togoland. The discussion in this chapter is limited to colonial town planning activities in Gambia, Sierra Leone, Ghana, and Nigeria. I begin by briefly discussing the colonial history of these countries.

Colonial history of Gambia, Sierra Leone, Ghana and Nigeria

Gambia

The British colonization of (The) Gambia dates back to 1816, when a settlement was founded on St Mary's Isle. Long before then in the seventeenth century, the British had set up a number of trading posts and forts at the mouth of the River Gambia. British interests in the area were constantly under threat from other Europeans, particularly the Dutch and Portuguese. This prompted the British in 1664 to erect yet another fort, Fort James. Initially, the British administered the colonial territory through Sierra Leone, their neighbouring colony to the west. In 1843, Gambia became a separate colony, complete with its own colonial government capital in Bathurst (present-day Banjul). The country gained its independence from Britain and became a member of the Commonwealth on 18 February 1965.

Sierra Leone

The first known European to have expressed more than a passing interest in the general area occupied by present-day Sierra Leone is a Portuguese navigator named Pedro de Sintra. He named the area Sierra Leone after the territory's hilly terrain, which he thought, together, strikingly resembled a lion. The territory played a crucial role in the struggle to emancipate slaves. In 1772, the British government declared that any escaped slave was automatically eligible for asylum in Britain. Subsequent to the enactment of this policy, several slaves became destitute in Britain. In an effort to improve the lot of the destitute slaves, the Anti-Slavery Society bought the coastal territory from the native Timni chief in 1787. With the assistance of a group of British philanthropists, the freed slaves were transported to Cape Sierra Leone, which thenceforth assumed the name Freetown. The British government was not formally in control of the territory until 1807. This was when the Sierra Leone Company transferred its rights over the territory to the (British) Crown. In 1895, Britain and France entered into an agreement delineating the territory's frontiers. The territory became a British protectorate one year later but remained a separate entity from the colony of Freetown. The British protectorate of Sierra Leone and its colony of Freetown were reunited in 1951 and became an independent member of the Commonwealth on 27 April 1961.

Ghana (The Gold Coast)

As elsewhere in West Africa, the Portuguese were the first Europeans to set foot on the soil of the area presently known as Ghana. The British colonial authorities arrived in Ghana, or what they called the Gold Coast, in the sixteenth century. English ships had arrived at the Island of Elmina as early as 1553. However, constant wars amongst European powers made it difficult for the British to exercise any meaningful control over the territory for a long time. The Gold Coast in general, and Elmina in particular, rose to prominence during the slave trade era. Accordingly, slave merchants controlled most of the territory. When the slave trade was abolished in the early 1800s, the merchants transferred control, which was mostly in the coastal region, to the (British) Crown. For a long time, the British failed at their efforts to extend control to the hinterland areas despite the support they had secured from the Ashanti Kingdom. If the British had initially failed to effectuate control over hinterland regions, it is because of the fierce opposition mounted by one of the main native groups, namely the Fante. This opposition lasted until the merchants brought in an administrator by the name of George Maclean. This administrator succeeded in convincing the natives to sign treaties amongst themselves, particularly between the Fante and Ashanti and between the natives and Europeans. In 1850, the British Colonial Office decided to compensate other Europeans for any interests they might have had in the territory. In this regard, they bought the interest of the Danes (1850) and that of the Dutch (1871). By 1897, the British had extended control to the northern hinterland regions. Following the outcome of World War I and the economic growth of the immediate post-World War II era, the cry for independence grew louder. This resulted in the granting of independence to the Gold Coast, which became Ghana on 6 March 1957. It combined with parts of Togoland, which until World War I was a German colony, to become one independent country, the Republic of Ghana. Ghana thus effectively became the first independent erstwhile colony in sub-Saharan Africa.

Nigeria

European presence along the coast of the territory occupied by present-day Nigeria, dates as far back as the fifteenth century. Europeans were in the region largely to participate in the slave trade. Prominent amongst the early Europeans in the region were the Portuguese. The British, who came in mostly as slave buyers, did not arrive in the area in any significant numbers until the seventeenth century. When the slave trade was abolished in 1807, the British adopted other areas of commerce, particularly trade in agricultural products. Over time, the British began venturing into the hinterland, travelling on the River Niger. However, they were greatly discouraged from going too far into the interior by tropical diseases, particularly malaria. However, with the discovery of Quinine in 1854, it was possible for Europeans to make trips and spend longer periods in the hinterlands in particular and the region in general.

In 1861, the British decided in favour of colonizing Lagos. Administratively, Lagos was made part of Sierra Leone and later it became part of the Gold Coast. As time went by, the British colonial authorities signed treaties with other European colonial authorities, especially France and Germany, which owned colonies in the general area. The treaties gave Britain colonial rights to the area stretching from the colony of Lagos in the west to the border of German Kamerun (now Cameroon) to the east, and the area from the colony of Lagos to Abomey (present-day Benin) under French control to the west. The Royal Niger Company, comprising a number of the trading companies operating in the Lagos Colony at the time, was established in 1886. This company soon moved to secure territories inland and eventually converting the territories into (British) Crown property. In 1893, these territories were granted protectorate status. The southern region of the territory became the Protectorate of Southern Nigeria in 1900. The colony of Lagos became part of this protectorate in 1906. The northern portion of the region was granted protectorate status in 1903 as the Protectorate of Northern Nigeria, following treaties between Lord Frederick Lugard and Islamic Fulani and Hausa natives. The British established the colonial administrative strategy of 'indirect rule' in Northern Nigeria, particularly for purposes of administrative expedience. In practice, the British colonial authorities had to do little more than simply supervise a pre-existing highly effective authoritarian governance structure controlled by emirs and other traditional leaders. In the south, the British employed a more direct rule strategy, especially where there was an absence of pre-existing centralized governance structures. In such settings, they created one. Resulting from efforts in this connection, for instance, are the infamous Warrant Chiefs of colonial Eastern Nigeria. In 1914, Northern and Southern Nigeria were amalgamated to constitute the Protectorate of Nigeria, Britain's most populous colony in Africa. The chiefs, emirs and other major institutions of the colony's almost 200 tribal groups were left in tact. Colonial rule ended in Nigeria in 1960.

Trade, physical and spatial development

The 1500s–1600s

An examination of the 'European trade and commerce' period, beginning from the time the first known Europeans set foot on West African soil, is a worthwhile exercise for efforts to fully understand how African spatial structures have been historically manipulated in a bid to gain and consolidate power. Prominent amongst the first Europeans to visit West Africa were traders, particularly those with interest in human cargo or slaves. Some of the earliest European physical structures in British West Africa had something to do with the slave trade. A number of these structures, particularly the forts, are of great significance in the context of the discussion in this book not only because of the impact they had on the growth and development of the surrounding areas but also because of their implications for exercising power, control and dominance. Some of the earliest fort-building activities by the British (especially private English companies) took place in Ghana and date as far back as the seventeenth century. The British are credited with constructing forts at Kormantine (1651), Cape Coast (the Cape Coast Castle, 1661), Dixcove, Sekondi, Accra, and Whydah (from 1672 on). Credit for a majority of the forts built in the region goes to the Dutch, although it is necessary to note that the English acquired all of the forts, castles and other possessions belonging to the Dutch on the Gold Coast in 1872.

It is unlikely that Accra would have risen to prominence without the forts that were built in the city and neighbouring areas. In fact, prior to the transatlantic slave trade era and before the first forts were ever constructed in the region, the port towns of Ada and Prampram, as well as the inland trading centres of Dodowa and Akusa to the east, commanded more prominence. However, when the transatlantic slave trade began, and as soon as the Dutch completed the first forts in and around Accra, the town soared to prominence, becoming the most important town in the region until the slave trade was abolished in 1807.

The fortified massive buildings called forts were designed especially to house troops and defend European traders and trade from other European rivals and hostile members of the indigenous populations. The immediate, but perhaps not so obvious, objective of the structures – that of demonstrating Europe's technological and industrial might to Africans – was achieved by the use of European construction materials that were hauled some 6,000 km across the sea and the domineering size of the structures.

Apart from serving as temporary warehouses for goods, including slaves bound for Europe and the Americas, and the territorial defence purposes for which they were originally created, the forts played an indispensable role in Britain's efforts to expand her colonial possessions in the region. In this connection, it is instructive to see how Britain employed the forts to consolidate her colonial and imperial powers in the region once slavery was abolished in 1807. The demise of the slave trade prompted fort-owning companies such as the Royal African Company to fold up. Beginning in the nineteenth century, the British government took over the abandoned forts and began exercising territorial control over the towns in which the forts were located. Subsequently, the natives of these towns, most of which were located on the coast, accepted formal British control in 1817. The forts have played and continue to play a significant role in the growth and development of the towns in which they are located. This role has certainly not gone unnoticed considering the fact that Ghana's Coat of Arms includes the picture of a fort.

The slave trade, perhaps the most notable event of the period in question, also had spatial development implications. For example, Sierra Leone's capital was named Freetown as a tribute to its role as a refuge for rescued slaves. With the passage of time, and especially as the slave era drew to a close, the British and other Europeans began contemplating other means of exploiting the African continent. Colonialism presented itself as ideally suitable to the task and was widely adopted by the European powers. Initially, British colonialism entailed conquering coastal regions. In some cases, particularly those that fiercely resisted British control, it was necessary to annihilate the indigenous population and rule directly with no local authority. In others, the British found it possible to control by simply impressing upon the natives the futility of any attempts to resist. In such cases, town planning played a symbolic role by creating new human settlements or restructuring existing ones along British spatial design principles. A large number of the public infrastructure projects, particularly roads and railways, that were completed during the pre-World War I era were designed to accomplish military (territorial defence and conquest) objectives. For instance, the British constructed a railway in 1874 for the sole purpose of transporting troops that were necessary in executing the Ashanti War (Stark, n.d.). The railway's subsequent use for commerce and agriculture was only incidental.

Colonial town planning in British West Africa

West Africa was always known to be a risky destination for Europeans during the colonial era, and especially before the advent of sound methods for dealing with the anopheles mosquito, the vector of the malaria-causing parasite. Hence, there has never been a significant resident European population – at least not anything near the number that had been encouraged to relocate to the southern African region from Europe during the heydays of colonialism. On account of this, one would have expected colonial planners in the region to be unlikely architects of racially segregated urban design schemes. This was certainly not the case. Colonial urban planners in West Africa, like their professional colleagues elsewhere on the continent, played a potent role in creating racially segregated spatial structures. The early schemes that were designed to combat the spread of diseases, particularly those that professed to combat the spread of malaria (see Chapter 11), epitomize planning designed to accomplish the goal of racial residential segregation.

Planning laws were designed to protect the interest of the colonial officials and other Europeans resident in the colonial territories. For this reason, measures that were designed to protect human health and welfare were applied almost exclusively in the colonial towns or European districts. Thus, the native settlements or the native segments of urban areas were generally ignored. To the extent that urban planning was considered a strategy for combating health problems, it is arguable that European planners were concerned not with the health of everyone. Rather, they were concerned exclusively with the health and safety of Europeans. It is therefore not surprising that a major city such as Accra, Ghana did not have a citywide building control ordinance until 1907 and only then as a reaction to an epidemic outbreak – the bubonic plague – which claimed hundreds of lives (Konadu-Agyemang, 2001: 137).

As the colonial period progressed, town planning in the different colonies became increasingly varied, reflecting the preferences and proclivities of the different colonial administrators and, to some extent, prevailing local conditions. For this reason, I will discuss the town planning experience of each of the former British colonies in the region, including Gambia, Ghana, Sierra Leone and Nigeria, in turn. However, by compartmentalizing the discussion along the afore-stated lines, I am not ignoring the fact that for a significant portion of the brief European colonial period, the colonies were treated as an administratively unified entity despite the lack of geographical contiguity. For example, Maxwell Fry was appointed to serve as the Town Planning Adviser to the Resident Minister for the entire British West Africa region in the years leading up to World War II. In 1943, Fry proposed creating new planning posts. If nothing else, Fry's appointment and his subsequent recommendation that more planners be hired attest to the important role that colonial authorities assigned town planning as a tool of the colonial enterprise. However, in the eyes of the colonial authorities, planners and planning did not necessarily command the same degree of importance.

To be sure, colonial authorities were known to harbour serious misgivings about the town planners on assignment as consultants in the colonies (Home, 2000). Whereas these planners saw themselves as the consummate professionals that they were, the career colonial civil servants viewed them otherwise. Thus, when Maxwell Fry proposed hiring more town planners in 1943, one colonial authority lashed out saying, as a consultant, Fry had no business assuming the role of an adviser. According to the colonial officials, consultants such as Fry were to act as no more than executive officers just in the same manner as the health officers, engineers and architects who had been recruited to serve in the colonial administration. Notwithstanding, Fry initiated a number of pieces of new town planning legislation in British West Africa before the end of his tenure in the region after World War II. In this regard, he is credited with playing a leading role in crafting the first comprehensive town planning legislation for the Gold Coast (Ghana) in 1945, a similar legislation for Sierra Leone in the same year and another for Nigeria in 1946. These developments constituted part of the flurry of planning activities that were initiated once town and country planning was revived in the colonies during the post-World War II period. As part of efforts to resuscitate planning, which had been suspended throughout colonial Africa as a result of financial difficulties occasioned by the Depression, funds were set aside specifically to finance planning projects. The funds were made possible through the Colonial Development and Welfare Act of 1940.

Town and country planning in Gambia

H. Reginald Jarrett, who, before heading the Geography Department at Fourah Bay College, was the Senior Geography Master at the Methodist Boys' High School in Bathurst (present-day Banjul) from 1941–4, once qualified Gambia as a 'slender strip of land that stretches over 200 miles into the West African interior' and comprised mostly of mangrove swamps (Jarrett, 1948: 633). By the time of Jarrett's remarks, the British had been present on the territory for far more than a century. Given not only its diminutive size of 4,000 square miles (Southorn, 1944:10), but also its lack of mineral resources, one cannot but ponder why the British decided in favour of colonizing Gambia. A permanent British presence in this small country dates back to 1816 when they established a military outpost in Bathurst.

European activities with significant implications for spatial development in the country can therefore be traced to 1816. The first Europeans to take up permanent residence in Bathurst were British and French traders who wanted to benefit from the protection afforded by the military outpost. In 1821 Bathurst was designated as a Crown Colony. Due largely to this designation and its status as a European settlement, Bathurst became the de facto beneficiary of all development projects in Gambia. Two other factors accounted for the exclusive focus on Bathurst, which invariably entailed neglecting the rest of the country. One of these factors was the sheer scarcity of resources. The other was related to the British government's unwillingness to incur further responsibilities in West Africa. Gambia, after all, was, as Sir Thomas Southorn, one of its colonial governors noted, often regarded in Britain as an expensive nuisance rather than an asset (Southorn, 1944). The colonial governors were, for a long time, given specific orders not to interfere with the activities of the indigenous people, or what the colonial authorities called 'tribes'. This gave rise to the growth and development of two societies in one – the European settlement on St Mary Island, Bathurst on the one hand and the settlements of members of the indigenous population on the other. The contrast was dramatic, with the domineering and flamboyant structures of the European settlements set on the island as a conspicuous symbol of European power, while the dwelling units or the so-called 'huts' of members of the native population stood unimpressively in the outlying countryside. In 1851, the entire Gambian territory had only 5,500 Africans and 190 Europeans (Southorn, 1944: 12).

The first significant formal attempt at country planning in the colony took place in 1894, when the Crown Colony was divided up into districts with each district placed under the administrative jurisdiction of a local chief. The chiefs were supervised by colonial government commissioners and were responsible for 'good government'. Under this Ordinance, Native Laws and Customs were supposed to be in full force and effect as long as they were not repugnant to natural justice or incompatible with the laws of England or local laws applicable to the Protectorate (Southorn, 1944: 14). The status of 'Protectorate' was extended to the entire territory of Gambia in 1901.

In addition to enacting the Council Ordinance, the colonial government in Gambia took bold steps to develop policies designed to convert most tracts of land in the territory into Crown Land. In this regard, the Governor was given inordinate powers over land (Gray, 1904). For instance, he had the authority to appropriate any land for public use. In addition, the colonial Governor was authorized to make rules governing the sale, transfer and alienation of all land within the territory.

It was not until after World War I and especially after World War II that some of the most significant town planning initiatives were undertaken in Gambia. Shortly prior to World War II, the colonial territory boasted over 1,000 miles of roads and several bridges (Southorn, 1944). Between October 1943 and October 1945, Maxwell Fry, as Town Planning Adviser to the Resident Minister of the Colonies for British West Africa, had studied a number of the colonial capital cities, one of which was Bathurst. The ultimate objective was to advise the colonial government on crafting appropriate town planning legislation and the machinery for implementing it. Fry summarized the results of his findings in an address he gave to a meeting he had with the Royal Empire Society on 26 June 1946 (see Fry, 1946). In the segment on Bathurst, Fry paints a vivid picture of the genre of problems colonial planners faced or were likely to face in their efforts to design a functional plan for the city. The construction of the country's main airport in that colonial capital city, Fry noted, constituted a nightmare for the planners. This, he explained, was due to the fact that the airport had occupied virtually all the usable space in the tiny city, which was situated on a low altitude and saddled with acute drainage problems. Fry recommended relocating the colonial government to a new site. This recommendation was rejected by colonial authorities not only because of the enormous cost of executing such a proposition but also, and perhaps most importantly, because of the historic value of Bathurst as a symbol of colonial power in the territory.

In addition, a number of studies whose results constituted vital input into the colonial government town planning process had been commissioned and completed. At least two such studies come to mind. One of these was designed to generate a land use map for Kuntaur Village. The study was carried out by a team of researchers from Oxford University as part of the 1948 'Expedition to the Gambia' (see Gordon, 1950). Another is J.G. Reese's study, 'Housing in a Gambian Village', which was conducted following the conclusion of World War II (Reese, 1952).

As mentioned earlier, Bathurst, the colonial capital, like colonial capitals elsewhere, benefited from a lot of infrastructure investment projects. However, unlike other colonial capitals, Bathurst experienced relatively little racial spatial segregation (Curtin, 1985). This was not because of a lack of the desire by colonial authorities to implement racial spatial segregation schemes. Rather, it was because of the counterproductive and fastidious nature of such schemes in a town whose European population was rapidly dwindling. At one point, the population of Europeans in Gambia was estimated to be fewer than 100 with those who called Bathurst home numbering only in the twenties (Curtin, 1985: 601). In addition, the town boasted a significant number of economically well-to-do Africans. This rendered the task of designating the more desirable areas of the town as 'European Only' districts more complicated.

A perusal of the chronology of events that transpired in the town and country planning arena in Gambia reveals an obvious progression from a point where the territory was virtually ignored to one where colonial authorities made some arguably serious efforts to improve living conditions in the territory. Why the policy changes? Although apparently not obvious, the changes were in concert with the goals of Britain's colonial enterprise. First, there was a need for British colonial authorities to assert control over the territory, which was constantly being threatened by the French who occupied surrounding territories and had on several occasions hoisted the French flag on territory believed to be part of Gambia. Second, the war had given Britain an opportunity to appreciate the loyalty of her colonial 'subjects', including the people of Gambia. Thus, Britain saw herself, and rightly so, as owing the people of Gambia and those of her other possessions in Tropical Africa a debt of gratitude. Colonial government public infrastructure development projects such as those that were undertaken during the post-war era can therefore be seen as constituting Britain's effort to acknowledge her indebtedness to the Gambians.

Finally, the British colonial policy that required each colony to be self-supporting resulted in the mother country neglecting the social and other needs of impoverished colonies such as Gambia. This had become a source of increasing embarrassment to Britain amongst her peers such as the French and the Portuguese, who did well to carter to the socio-economic needs of their own possessions. Accordingly, the British government enacted the Colonial Development and Welfare Act of 1940, which enabled her to address the social and other problems of people in her needy possessions such as Gambia.

Town and country planning in colonial Ghana

Town planning

Ghana boasts a long and rich history of large and well-planned human settlements that pre-date the arrival of the first wave of Europeans in the region. Kumasi, the capital of the ancient Ashanti Empire, served as a point of convergence for an extensive series of roads that connected different parts of the empire (Herbst, 2000). Not to be outdone by so-called modern town and country planning, the ancient Ghanaians created written versions of their plans. In this connection, the Mankessim Constitution, which was adopted by the Fante Confederation in 1871, contained detailed information pertaining to town and country planning. As Jeffrey Herbst (2000: 42) notes, Article 8, Section 3 of the Constitution pertains to matters relating to circulation, while Article 26 stipulates the width of roads to be 15 feet (4.50m).

It was, however, not until 1907 that the first significant piece of modern town planning legislation was enacted in Ghana (Konadu-Agyemang, 2001; Tipple, 1987). Adopted primarily as a reaction to the outbreak of the bubonic plague that wreaked havoc, claiming hundreds of lives in Accra in 1907, this piece of legislation stipulated minimum plot sizes (50ft × 75ft or 15.00m × 22.50m), regulated the alignment of streets and back-lanes, and controlled vegetation and water quality (Konadu-Agyemang, 2001: 137–8; Tipple, 1987). In 1945, and as noted earlier, Maxwell Fry initiated Ghana's first comprehensive Town and Country Planning Ordinance. This ordinance drew its inspiration from, and mirrored, the British Town and Country Planning Act of 1932. Like the English Town and Country Planning Act, the Ghanaian Ordinance of 1945 had the goal of promoting health, hygiene, and safety, and ensuring the orderly development of land. In practice, the legislation focused primarily on controlling and regulating the development of planning schemes, layouts, plot sizes, and zoning, *inter alia*.

Apart from the enactment of town planning legislation and ordinances, colonial authorities influenced spatial development and structures in many other ways. Prominent in this regard was the practice of creating anew, or designating some existing towns as colonial administrative centres. In this latter case, colonial authorities endeavoured to avoid designating towns that served as the headquarters of pre-existing indigenous empires. To designate a town that played no significant role prior to European conquest was necessary as a means of accentuating the supremacy of the conquering colonial master nation over the conquered subjects. Thus, once the British had gained complete control over the Ashanti and neighbouring kingdoms, they immediately proceeded to designate Accra as the capital of the Gold Coast. This decision resulted in, amongst other things, a significant slow-down of the growth and development of Kumasi, the headquarters of the Ashanti Confederation. An examination of the evolution of Accra will serve to illustrate a number of the town planning decisions and actions that the British colonial authorities took during their reign in Ghana.

Cape Coast

This was the first colonial capital of the Gold Coast (present-day Ghana). Initially during this era, two types of local governance systems had been set up to govern towns in the colony. One of these involved town councils and the other involved traditional or native authorities (NAs). The town councils were made up of elected representatives and some government ex-officio members, while the native authorities comprised traditional chiefs and/or rulers. Management of the affairs of the towns fell directly under the charge of the town or municipal councils. The Town Council Ordinance of 1858 created these municipal councils. Initially, the councils were created only for Cape Coast and Accra. However, the Town Council Ordinance of 1894 added Sekondi to the list of towns with town councils. The 1894 Ordinance emphasized the councils' responsibilities of conservancy and protection of public health.

The traditional authorities, which were comprised of local chiefs, had very little or no role to play in managing the affairs of the towns as stipulated by the ordinance. In theory the decision-making powers were supposed to reside in the hands of the elected members as opposed to the government appointees, who had ex-officio member status in the council. However, in practice, government ex-officio members, usually made up of European district commissioners of the areas concerned, were in the majority and tended to dominate all council deliberations. This point is particularly worthy of note in light of its implications for the distribution of power in the town planning arena in colonial Ghana.

Accra[1]

In the 1870s, the British colonial authorities reached a decision to relocate the colonial capital of the Gold Coast from Cape Coast to Accra. Resulting from this was a rapid increase in the population of Accra, *inter alia*. Prominent amongst the new members of Accra's population were Europeans working either for the colonial government or in the private sector. The colonial government was faced with not only the problem of providing housing for a growing and proliferating population but also that of satisfying the special spatial needs of the European population. The colonial government's racial spatial segregation policies and a preference for panoramic sites by members of the European population conspired to complicate the task of addressing these needs.

The problems notwithstanding, colonial authorities initiated a number of projects with the objective of eradicating the growing housing problem of Accra in the late-nineteenth century. In line with the avowed colonial government policy of spatially segregating the races, Africans and Europeans were assigned to different areas of the town. To satisfy the European craving for panoramic sites, the authorities decided in favour of designating Victoriaborg, a breezy area to the east of what were the city limits at the time, as an exclusive European residential district. Following the outbreak of the bubonic plague in 1908, the town was expanded. This expansion entailed the creation of a native-only neighbourhood, designed to accommodate members of the native population as a means of relieving congestion problems in overcrowded inner city areas. A second neighbourhood, Adabraka, was established to the north of Accra to serve as an enclave for the town's growing Muslim population.

Apart from the bubonic plague, another development that occurred in 1908 and had far-reaching implications for the spatial structure of Accra in particular and colonial Ghana in general, was the decision to construct the Accra–Kumasi railway. This railway effectively linked Accra, which at the time was the main port of the Gold Coast, to the colony's main cocoa producing regions. The railway construction project was completed in 1923, and by 1924, barely one year later, Accra had emerged as the colony's most important township. A little less than a decade earlier in 1915, Accra's pipe-borne water supply project had been completed. This, coupled with the ease of travelling to and from the hinterlands afforded by the new railway system, served to attract large numbers of rural immigrants to Accra.

Racial residential segregation laws were officially no longer in effect in Accra as of 1923. In theory this meant that members of the native population were free to live wherever they wanted in the city thereafter. In practice, building regulations requiring that all buildings be constructed of stone, burnt bricks or concrete and roofed with corrugated aluminium sheets, made it difficult at best and impossible at worst for members of the native population to live in European neighbourhoods. Although the colonial state was quick at enforcing the building and other regulatory measures, it made barely any efforts to maintain and/or improve the public infrastructure. The exception here was the European neighbourhoods whose services were always in excellent functional order.

Accra continued to experience tremendous growth in its population, prompting the colonial governor, Sir Frederick G. Guggisberg, in 1923 to initiate actions designed to expand the city. Prominent in this regard was the construction of a bridge across the Koole Lagoon and the opening up of the land west of the lagoon for human settlement. A number of other public works projects, including the construction of schools, hospitals, and government offices were also completed in Accra during Guggisberg's governorship. These projects contributed not only to altering the town's spatial structure but also to significantly increasing its population size. Thus, between 1931 and 1948, the population of Accra more than doubled from 60,726 to 133,192 (Ghana.co.uk). Equally increasing was the resident European population.

The significant gains experienced by the town's European population led authorities to embark on more racially segregated planning schemes despite the fact that the law no longer mandated such schemes. Thus, two new low-density neighbourhoods, the Ridge and Cantonments, designed to exclusively accommodate Europeans were created. The efforts to accommodate the town's European population were not matched by similar efforts to provide housing for members of the native population migrating from the rural areas. The new immigrants were expected to find accommodation in areas such as Nima or Accra New Town, which at the time had not yet been incorporated into Accra City proper. Essentially therefore, the areas in which the new immigrants sought accommodation were outside the jurisdiction of Accra and were therefore not regulated. In a sense, these areas would qualify as contemporary squatter settlements or shantytowns. That the colonial government virtually ignored the presence of such residential areas on the urban fringes is not at all surprising given that the areas served as reservoirs for the labour power that was necessary for Accra's fledgling capitalist economy to function.

Accra enjoyed further growth after World War II. Maxwell Fry crafted Accra's first comprehensive master plan in 1944. B.D.W. Treavallion and Alan Flood revised said plan in 1958, one year subsequent to the country's independence from Britain. The immediate post-World War II period witnessed the development of huge and architecturally sophisticated public and private commercial buildings, with at least one that comprised multiple storeys in Accra's central business district.

Housing

Regulatory measures specifying building standards and permissible building materials had been promulgated and were in force in major Ghanaian towns, including Accra, Kumasi, Cape Coast and Sekondi-Takoradi quite early during the colonial era (Konadu-Agyemang, 2001). Only building units of concrete, stone or burnt bricks that had metal sheets as roofing materials were permitted. For a while, the measures were applicable exclusively in the towns. Even then, only certain portions of the towns were affected. It was not until after, and as a reaction to, the outbreak of the bubonic plague of 1907 that the purview of the regulations was broadened to cover housing units belonging to members of the native population. It took about sixteen years before the colonial government of Ghana initiated any action with implications for all in the housing market. One such action had to do with the Dispossessed People's Housing Scheme that was instituted in 1923. The scheme was designed to provide housing to families whose housing units were collaterally damaged in the process of colonial government development projects. The scheme permitted the colonial government to provide loans enabling affected families to purchase building materials. By the time the scheme experienced funding difficulties and was discontinued in 1933, it had provided loans amounting to a total of £9,280 to 118 families (Konadu-Agyemang, 2001: 138).

The colonial government of Ghana took another noteworthy action in the housing policy field in 1939. This action entailed instituting a scheme, the Accra Earthquake Victims' Housing Scheme of 1939. As its name suggests, the scheme was designed to rehouse individuals rendered homeless by the earthquake disaster that was visited upon the city that year. The scheme largely comprised the development of three new housing estates, namely the Osu, Mamprobi and Chokor Housing Estates. Implementing the project necessitated intense collaboration between the colonial state and local traditional authorities, particularly the local chiefs. On its part, the state provided the necessary funding, while the traditional chiefs furnished the building land. Project beneficiaries were charged a nominal customary fee of £5/10/– for each parcel of land. This amount was payable to the appropriate Stool only at the time of effective occupation. Additionally, beneficiaries were charged an interest rate of 4 per cent on the loans. To put this in perspective, Konadu-Agyemang (2001) draws attention to the fact that the prevailing interest rate at the time was only 2.5 per cent. Thus, the colonial state seized the opportunity presented by a natural disaster to exploit an already disenfranchised native population. Here, I would be remiss if I failed to draw attention to the paradoxical fact that the Ghanaian colonial government had since the 1890s operated a programme that provided housing free of charge to senior colonial civil servants, all of whom for a better part of the colonial era were Europeans.

A number of specific features of the Accra Earthquake Victims' Housing Scheme of 1939 deserve further attention here. First, it is worthy of note that the housing estates developed as part of the scheme contained barrack-style residential facilities – single attached rooms, communal toilet, kitchen facilities and courtyard, with each estate being located in a geographically well-defined area. Some of the buildings in the estates contained as many as twenty-four separate one-room housing units served by a common veranda. Although the buildings were constructed of so-called modern building materials, they deprived the residents of the freedom they enjoyed in the traditional African units they occupied prior to the earthquake. For the colonial state, it took an Act of God to provide an excuse for confining the 'natives' to an environment in which they could be under the constant gaze of the colonial police. Furthermore, the stark contrast between the barrack-style housing facilities of the estates afore-described and the luxurious residential facilities of European-only neighbourhoods cannot be ignored. Such a sharp contrast served to brutally express and concretize the European's perceived supremacy over members of the native population.

The immediate post-World War II era is also of interest in any meaningful discussion of housing policy in colonial Ghana. This period witnessed a wave of veterans returning from the battlefields – a phenomenon that created an unprecedented demand for housing in and around the major towns. In an effort to address this problem, and as a means of rewarding the returning soldiers for their valiant role on the battlefields, the colonial government embarked on a programme to directly inject new units into the housing market. The efforts in this regard were calculated and directed towards constructing small estates of 'modern' housing units for the veterans. These estates eventually evolved into what became known as 'Legion Villages'. Like the 'barracks' of the earthquake victims, the Legion Villages comprised buildings of single rooms served by communal toilet, kitchen and other facilities.

The post-World War II era also saw the enactment of a piece of legislation with profound implications for housing in colonial as well as post-colonial Ghana. This piece of legislation, the Municipal Council Ordinance of 1953, was designed to regulate all building and construction activities in municipalities throughout the colony. More importantly, the ordinance stipulated the cumbersome and complex procedures for obtaining the building permit, minimum plot sizes, floor area ratio (FAR), building height, building line, and the standards and materials for all building works. Here, it is important to note that the stipulated building standards and materials pertain to Britain, and were transplanted to Ghana without due regard to context. One analyst of the document containing this ordinance has drawn attention to this fact. He noted that the document makes frequent references to 'British Standards' and 'British Codes of Practice' defined in Section 2(2) as 'publications by the British Standards Institution, British Standard House, Park Street, London' (Konadu-Agyemang, 2001: 170).

The land question in colonial Ghana

The British colonial authorities in Ghana were faced with unique problems, particularly because they had to deal with a territory with an extensive history of organized settlements and sophisticated political organization. The Ashanti Empire, for instance, was already versed with, and had in fact employed, complex strategies for broadcasting authority over extensive regions for centuries pre-dating the European conquest. In addition, they were fully aware of the importance of land and territorial control – although not in the same manner as the Europeans. For one thing, the Ashanti and other members of the native population in colonial Ghana were more interested in the use value of land than in its economic or commercial value, which was of utmost importance to the Europeans. For another thing, all land in the territory was communally controlled and vested in the Stool. This means that land was neither individually owned nor available for sale. This contrasted sharply with the British conceptualization of land, which saw land as a commodity that can be sold and/or exchanged on the market.

These conflicting conceptualizations of land and its role in society clashed violently in the 1890s when the British colonial government enacted a bill, the Lands Bill of 1897, which sought to convert all so-called 'vacant lands' into property of the Crown. In their effort to prevent the British from implementing their imperialist plan, the kings, chiefs and other local leaders constituted an ad hoc group, the Aboriginal Rights Protection Society (ARPS). The ARPS's sole mission was to prevent the British colonial authorities from implementing their perfidious land tenure reform schemes in Ghana. Were it not for the organization's efforts, the British colonial government would have succeeded in converting all of the country's lands into Crown property – a euphemism for the colonial state. Foremost amongst the factors that contributed towards bolstering the ARPS's efforts and conversely obfuscating the colonial government's fastidious land conversion or acquisition schemes was Ghana's rich and extensive history as a territory of well-established traditional states (kingdoms and chiefdoms). As a basis for comparison, note that similar efforts on the part of colonial authorities paid huge dividends in East and Southern Africa, where powerful pre-colonial states were rare.

Town and country planning in colonial Sierra Leone

Some of the best-known formal efforts to plan human settlements in Sierra Leone occurred as far back as the 1700s.[2] The plan which was drawn for Freetown between 1792 and 1794 is illustrative. In 1792, Governor Clarkson enlisted the technical assistance of surveyor Pepys to produce a layout for a site to accommodate 1,131 freed slaves from Nova Scotia (Olu-Wright, 1968: 25). In 1794, a French raid destroyed the town, including the layout, and a new plan was crafted that same year (Fyfe, 1968; Olu-Wright, 1968). The plan of 1794 constituted a significant improvement over its predecessor, particularly because it covered an area of about 80 acres (about twice as much as the initial layout) and included streets that were wider and more aligned. With a width of 24 metres (80 ft) and twice as wide for at least one, the streets would be considered vast even by present-day standards. The plan divided the town into two physical and functional parts – east and west – and included streets that were laid south-north.

The plan also prescribed ample distances between houses. These two requirements, wide streets and spaced-out houses, are of particular interest here because of their function as tools of power, control and domination. Wide streets flanked by amply spaced structures facilitate policing and surveillance. It was essentially the need to improve policing and surveillance in an effort to avert another revolution that led Emperor Napoleon III to replace France's narrow alleyways with wide boulevards.[3] A further feature of Freetown's street system of the colonial era that cannot be ignored is the fact that the streets were set at right-angles to each other, thus forming a gridiron pattern. This pattern is famous for its ability to facilitate military intervention and control, particularly the entry and exit of military vehicles. As a colonial town, Freetown is exemplary in manifesting the (colonial) state's propensity to employ spatial planning as a tool for attaining its objectives in society. It is, as Christopher Fyfe (1968: 4) accurately observes, 'a colonial city planned by authority in orderly fashion, according to the convenience of the Government rather than of its inhabitants'.

However, to see Freetown's 1794 plan uniquely as a tool for facilitating policing and surveillance is to ignore some of its other strengths. The plan, perhaps above all else, was designed to accomplish an important ideological objective. John Peterson (1968: 10) notes that prominent amongst the factors that led to the founding of Freetown in 1787 was the Enlightenment philosophy of eighteenth-century Europe – particularly the quest for the 'perfect society', which British humanitarians pursued with unparalleled gusto. In Africa, the quest for the perfect society drove the English humanitarians to strive towards abolishing slavery and subsequently seeking a perfect haven for the freed slaves. Thus, the surveyors (planners) who set out to design the city were bent on transforming into reality the utopian dream of building the 'perfect city' or as Peterson (1968: 11) puts it, 'the heavenly city of eighteenth century philosophers'.

Land and housing

To appreciate colonial town planning legislation in Sierra Leone it helps greatly to focus on the country's capital city, Freetown. An Ordinance of 1893 made Freetown a municipality comprising three wards, namely East, Central and West (Olu-Wright, 1968). The three wards aforementioned were significantly larger than the five that were initially created when Freetown was made a Crown colony in 1808. An important aspect of the 1893 plan relates to the land distribution pattern. The ordinance specifies two main categories of land – Crown land and freehold land.

Prior to the European conquest, houses were constructed of local materials, including wattle, clay, rocks and wood for the walls and grass and clay as roofing materials. The Europeans introduced so-called modern building materials and techniques. It did not take long for the new materials and techniques to supersede the local varieties. With the influx of freed slaves, the influence of European and North American construction techniques and materials was amplified. Thus, quite early during the colonial era, housing units of burnt bricks, plywood, roofed with shingle and raised a few centimetres off the ground had become more common in Freetown than the 'native-style' housing that could be seen in the hinterland regions. The exclusive European districts such as Hill Station as well as the administrative district boasted houses and other buildings that were prefabricated in England. The desire on the part of European powers to 'Europeanize' Africa was given physical expression in Freetown when colonial authorities imported prefabricated structures, complete with fireplaces, from Britain to construct the Tower Hill Barracks and the Upper and Lower Commissariat buildings (Olu-Wright, 1968: 32).

Country planning

Roads and transportation facilities in general are widely recognized as instruments for broadcasting authority (Herbst, 2000). Thus, in colonial Africa, it was commonplace for colonial authorities to embark on the development of transportation facilities as a means of extending the locus of colonial power. In this context, transportation facilities constitute part of what Michel Foucault once referred to as projects for territorial governance (Faubion, 2000). This territorial governance model functions 'on the premise that a state is like a large city; the capital is like its main square; the roads are like its streets' (Faubion, 2000: 351).

On account of their investment priorities, it would appear that the British colonial authorities in Sierra Leone were amply aware of the potency of transportation infrastructure as an instrument for broadcasting and consolidating power. The railway, whose role in facilitating the exploitation of natural resources is well established, assumed heightened importance in colonial Africa. Railways were supposed to serve as a tool for winning the hearts and minds of the native leadership and as a bulwark against the territorial ambitions of competing European powers, particularly the French. As far back as 1872, E.W. Blyden (per the 'Report on the Falaba Expedition') as a goodwill gesture to the king of Falaba, proposed to link Freetown by rail to the northeastern part of the country (Ridell, 1970). This proposal was never accorded serious attention until 1890. At this time, due to intense and widespread public pressure, backed by legislative support, the proposal was seriously reconsidered. The need to do this was accentuated by the fact that the French had penetrated nearby Guinea. Thus, the British colonial authorities saw such a railway as a necessary component in British efforts to establish sovereignty over the entire protectorate of Sierra Leone. Accordingly, railway construction began in the colony in earnest in 1895. The Hut Tax War of 1898 interrupted the railway building efforts. Ironically, the war gave the colonialists an opportunity to demonstrate the effectiveness of transportation facilities in facilitating the movement of troops. The interruption was brief as work on the project soon resumed and by 1899 the railway had reached Songo Town. By 1904, 220 miles of railway had been added extending the line to Baiima in Upper Mende country. Military concerns, particularly fears of possible attacks by the French in neighbouring Guinea, *inter alia*, compelled authorities to develop a narrow gauge railway system to avoid having the same gauge as the French.

As mentioned earlier, transportation facilities are very effective in their role as tools for broadcasting state authority and facilitating territorial control. A rigorous analysis of colonial Sierra Leone's transportation network reveals that the network was developed with a view to reinforcing the colonial government's power and facilitating its control of the territory. In discussing the 'areal organization' of the country's colonial administration, Ridell (1970: 14) states as follows:

> The transport and communications networks were structured, at least partially, with reference to the district and provincial capitals; it was within the headquarters towns that many of the modern institutions and services were located; and it was from these centres that policies were implemented and information spread.

For almost a decade after the declaration of the Protectorate of Sierra Leone in 1896, the colonial authorities encountered enormous difficulties controlling especially the hinterland regions. These difficulties subsided significantly with the opening of the country's first railway and the construction of a series of feeder roads in 1907. In time, the railway rose to become a critical element in the command and control calculations of the British colonial authorities. In this regard, soon after the railway project was completed, a number of administrative districts were re-constituted with locations along railway lines or railway terminals serving as their headquarters. For instance, the Panguma and Bandajuma Districts were combined to constitute one district, the Railway District with a railway town, Kenema, designated as its headquarters; while the northern part of Panguma District was amalgamated with parts of a number of adjacent districts to constitute the Central District. In 1909, this latter was dissolved and made part of the Railway District. This suggests that as transportation improved, it took increasingly less (i.e. fewer administrators) to control the colony.

Town and country planning in colonial Nigeria

Nigeria, like the other British colonies in West Africa, was never a destination for Europeans who wanted to relocate permanently to Africa. Foremost amongst the factors that served to discourage the permanent settlement of Europeans in the region was the prevalence of anopheles mosquitoes. Legend has it that a proposed but rejected design for the national flag of Nigeria as it prepared for independence contained the picture of an anopheles mosquito. Inclusion of the insect's picture was, according to the legend, intended as a gesture to acknowledge its indispensable role in preventing the permanent settlement of Europeans on Nigerian soil. The apparent sarcasm inherent in the afore-narrated legend notwithstanding, it is important to appreciate the fact that the anopheles mosquito posed an enormous threat to the health of Europeans who dared to make it to West Africa. It is therefore understandable that health planning emerged as a major component in colonial town planning, especially in the early 1900s (DeLancey, 1978; Curtin, 1985; Aka, 1993). Thus, although the absence of a significant resident European population would have nullified the need for segregationist planning, colonial planners in the region invoked concern with mosquito-related, and other tropical, diseases as a pretext for racial spatial segregation. Therefore, colonial planners in Nigeria wrestled with problems identical to those faced by their professional colleagues in colonies with significant European settler populations and where the apparatus of colonial governance was based on apartheid or racial principles. Essentially therefore, issues relating to racial residential segregation, which would have taken a back seat given the scant presence of Europeans in the region, were given an artificial life by colonial authorities with rigid ideological agendas. Lord Frederick Lugard, the colonial official credited with actuating the indirect colonial rule strategy in Nigeria was adamant about keeping the colonial physical presence segregated as far as possible from the indigenous population or what he called the 'natives' (see Lugard, 1922). Lugard summarized his views in this regard in one of his memoranda as follows (quoted in Home, 1983: 166):

> The British role here is to bring to the country all the gains of civilization by applied science (whether in the development of material resources, or the eradication of disease, etc.) with as little interference as possible with native customs and modes of thought.

Thus, for Lugard, the physical separation of Africans and Europeans was not to be construed as constituting a manifestation of racist tendencies. Rather, such separation, as Lugard would want us to believe, was simply a means of ensuring as little interference as possible with the physical, social and intellectual activities of the 'natives'.

A perusal of colonial government activities in the urban planning and related fields in Nigeria during Lugard's tenure (1900–19) can be very revealing. To be sure, his indirect rule doctrine, as articulated in *The Dual Mandate in British Tropical Africa*, was invoked only when it facilitated attainment of colonial/imperial development objectives. It is therefore hardly any wonder that while the doctrine found expression in the northern portion of the protectorate, where there was a well-organized and highly centralized administrative structure in place, it was only scantly applied in the historically stateless regions of the south. Here, the Lugard administration found it more expedient to adopt 'direct rule' strategies entailing the creation of colonial chiefdoms or what went under the appellation 'Warrant Chiefs' (e.g. for the Igbos in the southeast and the Tivs in the lower northeastern belt). It is also worth noting that before the amalgamation decision that unified the different parts of Nigeria in 1914, 'indirect rule' was applied only in the Protectorate while the Crown colony of Lagos remained under 'direct rule'.

Town planning

Town planning had been going on, particularly in Lagos colony, long before the protectorate was amalgamated and long before Lugard became governor of colonial Nigeria. An examination of some of the most prominent planning schemes that were conceived and implemented during the early days of the British colonial epoch in the region can prove very informative, particularly with respect to how colonial authorities, local elites, and members of the native population at large contested the space. Such an examination also promises to be useful in deconstructing and illuminating power relations in the built environment of colonial Nigeria.

Formal town planning in Nigeria is of more recent vintage than in other erstwhile British possessions in the region, such as Sierra Leone and Ghana. Although some analysts erroneously trace the earliest formal town planning initiatives in Nigeria to the early 1900s (see e.g. Aka, 1993), such initiatives date as far back as the mid-1800s. For instance, the colonial government of the Crown colony of Lagos enacted the Town Improvement Ordinance in 1863. This was followed thirteen years later by the passage of the Land Act of 1876. This Act gave the Colonial Secretary the authority to acquire for public use either by agreement or compulsorily, any land within the Crown colony of Lagos.[4] One year later, the Swamp Improvements Ordinance of 1877 was passed. However, it took until the early 1900s for a flurry of consequential town planning ordinances with far-reaching implications to be enacted in colonial Nigeria (Home, 1974, 1983; Omotola, 1991; Aka, 1993). In 1902, an ordinance establishing 'European-only' reservations went into effect in major towns throughout the colony. Intended in part as a social control device, the 1902 ordinance was accorded legal backing fifteen years later by yet another ordinance, namely Ordinance No. 29 of the Township Act of 1917. The Act, which professed to focalize on matters relating to health, hygiene and sanitation, provided for, amongst other things, the physical separation of European residential districts from 'native' settlements. The British colonial authorities saw native areas as havens for treacherous diseases and therefore a health hazard. Most dreaded in this regard was the anopheles mosquito, which by that time had already been incriminated as the vector of the parasite that causes malaria. The requirement for a buffer or natural vegetation separating native settlements from European districts, the colonial authorities claimed, was designed to protect Europeans from infected anopheles mosquitoes. The required width for the buffer zone of no less than 440 yards (396 metres) is a distance that was believed to be greater than an infected anopheles mosquito could traverse. In addition to segregating human settlements by race, the Township Act also stipulated segregation by class. Thus, within the European districts, Europeans engaged as clerks, drivers, storekeepers, nurses and so on, were physically separated from their middle- and upper-class counterparts engaged as functionaries in the colonial civil service or managers in European firms and corporations. The African districts were also spatially segregated along class lines.

Apart from its role as a social control device, the Township Act facilitated and institutionalized the colonial practice of disenfranchising and oppressing the poor in particular and members of the indigenous population in general. Thus, for example, African neighbourhoods were systematically underserved in terms of infrastructure and social amenities. In fact, an indigenous neighbourhood was unlikely to attract any planning activity, let alone infrastructure and social amenities unless it served some role of the colonial administration or unless it was strategically located (Home, 2000). To put this in perspective, it must be noted that the colonial government of Nigeria ensured that the European districts were well served. Throughout the colony, such districts boasted tree-lined streets, wide and well-lit paved streets or avenues, large lots, recreational facilities (e.g. swimming pools, golf courses and tennis courts, country clubs), and a plethora of social amenities.

The buffer zones that separated the European from the native areas were usually selected with no regard for topography or other important features necessary for the proper functioning of the built environment. For instance, efforts on the part of colonial authorities to racially segregate Sapele Town resulted in isolating the wholesale trade area located in the European district from the retail market, which was located in the native district.

Another noteworthy aspect of colonial town planning activities in Nigeria is the fact that like similar activities elsewhere in colonial Africa, they were based on ideological principles and greatly influenced by the ideas of Ebenezer Howard and Patrick Geddes. In the first instance, town planning was supposed to constitute a tool for giving urban form to human settlements – a reflection of the greatness of the British empire. On the second count, the influence of Howard is easily discernible from the fact that none of the four priority towns targeted for planning by colonial authorities in Nigeria in 1928, including Enugu (27,000), Warri (10,000), Benin (8,000), and Sapele (4,000), exceeded 30,000 (Home, 2000). It is important to note that colonial planners in Nigeria virtually ignored large pre-colonial or traditional towns such as the Yoruba towns of the western part of the territory and major Hausa towns such as Kano and Zaria in the north. Targeting the indigenous settlements, the colonial authorities probably thought, would have resulted in squandering a great opportunity to dramatize the perceived contrast between what they saw as the dazzling elegance and splendour of modern spatial structures and the repellent drabness of the primitive African varieties.

The British colonial town planning policy of ignoring traditional towns resulted in the development of sprawling communities at the fringes of these towns. In the Hausa towns of the north, these communities, which were usually populated by non-Hausa persons or 'strangers' from other parts of the country, became known as *Sabon Garis* (a local term for 'stranger quarters').

Professional planners in Nigeria often had to wrestle with striking a delicate balance between two diametrically opposed philosophies: Ebenezer Howard's garden city ideal of efficient, harmonious communal living and the segregation principles, which their main client, the colonial authorities, expected them to adhere to. Gurus of colonial administration, especially staunch proponents of the indirect rule strategy such as Lord Lugard, believed strongly that the success of colonial rule was contingent upon the degree to which the colonialist could maintain a social distance from the 'natives'. In practice, social and physical distance were taken to be synonymous, hence the need for racial spatial segregation.

A piece of legislation, the Public Lands Acquisition Act, was enacted in 1917 to replace the Land Act that had been enacted for the Crown Colony of Lagos in 1876 and made applicable in the Protectorate of Southern Nigeria in 1906. The 1917 Act, which was applicable throughout the entire colony of Nigeria, authorized the colonial government to acquire compulsorily or by agreement any land within the colony for public purposes. The term 'public purposes' was vaguely defined to include, but not be limited to, the following: the establishment of new layouts or towns, the development of government stations, districts or facilities, the creation of new settlements, and the extension of existing towns or human settlements and road/street construction.

The Township Ordinance of 1917 also conferred yet another set of inordinate powers on the colonial Governor. As per this Ordinance, the Governor was empowered to create townships. The townships were divided into three main classes, namely First Class (including Lagos, Ibadan, Kaduna), Second Class (e.g. Aba, Ilorin, Jos), and Third Class (e.g. Abakiliki, Benin, Ife, Ekot Ekpene). The classes depended on their degree of municipal responsibility and, above all, their relative roles within the colonial economy. In this latter regard, Class 'A' townships were critical to the functioning of the colonial economy, while Class 'C' townships were small and played limited and non-essential functions in the economy. The functions of Class 'B' townships ranked between those of Class 'A' and Class 'C' townships. The townships fell under the administrative jurisdiction of a local authority. The executive bodies of the townships comprised members appointed by the Governor. Note the extent to which the Ordinance endowed the colonial Governor with power. Not only was the Governor given the power and authority to elevate or demote any town, he was also empowered to appoint members to the executive body of the towns.

The main functions of the townships included the provisioning of utility services, the maintenance of public infrastructure and the enforcement of rules made by the Governor. The main sources of revenue for townships included rates, fees, charges, grants and rents from colonial government property. An important objective of the Ordinance was to separate the physical presence of the colonial power from the native population in line with the 'indirect rule' colonial administration policy. The policy of segregation, in practice, set aside different areas in towns for different groups. In Nigeria, such segregation was not limited to race. It extended to 'native strangers'. Thus, 'native strangers' were separated from 'local natives', who were confined to 'native reservations'. The two groups were then spatially separated from the European districts. Segregation worked well in the northern part of Nigeria but was never quite successful in the south due to the fact that the south has always known non-local populations. In the south, including the UN Mandate Territory of British Cameroons, however, areas were set aside for northern immigrants. These areas, which went/go under the name 'Hausa Quarters', exist to date.

The policy of land use compartmentalization marked the official beginning of town planning in Nigeria. The policy necessitated the planning of sites in conformity with predetermined standards. The standards were, as stated before, tailored after those that were in force in Britain at the time. In a number of cases the standards would have been slightly modified and applied in a British colony somewhere and then later transferred to Nigeria. For instance, the standards that were adopted in designing layouts in Northern Nigeria, particularly in Kano and Zaria under provisions of the 1917 Township Ordinance, conformed to the principles of British colonial cantonments in India (Home, 1974).

The early layouts emphasized such features as plot size, floor area ratio, building heights, and set back. The streets assumed what C.L. Cox, a colonial civil engineer who at the time was the Director of Public Works, had criticized as 'the unimaginative grid-iron pattern'. Cox went on to collaborate with H.A. Foy, then Deputy Director of Medical and Sanitary Services, to apply pressure on the concerned authorities to create a Town Planning Committee. To their credit, the committee was established and met for the first time in Lagos on 14 July 1922. During this maiden meeting, a decision was reached to appoint local planning officers who would be under the purview of the Public Works Department. The main objective of the committee was to develop Nigerian towns 'along modern lines, emulating the principles and practice of Town Planning followed elsewhere' (Home, 1974: 226).

The afore-cited developments occurred without the benefit of a resident professional town planner. Nigeria did not have a resident professional planner until 1928. This is when Albert J. Thompson, a planner with extensive experience in planning garden cities, was appointed as the colony's Town Planning Officer. Prior to arriving in Nigeria in 1927, Thompson (1878–1940) had worked in South Africa, where he designed the Pinelands Garden suburb of Cape Town and the Durban North Estate. In Nigeria, Thompson redesigned the Yaba (Lagos) Housing Estate (1927) and prepared a report proposing strategies for economizing on layouts (1928). In 1928, a memorandum, which set out the general principles governing layout, was prepared. The document was revised and reissued a decade later in 1939. Two junior town planners, R.B. Walker and C.L. Waide, were appointed in 1930, two years after Thompson's appointment.

Some of the major projects initiated by colonial town planners in Nigeria are as follows (Home, 1974): the construction of an African staff housing scheme in Lagos in 1926; and a project to improve drainage on Lagos Island subsequent to a series of plague outbreaks on the Island. Under the provisions of the Lagos Town Planning Ordinance, the Lagos Executive Development Board was established with an initial fund of £200,000, earmarked for covering the cost of drainage, swamp reclamation, slum clearance, market planning, and the development of suburban estates for African employees of government and European firms at Apapa, Yaba and Surulere on the Lagos mainland. The Board, it must be noted, was modelled along the lines of similar boards in India and Malaya (present-day Malaysia).

After a brief hiatus, caused by the Depression, town planning activities were rejuvenated in colonial Nigeria during the post-World War II era. One of the most significant events in this regard was the enactment in 1946 of the Nigerian Town and Country Planning Ordinance. The Ordinance was essentially a piece of planning enabling legislation in the country and was based on the planning concepts of Britain's Town and Country Planning Act of 1932.

Land tenure legislation

The Public Lands Acquisition Act, which originated in the Land Act of 1876, authorized the Colonial Secretary to compulsorily or by agreement acquire any land in the colony and the protectorate. The application of this Act was restricted to the southern region as the north was governed by a completely different set of land laws, particularly those contained in the 1910 Land and Native Rights Ordinance of Northern Nigeria. The Ordinance, which drew its inspiration from the principle of 'indirect rule', had declared all land in the northern region Native Land and placed it under the administrative jurisdiction of the Commissioner for Lands. In effect, the lands in the Hausa-dominated northern states were not governed by the same laws as those of the less homogeneous and less centralized areas of the south. It is important to note that the colonial land laws that were in force in the north were markedly more sensitive to traditional or native land tenure systems than the sweeping land laws of the south. As I have noted elsewhere (Njoh, 2003: 86), 'land legislation in British colonies, where indirect rule was prevalent, embodied elements that explicitly gave due regard to native customary laws of tenure'. The sensitivity of the 1910 Land and Native Rights Ordinance of Northern Nigeria to customary laws of tenure caught the attention of League of Nations authorities, who prescribed a replication of the ordinance in erstwhile German possessions that became Trust Territories of the League of Nations subsequent to the outcome of World War I.

The obvious question here has to do with why the British colonial authorities decided in favour of crafting land laws that appear sympathetic to customary land tenure principles in the northern states of Nigeria. The motives of the colonial authorities in this case can be better understood within the context of the broader objectives of the colonial enterprise. The authorities were interested in controlling and dominating but not alienating the natives. This meant striking a delicate balance between the important colonial objectives of 'goodwill' and 'rule' (Myers, 2003). The objective of striking a delicate balance between 'goodwill' and 'rule' was at the root of the 'indirect rule' strategy. Attainment of the objective depended to a great extent on the degree to which the British colonial authorities could persuade members of the indigenous population. Thus, the 1910 Land and Native Rights Ordinance can best be seen as a tool of association and persuasion rather than one of overt domination. Note that the ordinance only appeared to be sensitive to customary and indigenous claims of entitlements to land. However, in reality, it concentrated all authority and control over the lands in the colonial Commissioner for Lands.

Discussion and conclusion

Formal town planning pre-dated the European colonial epoch in the territories discussed here under the general rubric of British West Africa. In Sierra Leone, for instance, such activities go as far back as 1792, when the city's first layout plan was produced. Before then, European traders had been undertaking a lot of activities with implications for spatial structures in the region. Most remarkable in this connection are the many forts and castles that were constructed in the coastal areas of Ghana. It was, however, not until the advent of formal colonization that Euro-centric planning schemes began finding expression in the region. An examination of some of the schemes described in this chapter affords ample opportunity to appreciate the political nature of colonial urban planning. More importantly, it facilitates our appreciation of a number of essential but generally ignored objectives of urban planning, namely power, social control and domination.

The official rationale for the colonial town planning schemes described here, including those that sought to segregate residential areas by race – or more straightforwardly, isolate Europeans from Africans – was to protect the health of the general public. However, a more critical examination of the motives of such schemes reveals that they were designed to facilitate accomplishment of a number of specific goals of the colonial enterprise. The most notable of these goals in the context of this book are power, domination and control. Therefore, efforts to mould human settlements in the image of town planners, establish administrative headquarters, develop public infrastructure and so on must be seen as part of the colonialists' efforts to assert power, control and dominance over colonial space and subjects.

From this vantage point, the urban plans and layouts of the British colonial authorities constitute a framework through which they expressed colonial power. To be sure, the British colonial authorities in West Africa were not the first, and certainly not the only colonialists to manipulate urban space with a view to asserting power and effectuating control. The French, as Nicola Cooper (2000) notes, did this in Indochina. Just as 'Hebrard's zoning of city space created indigenous ghettos' in Indochina (Cooper, 2000: 92), the British residential segregation schemes that relegated members of the native population to the least desirable areas created indigenous ghettos in Accra, Kumasi, Freetown, Zaria, Kano, and Lagos, to name just a few. The *Sabon Garis* of Northern Nigeria and the shantytowns on the fringes of Accra exemplify these ghettos. Similarly, the wide and orderly arranged streets constituting a conspicuous element of the colonial towns that were developed by the British colonial authorities served to facilitate police and military control of the colonial subjects. In this regard, the streets were necessary to permit accessibility by the military and the police whenever there was a need to quash any civil unrest, revolt or political upheaval.

Land was at the heart of colonial town planning activities in British West Africa. Although the British 'indirect rule' policy showed some sensitivity towards customary land tenure systems, British colonial authorities strived to gain as much control as possible over land in the colonies. The British appreciated such control not only for its symbolic value but also, and perhaps above all, for its ability to guarantee political power. Here, the many land reform measures that the British enacted during their tenure as colonial authorities in the region enabled them to appropriate and redefine the indigenous people's relationship to land. To the extent that the reforms designated the colonial state or her agents, such as the Governor or Commissioner for Lands, as custodian of all land, it effectively placed the colonial state in control of the most critical factor of production. Economic power in any society is a function of the extent to which competing entities within that society control land. Therefore, any societal entity that possesses the authority to determine the ownership, succession and disposition of land emerges as the most powerful entity in society.

Apart from its utility as an economic tool, planning served as an important element in efforts on the part of British colonial authorities to achieve essential European ideological objectives such as 'Europeanizing' or 'Westernizing' the rest of the world under the oft-used euphemism, 'civilization'. Maxwell Fry, who served from 1943–5 as Adviser to the resident Minister for British West Africa, articulates this objective of colonial town planning in an address he gave 'to a combined meeting with the Royal Empire Society on the 26th June' 1946 (see Fry, 1946). Fry was so fascinated with what he saw as the potentiality of town planning to 'modernize' Africa that he recommended that the orbit of town planning in colonial Africa be expanded to incorporate villages. This is what he branded 'village planning'. He recommended developing plans for villages with a view to transforming them into 'young and growing towns', complete with the amenities afforded by Western civilization.

Notes

1   This segment draws largely from Ghana.co.uk, a UK-based informational website on Ghana. The URL for said source is as follows: http://www.ghana.co.uk/history/history/colonial_rule.htm.
2   The reference to 'formal efforts' is meant to distinguish planning based on European principles and concepts of spatial organization from spatial designs that adhere to traditional African principles. This latter, as I have argued elsewhere (see Njoh, 1999b), has always taken place in Africa. This is despite the fact that it has often been discounted.
3   That Napoleon III did not succeed in averting a revolution does not discredit the important policing and surveillance function of wide streets and spaced-out housing.
4   The Act's coverage was extended to the Protectorate of Southern Nigeria in 1906.

5 Planning in French West Africa

Introduction

Activities designed to promote as well as control urban growth and development occupied a priority place on the French colonial development agenda. The ultimate goal of these activities can be summarized under the following categories: social, economic, politico-administrative and psychological. From a social perspective, the French were bent on transforming human settlements in Africa into mini versions of French towns. To the extent that this goal was attainable, it helped in efforts on the part of French colonial authorities to recruit the calibre of officials required for efficacious administration in the colonies. From an economic perspective, urban centers were seen as critical engines of colonial development. The concentration of physical and social infrastructure in one place permitted colonial authorities to reap the benefits associated with economies of agglomeration and scale. Politico-administratively, urban areas served as locations for government administrative activities and centres for the diffusion of the political culture of preference. This culture was rooted in the French politico-administrative philosophy, which emphasizes the centralization of power and authority. The French monarch, Louis XIV, once made the following proclamation, 'l'état c'est moi', implying that there was no distinction between himself and the state. Psychologically, French colonial authorities considered the introduction of so-called modern concepts and principles of spatial organization, as well as the concomitant utilization of Western building materials and techniques, as a necessary instrument in their bid to portray French culture as superior to that of Africans.

Although works on European colonialism only rarely draw attention to this, urban development policy and projects occupied a prominent place on the French colonial agenda. This chapter is dedicated to examining the most important of these projects. The focus is on urban development and related projects that were executed prior to the end of the French colonial era in sub-Saharan Africa. The projects are grouped by colony. The discussion in this chapter is limited to projects that were executed in what used to be called the Federation of French West Africa, including Senegal,

Guinea, Côte d'Ivoire, Dahomey (present-day Benin), French Sudan (present-day Mali), Mauritania, and Niger. These erstwhile French colonies are examined below in alphabetical order.

Benin

Cotonou

By the middle of the nineteenth century Cotonou was just a small village largely inhabited by fishermen. Around that time, there were a lot of skirmishes between different groups (e.g. the Franco-Anglo squabbles over control of the territory which later became Dahomey; the inter-tribal feuds involving Porto-Novo and members of the Abomey Kingdom). Cotonou, which did not belong to any particular kingdom and was ruled by a relatively less powerful chief, was deemed safe as a site for the location of colonial government activities as well as a place of residence for European inhabitants. Account was also taken of other factors such as the relative ease of negotiating land and other treaties with members of a less powerful chieftaincy as opposed to doing so with elements of the Abomey Kingdom, a larger, well-organized and more powerful group. Despite all the advantages offered by Cotonou, it was not chosen to serve as the seat of the government of the French colonial territory of Dahomey. Instead, in 1884, colonial authorities designated Porto-Novo as the territory's capital. This decision did not, however, go unchallenged. Opponents of the decision considered Cotonou a better and more logical choice. First, the opponents contended, Cotonou was cleaner than Porto-Novo. Second, they went on, Cotonou was more aerated than Porto-Novo. Finally and above all, it contained fewer members of the indigenous population as well as fewer man-made structures than Porto-Novo. Thus, according to the opponents, colonial authorities were in a better position to shape the spatial structure and development of Cotonou to conform to their own proclivities and less able to do so in the case of the more developed Porto-Novo.

Although Cotonou was not the chief administrative centre of the colonial territory of Dahomey, it remained a very important city to the French colonial administrators. Earlier on, the city, or what was then a small village of fishermen, had played a crucial role in the efforts of the French to capture the Kingdom of Abomey as a colony. It served not only as the point at which French troops entered the territory but also became a French military post. Furthermore, the city's location on the coast had contributed to making it an important commercial centre since the beginning of the twentieth century.

In 1892, a sub-division plan was drawn for the city. This was part of efforts by the French colonial authorities to influence the city's spatial growth. Also as part of these efforts, the authorities had constructed or encouraged the construction of buildings as well as facilitated the development of commercial activities in the town. These efforts initially yielded only minimal dividends. As of 1905, the town's population was only about 1,000. Several years were to elapse before earlier investments in the town began registering positive results. By the 1920s the town's seaport had grown in prominence and had become more active than that of Porto-Novo. Between 1932 and 1938, the town's population grew from 5,000 to 10,000. By 1945, the population stood at 16,000. This population, however, remained inferior in comparison to that of Porto-Novo. It was not until the eve of independence that Cotonou's population, which was recorded as 50,000, surpassed that of Porto-Novo for the first time. Apart from some of the factors already mentioned, the fact that a lot of economic and administrative activities were increasingly being located in Cotonou contributed to accelerating the pace of the city's growth.

Spatially, the city developed longitudinally stretching from the sea to the lagoon. Unlike other urban areas of that era, Cotonou lacked a discernible racially segregated urban pattern. One particular factor, the fact that the city contained an insignificant European population, explains this phenomenon.

Porto-Novo

European contact with the general region of which Porto-Novo is a part, dates as far back as the seventeenth century. These were the heydays of the infamous trade in human beings from the African continent. European slave traders had established an outpost in the region. The outpost doubled as their place of residence and business in a village called Judah or Ouidah. The first European inhabitants of said village were of Portuguese extraction. With the passage of time, the French and the English, in that order, joined the Portuguese. It was not until the end of the eighteenth century that Europeans, again led by the Portuguese, began inhabiting another village in the region. This latter village went by the name Hogbodou. Hogbodou, which was later christened Porto-Novo, was important not only because it was a European outpost, but also because it was the capital of the Abomey Kingdom. Furthermore, the village also played a crucial role in the lucrative slave trade of that epoch. In fact, the town's rapid transformation from a village to a town of respectable size at that time was due largely to its identity as a launching pad for slave-hunting expeditions and a temporary holding place for slaves. By 1820 the town boasted a population of between 7,000 and 10,000 (Sinou et al., 1989: 31). By 1860, the slave trade had experienced a sharp decline and was rapidly losing its status as a lucrative commercial activity. The demise of this trade did not spell doom for the town as it soon rose to prominence as a centre for the production and processing of palm oil and related products. The economic importance of these products, especially at that time, cannot be overstated. As the town became more prosperous, its population continued to grow and proliferate. Initially, the buildings vacated by slave traders served to absorb the new immigrants. Thus, the increase in the town's population was not matched by significant transformations in its spatial structure.

One unique feature of Porto-Novo as a colonial capital had to do with the fact that unlike its peers, it possessed all the characteristics of a traditional African human settlement. In other words, Europeans had little influence on the town's spatial organization. This was largely a function of the fact that the town's existence, albeit as a village, pre-dated the arrival of Europeans. The problem of resource scarcity dictated a need for the French colonial authorities to utilize existing infrastructure as opposed to embarking on new construction projects. In this regard, colonial authorities are on record for renting facilities such as housing units for colonial officials from members of the local population, especially the Afro-Brazilians. Another factor that worked against any attempts on the part of the colonial authorities to significantly influence the course of the town's spatial development is related to local norms and practices governing the use, alienation and possession of land. Particularly, these norms and practices rendered difficult at best and impossible at worst, any efforts to proceed with drawing up and subsequently implementing sub-division plans as they had done in Cotonou.

The foregoing notwithstanding, colonial authorities were able to craft plans designed to influence the course of the town's spatial development. In this regard, a plan indicating existing structures as well as charting the city's future spatial growth path was drawn up in 1904. The plan contained proposed modifications, especially with respect to access roads, for some of the older portions of the town. The proposed modifications were limited to areas inhabited by Europeans. Of interest to the colonial authorities as far as the communication infrastructure was concerned was the linking of important points throughout the territory. This concern led to, amongst other things, the launching in the early 1900s of major projects such as road building and especially the Porto-Novo–Sakete railway project. This latter was completed in 1907. Other major projects in the town included the extension of a hospital (around the end of the nineteenth century) that was originally constructed for members of the colonial armed forces, and the construction of schools. One of the best known of these schools, the Victor Ballot Senior Primary School, was completed and inaugurated in 1913. Furthermore, a number of administrative facilities were added to the old stock of colonial government buildings in the city.

Côte d'Ivoire

Grand Bassam

The French were present in Côte d'Ivoire long before the territory became a French colony. The first treaty between the French and local authorities in the territory was signed in 1824. The treaty effectively transferred control of Grand Bassam to the French. The ink on the treaty papers was hardly dried when the French moved to construct a wooden fort, Fort Nemours, on the Grand Bassam River. Following this, the French established a military post in the area. An important objective of the treaty and the military post was to prevent the English from establishing trade and other relations with groups in the region. The treaty notwithstanding, the French population in the area grew very slowly. The major reason for this slow growth had to do with the high incidence of yellow fever, which was a leading cause of death amongst Europeans in the region. In this respect, it is worth noting that a yellow fever outbreak occurred in Grand Bassam in March 1899.

The earlier treaties between the French and local authorities served to facilitate France's efforts to colonize the territory. When the territory was effectively colonized in 1884, Grand Bassam was selected to serve as its administrative capital. This decision was contingent largely on the fact that the town boasted a few permanent buildings and other infrastructure designed to accommodate its, albeit small, European population. Mostly because of concerns with the danger posed by the incidence of yellow fever mentioned earlier, colonial authorities were unsatisfied with Grand Bassam and accordingly sought to find a safer location to serve as the colony's administrative capital. In 1887, the site whereupon sits present-day Abidjan, some 40km west of Grand Bassam, was proposed to serve as the location of the colony's administrative capital. The identification of the new site did result in the immediate termination of colonial government urban development work in Grand Bassam. In fact, in 1890, three years after Abidjan was proposed as the new capital of the colonial territory, the first urban development plan (Plan d'implantation de la capitale de la colonie de Côte d'Ivoire) for Grand Bassam was completed by the Topographic Service of the French Army Corps of Engineers (Service topographique du Génie Militaire). The project was financed with funds from the colonial budget under the auspices of the governor of the colony.

Bingerville

Up until 1900, Bingerville was known as Adjamé-Santey. It was renamed Bingerville in 1900 in honour of the first governor of the colony. The importance of Bingerville resides in the fact that it was selected to serve as the colonial capital of Côte d'Ivoire after the decision was reached to relocate the capital from Grand Bassam, which had become unsafe due to the frequent outbreaks of yellow fever. Initially, Abidjan was proposed to serve as the new capital. However, Abidjan was later rejected in favour of Adjamé-Santey, later renamed Bingerville, which was located at an altitude of about 70m above sea level. Bingerville's high elevation meant that it was less susceptible to diseases such as yellow fever. Another advantage associated with Bingerville relates to the fact it was closer than Abidjan to Grand Bassam from where the capital was being transferred. Based on especially these two factors, that is, its elevation and proximity to Grand Bassam, General Capest, at that time Lieutenant Governor of the Colony of the Côte d'Ivoire, wrote a letter dated 20 June 1899 and addressed to the Minister of the Colonies, recommending that the transfer be effectuated. The Minister wasted no time in approving the transfer and in the same year, 1899, a plan, 'Plan d'implantation de la ville de Bingerville (ex. Adjame-Santey)', for the city was completed.

Odienné

This town constitutes yet another important urban development project of the French colonial authorities in Côte d'Ivoire. In 1898 these authorities had established a military post in the general region of Odienné. The site upon which Odienné sits is to the north of this post. The site was selected for development particularly because it commands a magnificent view of the surrounding areas. In this regard, it is worth noting that Odienne sits atop a hill with altitude of 437m. The actual development, particularly as regards the provision of urban infrastructure, started in 1900, when the first residential property and a few administrative buildings were constructed.

It was, however, not until 1911 that Odienne's first colonial civil administrator, Commandant Pitchot, proposed a spatial development plan for most of the town. The plan, entitled 'Premier plan d'alignment et de lotissement d'une ville moyenne', was drawn and implemented under the auspices of Commandant Pitchot. It was financed with funds from the colonial territory's own budget. The entire town of Odienné at the time comprised ten neighbourhoods grouped around the town's mosque and main market. The town was divided into two main sections. The one contained traditional buildings, which were inhabited by members of the indigenous population, while the other contained units of so-called modern building materials. This latter section contained the residential units of the resident European population as well as colonial government offices.

Régie Abidjan

Designed in 1923 to house members of the workforce that constructed one of colonial Côte d'Ivoire's main railways, this project, Campagnes des chantiers de chemin de fer, is deemed important for the purpose of the discussion in this book. This is particularly because of the project's far-reaching spatial and physical development implications.

The railway project's execution depended largely on the forced labour of the members of the local population as well as natives of neighbouring colonial territories. Initially, the workers were left to their own devices as far as housing was concerned. However, adverse weather conditions, particularly very cold night-time temperatures, resulted in the death of several workers. To stem this tide, the colonial authorities decided in favour of constructing a workers' camp to house employees of the railway construction project. The units were of different sizes and quality. These and other features of the units differed based on the rank and status of their occupants. Similarly, the units were grouped to ensure that employees of different ranks within the organization's hierarchy did not live in the same section. Accordingly, some sections were designed to house exclusively labourers while others were designed to house team headmen, foremen, and supervisors. The units designed to house labourers measured 6.5m × 5.5m (out-to-out) and had a small vent between the wall plate and the roof. However, apart from the fact that the units were constructed of relatively durable materials, no provision was made for heating despite the expressed concern with cold night-time temperatures. As a result, the workers continued to suffer, although not as much as was the case when they housed themselves, during the cold nights characteristic of the Sudano–Guinean climate.

All told, the camp contained 30 units distributed on a surface area of 10ha. The density or average number of residents per hectare was 3.5. The floors and walls were of earth. The communal kitchen and toilet facilities were detached and located a considerable distance away from the residential units. Furthermore, the units lacked basic utility services, including electricity.

Abidjan

Following World War II, Abidjan assumed a more important role within the political economy of the colonial territory of Côte d'Ivoire as well as that of neighbouring landlocked territories such as Upper Volta (now Burkina Faso). This role was accentuated by the creation of the seaport, which had been planned and awaited during the preceding 40 years.

The elevation of the Abidjan's status to that of the territory's political and economic capital necessitated a lot of urban and spatial planning activities. Paramount amongst these activities was the drawing up in 1949 of an urban management and extension plan (Projet d'aménagement et d'extension de la capitale économique et administrative de Côte d'Ivoire). The plan comprised three components. The first was the urban master plan, which was drawn to a scale of 1:10,000. The second constituted the urban management plan, which was drawn to a scale of 1:5,000. The third component was a document containing a description of, and rules governing, physical development activities in the city.

The plan, amongst other things, divided the city into four distinct parts or zones as follows: industrial zone, commercial and administrative zone, residential zone and reserved zone. The industrial zone comprised separate sections for:

- crafts or artisan activities;
- small-scale industries;
- semi-heavy industrial activities;
- heavy industrial activities; and
- wood and related industrial activities.

The commercial and administrative zone comprised two main districts, namely the administrative and commercial districts. The residential zone comprised six districts, respectively containing: single and multi-family housing units, low density single-family housing units, multi-family housing, mixed housing, light industrial activities, and native residential housing. The reserved zone was largely an undeveloped stretch of wooded land at the outskirts of the city.

Cité Foulon

This project was designed as a low-income housing community (*opération d'habitat économique groupé*). Developed in 1950, it constitutes a good example of the low-income housing projects that were developed by French colonial authorities in sub-Saharan Africa. The Cité Foulon project comprised two parallel rows of housing units separated by an island of trees and flowers. The project was designed to house both single individuals and families. The units destined for individuals measured approximately 7m², while those designed to house families were about 20m². Units in this latter category were provided with a veranda apiece. Basic facilities such as kitchen and latrine were detached and shared by multiple households while the density was extremely high. In this regard, there were 26 buildings for single individuals and 26 buildings for families – that is, a total of 52 buildings located on a piece of land with an area of approximately 1.5ha. Thus, on average, there were about 50 housing units per hectare containing a population of about 200 persons.

Azopé

The desire on the part of French colonial authorities to transform human settlements in Africa into mini versions of communities in France found expression not only in urban centres but also in rural enclaves. Designed in 1953, Azopé stands out in this regard particularly because it was a pilot 'model village' project under the title, 'Plan de lotissement de villages pilotes, modernisation de l'habitat rural'. As the title suggests, the model village project was part of the larger French plan to 'civilize or modernize' Africans. The project was therefore designed to introduce not only so-called modern building techniques, materials and housing standards, but also Western concepts of spatial and environmental design. In this connection, the 'model village' plan included subdivisions, subdivision regulations, a system of well-aligned streets, public infrastructure such as potable water fountains, schools, markets, health centres, town hall, and post and telecommunication facilities. The project was designed by the Topographic Service of the Colonial Department of Public Works. The 'model village' projects were supposed to be financed with funds from several public sources including, but not limited to, the local housing corporations, the Crédit de la Côte d'Ivoire, and commercial and other banks.

It is important to note that Azopé constituted only one of about fifteen planned village projects that were developed in Côte d'Ivoire by French colonial authorities. The following five of these projects stand out and are worth mentioning here:

- the Bénéné, Dimbokro project, which essentially entailed the construction of permanent residential structures;
- the Ousrou project, which constituted the construction of housing units of bricks;
- the Dougbafra, a project designed to rebuild a village destroyed by fire;

- the Abongoua, which entailed the construction of low-income housing;
- the Yamoussoukro project, which entailed the design of a subdivision plan for 3,000 inhabitants.

The Azopé project, as well as the other 'modern village' projects that were completed by the French colonial authorities, suffered from several problems. These problems included, but were not limited to, the fact that they were: (1) not affordable by members of the target population, (2) not adapted to the conditions and needs of the villagers, and (3) not adapted to the natural environment. Additionally, the projects experienced many problems relating to cost recovery.

Yamoussoukro

Developed in 1954, Yamoussoukro was one of the many 'modern village' projects executed by the French colonial authorities in Côte d'Ivoire. The Yamoussoukro project was unique particularly because its conception and realization were influenced by a member of the indigenous population and native of Yamoussoukro, Mr Houphouet-Boigny, who was at the time a minister in the colonial government. The village was designed to serve as a camp for coffee and cocoa planters (*construction d'un nouveau village pour planteurs de café et de cacao*). The local housing corporation, Société Immobilière et d'Habitat de Côte d'Ivoire (SIHCI), played an important role in this project. It is important to note that SIHCI became interested in construction and cognate projects as from 1952. However, this interest was not matched by the availability of the funds necessary for financing such projects. To be sure, the financing of the Yamoussoukro project would not have been possible without the participation of the then newly created African Rural Housing Association (Société de l'Habitat Rural Africain) and the real property insurance company, l'Urbaine et la Seine, which made available 50 million CFA francs for the purpose of funding the project.

The Yamoussoukro project, which was located along the Abidjan–Bouaké highway, comprised 625 lots. Initially, it contained, amongst other things, a commercial zone, a fuel station, a parking lot, and an area of six hectares reserved for the construction of a market.

Guinea

The *raison d'être* of most early European contacts with territories on the coast of West Africa was commerce. This was the case with the territory which later became Guinea. Prior to the nineteenth century, the Kaloum peninsula and the islands of Los in present-day Guinea served as venues for the exchange of African goods, including human cargo, bound for Europe and the Americas. In addition, these two locales served as a refuge for sea pirates, slave traders and European commercial ships. Later, the locales became the meeting points for people involved in illicit business along the West African coast. By the beginning of the nineteenth century, the area had become the home of a number of legitimate commercial companies. The area became more prominent as a commercial venue as time went on and by 1865 almost all ships passing through the coast of West Africa made a stop over at the Los islands. European expeditions into the hinterland region off these islands, especially the area adjoining the Kaloum peninsula, did not occur until 1885. At the time, the largest human settlement in the region was Dubreka.

Conakry

Europeans had more than a passing interest in the mentioned islands and peninsula. They were interested in the outright possession of the region as a whole. Accordingly they embarked on a course to attain their objective in this connection by all means necessary. In 1887, the French succeeded in gaining total control over Kaloum. Two years were to elapse, however, before they initiated any development activities in the region. The first of these activities, particularly construction, took place on Tombo Island. French occupation of the territory which later became Guinea began in 1889. At the time, Tombo Island, which was home to 300 residents in 1885, comprised two villages, namely Conakry and Boulbinet. French colonial authorities designated Conakry, which at the time had at most 30 buildings, as the chief administrative and commercial centre for the territory soon after they gained control of the island. The six-year period that followed this decision witnessed a flurry of construction and other development activities on the island. The orthogonal shape of the island acted as a constraint on these activities. To maximize utility of the limited space, developers arranged the buildings in small squares. The plan of this unplanned community looked like a chessboard. Access roads were terribly narrow, thereby inhibiting movement throughout the island.

To remedy the situation, colonial authorities drew up a plan, the first urban master development plan for Conakry (Premier plan d'implantation de Conakry) in 1895. The plan made provision for wider streets and boulevards generously lined with rows of trees that provided badly needed shade in the daytime when heat from the tropical sun is at its peak. Construction work on most of the administrative units and other public infrastructure in the town was begun in 1895. The first phase of work on the Conakry–Niger road was also begun in the same year. The period between 1895 and 1910 marked the intensification of development activities in the city both by private and public entities. In 1900, work started on the railway linking Conakry to the River Niger. By 1904, the line had reached Kindia and in 1910, it had been extended to Kourouscou on the Niger. Work on the seaport was also completed in 1910. The completion of these two projects constituted a mixed blessing. Paradoxically, the railway effectively disconnected the southern part of the island from its northern end, which thenceforth depended almost exclusively on maritime and other activities associated with the seaport. Efforts aimed at developing the town's public infrastructure, especially the communication network, were in progress simultaneously with some of the activities aforementioned. Here, attention is drawn to 1903, the year in which the first aqueduct was constructed, and the first telephone and telegraph lines were installed in the town.

In 1904, the islands of Los, which until then were under the control of the English, became part of the urban area of Conakry. A notable feature of the built environment of Conakry, especially during the years following 1910, was the architectural style assumed by the buildings. The style known as 'casa', drew its inspiration from oriental architecture and remains a distinct characteristic of human settlements in the Gulf of Guinea.

It was not until the end of World War II that colonial authorities undertook a number of other major urban development projects in and around Conakry. One such project involved using stabilized soil to construct low-income housing units for members of the indigenous population ('Opérations d'habitat en terre stabilisée pour les Africains'). The Guinea Housing Authority (Société Immobilière de Guinée – SIG) undertook this project. The stabilization entailed the addition of 80kg of cement and limestone to a cubic metre of soil. The material was then compacted to mould blocks used in constructing the housing units. Bricks used for flooring were also of stabilized soil. In this case the bricks were made from an aggregate consisting of 100kg of cement added to a cubic metre of earth. This strategy resulted in enormous cost-saving as the total cost of producing a two-room housing unit was only 145,000 CFA francs or 4,700 CFA francs per square metre. This translated into savings over conventional materials of 50 per cent for the walls and 20 per cent for the unit as a whole.

In 1956 SIG completed the plan for a major project to provide temporary housing (for an estimated period of three years) to residents of a neighbourhood that was made unsafe for habitation by floods. Although the project, entitled 'Operations de restructuration d'un quartier insalubre du centre-ville', was never realized, its ambitious plan deserves more than a passing observation. According to the plan, the project was designed to construct 300 housing units to accommodate residents evicted from the unsafe neighbourhood for a period of three years. Each unit was comprised of one room of 3m × 3m and a veranda of the same size. Facilities such as toilets and bathrooms were shared in the following order: 4 toilets and 4 showers for every 25 housing units.

One of the last projects with spatial implications undertaken by colonial authorities in Guinea was the drawing up of a master plan for a new town ('Création d'une ville nouvelle suite à la construction d'une usine d'alumine') located some 155 km from Conakry. The project was designed to respond to the housing demand generated by what was at the time a newly constructed aluminium factory. Although the new town was located at a considerable distance from the heart of Conakry, it soon became the administrative and political capital for the region. The town, which was located on a plateau, was originally designed to accommodate 25,000 inhabitants. A generous allowance was made for streets, green areas and public facilities. An important and unique feature of the plan is the fact that it included four quadrants (numbered Units I to IV) and a downtown area (*centre ville*) located literally at the heart of the town.

Mali

Bamako

Bamako was initially a military base established by the French colonial authorities on the banks of the River Niger in 1884. It was from this base that the French organized and launched the military missions that were necessary for conquering the territory. The first major project with spatial and physical development implications for Bamako was the drawing up in 1894 of a plan for a new system of streets to replace the access roads that had developed spontaneously prior to that time. Later on, the colonial authorities crafted a system for distributing land through concessions. In 1895 the governor of the territory, Governor Trentinian, proposed the relocation of government and military administrative facilities to Bamako. These facilities were to be located at Kati, a plateau at the highest elevation in the area. The site was actually a few kilometres from the Bamako city centre in the direction of Kayes City. It was not until 1903 that the plan for the proposed complex ('Plan d'une cité administrative – un quartier de Bamako') was completed. The plan, which was drawn up by the Topographic Service of the French Military Engineering Corps with funds from the colony's budget, was unique in two important ways. First, it was, at least at the time, the only colonial government administrative complex that was geographically far-removed from the city of which it was a part. Second, the complex was designed along the lines of ancient acropolises. A single road flanked by government buildings led in and out of the complex. The governor's mansion constituted the terminus for said road and served as the focal point of the complex.

Prior to the completion of the aforementioned plan, the French colonial authorities had implemented other projects with spatial and physical development implications for Bamako and the surrounding region. Two of these projects warrant some attention here. One constituted the creation of a village for freed slaves (*village de liberté*) in 1896. This village was located along the Kayes–Bamako railway and could be considered an urban management scheme as it was designed to contain members of the growing immigrant African population in Kayes and Bamako. The other comprised the construction of an identical village in Bamako.

The village comprised four large squares that were separated by wide streets flanked by banana trees and cassava plants. Each square contained 24 circular housing units, each of which had an interior diameter of 5m and a height of 2.5m. The walls of these units were of mud and plastered with white sand. A wall of burnt bricks enclosed each of the four squares and access into the village was possible through only three gates. Units were assigned to residents according to gender and age without any regard to marital status. The movement of residents was strictly controlled and no one was permitted to leave or enter the camp at night. Four headmen (one for each square) maintained order in the camp. Thus, by constructing these so-called 'villages of freed slaves', the colonial authorities not only ensured the exclusion of members of the native population from the cities, but also assured the availability of a steady supply of the unskilled labour necessary for urban functioning at close to no cost.

As a colonial military post, Bamako was only one of several which the French had established between the River Senegal and River Niger. The other posts later became transit points while Bamako served as the terminus when the railway linking the two rivers was completed. (Bamako was the final stop on the rail line until the line was extended into Koulikoro, where the River Niger becomes navigable.) In 1906, Bamako was designated the capital of French Sudan (present-day Mali). Prior to that time, the capital of the territory was located in Kayes. Soon after Bamako became the capital, its status increased tremendously. The city had become not only an important administrative centre but also a dominant commercial city in the territory. Most of the commercial development took place along the river near two important landmarks, the railway station and the old fort. As was the case in other colonial administrative centres, the colonial authorities carried out a number of projects with spatial and physical development implications. Noteworthy in this regard is the construction of the following facilities: a colonial government station on the Koulouba Hill overlooking the rest of the city, a hospital, the governor's mansion, and residential units for colonial civil servants. Later, in 1919, the colonial government began developing sub-division plans for the city, especially the area surrounding the government station. These plans were designed to control the nature, direction, rate and timing of growth throughout the city.

Mauritania

Europeans had been present in the territory which came to be known as Mauritania since the latter part of the nineteenth century. Initially, European explorers had made contact with residents of the ancient town of Ksar. It was, however, not until the early part of the twentieth century – in 1903, to be more precise – that they decided to manifest their presence by establishing a trading outpost in the region. The outpost was located at Trarza. The establishment of the outpost was followed immediately with the construction of a fort in the same general area.

Apart from Ksar, the territory comprised mostly small villages. Thus, urbanization was unknown throughout the territory until the creation of Nouakchott towards the end of the colonial era. Nouakchott was designed to serve as the territory's capital. It is noteworthy that on 24 July 1957, when Nouakchott was designated as the capital of what was to become the independent country of Mauritania, it had nothing in the way of man-made structures. In selecting the site for the new capital city, care was taken to ensure that it served to unite rather than polarize the entire country. A number of specific factors were considered. One of these factors was political in nature. In this regard, the capital of the territory had to be located neither too close to the south nor too close to the north. Locating it further south would have infuriated the Maures, while locating it further to the north would have angered the Blacks, who were based largely in the southern part of the territory. Another factor that was considered had territorial administrative implications. In this connection, efforts were made to ensure that the capital of the territory was as close as possible to Dakar, Senegal, the seat of the government of the Federation of French West Africa of which Mauritania was a part. Additionally, the choice of the site was contingent upon its location on the coast, hence accessibility to the outside world.

The decision to designate Nouakchott as the capital slowed growth in some of the territory's older human settlements such as Rosso and Nouadhibou (then, Port Etienne). Apart from its location, Nouakchott proved ideal as the territory's capital because of its favourable geographic conditions, geology, littoral climate and weather. The initial development of the city was financed with funds from the French Cooperation and Assistance Fund (Fonds d'Aide et de Coopération Français).

One of the earliest projects with far-reaching spatial and physical development implications undertaken by the French colonial authorities in Mauritania was initiated in 1954. Under the auspices of the Federal Office of Housing (Bureau d'Etudes du Service Fédéral de l'Habitat), and with a loan of 77 million CFA francs from the French Overseas Central Funds (Caisse Centrale de la France d'Outre-mer), a plan was crafted to develop a number of low-income housing units ('Plans types de logements économiques'). The project included four main categories of housing, coded thus: M1, M2, M3 and M4. Units in the M1 category measured 30m^2 and cost 135,000 CFA francs each, while those in the M2 category had an area of 46.5m^2 and cost 185,000 CFA francs each. The units in the M3 category measured 61m^2 and cost 200,000 CFA francs and those in the M4 category had an area of 91m^2 and cost 360,000 CFA francs each.

Once the decision to develop Nouakchott as the capital of the colonial territory of Mauritania had been reached, the attention of colonial authorities was turned to crafting a suitable urban development plan for the city. The French colonial government decree of 18 June 1946 established the modalities, guidelines and conditions for drawing up such plans. According to the Committee on Urban Planning and Housing, urban development master plans, which were required especially for colonial capital cities, were supposed to spell out guidelines and rules for developing urban land as well as map out the necessary network of urban infrastructure. The arrêté of 8 August 1946 further specified the various elements that must be included in each urban master development plan (plan directeur). Prominent amongst these elements were the following:

- a feasibility report;
- a regional master development plan drawn to a scale of 1:20,000;
- a comprehensive physical development plan drawn to a scale of 1:50,000;
- an implementation plan; and
- a land-use plan showing public infrastructure and services.

Several urban master development plans were proposed for the city of Nouakchott in the 1950s. Governor Mauragues proposed the first such plan in 1957. This plan neither benefited from the services of a trained urban architect nor took into account prevailing local conditions. Cognizant of the deficiencies of this first plan, the Director of Public Works for the colonial territory at the time, Hirsch, proposed a second plan. While efforts were made to adapt this second plan to the physical environment, the plan lacked a lot by way of detail. This rendered implementation rather difficult. In May 1957 yet another plan was proposed. The architect of this plan was Cerutti Marri, who was the official architect of the government of French West Africa based in Dakar. This plan, while more detailed, was nevertheless inspired by the earlier plans produced by Governor Mauragues and M. Hirsch respectively. Lainville, an architect at the Colonial Government Central Office of Public Works and Planning in Dakar, proposed a fourth plan for the city. On 4 July 1957, the General Assembly of the colonial territory favourably evaluated and recommended a few modifications to the plan. After the modifications were effectuated, the plan was adopted on 11 June 1958. Prior to that, Gerard Jacquet, Minister of French Overseas Territories, had visited Nouakchott on 5 March 1958 to launch the urban development project as well as lay the proposed city's foundation stone. In March 1959 two architects, Leconte and Lafon, were assigned the responsibility of updating the Lainville plan. The updating entailed modifying the road and street network, and creating additional zones.

Niger

What was later to become the French colonial territory of Niger was initially a military post established by a French government decree of 18 December 1904. The administrative capital of the new territory was located in Niamey while Zinder was designated as the military headquarters. The decision to assign important roles within the colonial government to these two towns had far-reaching spatial and physical development implications. For example, the elevation of the status of Niamey especially, which until then was nothing more than a village, correspondingly lowered the status as well as stifled the growth of Tahoua, which was one of the few well-established and populated human settlements in the region. For mainly strategic reasons, the administrative capital of the territory was transferred from Niamey to Zinder on 1 January 1911. On 26 December 1926, the colonial authorities decided to return the administrative capital to Niamey, where it remained throughout the colonial epoch and beyond. As was the common practice, colonial authorities concentrated their urban development efforts on the administrative capital. Thus, Niamey was the primary beneficiary of such efforts on the part of French colonial urban planners and administrators.

Niamey

One of the first actions taken by colonial authorities to promote the growth and development of Niamey was the non-taxation of the town's residents. Other actions, including the construction of a large market, government buildings and public infrastructure, soon followed. Perhaps more noteworthy is the fact that the colonial authorities actively discouraged the growth of other human settlements in the region as they strived to accelerate the pace of Niamey's development. For instance, they instituted a market tax on all transactions in markets in the region except those within the Niamey city limits.

Before the end of the colonial era, colonial urban planners had drawn up two urban plans for Niamey. The first of these plans was completed in 1905 immediately following the designation of Niger as a military territory. The plan was designed to, *inter alia*, extend the city, which at the time was no more than a village. The extension was envisaged to promote growth in the areas along the River Niger. The second plan was completed over thirty years later in 1937. This plan entitled, 'Urban Development Plan for the City of Niamey, Capital of the Territory of Niger' ('Plan d'aménagement de la ville de Niamey, chef-lieu du territoire du Niger'), was relatively more elaborate than its predecessor. It covered a superficial area of 617 hectares and stipulated conditions and specific geographic locations for the following developments (Sinou *et al.*, 1989: 154):

- a European district (*ville européenne*), comprising 80 parcels of 3, 4, 5 and 6 lots each;
- a 'native' district (*ville indigène*), separated from the European district by a green belt measuring 350 metres wide, and comprising 600 lots (for the first phase only) of four parcels each, and 28 lots set aside for the construction of stores serving the native population;
- a commercial and administrative district located in the European area of the city, and bordered by the green belt. The district comprised 44 lots of which 32 were set aside for commercial purposes while 12 were allotted to the development of future administrative facilities.

The plan also made provision for commercial development on 6 hectares of land along the River Niger. For aesthetic, safety and health reasons, the plan required that all dwelling units in the 'native district' be constructed of permanent materials and must be at least 3.50m in height. The plan also required the enclosure of all dwelling units within a fence of at least 1.50m high.

Apart from the requirement for fences, the plan was typical of all French colonial urban plans as it strived to reproduce a mini version of European cities by requiring the spatial segregation and compartmentalization of functions. Another aspect of the plan that was in line with colonial urban plans was the spatial separation of residential areas by race. Yet another typical feature of the plan is the fact that it set vast areas of prime, well-situated and aerated land for exclusive use by the European population. Here, attention must be drawn to the fact that the building lots in the European district were excessively large and located on the plateau, which is the highest and most ventilated area of the city.

Senegal

The importance of Senegal in French colonial adventures in sub-Saharan Africa cannot be overstated. As noted in Chapter 2, the French were present in Senegal long before they decided to acquire colonial territories in the region. Once the decision in favour of colonialism was reached, French colonial authorities found it judicious to use Senegal as their base of operation. The status of Senegal was elevated in 1895 when its premier city, Dakar, was designated the capital of the then newly constituted Federation of French West Africa (FWA). Accordingly, most urban infrastructure development projects for the Federation were concentrated in Senegal in general and Dakar in particular. Before delving into the details of these projects, we examine French urban development efforts in two of Senegal's historic island cities, Gorée and Saint-Louis.

Gorée Island

This island, which was occupied by the Portuguese, and then the Dutch, became a possession of France in the seventeenth century. In order to protect the island from possible attacks, the French moved speedily to fortify it. At the time the island was barely an outpost. Throughout the eighteenth century, several urban design plans were drawn for the island. However, none was ever implemented. It was not until the end of the century that the French asserted their presence and interest in the growth and development of the island by constructing two forts there. One of the forts was located at the lower end of the island while the other was situated on the cliff. Thereafter, the French authorities carried out a number of urban infrastructure development projects. By 1842, the island contained, amongst other things, a hospital and a church. With the passage of time, the authorities became preoccupied with bringing some degree of spatial order to the island. In this regard, they drew up plans designed to re-align the buildings along streets that traversed each other perpendicularly. The plan revealed a gridiron pattern of streets. The housing units were set back at a generous distance from, and facing, the streets.

Saint-Louis

The French took over control of the island after the British left in 1817. It did not take the French authorities long to notice that the island was suffering from physical and functional obsolescence and therefore required a lot of urban redevelopment work. This daunting and arduous task was rendered more complicated by the scarcity of necessary materials on the island and in surrounding areas. Despite this, the French embarked on redeveloping the island. The island's first official urban development plan ('Premier plan d'urbanisme pour l'île de Saint-Louis') was completed in 1828. The plan, which was adopted on 23 July of the same year, was drawn by the Topographic Department of the French Army Corps of Engineers (Service de Topographie du Génie Militaire) and financed with funds from the colonial budget. The results of the efforts of French authorities were hard to miss. When the urban plan was adopted in 1828, the island had only 200 houses of permanent materials, particularly bricks. A decade later in 1838, the island had as many as 320 such structures. Of these, 229 were storey buildings.

A second major project with physical and spatial implications on the island was the Saint-Louis Realignment and Extension Plan ('Plan de réalignement et extension du quartier Point-nord de l'Île Saint-Louis'). The plan, which was designed to realign the developed area as well as develop the undeveloped northern portion of the island, was completed in 1843. The objective of the project was double-pronged. On the one hand, it was aimed at facilitating traffic flow on the island. The fact that most development on the island had occurred spontaneously significantly hindered the free movement of people, goods and services on the island. On the other hand, the project was designed to relieve the developed portion of the island of the problem of population congestion from which it was already suffering. The extension project consisted mainly of sub-dividing the northern tip of the island into building lots. The lots were assigned to willing and able inhabitants of the island on condition that they would be developed with minimal delay. Failure to embark upon and complete approved development projects on any assigned lot resulted in the assignee's rights over the lot being automatically revoked. The island witnessed yet another important development with spatial and physical implications on 27 November 1849 when Governor Baudin announced the creation of a village for freed slaves (*village de liberté*).

Yet another important urban development project, an extension plan for Saint-Louis, was completed in 1919. The plan, which underwent a lot of modifications during implementation, was essentially designed to sub-divide part of the island into building lots. The need for the plan was triggered by amongst other things the fact that the island's population had grown significantly over the years and building activity in many areas had encroached on what was supposed to be the public right of way. In this way, the plan was designed to re-establish some spatial order on the island.

In 1931, the colonial government, with funds from a public works loan, undertook a project to develop 50 housing units for members of the indigenous population resident on Saint-Louis. The units were arranged into clusters separated from each other by a distance of 12m and set up in parallel rows. Each unit measured 5m × 4m and had a veranda that was 1.50m in depth. The clusters were arranged to form two main groups of homes occupying two lots, separated by an access road that measured 15m in width.

Dakar

Dakar, particularly because it was the seat of the government of the Federation of French West Africa, was the target of most French colonial government urban planning activities in sub-Saharan Africa. In 1847, what is presently the city of Dakar was a village of only 1,000 people, who were mostly fishermen and peasant farmers. It was after 1850 that the first military barracks and religious facilities were constructed in the city. These facilities were largely located between Place de Protêt, what is now the Independence Square (Place de l'indépendance) and the port. In 1862 a French military engineer named Pinet-Laprade drew the city's first master plan. The plan's main elements were a central boulevard, which bears the engineer's name, Esserts Street (Rue Esserts), Kermel Square (Place Kermel) Protest Square, and the Military Circle located at the site presently occupied by la Banque internationale pour l'Afrique Occidentale (BIAO). According to the plan, streets were supposed to be between 8m and 10m wide. The plan also set aside land for religious purposes, the construction of a market and buildings.

In May 1914, there was an outbreak of a plague epidemic in portions of the territory which later became Senegal. Dakar was affected. Colonial authorities, concerned with consequences of this plague and similar future situations for the city's European inhabitants, decided to physically separate the races. Consequently, a decree creating a 'native-only' district was promulgated on 24 July 1914. A sub-divison plan was drawn up for this district, known as Medina, in 1915. The district's physical parameters were established by a local decree of 6 November 1916. The plan effectively divided up the city into two main districts, the one for Europeans and the other for the 'natives'. The physical separation of the two districts notwithstanding, both were considered part of the same city. Thus, Medina was subjected to the building code and other development regulations that were in force at the time in Dakar. The said regulations, because of the plague, were tightened and later applied to other colonial territories.

By 1931, Dakar boasted a total of 24 km of street network. The streets had a width of at least 10m, with as much as 16 of the 24 km having a width of 10 to 20m. Of the 24 km of street network, 16 km were paved in stone while the remaining 8 km were tarred. Most of the streets were flanked by rows of trees. The trees served to shade the streets during periods of intensive solar radiation. This account gives the false impression that the entire city was well served by a network of streets. In fact, these streets were located mostly on the plateau, which was the area of town inhabited by Europeans and in which colonial government offices were located.

Discussion and conclusion

An important but oft-ignored objective of European colonialism in Africa was self-preservation. I use this term not in the strict biological sense connoting the instinct of an animal in pain to attempt to stop the pain and seek safety. Rather, I employ the term to refer to the proclivity to avoid being injured or to try to survive at all costs on the part of humans and human institutions.

With this in mind, I interrogate the French colonial town and country planning activities in West Africa to see how these activities helped the French realize their colonial objectives. I focalize on those activities, that by design or not, helped the colonial institution to protect and preserve itself, those that helped protect, preserve and promote the French culture, and finally the activities that colonial authorities indulged in as part of strategies designed to protect and preserve themselves.

Preservation of the institution of colonialism

The initial phase of the European colonial era in Africa was characterized by constant skirmishes between rival colonial powers and between colonial powers and members of the indigenous population. It took not only the firepower of the military but also the professional and technical ingenuity of colonial environmental designers, including architects and town planners, to conquer and protect the colonial territories. The important role of these professionals manifested itself through the selection of appropriate sites for colonial administrative stations and designing and constructing the forts that protected the conquered territories. The relocation of the colonial capital of Niger from Niamey to Zinder and then back to Niamey was part of an effort to defend the colonial territory of Niger from rival European powers. Once conquered, a lot of spatial strategies were put in place to protect and preserve the territories. For instance, one reason for choosing locations at high altitudes (e.g. Dakar, Abidjan, Conakry, Yaoundé, Bamako) to serve as the sites for colonial government stations had to do with the view that such areas command their surroundings. Thus, such locations facilitated accomplishment of the colonial government's task of keeping constant watch over members of the indigenous population. Members of this population were usually located at the foot of hills upon which reposed colonial government stations. To further facilitate the colonial state's ability to control members of the indigenous population, the colonial planners and civil engineers provided wide and well-aligned streets. Such streets were necessary to facilitate the movement of the colonial government security operatives.

The need to protect and preserve colonialism occupied an important place on the French colonial power's priority ladder even during the twilight of the colonial era. A conference that brought together French colonial authorities and representatives of all territories within her colonial empire was held in Brazzaville in 1944. The meeting had as its main purpose deciding the post-war future of the French colonial empire. The final resolution of this major conference says a lot about how badly the French colonial authorities wanted to protect and preserve the institution of colonialism. The resolution reads thus (quoted in Lewis, 1962: 130):

> The aims of the work of colonization which France is pursuing in her colonies exclude any idea of autonomy and any possibility of development outside the French empire bloc; the attainment of self-government in the colonies even in the most distant future must be excluded.

Thus, efforts such as those involving infrastructure development in the colonies must be seen as constituting part of the strategies that were designed to ensure the survival of colonialism in the French empire.

Racism or 'preservation of culture?'

French policymakers have always wanted the rest of humanity to believe that they find racism contemptuous. This is the case even when, under the pretext of race-neutrality, they fail to acknowledge the problem's prevalence in French society. What is more interesting is the bizarre view that the French typically harbour about racism, which makes the mere mention of the word itself 'racist'. This is true today as it was back in the colonial era.

The roots of the Protestant ethic and capitalism, which place much premium on capital accumulation and individual material wealth, are traceable to European culture. Appreciating this point is of essence particularly because it facilitates understanding of the motives of colonial projects with capitalist overtones, such as those that strived to commodify land in Africa. Assimilation and acculturation as goals of French colonialism were meant to transform the colonized into 'Frenchmen'. The primordial goal in this regard was, as Jacques Stern, a former French Minister of Colonies, said during World War II, to bind together through material and moral bonds 40 million continental Frenchmen and 60 million overseas White and 'Coloured' Frenchmen (Lewis, 1962).

The strategies that were adopted in such cultural usurpation efforts were plentiful and incorporated into educational, religious, commercial and spatial development programmes. In France the educational, social and military policies of the Third Republic had ensured the transformation of France from a country of peasants into a nation of Frenchmen by 1914. Concomitant with this development had been the accentuation of the role of the increasingly centralized French state and its capital, Paris, in the country's politico-economic life.

In French colonial Africa, school children were compelled to recite the same lessons as their counterparts in Paris. Lines such as 'Our ancestors had blue eyes and blond hair …' despite their undisguised absurdity, were commonplace. For French colonial authorities, such lines were anything but absurd as long as they helped to keep French culture and the French identity alive. Hardly any effort was spared to create a class of Africans who could function as Frenchmen. Efforts in this connection led French colonial authorities to confer French citizenship on literate African residents of the early Senegalese cities of Saint-Louis, Gorée, Rufisque and Dakar (Winters, 1982).

Apart from conferring citizenship on the 'assimilated' African elite of French colonies, the policy permitted the colonies to be represented in the French National Assembly. Thus, based on available evidence, there is hardly any reason to believe that French colonial policy was driven by racism, that is, discrimination, hatred or dislike of a people because of the colour of their skin. It is true that efforts to usurp indigenous culture in colonial Africa possess the hallmarks of racism; however, we cannot ignore the fact that central authorities in Paris have also spared no effort at 'assimilating' French people in the provinces – a move that has historically infuriated French traditionalists and progressivists.

Preservation of French culture

The need to preserve, maintain and promote French culture with the concomitant living standards meant that only those who had gained adequate mastery of, and were prepared to maintain these standards were allowed in 'European-Only' districts. This explains the presence in early European settlements such as Rufisque, Gorée, Saint-Louis and Dakar, of literate middle-class Africans. In contrast, so-called 'civilized and cultured' Africans in British colonial Freetown, who had served or were serving as colonial auxiliaries were excluded from Hill Station, that town's exclusive European residential district (Goerg, 1998). The need to preserve a 'pure French culture' was also at the root of policies that located Africans in areas far-removed from European quarters and outlawed dancing and drumming in urban centres in Brazzaville (Martin, 1995) and Abidjan (Freund, 2001). It is therefore quite likely that what found expression in the built environment of French colonial Africa as 'racial spatial segregation' was an unintended consequence of policies designed to promote French living standards and cultural values amongst urban dwellers.

The promotion and preservation of French culture and living standards is also very likely at the root of policies that supplanted African urban design structures with French varieties. Throughout francophone Africa one sees urban design structures that bear a striking resemblance to Haussmann's design for Paris. Efforts to promote French building practices and materials on the continent should also be appreciated from this perspective.

Self-preservation

Efforts on the part of colonial officials to protect themselves from danger led to the enactment of a multitude of policies that left their mark on the built environment. Included in this fold are building codes that prescribed non- or less-combustible building materials for all buildings in urban areas, particularly the 'European districts'. This category also includes the flurry of spatial policies that were enacted throughout colonial Africa subsequent to Dr Ronald Ross's 1899/1900 studies, which incriminated the anopheles mosquito (*Anopheles gambiae/Anopheles funestus*) as the vector of malaria. Physical separation of Europeans from Africans was prescribed as a 'prophylaxis' against the deadly disease. Prior to Ross's revelation, racial cohabitation was not uncommon in French colonial Africa. However, soon after the revelation, such living arrangements were discontinued. To the extent that very little was known about the transmission and prevention of malaria, it is safe to attribute the apparent segregationist policies of French colonial authorities to a need to protect their lives and those of other Europeans in the colonies. It was also believed that mosquitoes had a low survival rate at high altitudes. This constitutes a plausible explanation for the tendency on the part of French and other colonial authorities to locate colonial administrative offices and European residential districts on plateaus at high altitudes. Although in this instance the line between doing so as a survival strategy as opposed to a strategy to preserve French culture is severely blurred. Christopher Winters (1982: 141) lends credence to this assertion when he characterizes the choice of locations for colonial capitals in francophone Africa in the following terms:

> In Bamako many governmental buildings and the villas of a large portion of its officers were in Koulouba, a cliff high above the African neighborhoods. Similarly in Dakar, Abidjan, Libreville, and Brazzaville, French residents took the highest land as their quarter and called it the Plateau. Did the name alone confer some protection? Niamey had a Plateau, but no plateau.

The line is further blurred when one acknowledges the fact that French colonialism also had as an important objective, that of advertising France's might and grandeur. Therefore, it is also possible that selecting locations at high altitudes was designed not as a strategy to prevent disease but as a strategy to affirm the supremacy of France in particular and Europe in general. In this case, one must agree with Christopher Winters (1982) that Europeans sought high altitudes as a means of symbolically asserting power and separating the colonizer from the colonized. It would therefore appear that consolidating power occupied a higher rung on the priority ladder of the colonial authorities than any other objective.

6 Planning power in French Equatorial Africa and Madagascar

Introduction

I now pass from the Federation of French West Africa (FWA) to the Federation of French Equatorial Africa (FEA), and Madagascar. The two federations, FWA and FEA, differed considerably not only in geographical terms but also, and more importantly for the purpose of the present discussion, in the level of attention each received from the metropolitan authorities. For its part, Madagascar was administered as a separate colonial entity. French Equatorial Africa (FEA) was virtually ignored in relative and absolute terms until the twilight of the colonial epoch. In fact, the region constituted a source of embarrassment to French colonial authorities because of its poor living conditions occasioned by a lack of basic infrastructure. French colonial officials stationed in Brazzaville, the administrative capital of FEA, across the Congo River from and within plain view of Léopoldville in neighbouring Belgian Congo, often recounted tales of the acrid pinch of relative deprivation they had to endure. The French colonial officials in Brazzaville had to live in makeshift housing lacking even basic services while their Belgian contemporaries across the river enjoyed living conditions approximating what they were used to in Europe.

A case study of town and country planning in FEA is of interest because it affords us an opportunity to compare the colonial infrastructure investment policy of France with colonial powers other than Britain. Such an exercise is also important in promoting understanding of how colonial authorities consolidated power in the built environment in the face of resource scarcity. A case study of planning policies in French Equatorial Africa is of further importance because it gives us an opportunity to examine evidence that undermines the popularly held belief that only British colonial authorities practised racial spatial segregation. One analyst harbouring this belief has gone so far as to state that 'segregation helps explain why the British failed to build attractive colonial towns as did the French', 'while French town-planning ... aimed at safeguarding the lives of all people' (Goerg, 1998: 1, quoting Gale, 1980: 505–6). I marshal evidence below to show that contrary to this belief, the French also enacted racial spatial segregation policies. In Brazzaville, the capital of FEA, French colonial authorities enacted racial spatial segregation policies to manipulate space in a manner designed to ensure not only that Europeans occupied the most desirable parcels of land, but also that they maintained a socio-psychological advantage over members of the indigenous population. To provide some background to the discussion, I begin by briefly discussing the history of French Equatorial Africa (FEA) or l'Afrique Equatoriale française (AEF).

Background

While the French had established a presence in West Africa, particularly in Senegal (Gorée, Saint-Louis and Rufisque) as far back as the sixteenth century, they did not begin exploring the equatorial region until the 1800s. In fact, it was not until the early-nineteenth century that French explorer Savorgnan de Brazza arrived in the interior of the region, establishing French stations in Brazzaville (which he named after himself) in present-day People's Republic of Congo, and Franceville and Lambaréné along the Ogooué River in present-day Gabon. By 1890, French explorers had reached the upper reaches of the Ubangi River in present-day Central African Republic. In the process, they signed treaties with many chiefs in the hinterland. The French were interested in establishing 'an axis across Africa as far as the borders of what was then Abyssinia' (present-day Ethiopia) – a feat they accomplished, if only briefly as they were soon 'forced to withdraw from the entire Nile Basin' (de Blij, 1964: 205).

French Equatorial Africa, referred to in French as Afrique Équatoriale française (AEF), was established in 1908 as a federation of French colonies, including Gabon, Middle Congo, which later became Congo Brazzaville (present-day People's of Republic of Congo), Ubangi-Shari (now Central African Republic), and Chad. These territories were known as *régions* (i.e. regions). Until 1934, when FEA was unified as a single colony, each of these territories had its own lieutenant governor, a budget and was relatively autonomous. As of 1934, the regions were renamed *territoires* (i.e. territories) and Brazzaville in Moyen Congo became the capital of the entire colony. Each territory had a governor stationed at the territorial headquarters, Libreville (Gabon), Bangui (Ubangi-Shari), and Fort Lamy (now N'Djamena, Chad). Under the jurisdiction of each governor were different units of colonial governments, including divisional and sub-divisional services, which were respectively under the charge of colonial divisional and sub-divisional administrators (Perlstein, 1943).

Country planning in French Equatorial Africa

As noted at the outset of this chapter, French Equatorial Africa, as a region and as a colony, benefited from very little investment by the French colonial authorities. Thus, not very much was accomplished by way of infrastructure development at the urban or regional level. French colonial authorities can point to only one large-scale regional development project, the Brazzaville–Pointe Noire railway, which was completed in 1934. Even here, the efforts of French colonial authorities are almost invalidated by the fact that the project was completed with the forced labour input of members of the indigenous population, of whom as many as 20,000 died in the process (USLC website). As an economic development initiative, the project cannot be faulted as it did well to open up the hinterland regions. However, due to the sluggish pace and the enormous human cost at which it was executed, the project raised more questions than it answered. What was the real motive of French involvement in the region? It would appear that the absence of any viable internal and/or external threat to French interest in the region meant they could get by with minimal investment in infrastructure for civilian or military purposes. Within the framework of French colonial thinking, colonial territories were only as important as they were worth in economic terms. Accordingly, the level of attention, investment or resource commitment to any colonial territory was always computed as a function of the territory's real or potential political and/or economic worth.

The political value of a territory or town was seen in terms of its place within the colonial organization structure, while its economic value was computed in terms of its resource base. This philosophy explains in large measure the fact that hardly more than the funds necessary for developing the Brazzaville–Pointe Noire railway were committed to French Equatorial Africa between 1925 and 1940 (Sinou *et al.*, 1989). It also explains the disparity between the size of funds destined for the coastal regions, which were viewed as the colonial cash cows, and the meagre amounts committed to resource-scarce hinterland regions such as Chad. As a general rule, French colonial investment projects invariably targeted port cities and colonial government headquarters. Phyllis Martin (1995) takes this line of thought a little further by noting the tendency on the part of French colonial authorities to ignore colonial territories or regions once they had outlived their military, political or economic utility. She bolsters her contention by invoking France's ostentatious display of disinterest in her colonial possessions in equatorial Africa. She notes that:

> Once the backdoor to its important West and North African possessions had been secured through the occupation of Chad and Ubangi-Shari, Equatorial Africa lapsed into obscurity in the official mind. ... French lack of interest resulted in most of Congo, although not Brazzaville, being turned over to rule by concessionary companies.
>
> (Martin, 1995: 19)

French colonial authorities decided, especially during the first 50 years of the colonial era, to concentrate on the extraction and exportation of natural resources from the region.

A number of other infrastructure development projects of lesser magnitude than the Brazzaville–Pointe Noire railway took place in Gabon, which had a pre-colonial history of densely populated human settlements and inter-regional trade. Here, three major projects were completed (Gray and Ngolet, 1999). The first is a road connecting Lambaréné to Libreville (now capital of Gabon), which was completed in 1939. Another is a 50 km stretch of road constructed between Lambaréné and the village of Fouramwanga (1940–3). The third project is a stretch of road that was added to the latter to complete the network linking Dolisie in Congo Brazzaville (now People's Republic of Congo).

Some of the territories that comprised French Equatorial Africa were almost completely ignored by French colonial authorities. Chad, for example, ranked near the bottom on the French colonial authorities' scale of priorities. It is therefore hardly any wonder that progress in Chad during the colonial era and beyond was at an exceptionally slow pace. The French came to see Chad primarily as a source of raw cotton and manpower to be conscripted into the forced labour camps in the coastal regions. Territories such as Chad that were not endowed with natural resources were ignored to the point that basic functions of governance such as the maintenance of law and order were neglected. An important factor that compounded the resource-scarce region's difficulties was the absence of qualified colonial officials. In fact, it was never easy to find qualified colonial officials for a territory such as Chad. 'Officials in the French colonial service resisted assignments to Chad, so posts often went to novices or to out-of-favour officials' (USLC website). In the end, the region was seen as no more than a source of raw materials – cotton from Chad and timber from the Central African Republic (at the time, Ubangi-Shari), Gabon and Congo.

It is not so much the fact that they extracted the natural resources as it is the fact that little if anything was invested in developing urban and regional infrastructure in the region that is of concern here. One analyst lambastes the mediocre performance of the French colonial authorities in the area of infrastructure development in Congo by comparing it to the more serious efforts of the Belgians across the Congo River in Belgian Congo. This analyst notes that, 'it is a reflection of the contrasting conditions in French Equatorial and Belgian Africa that the French railroad was completed more than thirty years after the Belgian one' (de Blij, 1964: 208).

The paucity of public infrastructure, especially roads, severely limited the ability of the French colonial authorities in Equatorial Africa not only to broadcast authority and consolidate power but also to execute the regular duties of colonial administration in the region. For instance, the problem of few all-season roads and, in some cases, no roads at all, conspired to thwart the colonial administrators' ability to travel from the regional headquarters to divisional headquarters (*circonscriptions*) or to sub-divisions (*subdivisions*). Yet according to Martial Henri Merlin, the first Governor-General of French Equatorial Africa, effective colonial administration was contingent upon the extent to which central and regional colonial administrators made contact with populations in the hinterland (Weinstein, 1970). For Merlin, colonial administration largely consisted of travelling. He underscored the importance of colonial administrators taking 'tours' to the provincial enclaves under their jurisdiction when he said 'administrer c'est essentiellement se déplacer' (Weinstein, 1970: 108). The Governor-General was also acutely aware of the difficulties inherent in implementing 'direct rule' in the colonies. 'Direct administration', he once opined, 'is impossible in the colonies. ... Therefore, we must institute a policy of help and collaboration with the native chiefs' (quoted in Weinstein, 1970: 108). Thus, like the British, Merlin was advocating the adoption of the 'indirect rule' administrative strategy. However, he was careful not to let power slip away from colonial authorities in the process. Accordingly, he prescribed the role of 'subordinate collaborators' as opposed to 'protected potentates' for the chiefs. Brian Weinstein (1970) summarizes Governor-General Merlin's view of the place and role of the local chiefs within the framework of French colonial administration as follows. Chiefs constituted an extension of the French colonial administrative machinery. They had the power to give certain orders as well as to execute certain policies with colonial administrative support. More importantly, chiefs had the responsibility of collecting taxes. In the event of non-compliance, the administrator had the Governor's permission to 'accompany the chief and affirm chiefly authority before the people' (Weinstein, 1970: 109). Here, the Governor left no doubt in anyone's mind with respect to the fact that power resides ultimately in the hands of the colonial establishment.

The land question

As mentioned in previous chapters, control over land was a central objective of the colonial enterprise in Africa. A common strategy that was repeatedly adopted by the French colonial authorities was the classification of land into two distinct categories, namely public and private lands. Two decrees, one enacted on 8 February and the other on 28 March 1899 did just this for lands in Congo. The decrees contained provisions requiring the formalization of claims of entitlement to any piece of land within the territory. Such formalization entailed applying for and securing land certificates and duly registering all land titles (*titre foncier*) in the Land Register. The objective of the colonial authorities here is easy to understand once we appreciate the socio-economic, political and cultural value of land. France's colonial land policies were motivated by two concerns that were central to the French colonial enterprise. One of these concerns had to do with France's civilizing mission. In this case, French colonial authorities considered the African land tenure system inherently 'primitive' and therefore antithetical to development. Thus, to 'Europeanize' the system was essentially to 'modernize' it – something the French viewed as their pre-ordained task to accomplish. Second, the idea of 'communal ownership' of property did not bode well with French capitalist ideology, which advocated individualized ownership. Thus, they also deemed it necessary to transform the system. In this case, French colonial authorities were allured by the English and Australian land tenure systems, which themselves drew inspiration from the Torrens Act. This system focalises not particularly on the rights of individuals but rather on those of the piece of land itself as accorded expression by a land title registry.

To underscore the importance of land in the colonial development calculus, French colonial authorities in the centre worked indefatigably to ensure that they played a central role in decisions relating to the management and control of land, and transactions relating to land. Their efforts in this connection resulted in the curtailment of the amount of power colonial authorities on the ground had over land in the colonies. In 1928 a Central Committee of Public Works and Mines for the colonies based in the metropolis was created. This was done on the pretext of ensuring the judicious utilization of land throughout the colonies. In reality, what was at play was a struggle over control of a vital resource, namely land. Control over land spelled the difference between the 'powerful' and the 'powerless'. Creation of the committee was thus meant to, *inter alia*, ensure a significant level of central control over the vast lands in colonies and conversely curtail the level of autonomy enjoyed by colonial government units on the ground. The committee was a consultative body charged with the task of coordinating public works activities in all the French Overseas Territories. This was in line with France's well-known propensity to concentrate power in the centre.

Urban planning and governance

Municipal governance or urban administration was a priority area for French colonial authorities. Several colonial legislative actions focused specifically on improving municipal governance in French tropical Africa. In this section I concentrate especially on those legislative actions that targeted municipalities in French colonial possessions in equatorial Africa. The pieces of legislation under consideration, like others dealing with aspects of urban planning in the colonies, are facsimiles or clones of legislative pronouncements that were, or had been at some point, in force in the metropolitan country.

For example, the enactment of the Municipal Law of 5 April 1884 was designed to accord French towns a 'special status' that permitted them to have some level of budgetary autonomy. Not long after being exclusively operational in metropolitan France, its locus was extended to include a few towns in certain colonies on 31 July of the same year. On 13 December 1891, the same law was adopted in at least three towns, namely Gorée, Rufisque and Dakar (Senegal), in French West Africa. It was not until 1904, two decades after it was initially promulgated and enforced in France, that the law was adopted in French Equatorial Africa (FEA). Three towns in the Federation, Libreville (Gabon), Bangui (Central African Republic) and Brazzaville (Congo), were the first to benefit from the law as they were accorded a special status. As intended under the mother law, FEA's law gave the named towns some degree of budgetary autonomy. However, in FEA, an important provision was added to the original law. This new provision endowed the towns with more than relative budget autonomy. It transformed the towns into self-governing local government units (*communes*) whose administrators were drawn from the local community as opposed to being appointed by some central authority.

Initially, Africans did not play any role in these local governmental bodies. Such bodies drew their members exclusively from the resident European population. However, subsequent to World War I, French colonial authorities in the metropolis felt indebted to the people of colonial Africa because of their valiant role in the war.

Consequently they felt obligated to reward the Africans, especially the African elites, by assigning them a role in local urban governance. Accordingly, a number of urban reform measures were initiated. Principal amongst these were a series of legislative actions that culminated in the issuance of an *arrêté* defining the parameters and modalities of 'mixed communes' (*communes mixtes*). Essentially, these were local governmental bodies which, contrary to their predecessors, were bi-racial, drawing their members from both the African and European districts.

Recognition of the importance of urban centres and increasing interest in urban management also led to the creation of consultative commissions in the colonies. The earliest and best known of such commissions was established in the Federation of French West Africa by a colonial government Legislative Order of 15 November 1909. The commission comprised mainly business people (traders). These traders shared one common interest, namely making a positive contribution to the development of their towns. Growing concern with health and hygiene matters prompted the inclusion of a physician on this commission in 1910. A decree of 1911 extended the powers and relative autonomy of urban governments. The increased autonomy over administrative and financial matters meant that urban residents could play a role in local governance. A decree of 27 November 1929 further strengthened urban governments.

It is important to note that towns in colonial Africa were not for Africans. This said, I hasten to note that the French differed, at least in theory, in the way they related to 'colonial subjects'. Christopher Winters (1982: 140) echoes this point when he states that, 'the French attempted, at least in theory, to create a class of Africans who could function more or less as Frenchmen'. However, the difference does not go further than that. Certainly, there were more similarities than differences between colonial powers and the manner in which they related to the colonized. For instance, the French were just as likely as other colonizers to use their privileged access to resources and other real or perceived advantages to symbolize the unequal distribution of power that has historically characterized the relationship between Africans and Europeans.

As implied above, the French encouraged urban living for African elites or 'evolved' Africans (*les évolués*). Colonial authorities in metropolitan France gave members of this group an opportunity to participate in urban governance after World War I. This should not be taken to mean that French colonial authorities saw the colonized as their equals in political, social, economic or any other terms. In fact, while the two groups could hold membership in the town or urban council and attend common meetings, they retired to different locales – the African to the African district and the European to the European district – at the close of the day or meeting. Here, the real or perceived power differentials were not only symbolized by the different locales they called home but also by the terminology used in reference to the one versus the other (Winters, 1982). In French Equatorial Africa, the African district was referred to as *la cité*, a word with medieval roots. In the colonial context it was used to patronize Africans. More commonly, African neighbourhoods in the region were referred to as villages (*les villages*), itself also a 'condescending term' (Winters, 1982). More glamorous terms such as city (*la ville*) and residential districts (*zones résidentielles*) were reserved for European neighbourhoods.

Planning commissions

Initially, urban commissions were active only in metropolitan France. They did not become part of the urban planning policy field in colonial Africa until 1945. They were originally created in 1938 and charged with the responsibility of managing and implementing urban development projects. As the colonial era drew to a close, planning increasingly assumed an unprecedented level of importance. Almost every government service had a unit of architecture and/or planning. The purpose of these units was mainly to maintain and repair existing structures within their respective colonial services. The architectural units of municipal authorities and the Military Corps of Engineers had broader responsibilities. They were responsible for examining, recommending revisions to, and approving architectural designs for proposed buildings. A major objective here was to promote the development of only architectural styles deemed to be in line with France's notion of modernity and sophistication. Earlier in the colonial era, the preference was for purely European style architecture. In this case, the aim was to assimilate Africans without regard to their indigenous culture. This approach had the effect of alienating Africans – something that became apparent before long to French colonial authorities. Later in the colonial era, French colonial authorities decided in favour of a more subtle approach to assimilation – association – especially designed to assuage Africans. Accordingly, they adopted and promoted designs that incorporated elements of local architecture. The promotion of elements of neo-Sudanese architecture in places like Bamako, Mali is a case in point.

Urban spatial organization

Policies in this domain span the gamut of physical activities in the built environment from sub-division regulations to building codes, from the location and timing of land development activities to the formulation and implementation of public health policies. At the top of the priority ladder of colonial authorities were issues of health and hygiene. These issues or concerns constituted the driving force behind town planning and especially building codes and regulations from the formative years of the planning profession in England in particular and Europe as a whole. Thus, when the issues surfaced in Africa, French colonial authorities found it convenient to simply transplant to the continent laws that were already, or had been at some point in force in France. Therefore, as a means of dealing with issues of health and hygiene in housing, the colonial authorities in tropical Africa adopted in 1889 a law that had been enacted to promote and protect salubrious environments in France since 13 April 1850. However, a number of specific circumstances arose or were created to necessitate the enactment of policies in the health and hygiene domain with specific and unique application in Africa. One example comes to mind here. This has to do with the Legislative Order of 27 July 1881, which was specifically designed to deal with the movement of people during periods of epidemic outbreaks. Isolation and quarantine were often the strategies of choice. Specific units within the colonial governments were responsible for health and hygiene from 1904 onwards.

Racial spatial segregation

On the pretext of protecting the health of the general public, the French colonial authorities adopted many ostentatiously racist policies. On this score, the policy to segregate living areas by race was the most blatant. There is no shortage of areas throughout colonial Africa where the French implemented or attempted to implement such policies. Before identifying and discussing some of the locales in which such policies were implemented, I examine some of the legislative pronouncements that articulated the policies. In 1860, a decision was reached to forbid the construction of housing by Africans and to destroy all existing houses belonging to Africans within a specified distance of the European district in Saint-Louis (Senegal). This act was resuscitated and adopted in Bamako (Mali) on 20 January 1910. Some years subsequent to that, the policy of racial separation became commonplace in the two federations. Racial segregation policies did not sit well with the republican ideology of the time. However, that and passive resistance as well as active opposition from members of the indigenous population did not prevent the policies from being enacted or implemented. Across the federations there were distinct European 'residential zones' and African 'villages'. A Legislative Order of 23 March 1908 provided the legal and institutional backing – as if one was needed – for this practice. The Order stipulated the width of the band of natural vegetation that must separate European from African districts.

Colonial policy reforms and the housing question

Africans attending the Brazzaville Conference in January 1944 left no doubt in the minds of their French colonial masters that they wanted to play a more active role in the management of their own affairs. The concerns that were raised by participants at the conference revolved more around institutional and structural reforms than about decolonization (Sinou *et al.*, 1989). These concerns did not fall on deaf ears as reflected in France's 1946 Constitution, which reformed the entire French colonial system. The reform measures introduced new structures for French intervention and identified areas in need of urgent attention. Prominent in this connection was the problem of urban development.

This problem was made urgent by rapid rates of urbanization and concomitant quandaries such as housing shortages, public infrastructure provisioning and urban governance in the colonial territories. One testament to the metropolitan government's awareness of the growing urban problems in the colonies was the creation in 1946 of a committee, the Committee on Town Planning and Housing for the Colonies (Comité de l'uirbanisme et de l'habitation aux colonies). The committee comprised mainly technical advisers from metropolitan France and French overseas territories. Despite its composition, which gives the semblance of power sharing between the metropolitan authorities and local officials on the ground in the colonies, it operated out of Paris. This did not bode well for local authorities. Despite the reform measures, these authorities continued to witness a continual erosion of their power. The struggle for power between the centre and the periphery characterized French colonialism and accounted for delays in the implementation of several projects and policies that were deemed rather too 'metropolitan' by local authorities in the colonies during the post-World War II era.

One aspect of the new orientation in French colonial thinking worth noting was the requirement for ten-year development plans for the overseas territories. The first such plan for a colonial federation was completed for the Federation of French West Africa (1947–57). The lion's share of the plan was taken up by economic development projects, to which as much as 78 per cent of the budget was dedicated while the rest was dedicated to social programmes and projects (Sinou *et al.*, 1989: 167). Housing and urban development, along with health and education, were considered part of the latter category. A total of 3,000 million francs was allocated to social programmes and projects in French Equatorial Africa. The ink on this maiden long-term development plan for a colony had hardly dried before authorities recognized the intricacies of long-range planning. This recognition resulted in a decision to generate intermediary plans. Accordingly, the major tasks of the ten-year plan for French Equatorial Africa were broken up into two main parts. The first part comprised capital improvement and economic development projects and covered the period 1947–52. Social development projects were subsumed under the second intermediary plan, which covered the period 1952–7.

Colonial authorities in the centre initiated a plethora of actions designed specifically to address the urbanization problem, which was growing increasingly complex. For instance, authorities created credit institutions and endowed them with the powers and resources to grant loans for new home construction and existing home rehabilitation. In 1949 one such institution was created and charged with serving the Federation of French Equatorial Africa. Named le Crédit de l'AEF, this institution had its headquarters in Brazzaville, the seat of government for the federation. A colonial government corporation, le Crédit de l'AEF was initially endowed with an operating capital of 120 million CFA francs (Sinou *et al.*, 1989: 196). Although in theory small and medium size businesses as well as individuals could qualify for these loans, in practice only businesses and individuals with verifiable sources of income – in other words, individuals employed in the formal sector – actually participated in the programme. By 1956, seven years after the programme was established, le Crédit de l'AEF had granted loans to 2,000 families for new home construction and existing home rehabilitation amounting to 600 and 200 million CFA francs respectively (Sinou *et al.*, 1989: 196).

Republic of Congo

Brazzaville

Paradoxically, the competition for power and dominance in the urban space in French Equatorial Africa was not between European and African symbols of power. Rather, this competition was often between two European entities, the Church and the colonial state. Two examples, one from Lambaréné (in present-day Gabon) and the other from Brazzaville (in present day Republic of Congo) are illustrative.

When Savorgnan de Brazza arrived in Lambaréné in 1883, he wasted no time in creating a French colonial post on the hill overlooking the island from where river traffic could be surveyed with facility (Gray and Ngolet, 1999). At just about the same time, the French Holy Ghost Fathers of the Catholic Church, which had been established in the local area three years earlier, were completing a chapel. The chapel, by all measures, was more impressive and more imposing than the colonial government station. The second case recounted by Phyllis Martin (1995), also involves the Holy Ghost Fathers and relates to Brazzaville. Here, the Holy Ghost Fathers had acquired a piece of prime land conspicuously located on a hillside overlooking the town of Mfoa. It was on this piece of land that Monseigneur Augouard, Bishop of Upper Congo (1890–1921) decided to erect the mission's gothic-style cathedral, capable of holding 1,000 people. The gargantuan stone, brick and wooden structure was surrounded by the Bishop's house, which stood two storeys high, schoolrooms, dormitories, workshops and gardens. Nearby and almost completely dwarfed by the domineering church structure, were the unimpressive tiny houses of the colonial officials. That the church and colonial state competed for power in colonial Brazzaville, as Martin (1995) states probably escaped the attention of members of the indigenous population. After all, to them, both entities symbolized European dominance.

Phyllis Martin (1995) has done a fine job tracing the evolution of town planning and urban conditions in colonial Brazzaville. Colonial authorities in Brazzaville continued to endure poor living conditions until 1909 when the colonial ministry provided a subsidy for town 'improvements'. In 1911, Brazzaville was elevated to the status of 'commune'. Thus, the town had become a distinct administrative unit, complete with a mayor and an operating budget. In addition, a town council of four members appointed by the Lieutenant-Governor of Middle Congo (now Republic of Congo) was created. The four members were drawn from the small population of Europeans in the town. One of the council's first most significant official actions was to racially segregate the town. This was the first instance in which the racial spatial segregation policy was given physical expression in Brazzaville subsequent to its enactment on 23 March 1908. In 1909, two African villages, Bacongo and Poto-Poto, were established. African villages were typically relegated to the least desirable sites. Nowhere else was this truism more brazen than in the case of Brazzaville's segregated settlements. One of the African villages, Poto-Poto, was literally located in muddy or swampy terrain. In fact, the word *poto-poto* means mud in Lingala (the lingua franca of Congo), Pidgin (the lingua franca of Anglophone West Africa), and in a number Bantu languages.

As for public security, French colonial authorities used this as a pretext for instituting draconian policies that strictly limited the movement of Africans. For instance, a law of 15 December 1926 forbade the movement of Africans in Brazzaville after 9 pm. In other words, they imposed a 9 pm curfew on Africans of all ages. This policy was a replica of one that was also in effect across the Congo River in Leopoldville (now, Kinshasa) in Belgian Congo. A number of issues, including prestige, health and culture, dominated the discourse on planning in colonial Brazzaville (Martin, 1995). The curfew policy was not the only draconian piece of legislation promulgated by colonial authorities in Brazzaville. In fact, prior to enacting the law imposing a curfew hour of 9 pm on Africans, a colonial decree of 1904 had forbidden Africans from playing drums and dancing at certain hours in Brazzaville. This decree had far-reaching implications for life in African communities given the role 'drumming and dancing' play in their lives. Drumming and dancing constitute a *sine qua non* in important ceremonies and occasions such as weddings, anniversaries, funerals, coronations, and so on in traditional African societies. It is necessary to peruse salient parts of the text of said decree, which Martin (1995: 37) has reproduced;

> Tams-tams and other noisy dances are formally forbidden within the urban perimeter of Brazzaville except in an area from the Felix Fauré bridge to the Dutch House and from the so-called Glaciere River to the Djoué river on the other side, where tams-tams and other noisy dances will be authorized in exceptional cases on advance demand, and all natives who want to obtain such permission must pay a fee of five francs ... these dances can only be authorized once a week from 6 p.m. on Saturday until Sunday morning and any contravening of this decree will be punished by a fine and 1–5 days in prison or either of these.

With respect to prestige, French colonial authorities in Brazzaville had hardly anything positive worth mentioning, especially with regards to infrastructure. As far as infrastructure and living conditions go, French colonial officials in Brazzaville were humiliated by the physical conditions they had to endure. The poor straw huts these officials called home certainly did not help matters. Nor was it any consolation for them that within sight across the Congo River their Belgian counterparts were living in luxury. Progress did take place in the area of infrastructure development in Brazzaville albeit slowly. By the eve of World War I, the town was beginning to assume the look of a colonial government capital. By 1912, the town already had a Governor's residence, the offices of the Lieutenant-Governor, a treasury, a law court, a post and telegraphs building, the Pasteur Institute, a military hospital, and a town hall (Martin, 1995: 34). Additionally, the network of streets was beginning to take form. One point worth noting here is the haste with which colonial authorities proceeded to immortalize the names of European explorers by naming the town's streets after them. In fact, even the name of the city, Brazzaville, itself was intended to immortalize the name of Savorgnan de Brazza, the French explorer credited with establishing a French presence in the region.

Gabon

Libreville

As was the case with Freetown, Sierra Leone, Europeans designated Libreville, Gabon as a refuge for freed slaves. Libreville – that is, *'libre ville'* – is French for 'free town'. This designation took place in 1849. This date is erroneously believed to be the date of the town's establishment. This error is not unique but warrants correction because it gives the false impression that the area was devoid of human activity or settlement prior to the arrival of Europeans. Yet the entire region of which Libreville is a part has a long history of human settlement and served as an important node for pre-colonial long distance commerce. Of course, crediting Europeans with the creation or establishment of important African towns such as Libreville is but a small part of efforts designed to bolster the ideological power of what Lucy Jarosz (1992:105) calls 'the metaphor of Africa as a Dark Continent'. Of crucial importance for the purpose of the present discussion is the fact that this metaphor has historically perpetuated and effectuated unequal power relations and domination by European authorities over Africans.

The site that constitutes the nucleus around which present-day Libreville developed is not the original site where the slave refuge was located in 1849. French colonial authorities later decided to relocate the town from its original site to the top of a nearby hill. This decision pivoted on a number of reasons, one of which was the medical thinking of that time which prescribed well-ventilated high altitude locations as a means of averting potential health threats. Another consideration hinged tightly on the widely-held belief that altitude constituted an important determinant of power. By 1850 a number of projects, including the construction of a hospital, military barracks and colonial administrative units, had been completed on the new site. The newly constructed structures and nearby Fort Aumalé conspired to symbolize power and announce the European presence in the area. Thirteen years later, in 1863, the Catholic Mission erected a monumental chapel next to the fort. The gigantic flamboyant stone church building dwarfed other structures, especially the small dwelling units of members of the indigenous population in the vicinity. Whether by design or not the chapel constituted a visible manifestation of European power and domination in the area for a long time. As time went by, the site was progressively subdivided into three main compartments or zones. One zone was assigned to freed slaves; another, which was located near the sea at the foot of the hill, was set aside for factories; and the third zone, which was located on the plateau on top of the hill, served as the locale for European housing and colonial administrative facilities. Structures in this district were constructed of solid materials – particularly stone or rocks.

In 1881, Libreville, the oldest French settlement in the region, was designated as the administrative capital of French Congo. Libreville lost this status when Gabon became part of the reconstituted Federation of French Equatorial Africa with Brazzaville, Congo as its capital in 1908. Prior to that, Libreville benefited from infrastructure development programmes and projects as a regional headquarters. For instance, housing and other facilities for colonial officials on the ground in the region, including the General Commissioner and the Lieutenant Governor, were located in Libreville. The town later became the headquarters of colonial Gabon and continued to be the beneficiary of the genre of development projects designed to facilitate colonial governance – colonial government offices, military post, colonial social service infrastructure, court houses, prisons and living facilities for colonial government officials.

Two specific projects in this regard are worth discussing in more detail, particularly because of their role in facilitating the consolidation of power by French colonial authorities in the territory. The first of these projects, completed in 1929, was the cadastral plan for the City of Libreville ('Premier plan de cadastre pour le chef-lieu du territoire du Gabon' or the First Cadastral Plan for the Capital of the Territory of Gabon). As a vital element in the colonial government's strategy to consolidate power, the cadastral plan served to provide detailed information on the extent, value and ownership of land. This information is critical for purposes of taxation and monitoring all transactions in land, an important factor of production.

The cadastral plan for Libreville was produced by F. Cheval under the supervisory auspices of the Directorate of Public Works and funded by the colonial government budget (*budget du territoire*). The plan, which was drawn to a scale of 1:5,000 and thirteen years after the first official land development permits were issued by the colonial government in Gabon in 1916, classified land in the City of Libreville into five distinct categories as follows:

- land for which a final ownership title has been issued;
- land for which a provisional ownership title has been issued;
- land without title but upon which a suitable building has been erected;
- occupied land with neither title nor seriously under use; and
- vacant land.

(Sinou *et al.*, 1989: 141)

According to the plan, no claims of land ownership or entitlement in Libreville were to be recognized unless the land in question fell under the first or second of the named categories. Anyone whose land fell under the third category had to apply for, and be issued, a land title to have any claims of entitlement to the land honoured. All lands belonging to the fourth and fifth categories were considered 'vacant' and/

or 'ownerless' and therefore property of the colonial state. These conditions were approved by an arêté of 3 September 1925 before being incorporated into the final plan in 1929. Other significant attributes of the plan include the number of lots – a total of 1,586 – that were demarcated (Sinou *et al.*, 1989: 141).

A second significant colonial development project was completed in 1939, ten years after the cadastral plan. This second project was the first master plan for the City of Libreville ('Plan directeur d'aménagement et d'extension du chef-lieu du Gabon'). Like the cadastral plan, the master plan was a vital element in the colonial powers' efforts to accomplish the broader goals of the colonial enterprise. The master plan, essentially a comprehensive guide to long-term development, does more than simply guide development. More importantly, the document stipulates the philosophy and manner of development as well as the methods and procedures that must be followed to accomplish the long-term goals of an area. In the case of Libreville, colonial authorities masterfully employed the master plan to influence the timing, location and juxtaposition of land use activities. The master plan served the important purpose of providing institutional cover to otherwise blatantly racist spatial segregation policies. Thus, as elsewhere throughout colonial sub-Saharan Africa, the master plan of colonial Libreville compartmentalized not only land use activities but also the races.

Port-Gentil

This is another town of colonial historical significance in Gabon. Its importance derives from the fact that it served as an important gateway into the region during Savorgnan de Brazza's exploratory missions. It began serving this role in 1880 and at one point was the base from which de Brazza and other early European explorers in the region operated. With time, it grew in importance and size, especially when exploration of the Okoumé area began. It became a centre of colonial administration in 1900. Among the first European structures constructed in the town were a customs post and a number of commercial facilities. Later on, colonial authorities adopted racial spatial segregation policies that were already in force in other parts of colonial Africa.

Town and country planning in Madagascar

Background

Although the French had been present in Madagascar in one capacity or another since the 1600s, they did not effectively control the island until the late 1800s. Other Europeans who had been on the island at one point or another were the Portuguese and the British. The French began effective occupation of Toamasina (previously known as Tamatave) in 1883 and established a protectorate over Madagascar two years later in 1885. French presence on the island faced fierce resistance from the natives. This resistance was quashed by French troops under General Joseph-Simon Gallieni in 1896. To prevent the possibility of future challenges to their authority on the island, French colonial authorities abolished the Merina Monarchy and deported the Queen, Ranavalona III, and the prime minister, first to the Indian Ocean Island of la Réunion and later to Algeria. France declared the island a French colony in 1896 and appointed General Gallieni as its first Governor-General. Madagascar gained independence from France in 1958.

As the first governor of the new colony of Madagascar, Gallieni had the unenviable task of 'modernizing' it. If anyone could be up to this challenge it was Gallieni. He arrived on the island on 27 September 1896 after serving in Indochina. Gallieni insisted on retaining Antananarivo, which had been the capital of the Merina Monarchy under Queen Ranavalona III and her predecessors, as the capital of the new colony. Military leaders, especially the engineers, disagreed with him on grounds that the site was rather too hilly and remote to effectively and efficiently serve as a colonial capital. Instead, they proposed Toamasina as an alternative but temporary colonial capital while awaiting the eventual development of Antsirabé as a permanent 'hill station' colonial capital. However, Gallieni had plans for Antananarivo that included transforming it into the clone of a typical French city as a means of advertising France's grandeur and cultural supremacy. He was certain that French colonial authorities could make the city highly visible at the centre of Madagascar's urban life.

Gallieni arrived in Madagascar at a time when French colonialism was undergoing an ideological transformation and French colonial authorities were becoming increasingly interested in 'winning the hearts and minds' of the colonized. Gallieni had always been positively predisposed to this philosophy and manifested this by leaving an indelible mark on many facets of the colony's social, political and cultural systems. He is credited with laying the foundation upon which reposes Madagascar's contemporary system of education, health, jurisprudence, and public infrastructure. He instituted some of the colonial programmes and development strategies he had developed during his tenure in Indochina. Cognizant of the need to control and dominate the colonial subjects while 'winning their hearts and minds', or at worst not alienating them, Gallieni instituted a number of outreach services through existing towns and new settlements. By 1903, barely seven years after colonial rule was declared on the island, Gallieni had already developed as many as 650 schools, which had trained 50,000 students (Wright, 1991). Furthermore, he instituted a system of 'quasi-indirect rule' in which he handpicked local leaders to implement French colonial government policies in their local areas. This strategy is identical to that entailing the use of appointed 'warrant chiefs' employed by British colonial authorities.

Urban governance

As part of the 'associationist' strategy that France had adopted during the waning days of colonialism, the colonial government revived the customary village council model or the *fok'olona*, that had been in use on the island during the pre-colonial era. In pre-colonial Madagascar, *fok'olona* constituted a forum through which traditional leaders settled disputes, collected taxes, and organized public works activities. Initially, the system had been revived only in the central region. However, Gallieni soon realized its enormous utility and decreed that it be revived throughout the territory and introduced in areas without a history of employing the model.

In the area of spatial design, Gallieni was allured by the concept of 'village squares', a prominent feature of the indigenous spatial structure of Madagascar. Again, as part of the 'associationist' strategy, and as a tribute to the indigenous culture of the island, Gallieni decreed resuscitation of the concept. One of the major endeavours in this regard was the revival and redesign of the village square or main open space, known as the *Andohalo*, of Antananarivo. In pre-colonial Madagascar, the *Andohalo* served as the venue for important occasions involving the assembly of the entire city or speeches and celebrations (*kabaries*). The *Andohalo* played a function akin to that of the *agoras* of ancient Greece. In redesigning this facility the French colonial authorities added landscaping, which Gwendolyn Wright (1991: 255) characterized as 'reminiscent of a nineteenth-century provincial capital' complete with a lawn divided up into three terraces, flowerbeds, trees, and a platform upon which the military band sat to entertain the crowd every Sunday afternoon. The French colonial authorities re-named the place 'Jean Laborde Square', after a French adventurer who had experienced problems and abandoned his vessel off the western coast of the island in 1831 and later owned and operated a number of factories on the island.

Not all the policies introduced by Gallieni would fall under the category of 'goodwill'. A good many of the policies were obviously designed to promote the colonial ideology of capitalism. For instance, he introduced private property to replace the island's traditional system of property holding. In the land domain, this meant commodifying land. Prior to that, land in Madagascar was vested in the Monarch, who held it in trust for the commonweal. Reforming the system as the French colonial authorities did, essentially made the colonial state the 'ultimate owner' of all land throughout the territory. In its capacity as the 'ultimate owner' of the land, the colonial state proceeded to lure French people to relocate to the island. With as little as 5,000 francs, a French national could acquire as much as 150 acres of prime land, particularly for agricultural purposes (Wright, 1991: 253). Despite this aggressive strategy, only 650 European farmers had taken up this offer by the time Gallieni's tenure as Governor-General ended in 1905. A perusal of the list of those who effectively benefited from the French colonial government's land grant scheme in Madagascar reveals that half of the grants, accounting for a total of 1.4 million acres, went to only five companies (Wright, 1991: 253).

Town planning

Gallieni, who had more than a passing interest in town planning, initiated and/ or completed many projects on the island before his tenure as the colony's top administrator had elapsed. I identify and briefly discuss some of the most significant ones here. In his effort to improve urban functioning, Gallieni appointed a commission comprising engineers, military advisors and commercial interests – but no Africans – to develop a system of streets for the city. The commission had several deliberations, which culminated in a set of recommendations, including the removal of all objects obstructing circulation throughout the city, the prevention of pigs from roaming the streets, widening of all thoroughfares, development of additional streets, and demolishing houses in the way of the Résidence de France and widening the approach to the same. Within one year of the recommendations, two wider thoroughfares had been developed, namely Rue Guillan and Avenue de France. It did not take long after that for evidence of European presence to manifest itself in the large number of ferroconcrete buildings, which began to appear and flank the wide streets. A few years later these structures, the tree-lined avenues and the meticulously aligned streets conspired to dramatically transform the heart of the fledgling colonial capital city.

The military played a leading role in the public works projects. In particular, they were responsible for widening the trail linking Antananarivo to Mahajanja on the western coast and then to Toamasina, a considerable distance away to the east. These projects went a good way in facilitating the movement of people and goods throughout the island. Developing railway lines to connect both coasts and the capital was slow and took about a decade to complete. This was largely due to the difficult geology, challenging topography, and the rudimentary technology of that time.

Gallieni appointed Hubert Lyautey, whom he had known as a friend and colleague from his days in Indochina, as the colony's urban designer. Lyautey's first assignment was to design and develop a military camp in Ankazobé. The plan Lyautey crafted had the hallmarks of classic French urban design – a grid system comprising diagonal streets that converge to a central point, a traffic circle or roundabout. Lyautey's next assignment had an unmistakable political ring to it – 'pacifying the south of the island'. Here, Lyautey was required to demonstrate his prowess as an urban designer to create a spatial structure capable of not only dominating but also assuaging members of the indigenous population. Lyautey's response was to design what was a 'true *ville nouvelle*' in Fianarantsoa, a town with a population of 5,000 at the time (Wright, 1991). In 1918, another commission was established to produce a plan for the capital. The commission was instructed to adhere to principles of modern hygiene and urbanism as it contemplated the scheme. The commission comprised health officers, government bureaucrats and businessmen. Again, conspicuously absent from this commission as in the one before, was a representative of the indigenous population.

Georges Cassaigne, a graduate of the prestigious Ecole des Beaux Arts in Paris, was assigned the role of principal designer on the project. Cassaigne proposed the use of traffic circles, one-way streets, specified crosswalks and off-street parking as a means of resolving the city's growing traffic quandary. Cassaigne was a proponent of racial spatial segregation and recommended this as part of his proposal for the city's new design. However, it is important to mention the fact that French colonial officials on the ground, conscious of the fact that rumours of such a scheme had already been negatively saluted in the metropolis, spared no effort in ensuring that the final plan excluded all overt racially discriminatory clauses. Instead, they used material-specification standards to regulate building activities in certain districts – districts located in the most desirable areas of the city.

Discussion and conclusion

In his analysis of 'urban morphogenesis in Francophone Black Africa', Christopher Winters (1982: 141) makes the following observation:

> Europeans used topography – real or imagined to symbolize the unequal distribution of power and wealth and the separation of the ruler from the ruled.

Based on the thinking of French and other colonial authorities such as the British, with whom the notion of 'hill station' is usually associated, altitude correlates strongly with power. The preference for locations on higher ground is thus rooted in the belief that such locations command power. In the colonial context, this power can be appreciated from a number of different but inextricably interconnected perspectives. For one thing, locations on higher ground afforded colonial authorities a commanding view of the surrounding areas. Thus, by locating the colonial government offices and European living quarters on hills while assigning the foot of the hills to Africans, colonial authorities were able to watch and monitor the movements of members of the native population. Thus, the colonized were under the constant gaze of the colonizers. From this vantage point, it is safe to conclude that higher ground facilitated spatial surveillance and control of the colonized by the colonizer. As Dovey (1999) persuasively argues, surveillance and control are both coercive. For another thing, higher ground symbolized power to the extent that in forested areas such as French Equatorial Africa – with the exception of Chad – such higher ground was (is) more suitable for human habitation than low-lying areas, which are likely to flood.

French colonial authorities, as the discussion in this chapter shows, used more than topography to underscore the historically uneven distribution of power and wealth between the ruler and the ruled. Whenever possible, they used sheer size to attain this goal. Thus, it is hardly any wonder that very early in the colonial era, when Christianity was only beginning to penetrate Africa, the Catholic Church had deemed it necessary to erect a monumental chapel with room for 1,000 in Brazzaville – what at the time was by any measure a remote locale. Similarly, one cannot but ponder the purpose of the gigantic church building in Lambaréné also constructed by the Catholic Mission (see above). Such monumental structures constituted tools of intimidation. As Kim Dovey (1999: 10) suggests, exaggerated physical scale dominates by belittling 'the human subject as it signifies the power necessary to its production'. As architectural symbols of power, the grandiose church buildings constituted what Nicola Cooper (2000: 77) would call 'a domineering and inviolable image of the imperial nation ... [and] a visible expression of the universality of Western concepts of beauty and order'.

Another effort at universalizing Western concepts of beauty was evident in the spatial design structures that were introduced in the region. All French-influenced major towns in Africa share a common characteristic. They have a gridiron street system, with the major streets converging in a radial pattern upon a central roundabout or traffic circle. The circle usually constitutes the heart of the town and often the location of important conspicuous structures such as a cathedral, the central post office, a court house or government ministry – all facilities that symbolize power, control and dominance.

As a further effort to impress upon the colonized the pre-eminence of European civilization, French colonial authorities in French Equatorial Africa, like their counterparts elsewhere in Africa, named streets and towns after Europeans who conducted exploratory expeditions in Africa as a means of immortalizing their names. It was, and has always been, important for Europeans to insist that they 'discovered' Africa despite evidence to the effect that long before they arrived, Africans and Arabs had travelled the continent extensively as long-distance traders. Several reasons are at the root of this tendency. One of these reasons, perhaps the most important one, has power implications. Here, power can be seen from two perspectives. First, it can be appreciated in the sense once employed by Francis Bacon in his familiar maxim of 'knowledge is power', which implies that he who has knowledge has power. Second, it can be seen in the Foucaultian sense of *savoir-pouvoir*, implying that knowledge and power enjoy a reciprocal relationship in which the one reinforces the other on a continuous basis (Foucault, 1980a; Yeoh, 2003).

Colonial authorities in French Equatorial Africa also spent a great deal of time and other resources formulating and implementing decrees aimed at controlling the movement of Africans, particularly with respect to when and how they could come and go from the colonial towns. It is informative to employ the space syntax methods (Hillier and Hanson, 1984; Markus, 1993; Dovey, 1999) to facilitate understanding of the power implications of such decrees.

Let me state at the outset that my use of the concept of space differs slightly from that employed by Hillier and Hanson, Markus, and Dovey, who concentrate on physical buildings and walls. Rather, I view space in the Foucaultian sense that sees buildings and physical walls as only one aspect of space. Allocation of people in space, particularly the canalization of people's circulation can take place without physical walls. In this case, space could be delimited with other physical markers such as streets, railway tracks, vegetation and topography. In some cases space may be psychologically delimited. To the extent that this is true, it is safe to conclude that space was a critical element in the exercise of power in colonial Africa.

Spatial syntax analysis reposes on two basic assumptions, both having to do with the use of delimited space. The first relates to the use of areas outside, and the second concerns the use of the area within, the delimited space. Within this framework, 'visitors' or 'strangers' have access to outside areas while the interior of the space is reserved for 'inhabitants'. The 'inhabitants' not only have an investment of power in, but are also the 'controllers' of, everything within the delimited space. Others such as 'visitors' may be permitted to enter the delimited space. When this occurs, the controller stipulates, a priori, the time of entry and exit, as well as the areas which the 'visitor' may visit while within the delimited space. Here, it is obvious that the 'controllers' or 'inhabitants' have an inordinate degree of power and control over the 'visitors'. Using the space syntax to analyse the relationship between Africans and Europeans in colonial towns portrays the latter as 'controllers' or 'inhabitants' and the former as the 'controlled', 'visitors' or 'strangers'. The depth to which any visitor was allowed to penetrate the delimited space was an indicator of his status vis-à-vis the other visitors. It is therefore hardly any wonder that members of the indigenous population who had 'culturally evolved' (*les évolués*) and/or worked for the colonial civil service or European companies, were allowed into areas within the delimited space (colonial towns) that were deeper than those which the non-evolved members of the population could access.

Colonial authorities in FEA did more than control 'where' in relationship to the delimited space – that is the colonial town – Africans could be. They also controlled 'when' they could come and go from this space. In Brazzaville, the time at which Africans must be indoors was established as 9 pm. In essence, colonial authorities literally placed all Africans in Brazzaville under house arrest. House arrest by definition is 'the situation where a person is confined (by authorities) to his or her house, possibly with travel allowed but restricted' (Labor Law Talk Forum website). Thus, colonial authorities in Brazzaville and other areas where such ruthless laws were in force (e.g. Léopoldville) possessed, and exercised, the same kind of power 'over' Africans that warders or prison guards have over prisoners.

Some of the reasons the colonial authorities advanced for instituting restrictions on the movement of Africans in colonial cities had to do with the fear of crime. Imposing a curfew on Africans was therefore considered a strategy for preventing crimes in the town and especially for protecting the safety of members of the resident European population. Ideally, the colonial authorities would have preferred facilities into which Africans could check-in and be locked up every evening and then released every morning. However, from a Foucaultian perspective, such a strategy would have been economically inefficient if not prohibitively costly. This had been evident in France as far back as the eighteenth century when authorities became aware that it was more economically efficient to place people under surveillance than to physically lock them up (Foucault, 1980a). Efforts to confine Africans to readily accessible and highly visible areas of town and the imposition of curfew hours must be seen as elements in the colonial authorities' surveillance strategy.

Apart from seeking to reinforce their socio-psychological power over the colonized, French colonial authorities also developed and implemented policies whose objectives were to promote the political and economic interests of France in particular and Europe in general. The programme to grant home-building and home rehabilitation loans to Africans following World War II exemplifies strategies in this regard.

To appreciate this line of thought, it is important to note that recipients of Crédit de l'AEF loans were mostly urban residents holding important positions in the colonial civil service and European companies based in the colonies. To the extent that this is true, I contend that the loan programme was designed to accomplish at least five objectives of the French colonial enterprise in Africa. First, it is certainly not by chance that only urban areas and the African elites resident there benefited from the programme. As noted above, not only were Africans increasingly expressing discontent and frustration with colonial policies, they were also clamouring for more participation in local affairs subsequent to World War II. Those at the forefront of these developments were urban-based African elite groups in colonial Africa. The loan programme was therefore part of metropolitan France's efforts to co-opt and placate members of these groups. Second, French colonial authorities had been accused of being derelict of their duties, especially in colonies which had little or no real or potential economic value. Here, it is worth noting that this dereliction reached its zenith in the case of the Federation of French Equatorial Africa (FEA), for which the first ten-year Economic and Social Development Plan in French colonial Africa was drawn. The loan programme can therefore be seen as constituting an effort on the part of French colonial authorities to keep abreast of their peers as far as catering for socio-economic well-being of colonial subjects was concerned. It would be recalled that the British Colonial Welfare Development Act was promulgated immediately subsequent to World War II as well.

Third, it is necessary to note that ownership of duly registered and titled land was a prerequisite for securing a loan from le Crédit de l'AEF. Therefore, the loan programme can also be seen as a tactic by the French colonial authorities to promote and accelerate the land tenure reform process in the colonies. Fourth, the loan programme constituted an element in efforts on the part of French colonial authorities to accomplish the avowed French mission of civilizing and assimilating the colonized. Here, it is important to note that the loan programme actively encouraged the development of so-called permanent building units. In the context of colonial urban planning, only structures constructed of materials imported from Europe such as cement, iron, tiles and aluminium sheets were labelled as 'permanent'. This leads us to the final possible rationale for the loan programme, namely the economic interest of the colonial power. To the extent that the loans insisted on, or favoured, non-traditional or imported building materials, it is safe to conclude that it invariably served the economic interest of the colonial authorities. The economic benefits accruing to these authorities due to the loan programme can be appreciated at two levels. In the first instance, the colonial master nation stood to benefit from taxation on the sale and export of building materials necessary to satisfy the heightened demand for housing rendered effective by the loan programme. In the second instance, the colonial governments generated significant revenues from duties on building materials imports and sales as well as taxes on professional services rendered by surveyors, architects, professional builders and tradesmen in the local construction and cognate industries.

The goodwill gestures of developing the colony's social and cultural infrastructure and the use of local leaders – albeit handpicked – to implement French colonial policy had several objectives with far-reaching implications for the success of the colonial mission in Madagascar. First, these projects were meant to 'frenchify' (or '*franciser*') Madagascar – in line with the French colonial civilizing and acculturating mission. Second, the projects were meant to humble or pacify the Merina elite. A third objective was to undermine earlier strong influences of the British who had occupied parts of the island before the French colonial epoch. Similarly, adopting the *fok'olona* or village council model was designed to give the semblance of local self-governance – another pacification strategy.

Gallieni's choice of Antananarivo as the capital of the new colony was founded largely on psychological grounds that dovetailed neatly into the colonial objective of domination. He was convinced that adopting the traditional capital of the Merina Monarchy was guaranteed to establish the political authority the French colonial authorities badly needed on the island. It was from that location, Gallieni was said to have argued, that the French colonial establishment, like the Monarchy, could assert its superiority over the local elite and the distant tribes (Wright, 1991).

Renaming the central square in Antananarivo after Jean Laborde was meant to immortalize the name of a French 'hero' while discounting the achievements of the indigenous people, whose idea it was to have the square in the first place. This was another instance of the colonial authorities brutally asserting their perceived supremacy over the colonized.

Although racial spatial segregation was not the official policy in colonial Madagascar, officials there succeeded in achieving the goal of segregation by stipulating the use of building materials in certain areas that were prohibitively expensive for members of the indigenous population. The proclivity towards pejorative treatment of the 'other races', evident in racially discriminatory policies such as this, or ostensibly racist behaviour, such as failing to include members of the native population in local town planning commissions, renders hollow claims to the effect that French colonial authorities were not racist while their British counterparts were.

7 Planning in the Cameroons and Togoland

Introduction

This chapter focuses on town and country planning in two erstwhile German colonies, namely the Cameroons (Kamerun) and Togoland, that did not constitute part of a distinct colonial administrative region or federation subsequent to World War I. Rather, they became mandated territories of the League of Nations, forerunner to the present-day United Nations. As part of the agreement reached at the conclusion of World War I, Cameroon was divided into two portions of one-fifth and four-fifths. The larger portion was placed under the colonial administrative tutelage of France while Britain was granted control over the smaller portion. Thus, we speak of the UN mandate territories of British Cameroons and French Cameroun. I discuss colonial town planning legislation in these countries with a view to showing how such legislation was used by colonial authorities as tools for establishing legitimacy and domination – or what some have called 'goodwill' and 'rule' (Myers, 2003).

Background: non-federated French colonies

At the beginning of the twentieth century, France was faced with the problem of crafting a suitable strategy for governing the growing number of territories she had amassed in Africa. Initially, the authorities in Paris decided in favour of a unitary and highly centralized system. Within the framework of this arrangement, the various territories subjected to French colonial rule were unified under a singular administrative umbrella with a governor who was directly answerable to the Minister of the Colonies at the helm in Paris. This arrangement soon proved to be not only cumbersome but also unmanageable. Consequently, it was abolished and in its stead, a decree of 1920 created a quasi-decentralized system comprising two federations, French West Africa (FWA) and French Equatorial Africa (FEA). French Cameroun, Togo and Madagascar were not officially part of either of these federations.

As colonies, Togo and French Cameroun had a unique status. Administratively, both were treated as separate units with commissioners instead of governors presiding over their politico-administrative affairs. The commissioner, who was the chief administrative officer in each of these trust territories reported directly to the Minister of French Overseas Territories. Some commentators (e.g. Cowan, 1959) draw attention to what they see as the distinct status of trust territories within the framework of French colonialism but acknowledge the fact that said territories were controlled in about the same manner as French colonies in the region. Thus, as in the French colonies, colonial authorities in the metropolitan capital played a dominant role in the affairs of the trust territories of Cameroun and Togoland.

Of more importance with respect to urban and regional governance, was the penchant for usurping all indigenous institutions on the part of French colonial policy. Part of the usurpation strategy employed in the trust territories entailed integrating the local chiefs into the colonial government bureaucracy as paid colonial civil servants. In this connection, traditional chiefs who exhibited any recalcitrant tendencies were immediately disposed of, and in some cases exiled, by the French colonial authorities. For instance, in Cameroun, the famous traditional leader of the Great Bamoum Sultanate, Sultan Njoya, was deposed and exiled to Yaoundé in 1931 for refusing to fully co-operate with French colonial authorities in matters of tax collection and the appointment of sub-chiefs, *inter alia* (Fonge, 1997; Le Vine, 1964). This example is noteworthy for at least two reasons. First, it betrays the unwillingness on the part of French colonial authorities to defer to local leaders even in matters of local significance such as town planning and administration. Second, it places in proper historical perspective the proclivity on the part of erstwhile French colonies, including Cameroon and Togo, for politico-administrative centralization. The implications of centralization for physical planning can hardly be overstated.

To be sure, no substantial decisions were possible on the ground in these territories during French colonial rule. This is particularly because power sharing was anything but a feature of French colonial policy. As Cowan (1959) notes, the problem in French colonies at the time was the fact that power sharing, particularly in terms of transferring any real legislative and executive power to the colonies, would have been incompatible with the principle of legislative responsibility centralized in Paris. 'The ultimate power of decision on matters of colonial administration was placed in the hands of the president of the Republic' (Ibid.: 53).

The centralization of power in Paris was glaringly reflected in the administrative structures of the trust territories, where the resident commissioners were not only the supreme heads of the colonial governments but also the direct representatives of the French President. All communications between the administrative services in the trust territories and Paris were channelled through him. The commissioners also constituted the channels through which the *arrêtés d'applications* and other communiqués designed to govern the territories were issued from Paris.

Town planning in Cameroon

Cameroon's status as a colony officially ended with the deposition of the Germans from the territory at the end of World War I. Thereafter, and as noted above, the territory was administered as a trustee of the League of Nations. French colonial authorities controlled four-fifths, while the British controlled one-fifth of said territory from 1919 until 1960 when the country gained political independence.

French colonial urban planning activities in Cameroon

French colonial authorities in Cameroon developed urban planning schemes that adhered strictly to the urban design blueprint established by their German predecessors. One reason for this had to do with the need on the part of French colonial authorities to avoid the costs associated with drawing up urban development plans from scratch. Another reason was related to the fact that the German and French views of colonial urban development coincided in several respects. For instance, like French colonial urban spatial design schemes, German colonial urban plans emphasized the spatial separation of land use activities. Also, both colonial authorities advocated, plausibly for different reasons, the spatial segregation of the races.

The Germans had initiated a number of projects with urban development implications prior to the end of their tenure in Cameroon. As implied above, these projects formed the foundation upon which French colonial urban planning schemes were developed. The most prominent of these projects were based in the territory's economic capital, Douala and deserve further discussion.

Douala

Significant human settlement activity pre-dated the advent of colonialism in the general area of present-day Douala. As far back as 1826, a British traveller, Richard Mother Jackson, travelling in the region, noted that 'Aqua Town' (present-day Akwa) was already a vibrant town equipped with two well-designed parallel streets, each measuring 10 yards wide and 250 yards long (Soulillou, 1989). The traveller also noted the elaborate nature and design of the palace of King Akwa. Furthermore, he drew attention to the exquisite design of the imposing residence of another neighbouring King, King Bell, whose house was a wooden storey building with glazed windows. By the traveller's account, the house bore a striking resemblance to the residences of British aristocrats of the time. The traveller also acknowledged the existence of at least three different densely populated human settlements, each with its own king, on the site currently occupied by Douala.

The indigenous settlements that pre-dated the colonial epoch, notwithstanding, colonial authorities, beginning with the Germans, and later the French, are credited with 'modernizing' the City of Douala. The earliest and best-known German urban development plan in Cameroon was designed to transform or 'modernize' one of the city's oldest neighbourhoods, namely Joss. The German Topographic Service drew up the first plan for the city of Douala in 1890. Some four years earlier, in 1886, the Germans had erected a few buildings in the area. A noteworthy feature of the buildings is the fact that they were constructed of materials such as tin (for roofing), metal and wood that were imported from the colonial master nation, Germany. The plan was typical of colonial urban development plans as it included features such as a spatially centralized governor's residence, a school, neighbourhood stores, a hospital, a prison, and an administrative office complex.

The second major plan with spatial development implications for Douala was completed in 1896. Although the plan, entitled the Urban Development and Seaport Management Plan ('Plan d'urbanisme et d'aménagement du port'), targeted the port of Douala, it was, for all practical purposes, an extension of the 1890 plan. A cursory examination of the 1896 plans reveals the materialization of significant aspects of the 1890 plan. For instance, the 1896 plan shows the existence of administrative, medical, military, educational and other facilities that were proposed as part of the 1890 plan. The 1896 plan also contained a number of features that were never proposed as part of the 1890 plan. Prominent in this regard are a military post, the wharf or seaport, and related facilities such as the customs house, warehouses and a number of commercial buildings.

By the 1900s, Douala was already experiencing significant spatial and demographic growth. This growth was particularly noteworthy in the New Bell area, which at the time was separated by a green area about 1km long. The New Bell area comprised at least four different neighbourhoods, namely New Bonandjo, New Bonapriso, New Bonaduma (otherwise known as Njo-Njo) and New Bonadumbe. The wider New Bell area was designated as home for Douala's non-indigenous African population. As the area grew in importance, it became necessary to draw up a plan to guide its spatial and demographic growth. Accordingly, in 1913, colonial authorities completed an urban management plan ('Plan d'aménagement d'un quartier á Douala') for the area. The plan took into account the importance of the River Wouri for the area's social and economic growth. According to the New Bell urban development plan as designed by German colonial urban planners, the area's western frontier was marked by the Free Zone (*Freine Zone*) and l'Avenue des Palmiers, while its southern boundary was marked by the old airport and the northern limit was marked by Kassalafam Street (rue de Kassalafam).

It is important to note that two other separate areas, one for members of the native Douala population and the other for Europeans, were set aside in other parts of Douala. At the end of World War I, a number of changes took place with respect to the spatial order that was created by German colonial authorities. Thus, for instance, once Douala fell into the hands of the Allies in 1914, the area that was initially set aside to serve as a green area separating the non-Douala population from the European residential area as well as the area occupied by members of the native Douala population, was immediately developed and occupied. Similarly, the area that had been set aside for colonial government offices was transformed into a residential area.

When the French took over control of the city, they selected an area in a neighbourhood known as Bali, to the south of Joss, to serve as the location for colonial government offices. In effect, the French colonial authorities had decided to designate the plateau to the north of Joss as the colonial government office park. This decision was soon followed by a number of other major developments. For instance, old New Bell was rapidly transformed into New Bell proper and witnessed a significant growth in its non-Douala population on the one hand and an equally significant decrease in its Douala population on the other hand. The growth of the non-Douala or stranger population was in large part a function of the rapid economic expansion that the city was experiencing. The expansion created a need for manpower. This need was responded to by an influx of workers from the hinterland region. Most of the workers originated from the grassland region, that is, present-day Western Province. This explains, at least in part, the dominance of natives of this region in Douala today.

Earlier on, the German colonial authorities had envisaged the growth and development of the city and accordingly drew up an extension plan ('Plan d'urbanisme et d'extension de Douala') for the city in 1914. An important objective of the plan was to facilitate the equipment and management of public infrastructure in the growing city. As noted above, the rapid growth of the city had orchestrated the expansion of human settlement and related activities into areas that were initially excluded from development and preserved as green space. The plan was also designed to manage the growing socio-economic needs of the city. These needs grew by leaps and bounds in response to rapid population growth rates in areas such as Akwa, Deido and Bonaberi. These population increases were triggered by the growth of economic activities occasioned by, amongst other things, improvement works on the Douala seaport and the construction of a railway linking the main city and Bonaberi. It was not until 1955 that these projects (the construction of the seaport, railway and railway station) were actually completed. An important aspect of the 1914 plan is the fact that it included green areas or wedges that physically separated New Deido and New Akwa from the areas occupied by Europeans, and commercial and administrative activities. The green area was at least 1 km wide and was slated to be developed as parks and sporting arenas.

As stated earlier, French colonial authorities inherited, and for a long time depended on, the urban development blueprint left behind by their German predecessors. In fact, more than thirty years went by before the French colonial authorities completed an urban development plan of their own for the City of Douala. This plan, 'Plan Directeur d'Urbanisme', completed in 1950, was in effect the first master plan for the city. The plan was drawn by Henri Calsat, a French colonial government architect and urban planner, under the auspices of the Governor-General of the colonial territory of Cameroon. It was financed with funds from Investment Fund for Economic and Social Development or FIDES (Fonds d'Investissement de Développement Economiques et Social).

A word on the goal and origin of FIDES funds is in order. FIDES funds were designed to finance the planning and implementation of urban infrastructure development and related projects. As time went on, the scope of projects that could be funded with FIDES funds was broadened to include long- and medium-term investments in areas such as public works, agriculture, industrial development and communication networks. Furthermore, the funds were used for social development, particularly in the provision of housing. The funds, which were distributed by sector, federation and colonial territory, originated in two major sources, namely the (French) state and contributions from French overseas territories. At the federation level, the funds were distributed into four major but unequal parts. The federation of French West Africa, federation of French Equatorial Africa, Cameroon and Togo each received one part. Until 1954, partial contributions to the funds originated from the Marshall Plan.

The completion of the master plan for Douala in 1950 coincided with the city's ascension to prominence as colonial Cameroon's economic capital. Several factors contributed to the city's economic growth and development. Primary amongst these is location. Located at an altitude of 15m, on the Atlantic Ocean and at the mouth of a major river, the Wouri, Douala occupied a key place on the colonial development agenda. Its economic progress was accelerated by activities in the agricultural (particularly fishing) and forestry sectors. If French colonial authorities had deemed it necessary to draw an urban master development and management plan for the city, it is partially because of the need to spatially and administratively organize and harness its growing economic and industrial activities. The city's rapid growth at the time is telling. Its population grew from 55,000 in 1945 to 110,000 in 1958 (Sinou et al., 1989: 258).

Major public and other infrastructure in Douala as of 1950 included the following: a Chamber of Commerce building, a post office, the headquarters of the Public Works and Railway departments, the office of the government delegation, the governor's office, the central police station, the French Customs Office, public security facilities (including the old court house and the old German police station), the mayor's office, the European hospital, offices of the Institute of Hygiene, the colonial civil servants' club house, offices of the water department, a cathedral, the Centenarian Temple, a Catholic Mission school, a radio house, a large market (the New Bell or Nkololum market), a mosque, a prison (i.e. the old German prison), the New Bell Police Station, the New Bell Railway Station, the Girls High School (New Bell), a hospital for members of the native population, the Laquintinie hospital, a school in Akwa, the Akwa-Deido Police Station, a professional school, offices of the electricity company, facilities of the Cameroon Brewery company (Brasseries du Cameroun), the Douala main railway station, the Besseke Market and the City School.

The following major public works and spatial organization projects were included in the 1950 master plan:

- construction of seaport and related facilities, including warehouses;
- construction of the 2,300m-long bridge across the River Wouri;
- construction of warehouses, workshops and other facilities for the railway;
- designating and organizing zones for secondary economic activities (e.g. New Bell);

- designating and organizing zones for commercial activities;
- spatial organization and location of housing and related activities in well-ventilated areas of the city such as the Joss and Akwa plateaus; and
- the construction of a hydro-electric power plant (on the River Sanaga in nearby Edea).

The plan was updated in 1959. The updated plan included plans to develop the following additional projects:

- an industrial park at Bonaberi;
- refurbishment and re-alignment of the New Bell neighbourhood;
- extension of a residential zone in the general area of Deido; and
- the construction of a road linking the northern and southern portions of the city.

In 1951, a project to construct a camp for workers of the Cameroon Railway Corporation (REGIFERCAM) was initiated. The project was designed to include 34 housing units on a 9ha piece of land with the average plot measuring 2,000m². Each hectare contained four units and the average unit measured 150m².

At about the same time (1951), another project, 'Cité Chardy: opération d'habitat individuel de bon standing pour les cheminots', was also started near Bassa. The aim of the project was to develop 1,000 additional housing units for workers at the National Railway Corporation. The units were of a variety of construction materials including wood, sandcrete blocks, and concrete. The railway corporation itself financed said project.

Edea

Another important project with spatial implications undertaken by the French colonial authorities in Cameroon in 1950 was the completion of the plan of a camp at Bilaceng, Edea for workers of the then newly established Cameroon Aluminium Company (Alucam). Some of the prominent features of the plan included a dispensary, a market, communal shower facilities and latrines and a green area for sporting activities. The residential area consisted of 222 housing units, at 450,000 CFA francs each, for a total of 99,900,000 CFA francs. Two entities, Alucam and the Crédit du Cameroun provided a total 105 million CFA francs to cover the cost of the project and related activities. The units were equipped with basic utility services including water and electricity.

Two other important projects worthy of note were launched in Douala in 1955 and 1956 respectively. The 1955 project constituted a set of physical and spatial improvement activities designed to construct affordable housing units for members of the city's African population. An area of 30 hectares located in Bassa, to the east of the city, was allotted to this purpose. In addition, 15 hectares of land were placed at the disposal of the Douala municipal government, while 25 hectares were awarded to the Cameroon Housing Corporation (Société Immobilière du Cameroun, SIC). This additional land was also designed to accommodate affordable housing units.

The 1956 project entailed the construction of a Customs barracks ('Opération d'habitat individuel groupe pour les fonctionnaires – agents des douanes'). This project occupied an area of 2.5 hectares. The project comprised 80 housing units, all of which were one-storey duplexes, arranged in blocks of two structures each. The ground floor of each unit contained amongst other things, a living room and a kitchen. There were three bedrooms in each unit and all were located on the first floor.

Yaoundé

The French colonial authorities were involved in a number of projects with spatial development implications in Yaoundé, particularly during the 1950s. Prominent amongst these projects was the drawing up of a plan in 1952 to develop a neighbourhood exclusively for the city's European population ('Opération d'habitat de bon standing cité de résidence pour Européens'). The first phase of this project, which was implemented under the auspices of SIC, comprised 21 self-contained residential units divided into the following subgroups:

- 5 units of 138m^2 each and rented out for 26,000 CFA francs per month;
- 5 units of 118m^2 each and rented out for 22,000 CFA francs per month;
- 5 units of 80m^2 each and rented out for 16,000 CFA francs per month; and
- 6 duplex units of 70m^2 each and rented for 14,800 CFA francs per month.

The units were each equipped with utilities such as electricity, water, access roads and gardens. The option to buy the units outright was also available to qualified applicants. In this connection, units from the first category above cost 2,230,000 CFA francs, while those in the second category sold for 1,900,000 CFA francs, and those in the third category cost 1,445,000 CFA francs, and finally, those in the fourth category cost 1,230,000 CFA francs each.

The second phase comprised seventeen units. Five of these were identical to those constructed during the first phase while six were 91m^2 each and an equal number had an area of 114m^2 each. In addition the second phase included a two-storey building. Each level of the building contained a self-contained residential unit with an area of 226m^2 and eight studio apartment units, each of which had an area of 53m^2.

In addition to projects such as the aforementioned that were designed to supply housing units of conventional building materials, the French colonial administration, through a number of private sector enterprises, carried out construction projects using local materials. Prominent in this regard were a number of projects initiated in 1953. These projects sought to construct wooden housing units in the cities of Yaoundé, Douala and Eseka. The Department of Water and Forest Resources (Service des Eaux et Forêts) implemented the Eseka project, while housing units at the Yaoundé project were designed by Wetter, SAFA, Société Camerounaise de Construction and built by SIC. Gatignol designed the housing units at the Douala project. The units in this latter category were rectangular in shape and occupied an area of 40m^2. Each had a gable roof of corrugated metal sheets. The front elevation showed one front doorway with one square window on each side. It is noteworthy that units in this category had no verandah, a feature that was common in housing units of the time. The housing units were delivered at a cost of 128,000 CFA francs (1953). This translated to about 3,200 CFA francs per square metre. The Wetter houses were equipped with a verandah that ran the full length of the building. The foundation was of sandcrete blocks. The Department of Water and Forest Resources units were almost completely of wood, save for the fact that they were suspended on concrete piers and had roofs of corrugated aluminium sheets.

Dschang, Bafoussam and Bafang

Following on the heels of the Germans, French colonial authorities were bent on promoting the cultivation of cash crops destined primarily for overseas markets. Primary amongst the cash crops of choice were bananas, oil palm trees, coffee and cocoa. Bananas and oil palms were encouraged mostly in the coastal regions while coffee and cocoa were promoted in both grassfield and coastal areas. With the growth and expansion of coffee and cocoa plantations in the Western Province of present-day Cameroon, French colonial authorities moved in 1958 to develop standardized conventional housing units in the cities of Bafoussam, Dschang and Bafang. The responsibility for developing the units was placed under the auspices of SIC.

Land legislation in colonial Cameroon

To fully appreciate French colonial land policies in Cameroon, it is necessary to understand the importance of land within the framework of early European expeditions in the territory. Although land was inalienable and not viewed as a commodity in pre-colonial Cameroon, some limited transfers of land from members of the indigenous community to European merchants and explorers did take place (Njoh, 2003). However, these transfers were initially free of charge and later in exchange for European products such as alcoholic beverages, cigarettes, gunpowder and clothing. In most cases, land was basically confiscated from the indigenous population. This practice was commonplace in the coastal region, where land was fertile and held enormous promise for plantation agriculture.

The desirability and especially commercial value of Cameroonian land explain the sweeping land reform initiatives undertaken by European colonial authorities beginning with the Germans in 1884 and later the British and French after World War I. Here, it is necessary to note that while the Germans were at liberty to do just about anything in the land policy field, the actions of their successors, the French and the British, were significantly scrutinized by the League of Nations. Among the many outcomes of World War I was the establishment of a condominium over Cameroonian territory by the British and French. The condominium had a very short life as it was abruptly abrogated in 1916. At this time, the two colonial powers agreed to divide the territory up into two unequal parts of four-fifths and one-fifth, with France assuming control over the larger portion while Britain controlled the smaller part. On the one hand, the British portion of the territory comprised two separate contiguous areas, known as British Cameroons, bordering Nigeria. On the other hand, the French controlled the remainder of the territory east of the River Mungo, known as French Cameroun. A few years later, in 1919, the entire territory, including French Cameroun and British Cameroons, became a mandated territory of the League of Nations. This arrangement remained binding until 1960/1 when the country gained political independence.

As noted earlier, League of Nations rules governing control over trust territories forbade France and Britain from behaving with the territory as they might have pleased. Thus, at least in theory, the colonial powers did not have a free hand over the territory's resources, especially land. In practice the story was, however, quite different. This is despite the fact that the League of Nations spared no effort to attempt to curb the excesses of the two colonial powers. One definite concern of the League of Nations was with the impending danger of colonial authorities usurping or overlaying traditional land tenure systems and land use patterns with European varieties. In fact, an important provision of the League of Nations trust agreement exhorted administering authorities to take the steps necessary to preserve native laws and customs as well as respect the present and future rights and interests of indigenous populations in the trust territories, especially with respect to land tenure and land use. Most importantly, the agreement stipulated that "no native land or natural resource may be transferred, except between natives, save with previous consent of the competent authority" (quoted in Njoh, 1998: 410; Fisiy, 1992: 30).

French Cameroun

As far as land tenure goes, two parallel systems of law were in operation in French Cameroun. One of these systems – *l'indigénat* – governed what the French colonial authorities branded, the 'natives' or *les indigènes*. These latter comprised members of the indigenous population who had not been exposed to, or influenced by, European and, particularly, French culture. The other system was designed to govern European residents as well as Western acculturated members of the indigenous population, or what the French labelled '*les assimilés*'. Land laws and legislation of the latter genre were crafted along the lines of the Napoleonic Code of 1810. The 'Napoleonic property doctrine' stressed individual, as opposed to corporate or communal, property rights. It should be noted that communal ownership constituted the king-pin of the indigenous land tenure system.

The laws that were applicable to the unassimilated members of the indigenous population (*l'indigénat*) had simply been transplanted to French Cameroun by a decree of 4 October 1924, from France's other colonies in the region, where they had been in operation since 1917. The distinction between the two systems of land law was one without a difference. Theoretically, the distinction suggests some degree of sensitivity to indigenous laws and customs. However, in practice the distinction faded into obscurity. The goal of the French in the land policy arena was hardly distinguishable from that of their German predecessors. In this connection, the French colonial establishment in Cameroon is on record for embarking on a massive campaign in the 1900s to consolidate and place under the direct control of the colonial state large parcels of land within the country.

It is in order, here, to examine some of the specific steps taken by the French to satisfy their voracious appetite for land as well as realize the objective of speedily supplanting the indigenous land tenure and land use systems with purely French varieties. One of the most prominent, and perhaps most consequential, of these steps entailed experimenting with several land tenure systems. These experiments were designed to determine the system with the highest probability of guaranteeing the colonial state a firm grip on all the land in the territory, while minimizing any chance of alienating the indigenous population. One piece of legislation introduced as part of these experimental efforts was the Land Law of 24 July 1921. This law, which went under the official appellation *la législation d'attente*, was simply an extension of a law that had been employed several decades earlier in 1855 to introduce the transcription system in France. The 1921 law was in operation for more than three decades until 17 June 1959, when law No. 59-47 of that same year repealed it.

Furthermore, the colonial authorities adopted a policy that converted all land that was neither individually owned nor duly registered throughout the territory into colonial government property. This policy was in line with a 1907 French West Africa Court of Appeal decision, which had ruled that all unregistered customary rights and interests in land were deemed null and void. The policy met with fierce opposition not only in Cameroon but also in other French colonies. This resulted in the law being rescinded in November 1935. In its stead, another policy declaring that all land left unused or unoccupied for a period of ten years – that is, what the French alluded to as 'terres vacantes et sans maître' – was automatically colonial state property. We will return to this policy later. For now, it is important to note the striking resemblance between the concept of 'unused and unoccupied lands' or 'terres vacantes et sans maître' and the notion of 'vacant and ownerless land' employed by the Germans (see below). From the foregoing account, it is easy to glean the fact that like the Germans, the French colonial authorities were bent not only on amassing as much land as possible but also on placing all land throughout the territory under the administrative control of the colonial state.

However, the French approach to land acquisition differed in one important way from that of the Germans. Rather than acquire large parcels of land as their German predecessors did, the French opted to secure small concessions of no more than 1,000 hectares at a time. At first glance, this has the appearance of a conscious effort to deviate from the path taken by the Germans and to honour relevant provisions of the League of Nations mandate agreement. In fact, the decision in favour of two systems of law, one for the 'natives' and the other for Europeans and *'les assimilés'*, on the part of the French colonial authorities was designed specifically to give the appearance of some degree of respect and appreciation for indigenous laws and practices. Upon further scrutiny, it becomes clear that the spirit and implications of the French strategy were hardly different from those of the Germans.

In addition, the French seldom took any steps to honour relevant provisions of the mandate agreement, especially with respect to land tenure and alienation. This is notwithstanding constant attempts on the part of the French colonial authorities to hide their otherwise egregious violations of relevant provisions of the League of Nations mandate agreement. The Decree of 12 January 1938, which declared all so-called *terres vacantes et sans maître* (unoccupied and ownerless lands) as property of the colonial state or territorial property, is only one manifestation of this tendency. According to the decree, *'les terres vacantes et sans maître appartiennent au territoire'*. This piece of legislation amounted to what some (e.g. Fisiy, 1992: 35) have called the 'colonization of customary lands' and triggered a series of protests on the part of concerned members of the indigenous population, particularly local chiefs and landlords. These parties construed the law as constituting a frontal assault not only on their ancestral lands but also on their system of property holding.

The notion of 'ownerless lands' was perceived as ludicrous and absurd, by members of the indigenous population, who consider land sacred and belonging to the entire community. It is basically this philosophy or view of land that comprised the strongest propellant of the wave of protestations that greeted the French colonial land reform efforts, particularly the decision to classify most land 'vacant and ownerless'. The protestations were not without impact. In 1955 the colonial authorities promulgated Statutory Order No. 55-580, which was designed to consolidate all previous acts and court rulings in the land policy field. Most importantly, the order explicitly recognized customary rights and interests in land throughout the territory.

Power and the land question in British Cameroons

Land was less significant as a basis of power in pre-colonial Africa, where land was more plentiful than in Europe, where it was scarce. How did this difference in the perception of land affect the struggle over legitimacy and control between the state and society in colonial Africa? I examine pieces of land use control legislation that were enacted in British Cameroons (i.e. some of the territory comprising present-day anglophone Cameroon) with a view to uncovering some answers to this question.

Europeans did not settle permanently in Cameroon. Therefore, inter-racial competition for space or land was non-existent. Yet, space remained a contested arena despite the fact that it was plentiful given the country's scanty population during the colonial era. The reason for this is simple. The colonial state, dating back to the German colonial era, viewed Cameroon as nothing more than a tropical trading and plantation colony. Accordingly, it moved to place all fertile land throughout the territory at the disposal of European plantation companies (Debussmann, 1996). The German colonial authorities are on record for concocting some of the most perfidious land acquisition schemes in Cameroon's colonial history. In fact German colonial emissaries and middlemen were specifically instructed to use all means necessary to amass lands in the colonies (Fisiy, 1992; Njoh, 2003). Under Governor Von Puttkamer, German colonial authorities in Cameroon had planned to herd villagers off to so-called 'Native Reserves', destroy their villages and make room for plantation agriculture on the fertile volcanic lands at the foot of Mount Cameroon. This was the proverbial last straw that broke the camel's back, as the villagers launched mass and violent protests to thwart implementation of the colonial government's treacherous plan. The villagers' efforts paid heavy dividends as the colonial authorities later called off the plan.

Subsequent to this, the German colonial authorities decided in favour of employing legislative and other mechanisms to satisfy their voracious appetite for land. The most prominent effort on the legislative front was the enactment of the Crown Lands Act of 15 July 1896, which converted all so-called 'vacant' and 'unoccupied' lands throughout the territory into property of the German Overseas Dominions. On the same front, the colonial government established twenty land commissions, and charged them with the responsibility of demarcating Crown lands and parcelling out areas to be used as 'native reservations'. Additionally, the rather meticulous plan stipulated that each 'native' be allotted 1.5 hectares of land for residential and related use. Furthermore, the plan required that all dispersed villages be consolidated into dense settlements complete with numbered and surveyed building and agricultural plots. It is difficult to miss the ultimate goal of this exercise on the part of the colonial state. It was precisely to free up as much land as possible for plantation agricultural purposes.

By all accounts, the Germans were very successful in their mission to endow the colonial state with inordinate amounts of land. By the time Germany's tenure as Cameroon's colonial master nation abruptly ended in 1914, it owned, operated and/or controlled several plantations on hundreds of acres of land in the coastal areas at the foot of Mount Cameroon. Some estimates suggest that the Germans owned as much as 300,000 acres of prime agriculture land and controlled as many as fifty-eight estates in the region by 1914 (Njoh, 2003: 79).

German plantations were largely located in the area that later became British Southern Cameroons (now anglophone Cameroon). On the eve of World War I, German companies controlled as much as 264,000 acres of land in Victoria Division (present-day Fako Division) and Kumba Division (present-day Meme and Ndian Divisions) (Meek, 1957). At the end of the World War I these vast areas of land were placed in the hands of the Nigerian colonial government. Recall that the British colonial authorities administered the League of Nations trust territory of the British Cameroons as an appendix of colonial Nigeria. Proclamation No. 25 of 1920 officially sanctioned this arrangement.

Based on agreements reached by the Allies subsequent to the outcome of World War I, ex-enemy property, such as German lands in Cameroon, were to be auctioned. Ex-enemy nationals were excluded from participating in the bidding process. It took two auctions to get rid of German plantations and other lands in Cameroon. The first auction failed, thereby prompting organizers to waive the clause that banned German bidders. It was upon doing so and permitting former owners of the plantations and other lands to re-acquire their property that organizers were able to register positive results. The auctions were held in London in October 1922 and November 1924 respectively.

No sooner had the German companies re-settled in Cameroon than World War II broke out in 1939 and displaced them once more. At the end of the war in 1945, colonial authorities took a number of major decisions with far-reaching implications for the plantation lands. Two of these decisions are worth discussing in some detail. The first was the decision that forbade the return of the plantation lands either to ex-enemy nationals or private individuals. The second relates to the fact that the lands were placed under the charge of the British Colonial Governor with jurisdiction over British Cameroons. This latter decision therefore effectively converted most of the land in the territory into property of the colonial state (similar to the 1896 Crown Lands Act) and conferred the status of 'super landlord' on the colonial Governor. Given the stipulations of the League of Nations, the Governor was supposed to administer the land for the common good and benefit of members of the territory's indigenous population. In reality, however, the decision to place the lands under the charge of the colonial Governor was part of a larger scheme to endow the colonial state with limitless control over land throughout the territory.

It is appropriate to acknowledge claims to the effect that the British government did in fact buy the lands in question and then placed them under the custody of the Nigerian colonial government (Meek, 1957: 356). This notwithstanding, it is important to note that the input of the natives was never sought at any point during the deliberations that culminated in the land transfer. This constituted an egregious violation of the League of Nations conditions for administering the trust territories. Whatever deal was struck had to have been between the British and the Germans. This fact is germane in efforts to pry into the mindset of colonizers, especially with regards to how they perceived the colonized. Here, there is little doubt that the colonizers were oblivious to the existence of the colonized and considered their views inconsequential.

At the end of the World War II, the land question in Africa in general and British Cameroons in particular was subjected to re-examination. This was in response to a number of developments that had occurred since the dawn of the colonial era in Africa. African colonies had experienced significant numerical gains in their populations. Rural–urban migration was picking up steam. In addition, colonial powers were re-examining their colonial development strategies – contemplating innovative ways of accomplishing colonial development goals without alienating colonial subjects. These factors conspired to prompt the colonial government to pay more attention to original League of Nations stipulations regarding the administration of trust territories.

The stipulation relating to land tenure is contained in Article 8 of the Trusteeship Agreement, which was approved by the General Assembly on 1 November and 13 December 1947. The article is important for the purpose of the present discussion and deserves being quoted in full:

> In framing land laws in the territories, the administering authority shall take into consideration native laws and customs and shall respect the rights and safeguard the interests, both present and future, of the native population. No native land or natural resource may be transferred except between natives.
>
> (Quoted in Meek, 1957: 370)

Thus, in keeping with stipulations requiring mandate territory administrators to preserve the customs and traditions of the 'native' people, authorities decided to treat British Cameroons as part of northern Nigeria. Thus, for instance, the southern portion of British Cameroons (British Southern Cameroons), which was administratively part of the Eastern Province of Nigeria, was considered part of Northern Nigeria in matters of land legislation. Accordingly, the Land and Native Rights Ordinance of 1927 that was already in force in Northern Nigeria became law in British Cameroons. This decision was crucial because applying the land legislation of Northern Nigeria, where the 'indirect rule' colonial administrative model was employed, guaranteed the preservation of traditional land tenure systems.

I have noted elsewhere that colonial authorities in Cameroon never went beyond rhetoric in their attempt to abide by the stipulations of the UN Trust Agreement in the land policy domain (Njoh, 2003). One reason for this has to do with the desire on the part of these authorities to consolidate power. A close read of the official pronouncements of the colonial government on the land question reveals an amazing level of consistency in the colonial government's efforts to guarantee itself infinite control over land. In this regard, Ordinance No. 38 of 1946 vested the colonial Governor with all native lands throughout the Cameroonian territory. This ordinance was in contravention of UN stipulations on administering mandate territories, which state for instance that land in the territories must be administered for the benefit of the 'natives'.

Vesting the colonial Governor with control over land made it possible for the colonial state to use land anywhere in the colony to attain colonial development goals. For instance, such control permitted the colonial state to use land to placate those who posed a viable threat to the political stability of the colonial polity. It was also able to employ land as a reward for political support for the regime in power in the metropolis. Finally, land was used as a tool to attain colonial economic development goals. It is therefore hardly any wonder that a lot of the ex-enemy lands that were never auctioned remain unaccounted for.

I began the discussion in this segment by stating that land did not command the same degree of importance in Africa that it did in Europe at the dawn of the colonial era. It is therefore safe to conclude that the struggle between the colonial state and society in Africa did not have the same objectives for both parties. There is reason to believe that the Europeans, perceived a direct relationship between control of land and power (economic, social, political, and otherwise). For Europeans, power was contingent upon the extent to which they controlled land.

The infatuation with land on the part of Europeans was a function of their environment and experience. They originated in a region that has historically experienced scarce habitable and/or agricultural land. Jeffrey Herbst (2000: 36) draws attention to this phenomenon by noting that the focus on the control of land as a basis of state authority by Europeans was not surprising on account of the fact that they were used to a region known for problems associated with high levels of population density and land scarcity. Underlying relevant analyses of the modern state is the assumption that land is scarce, thereby making control thereof a fundamental indicator of power (Herbst, 2000; Weber, 1991). Additionally, it is arguable that since states in Europe have a history of fighting for land, the control of territory is thus seen as invariably a defining characteristic of state authority. In colonial Cameroon, the British were conscious of the need to control land. However, they were also cognizant of the negative implications of alienating Cameroonians, especially at a time when people in the colonial territories were becoming increasingly apprehensive of colonial rule. Thus, British colonial authorities needed to strike a delicate balance between two competing philosophies – goodwill and rule – that characterized thinking during the waning days of the colonial era. Goodwill is evident in efforts to pay attention to indigenous land tenure practices, while rule or domination is obvious in the colonial policies that established 'native reserves' and colonial government actions designed to extend special favours to European plantation companies. Rule and domination are also evident in the colonial tendency of ignoring the colonized in rendering decisions on matters that directly impacted their well-being.

Togo

Lomé

Togo, as stated above, was a German colony until the end of World War I. In 1896, the German colonial authorities designated Lomé, which was at the time a small village, the territory's capital. The decision to make Lomé the chief administrative centre of the territory was accompanied by the drawing up of a master plan charting the course of the city's future spatial and physical development. The architects of said plan drew a lot of inspiration from the plan of the German city of Hamburg. The plan portrayed a city enclosed within a belt of semi-circular boulevards and divided into two main zones, the eastern and western zones, which were separated by a rail line. The eastern zone was set aside for commerce/industry and housing for members of the native population while the western zone was reserved for administrative activities and housing for Europeans.

Between 1904 and 1911 the German colonial authorities initiated a number of major activities with spatial implications. Prominent amongst these activities was the drawing up of a cadastral plan. The plan included 171 lots that were registered in a land title register (*Grundbuch*). By 1914 the city's population stood at 8,500. At that time the city contained a number of administrative buildings of permanent materials, particularly bricks. Also, an urban plan showing a network of existing and future streets for the city had been completed.

Togo came under the control of the French colonial authorities following the outcome of World War I in 1919. The French colonial authorities neither closely adhered to, nor completely discarded the master plan drawn for the city by the Germans. However, they proceeded to increase the stock of administrative buildings and in 1928 reconstructed the seaport. During this time, development activities along the circular boulevard had gathered momentum. The period also witnessed the sub-division of an area, Hanoukope, that had been reserved for members of the indigenous population according to the master plan for the city drawn by the German colonial authorities. It is worth noting that the French did very little with respect to proactive urban development in the city. Instead, most urban development activities were guided by the master plan drawn up during the German colonial era. Thus, the nucleus around which the city of Lomé has developed since Togo became independent in 1960 is an embodiment of German rather than French colonial urban planning ideology and principles. To be sure, the distinction between the two colonial authorities as far as urban planning goes is, for all practical purposes, blurred. After all, features such as the spatial segregation of the races as well as functions were common to the urban development plans of all European colonialists in sub-Saharan Africa.

Some final thoughts

The mandate and trusteeship system under which the Cameroons and Togoland were administered during the colonial era, constitutes a unique variant of colonialism. In theory, the power of the supervisory authorities, Britain and France, over the mandate territories was extremely limited by League of Nations provisions. For instance, the colonial powers were not allowed to incorporate the territories with other colonial possessions. Furthermore, as D.K. Fieldhouse (1981) noted, the transformation of these and other former German colonial territories into League of Nations trusteeships was designed to protect the territories from exploitation. In practice, this was not the case. For instance, as noted above, Britain opted in favour of administering Southern Cameroons as an appendix of Nigeria. In the planning domain, this meant, amongst other things, adopting many pieces of planning legislation that were already in force in Nigeria in British Southern Cameroons. One exception to this rule was noted above and bears reiterating here. The British colonial authorities went out of their way to recognize and even legitimize customary land tenure in the territory. This was despite the fact that such a system of landholding was widely considered a hindrance to the capitalist objectives of the colonial enterprise. To paraphrase Anne Phillips (1989: 59), a free market economy could never become reality while communal land tenure guaranteed access to land. In French Cameroun and Togoland a dual system of landholding, one for the urban areas and another for non-urban or rural areas constituted the norm. This suggest that by the time the British and French colonial authorities assumed control of the League of Nations mandate territories, they had become cognizant of the futility of indiscriminately adopting an alien system of landholding throughout their African colonies.

Accordingly, the colonial powers had decided to adopt a more pragmatic land policy – one that acknowledged and legitimized the traditional land tenure system. It is easy to misconstrue this policy change as constituting an erosion of the power of the colonial authorities. Yet nothing could be further from the truth. In reality, this change was essential to reinforce the colonial state's power in the land policy field in particular and the colony in general. There are at least three reasons for this (Phillips, 1989). First, the change served to prevent the imprudent alienation of land. Second, it averted such land-related problems as absentee landlordism. Finally, the change prevented the growth and proliferation of a landless proletariat. In contending that the reversal of policies promoting individualized tenure of land buttressed the power of the colonial state, I echo the sentiments of Phillips (1989). According to Phillips, this 'reversal of earlier visions for land reform' 'secured the chiefs in their traditional authority, and thereby strengthened their role as recruiting agents for the colonial states' (p. 59).

8 Town planning in British Southern Africa

Introduction

It is true that town planning in British colonial possessions was derived from British town planning legislation, principles and practice. However, it is erroneous to extrapolate from this basic fact that there was uniformity in town planning practice and legislation throughout the British colonies. In fact, Robert Home (1990) has drawn attention to the fact that significant differences characterized even the manner and process by which authorities transferred planning legislation from Britain to the colonies. Apart from procedural differences, we are safe to expect substantive differences as the colonies varied markedly in terms of climate, geography, population density, settlement patterns, history and/or levels of urbanization, and disease etiology and contagion. The fact that West Africa had a pre-colonial history of authoritative states (e.g. city-states), kingdoms and chiefdoms facilitated the functioning of the indirect rule colonial administrative model in the region. On the contrary, the absence of indigenous large-scale political units rendered the functioning of this model impossible in southern and eastern Africa. Sir Donald Cameron, Governor of British East Africa from 1925 to 1931, found this out when he attempted to rule Tanganyika 'indirectly'.

Thus, the British colonial possessions of East and Southern Africa experienced mostly 'direct' as opposed to 'indirect' colonial rule. As Home (1990) observes and I concur, these legal arrangements are by no means inconsequential for the exercise of town planning. Rather, they significantly affected town planning legislation and practice in the colonies. Also, West Africa's longer history of empire building and urbanization – pre-dating the European colonial era – quite possibly prevented British colonial town planners from realizing a number of preconceived projects. For example, the presence of well-established pre-colonial towns such as Kaduna, Kano and Zaria in Northern Nigeria meant that the British colonial authorities could only influence the structure of the built environment on the fringes of these towns. The spontaneous *Sabon Garis* or 'native stranger quarters', which developed on the outskirts of these towns, constitute a testament to the colonial planners' predicament.

Most importantly, while conditions such as the prevalence of anopheles mosquitoes prevented Europeans from permanently settling in West Africa, eastern and southern Africa constituted a popular destination for Europeans desirous of settling in Africa.

The Europeans did not arrive alone in eastern and southern Africa. Rather, they imported Asian slaves to work in the sugar plantations and later the mines. How did the presence of Europeans as permanent settlers and less powerful groups such as Asians and members of the various indigenous groups affect town planning legislation and practice in the region? How did colonial town planners manipulate space to bolster the power of the minority White settlers of the region? This chapter seeks to address these and cognate questions. It does so by interrogating specific spatial policies that were designed to enable the colonial state, and by extension the White minority, to exercise inordinate control over the built environment. In extreme cases, such as apartheid South Africa, Zimbabwe and others, towns were designed to be uninviting and threatening to non-Whites. Observed through the lenses of Lefebvre (1974) and especially Markus (1993), the towns became 'continuous structured entities', which allowed non-White groups in only as strangers or visitors. In the colonial towns, members of the powerful White minority population were always the inhabitants while individuals belonging to the majority but powerless groups were the visitors.

As Markus (1993: 13) would argue, 'the former have an investment of power and are the *controllers*, the latter enter or stay as subjects of the system – the *controlled*'. Before identifying and discussing some of the major pieces of town and country planning legislation and projects that were undertaken by colonial authorities, I provide some background information on the former British colonies in the region. Unlike the case of West Africa, many of the territories in this region were 'settler colonies'.

Town and country planning in settler colonies

To better appreciate the role and place of town and country planning in colonial southern and eastern Africa, one must first understand the nature of colonialism in this region. Colonialism in southern and eastern Africa differed markedly from what obtained in other parts of colonial sub-Saharan Africa. The colonial project in most of the southern and eastern African region epitomized the concept of colonialism in its strictest form. As an upshot of imperialism, colonialism may assume different forms. However, in its strictest sense, the notion of colonialism, derived from the term 'colony', is etymologically rooted in the Latin word, '*colonia*', which literally means settlement (Imperial Archives website). Thus, a defining characteristic of colonialism is settlement, which entails the movement of people from one place, a metropolis, to permanently live or settle in another locale, a peripheral territory. This type of colony, known as a 'settler colony'. is only one of two main types of colonies that European colonial powers established in Africa. Most of the colonies of Southern Africa, but particularly South Africa, Zimbabwe and Namibia, were settler colonies. The other type, the most common variant, is known as a 'colony of occupation'. Most colonies throughout Africa were 'colonies of occupation'. The difference between the two types of colonies deserves some attention, particularly because of the implications of this difference for public policymaking, power struggles and social control in the colonies. In 'settler colonies', as intimated earlier, the 'settlers' tended to remain permanently. Thus, in formulating laws, acquiring real property, and cultivating land, the settlers gave no thought to returning to their place(s) of origin. Rather, they typically made every effort to annihilate, displace, usurp and/or marginalize members of the indigenous population through institutional and other means. The situation was a little different in 'exploitation colonies' or 'colonies of occupation'. In such colonies, particularly those of West Africa, the European population was usually insignificant and was comprised mainly of colonial government officials, plantation farmers/managers, and businessmen concerned exclusively with protecting their individual interests or those of the colonial empire. Accordingly, their main focus was to exploit and ship raw materials from the colonies to the metropolis.

Settler colonies were not confined to the African continent. Rather, advanced countries, such as the United States, Canada, Australia, and New Zealand, were once settler colonies. However, the settler colonies of Africa were unique in many ways, especially because, unlike the US, Canada, Australia, and New Zealand, the European settler population in Africa never became numerically superior to the indigenous population. Nevertheless, the settler population managed to find ways to consolidate power and dominate members of the indigenous or native population.

Mahmood Mamdani (1996) has thrown some light on the status of settlers and the extent to which they wielded power in colonial southern and eastern Africa. Settlers, Mamdani contends, are a product not only of immigration, but also, and perhaps more importantly, of conquest.

Settlers are kept settlers by a form of the state that makes a distinction – particularly juridical – between conquerors and conquered, settlers and natives, and makes it the basis of other distinctions that tend to buttress the conquerors and politically isolate the conquered. However fictitious these distinctions may appear historically, they become real political facts for they are embodied in real political institutions (Mamdani, 1996: 2).

The state in settler colonies recognized two main types of political identities: civic and ethnic (Mamdani, 1996). The former was racially defined and encompassed within its orbit the identity of the citizen. Only those considered 'civilized' had the privilege of enjoying civil and/or political rights. The striking similarities between this philosophy and what French colonial authorities called les évolués or what the Portuguese dubbed the civilisados, is obvious. Here, I hasten to note that although the objective of 'civilizing' indigenous peoples is often associated with French colonialism, this objective was a common goal of all colonial powers. In fact, the Portuguese, who controlled a large portion of east and southern Africa during the colonial era, were actively 'civilizing natives' as part of their colonial project long before the French Revolution (Mamdani, 1996). A number of colonial administrative reforms that were initiated by the British colonial authorities, and later duplicated by others, including the Belgians (in Congo), the Portuguese (in Mozambique and Angola), and the French (e.g. in Senegal), had classified the African population into two main categories, namely the 'civilized' and 'uncivilized' or *les évolués* and *les indigènes* (French) or *civilisados* and *indigena* (Portuguese).

The rights of the civilized were stipulated and dealt with under the civil law of the colonial state. The enforcement of such laws fell directly under the responsibility of the central government. Members of the indigenous population, also known as the 'natives', were considered 'uncivilized' and were therefore neither governed by civil law nor fell under the direct auspices of the central state. This is not to say that no laws governed the space of members of the indigenous population or the natives. The natives belonged to a space defined by their ethnicity. The notion of ethnicity here is inextricably bound to the native's area of ancestry. Members of the native population fell under the jurisdiction of so-called customary law and were not affected by the Napoleonic Code or civil laws.

Throughout southern and eastern Africa, colonial law viewed native Africans as belonging to rural areas and not to the cities. Their presence in the cities or towns was considered temporary as they were expected to return to their ancestral lands in the 'villages'. This policy was not unique to British colonial Africa. Rather, the French, Belgians and others are also on record for formulating and implementing identical policies. In Belgian Congo, for instance, 'the notion of the native as permanently a peasant and only temporarily a worker was given legal reality through a series of decrees between 1931 and 1933' (Mamdani, 1996: 86).

The colonial administrative strategy of indirect rule, popularized in Uganda and other parts of eastern and southern Africa by Lord Lugard, treated the native as part of a community rather than an individual. As part of a community, the native was directly under the administrative auspices of a chief. He was always first and foremost, subject to African customary law. His access to land was limited to those parcels of land designated as communal property. Not only was the native required to pay taxes, he was also required to offer his labour services gratis to the colonial state. Pay taxes for what, one may ask, given that the native had claim to hardly any taxable possession. Well, the colonial authorities were very shrewd in this regard. First, they determined that each native of taxable age owned at least a hut and proceeded to levy taxes on huts – the 'hut tax'. When colonial local government revenues from this source were considered insufficient to meet the demands of colonial governance, they moved to levy taxes on every taxable native's head – the 'head tax'. With time, they decided in favour of taxing domestic animals (e.g. the 'dog tax').

Revenue generated through taxes on native property and activities contributed not only to colonial governance proper, but also to the development of public infrastructure in the very urban centres to which natives were denied access. The colonial state assumed the responsibility for providing public infrastructure and services in urban centres. However, when it came to similar provisioning in native areas such as the so-called rural villages and Black reservation areas, more often than not, the colonial state abdicated its responsibilities. Where it was necessary for the colonial state to broadcast its authority, it took advantage of an ancient African tradition, namely self-help or communal labour. This entailed free in-kind and financial input from members of the community towards the realization of communal or public projects. Rather early in the colonial era, colonial authorities had recognized this forté of Africans and proceeded to incorporate it into their development agendas. Joseph Nye, Jr (1963: 36) echoes this sentiment when he states (referring to Tanganyika, present-day Tanzania) that,

> Communal labour was not a new idea. It was an integral part of the traditional system of many tribes and as organized by the chiefs had been used by the colonial administration with varying degrees of success for a number of years

This means, amongst other things, that colonial authorities had come to focus on the so-called native communities not only as service delivery sites but also, and perhaps above all, as resources. In British East Africa, colonial authorities modernized and adopted the traditional African concept of community self-help. Furthermore, they fittingly attributed to this tradition a local appellation, *Harambee*, a Swahili word meaning 'working together for progress'. In other parts of colonial Africa, authorities were hard at work incorporating the labour input of the 'natives', especially through forced labour schemes, as they strived to develop the infrastructure that was necessary for the colonial enterprise's success.

The story of indirect rule in colonies such as South Africa and Zimbabwe (at the time, Southern Rhodesia) is at once complicated and intriguing. It was selective in its application. For instance, when it came to revenue generation for the colonial state, the local chiefs and headmen were depended upon to play an important role in taxation drives. In other respects, there was always a tug of war between the traditional leaders and members of the settler population who felt threatened by the apparent burgeoning power of indigenous groups or 'tribes'. Accordingly, colonial authorities in settled colonies ensured that indigenous institutions, including chiefdoms and kingdoms were transformed into toothless barking dogs. In the case of Southern Rhodesia, as Mamdani (1996: 87–8) observed,

> The 'cornerstone of all Southern Rhodesian law' was the provision that 'the law to be administered shall, as nearly as the circumstances of the country will permit, be the same as the law for the time being in force in the Colony of the Cape of Good Hope'. Here, as in South Africa, the president's power to appoint chiefs included 'the right to divide existing tribes into two or more' or 'to amalgamate tribes or parts of tribes into one'. Likewise, the line of native authority ran from chiefs to headmen to messengers and heads of kraals. As in the French colonies, where the chiefs had no status, Southern Rhodesian law books contained hardly a reference to the powers of native chiefs and headmen, but there was no shortage of clauses on their duties or obligations. Yet even if the

law was entirely silent on this question, it had long tolerated chiefs and headmen dispensing customary justice as part of an on-the-ground reality.

One exception, the case of Swaziland, is worth mentioning. Despite strong opposition from the large settler population, the British-controlled central state proceeded with reform actions that culminated in endowing the Swazi king and chiefs with complete autonomy of the genre for which non-settler colonies were well-known. A closer look at the case of colonial Swaziland is very revealing as it demonstrates the sharp contrast between 'true indirect rule' or 'autonomy' and 'centrally-controlled indirect rule' or 'semi-autonomy'. Two legislative pronouncements that occurred in Swaziland between 1944 and 1950 are worthy of attention in this regard. Under the Native Administration Proclamation of 1944, the British High Commissioner was endowed with the powers to appoint and depose all Swazi chiefs, including the paramount chief or king. This was 'centrally-controlled autonomy' at its best as only indigenous leaders who supported colonial state mandates had any chance of being appointed and retained as chiefs. This state of affairs, which endowed the colonial state with enormous powers changed dramatically in 1950 with Proclamation 79. This Proclamation recognized the Swazi king as the sole leader of the Swazi people. It further empowered him to make rules; with the only caveat being that the rules should not conflict with the laws of the colony.

One final aspect of the indirect rule strategy as it was applied in southern and eastern Africa that deserves attention here has to do with so-called native reserves. Native reserves and homelands were well-known features of the colonial landscape in settler colonies and almost completely absent in 'exploitation colonies' such as those of West Africa. Part of the colonial administrative reform actions that culminated in the institutionalization of indirect rule specifically targeted native reserves and/or homelands (Mamdani, 1996). In South Africa, for instance, the Bantu Authorities Act (No. 68 of 1951) sought to restore 'natural native democracy' in the native reserves by establishing a system of councils that operated under the leadership of chiefs and headmen. Similarly, an autonomous native treasury and a native administration with rule-making powers were created to facilitate the administration of customary law in Zululand (Natal) and other homelands. The Transkeian Territorial Authority, which was established in 1956, also had as a major objective decentralization and devolution of power as well as granting some degree of autonomy to members of the indigenous population.

Town and country planning in South Africa

Power struggles and evolution of the Union

Right from the onset, it was clear that the colonial enterprise in South Africa would bear hardly any resemblance to anything British colonial authorities, or any other colonial authorities for that matter, had known before. Pre-independence South Africa constitutes a unique case of a settler colony. The first recorded group of foreign visitors led by Jan van Riebeeck arrived at the Cape of Good Hope in 1652. This group of 90 persons, under the auspices of the Dutch East India Company, had two main missions – to construct a fort and develop a vegetable garden for the benefit of ships on the eastern trade route. No foreigner settled in the territory on a permanent basis until five years later in 1657, when nine Europeans were given land to farm in the area. At about the same time, the first wave of slaves was imported to the territory. By 1662, 250 Europeans had established permanent residence in the area. During this time, European powers were encouraging mass migration to the burgeoning colony. In the early 1700s independent farmers called Trekboers began pushing north and east resulting in the native Khoisans literally losing ground. By this time, a new group, which came to be known as 'coloured persons' – that is, descendants of inter-racial and/or inter-ethnic unions between Khoisans or Khoekhoe, slaves from other parts of Africa, Asians and Europeans – had gained numerical strength and had started seeking recognition within the geopolitical context of the colony.

By the mid-1700s, the colonists, mainly of Dutch, German, and French extraction, had begun losing their sense of identification with Europe. This period also marked the coming into being of the Afrikaner nation. The Cape went back and forth as a colony between the Dutch and the British from the late-1700s to the early-1800s until 1806 when it came under the control of the latter for good. This development did not bode well for the many Dutch settlers, the Boers. Consequently, they decided in favour of trekking north in search of territory to establish a new republic of their own.

In 1820, 5,000 new British settlers arrived in the area and were located on the eastern frontier. The decision to locate the new settlers in this region was based on a need to create a defensive buffer against the native Xhosa. The decision yielded no utility particularly because most of the new settlers were unwilling to make a living off the land. Consequently, they elected to settle in urban areas such as Port Elizabeth and Grahamstown, where they could secure jobs of the genre with which they were familiar in Europe. By the mid-1800s, what had started off as a tiny refreshment post at the Cape of Good Hope had blossomed into a huge European settlement spanning virtually the entire territory of present-day South Africa.

The discovery of minerals, including diamonds (1867) and gold (1886), contributed enormously to economic development and stimulated further immigration. Concomitant with this was the intensification of inter-group rivalries. Particularly noteworthy in this regard was the increased marginalization and subjugation of members of the indigenous population. The desire for autonomy and self-governance on the part of the Dutch settlers, or the Boers, led to acrimonious relationships and frequent skirmishes between them and the British colonial authorities. A Boer Republic was eventually set up in 1839. However, this republic was short-lived as it ended with the British annexation of Natal in 1843. Hostilities between the two parties, however, continued and culminated in a full-fledged war, the Anglo–Boer War (1899–1902), from which the British emerged victorious. Resulting from this was the creation of the Union of South Africa, which operated under a policy of apartheid until the introduction of majority rule in 1994. Thus, prior to 1994, the country was under the total control of members of the settler population.

Planning, power and race relations in colonial South Africa

South Africa provides an ideal context for examining town planning legislation as a tool for not only consolidating power, but also for privileging some societal groups while marginalizing others. South Africa has always been a contested terrain. In the pre-democracy days, the White powerful minority made indefatigable efforts to devise strategies to dominate and control all other societal groups. The laws and other government actions that were necessary to realize this objective had spatial implications.

Rapid economic development in the colony, which constitutes the present-day Republic of South Africa, resulted in the growth and proliferation of urban centres in the 1880s and 1890s (Parnell and Mabin, 1995). In response, local and national state colonial governments, which until then did little in the urban development sector, decided in favour of exercising more control over private developers. The colonial state saw countless opportunities for profit-making through the subdivision of land for urban use. Hence, local government after local government went to work in an effort to take advantage of the new opportunities. In January 1894, the Orange Free State (OFS) became the first state in southern Africa to create a system whose main purpose was to regulate urban spatial structure by promulgating the 'recognition of townships law' (Parnell and Mabin, 1995). The institution created by this law provided a formal structure for reviewing applications for establishing townships. Additionally, it provided a framework for more formal and coordinated state intervention during the period following the 1899–1902 war. The creation of the new local government structures was arguably the most important measure ever taken in the region to secure the powers necessary 'to recast urban society through the processes of social and civil engineering' (Parnell and Mabin, 1995: 49). Municipalities were also empowered under the Municipal Ordinance of 1903 to regulate building and related activities. With the passage of time, the colonial state found reason to be more assertive in the urban development arena. In urban Transvaal, authorities initiated actions to control many aspects of urban development. Prominent in this regard were actions designed to control the activities of citizens, including Blacks, the Coloureds and Whites, within urban centres. Initially, the responsibility for implementing policies aimed at realizing the colonial government's goals in this regard was given to municipal authorities. However, these authorities proved incapable of executing the task, and before long, the national colonial state decided to take matters into its own hands. Hence, aspects of urban control such as the Native Pass System came to be regulated directly by the central colonial government in Pretoria.

Several institutional reforms with the aim of improving urban governance were initiated in major urban centres within the colony. For instance, in 1903, a commission appointed by the Cape colonial government had recommended that the eight municipalities comprising Cape Town be amalgamated into one unified body. This amalgamation did not, however, take place until subsequent to unification of the four colonies in 1910. The amalgamation effectively transformed the Cape Town Council into a large and powerful city council. The 1920s and 1930s marked a radical departure from orthodoxy, which affected the entire character of towns. As elsewhere in the so-called civilized world, urban planning was viewed as a magical nostrum for all urban ills. This is evidenced by the many pieces of town planning legislation that were promulgated throughout the colony subsequent to the Public Health Act of 1919. Worth noting in this connection are the first major pieces of town planning legislation for the Cape Province (1927), Transvaal (1931) and Natal (1934).

The new attention to urban development contributed to raising the cost of urban land and consequently making it prohibitively costly or out of the reach of the indigenous Africans, and other non-Whites. As a result, only members of the European settler population could afford urban land at that time. Thus, urban land cost would have been quite successful in segregating urban space had formal colonial government laws failed to realize the objective.

The country's Master and Servants Act, and the Pass Laws of 1952, which restricted Black movement; the Native Poll Tax; the Group Area Act reinforcing the racial division of land; the Population Registration Act classifying citizens by race (1950); the Separate Amenities Act, which called for racial segregation on buses and in public places; and perhaps most conspicuous of all, the Land Act of 1913, which reserved 90 per cent of all land in the country for the minority White population, were all pieces of legislation designed to empower European settlers while disenfranchising native Africans.

It was common for European settlers to ally with the colonial powers to ensure the skewing of colonial policies in their favour. For instance, town planning laws and legislation, particularly those concerned with land administration, were deliberately biased in favour of the settlers. This invariably disenfranchised members of the native population. It was not unusual for this latter group of individuals to be herded into reserves, where they were confined and rendered impoverished and landless.

Town planning has always been an activity of the state. In colonial South Africa, it was never designed to serve the needs of members of the indigenous population. After all, the natives were never considered as belonging to the town. Whatever benefit might have accrued to any segment of this population was only ancillary. In other words, members of the indigenous population were hardly, if ever, the direct beneficiaries of any piece of planning legislation. In most cases, planning laws victimized members of the indigenous population. To be sure, this statement would constitute a gross understatement in the context of South Africa.

After all, one can state without equivocation that all pieces of town planning legislation in pre-democratic South Africa were enacted to protect one or another interest of the minority but socio-economically and politically dominant White segment of the population. The Public Health Act of 1919 and the Housing Act of

1920, both of which were aimed at entrenching urban privileges for Whites, are illustrative. Susan Parnell (1993) draws attention to a plethora of other major pieces of planning legislation that were formulated with the aim of ameliorating living conditions for White South Africans at the expense of their Black counterparts. In fact, the institution of racial spatial or territorial segregation in the 1900s was in response to 'the emergence of an unemployed class of unskilled whites in the cities of the Rand' (Parnell, 1993: 473). The manner in which planning legislation was invoked to address the so-called 'poor-White problem' in South Africa says a lot about the importance of planning as an instrument not only of social control but also, and perhaps more importantly, of power. Here, it is necessary to underscore the fact that poor South African Whites, as a proportion of the settler population, were by no means greater than the proportion of poor people in any typical European nation at the time. Thus, one cannot but ponder why colonial authorities deemed it necessary to confront the problem through the establishment of what Parnell (1993: 473) dubs 'a racial aristocracy'. I hasten to note that European settlers in Africa were generally unified in their determination to assert White supremacy even if this unity was hardly matched when it comes to questions of class and ethnicity. Parnell (1993: 473) provides a persuasive explanation, which reinforces the notion of town planning legislation as a tool commonly used by the powerful to consolidate power or create opportunities for members of preferred societal groups:

> Poor whites were most often Afrikaans-speaking unskilled workers who came to urban areas, most commonly those of the Rand, because they were forced from their position as bywoners, or tenant farmers, on the Free State and Transvaal farms by drought and the growth of capitalist agriculture associated with the mineral boom. Unlike the English-speaking working class, which came to South Africa with either mining or craft experience, the Afrikaner proletariat had few marketable urban skills. As basic wages for whites were between three and eight times those of African migrant labourers, the Afrikaner poor therefore found it almost impossible to find jobs on the open market.

However, to see the colonial state's efforts to speedily resolve the 'poor-White problem' simply in terms of an attempt to empower Whites *vis-à-vis* Blacks is to slightly miss the point. To fully appreciate the colonial state's motives in this case warrants a good understanding of the nature and *raison d'être* of the colonial state. The objective of the state, in its original Machiavellian sense, is, as Crawford Young (1994: 19) noted, 'to ensure its own reproduction through time'. State reproduction of itself depends largely on the extent to which it is able to consolidate power and maintain socio-political stability in society. Seen from this vantage point, it becomes clear that efforts on the part of the colonial state in South Africa to resolve the poor-White problem constituted part of the state's attempt to guarantee its own survival. One of the colonial state's main objectives was to impose racial order throughout the territory. The chances of realizing this objective would have been significantly reduced by rising levels of unemployment in White communities. Apart from the direct consequences of high unemployment levels amongst preferred societal groups such as Whites, failure to speedily address the poor-White problem risked transforming poor Whites into allies of other disenfranchised members of society such as the 'Coloureds' and Blacks. Such an alliance stood to pose a formidable threat to the colonial state's authority. This is certainly not a scenario the state in colonial South Africa wanted to deal with. Until later in the history of southern Africa, Whites, and not Blacks, constituted the most viable threat to the stability of the colonial state. In South Africa, German Southwest Africa (now, Namibia) and Southern Rhodesia (today, Zimbabwe), political struggles were rampant within the White communities. In German Southwest Africa, the Germans and Afrikaner settlers were frequently at each other's throats. In Southern Rhodesia, Afrikaner and British settlers were in a constant struggle for power and domination. Furthermore, the British South Africa Company and its White employees and farmers lived in uneasy tension. The struggle for space and/or power among Whites has a long history in South Africa: conflicts between settlers of British origin and Afrikaners; class warfare between white workers and mine executives on the Rand; the constant clamouring for a separate republic on the part of Afrikaners; the battle between White workers and government troops at the Witwatersrand in which 230 persons lost their lives.

The colonial state in South Africa also employed planning legislation to promote its economic interests. In this case, the participation of planners and professionals from fields outside the traditional orbit of town planning had to be enlisted. The role of Dr Charles Porter, Johannesburg's first medical officer, is worth noting in this regard. Porter introduced British town planning ideas in colonial South Africa. In this case, he was instrumental in extending municipal control of urban affairs (Parnell, 1993) and pushed for promulgation of clones of British town planning laws in South Africa. This latter was very important for at least one reason. It played a critical role in creating conditions that contributed to encouraging permanent European immigrant settlement in especially the mining towns in South Africa. Porter was also the architect of extensive anti-slum control measures in Johannesburg. He was quick to remark that these measures were similar to elements of the English Town Planning Act of 1909.

Porter exerted pressure on the Johannesburg City Council to develop 7,000 housing units specifically for members of the native population (Parnell, 1993). This, he argued, was necessary to free the Black slum, the 'Malay', for demolition. Although he favoured racial spatial segregation, he did not harbour the view that was so common amongst colonial authorities that Africans were any less hygienic than 'poor Whites'. He also deviated slightly from the orthodoxy of the time by not strongly advocating the spatial separation of the three racial groups, namely 'White', 'Coloured' and 'Black', that had been constructed by the colonial state in South Africa. Porter was for separate locations for 'Blacks', but not as much in favour of separate locations for 'Coloured and Indian'. He was deterred in fully supporting separate locations for this latter group by the fact that some earlier efforts in this regard had drawn unwanted heat.

Thus, it is safe to conclude that Porter subscribed to the idea of dichotomizing space. In this way, colonial space had simply two categories, the civic and the ethnic, with settlers or civilized occupying the former while the natives occupied the latter. This categorization schema differs slightly from that proposed by Mamdani (1996) in which the natives include only members of the local indigenous population, while settlers include Whites of metropolitan origin, Indians, Arabs, and Africans from other parts of the continent. Rather, my categorization schema considers all Blacks as belonging to the 'native group', and the rest as settlers.

Town and country planning in colonial Zambia

For a long time during the colonial era, active and passive efforts were made to ensure that the African population in urban centres in Zambia remained transient. This changed during the post-World War II era, when deliberate actions were taken to 'stabilize' the country's urban population (Heisler, 1971). Among the conspicuous features of the country's pre-war landscape were the many labour camps clustered in a ribbon-like fashion along the north–south rail line leading from the hinterland through Zimbabwe (then, Southern Rhodesia) to the sea. In 1946, at least 100,000 people resided in these camps (Heisler, 1971: 125). During the waning years of the war and by the time it had ended in 1945, a decision was reached to develop the infrastructure necessary to make the urban population more stable as opposed to transient. The decision was accorded official and institutional muscle in the colonial territory's Ten Year Development Plan (1947–57). Translating the plan into reality entailed, amongst other things, eradicating the camps' mosquito problem, providing pipe-borne water, improving sanitation conditions, building tarmac roads, and provisioning public transport facilities and services based on British and South African models.

Zambia's capital city, Lusaka

The garden city model served as the blueprint for Zambia's capital city, Lusaka. Before delving into details of the plan of Lusaka, a word on the garden city model is in order. The garden city model was not a town planner's invention. Rather, it was the brainchild of an obscure English court stenographer named Ebenezer Howard. The genesis of the garden city movement can be traced back to Howard's 1898 book bearing the title *To-morrow: A Peaceful Path to Real Reform*, better known under the title of the 1902 edition, *Garden Cities of To-morrow*. Although neither novel nor revolutionary (Schaffer, 1982), Howard's proposal advocated self-contained towns measuring about 5,000 acres, containing no more than 32,000 persons and boasting an assortment of quasi-urban institutions. In addition, Howard's model called for an area of dense settlement which should be located at the heart of each tract. A conspicuous feature of the garden city model is its prescription of a population ceiling of 32,000, with 2,000 of these engaged in agricultural activities and residing on the fringes of the residential area, and the remainder (30,000) living in the densely populated central portion of the town. As a self-contained scheme, the model was sensitive to the economic needs of the town. Hence, it provided for industries and factories to be located between the residential area and the agricultural/forestry lands. So located, the industries and factories would be close enough to be easily accessible to labourers but far-removed enough as not to inhibit residential and cognate activities.

Although the garden city model was not a planner's invention, professional planners throughout the Western world numbered amongst its most ardent advocates. Soon after Howard's classic publication, English town planners and policymakers embarked on ambitious projects such as the building of Letchworth and Welwyn. One of their aims was to demonstrate the workability of what they believed would be the model of choice for future towns throughout the world. British town planners had enormous confidence in the garden city model's ability to advertise Britain's creative prowess and supremacy throughout the world, and especially in the British Empire. This confidence was at the root of ostentatiously arrogant pronouncements such as the following, culled by Anthony King (1990: 44) from a 1907 issue of the journal, *Garden City*: 'We want not only England but all parts of the Empire to be covered with Garden Cities'. Five years later in 1912, Captain G. Swinton at the time, Chairman of the London County Council and member of the Planning Committee for New Delhi, stated thus (King, 1990: 44):

I hope that in New Delhi we shall be able to show how those ideas which Mr. Howard put forward ... can be brought in to assist this first Capital created in our time. The fact is that no new city or town should be permissible in these days to which the word 'Garden' cannot be rightly applied.

Robert Home (1990) asserts that the movement to universalize the garden city model assumed an evangelical posture between the World Wars. He bolsters his assertion by invoking the following title of a paper that was presented at the conference of the International Garden Cities and Town Planning Association at Olympia in 1922: 'How to get Garden Cities Established throughout the World' (Home, 1990: 28). If the garden city movement had become an evangelical mission, colonial planners constituted part of the most devoted missionaries. These planners sought every opportunity to demonstrate the viability of the garden city model as well as advertise Britain's supremacy.

The garden city model in practice

When S.D. Adshead at the time, Professor of Town and Country Planning at the University of London, was invited in 1931 to design a plan for the new administrative capital of colonial Northern Rhodesia (now, Zambia), he considered this one more opportunity to translate the garden city model into reality. Adshead was also a consultant, Past President of the Town Planning Institute and more importantly, a staunch advocate of the garden city idea. Collins (1980: 228) draws attention to Adshead's characterization of Garden City planning as 'a form of organized town development which is likely to have a great influence in the development of England in the future, to say nothing of the colonies'.

Before Adshead prepared the original plan for the new administrative headquarters, Lusaka was a small village along the rail line linking the mineral fields in Northern Rhodesia through Southern Rhodesia (present-day Zimbabwe) to the sea. Adshead recommended a site near the village to serve as the site for the new colonial capital to replace Livingstone. Amongst the reasons Adshead advanced to rationalize his choice were the following (Collins, 1980: 228):

- the fact that the site was part of Crown lands;
- the site's proximity to the existing village;
- the site's high altitude, which permits a clear view of, and visibility from, surrounding areas; and
- ease of drainage and suitability for residential use.

Adshead drew up a plan for a capital city that was designed to accommodate 13,000 people: 8,000 Europeans and 5,000 Africans. He did not deem it necessary to provide for economic activities, perhaps because he saw the planned city as having no more than an administrative function to perform. The plan did, however, provide for a shopping and business district, semi-official buildings, clubs and hotels. The colonial Government House was designed to be located about 2.4 to 3.2 km from the Government Centre. The Government House was supposed to be surrounded by the residences of other senior colonial government officials, such as heads of colonial government departments. Adshead envisaged that the town would develop in the direction of the railway line and station with factories developing in the area bordering the railway. The plan also called for a major street of 37m wide, linking the new capital and the old village of Lusaka. A 122m wide avenue was designed to run along the ridge, forming the backbone of the new capital city.

Adshead's plan was never implemented in its entirety thanks to the economic depression that was visited upon the global economy, and resulted in serious negative implications for the African economy from 1931 to 1933. It took four years subsequent to Adshead's plan before units of colonial government departments, including the Governor, were completely relocated from Livingstone to Lusaka. During this time, a number of deficiencies with Adshead's plan were becoming increasingly visible. The task of amending and updating Adshead's plan fell squarely on the shoulders of P.J. Bowling, the colonial government's town planning engineer. Bowling was compelled by the economic and other difficulties at the time to significantly reduce the scope of the original plan in his proposed amendments in 1933. Bowling's plan served as the template from which the new capital was actually developed (Home,

1990). The amended plan provided for 20,000 Europeans but was deafeningly silent about African accommodation except for designating an area as the 'African zone' on the actual blueprint. The plan that was guiding development activities in 1935 when the new capital was officially opened contained seven functional zones as follows (Collins, 1980: 230):

- special business zone, designed to contain offices but not shops;
- special shopping zone, containing shops but not offices;
- general business district, containing shops, offices, etc.;
- light industrial zone;
- heavy industrial zone;
- European residential zone, divided into 'first class', 'second class' and 'third class' sub-zones; and
- African zone.

The post-World War II era witnessed an influx of European settlers in the southern African region. One of the consequences of this in the colony of Northern Rhodesia was a marked increase in the demand for building plots in the urban areas, particularly Lusaka, the new capital. The post-war era also accentuated the need for industrial land in concert with the colonial development needs of the time. Accordingly, the original and revised plan for the city proved woefully inadequate for the growing residential, commercial and industrial needs of the city. Consequently, the services of professional town planners were needed. The colonial government authorities contacted and assigned the task of crafting a new city plan to Bowling, who at this time had established a private consultancy in Johannesburg. Bowling embarked on the project in 1947. The authorities, particularly the Lusaka Management Board, later contacted G.A. Jellicoe, a London-based planning consultant. Jellicoe began working on the plan in 1950. Jellicoe's plan was the first to explicitly pay attention to the city's mobility or transportation needs. However, like its predecessors, the Jellicoe plan provided for European residential facilities while trivializing the housing and cognate needs of members of the indigenous population. In this regard, a residential district of 2,800ha was reserved for 22,000 Europeans. The 'optimum' African population for the city was estimated to be 132,000 and as many as 80,000 Africans were already living at the outskirts or in the African zone within the city (Collins, 1980: 234). For this large number of Africans, the plan set aside only a meagre 1,500ha compared to the 2,800ha set aside for a projected European population.

Town and country planning in Zimbabwe

The land question and country planning

Land has historically been at the heart of most political conflicts, social upheavals and especially inter-racial feuds in Zimbabwe. More importantly for the purpose of the present discussion is the fact that White Zimbabweans have always enjoyed an advantage in access to, and control of land over members of the indigenous population. This invariably accounts for the relatively superior political power, social standing and material wealth of the country's European settler population. In other words, he who controls land controls power in Zimbabwe. Therefore, 'White domination and supremacy' in the region is certainly not due to what some (e.g. Bryce, 1898) have characterized as the superior intelligence, strength and will of Europeans.

Colonial authorities were amply aware of the importance of land as a source of political, economic and social power, and had decided quite early during the colonial era to place inordinate amounts of land in the settler colonies in the hands of Europeans. In Zimbabwe, groups of European settlers initially set out on their own to confiscate land throughout the territory in the late 1800s. In 1890, such efforts had reached significant levels in Mashonaland and other areas in the eastern part of the territory (Kay, 1970: 47). Not only did the colonial authorities acquiesce these blatantly illegal actions of the European settlers, they actually moved to encourage them.

In this regard, the British South Africa (BSA) Company, which had effective authority over Zimbabwe (then, Southern Rhodesia), decided in 1891 to begin selling and leasing large areas of land throughout the country to incoming settlers and companies. The BSA's actions are arguably the first official attempt at land management in the country. However, it must be noted that the actions were at best perfidious as they were meant to ensure the uninhibited access of Whites to land while disenfranchising the Africans. At least in one case, the BSA Company promised 2,420 hectares of farmland to members of the European settler population as a reward for helping defeat the natives during the campaign of 1894 (Kay, 1970: 49). The BSA Company's actions can be understood as part of the efforts designed to empower the settlers while enfeebling the Africans. Doing so was necessary not only as a strategy to bolster the economic power of the European settlers but also as an important element in the broader plan to transform the piece of African territory which at the time was known as Southern Rhodesia into a 'white man's country'.

Official policies were meant to consolidate state power and interests in all spheres in colonial Zimbabwe. Essentially, the laws sought to reinforce racial segregation in the urban and rural areas. To succeed on these fronts, it was necessary to have not only a strong local government system but also an elaborate set of planning laws. Fulfilling the first condition necessitated the enactment of a strong and all-encompassing municipal law. This feat was accomplished with the passage of the Municipal Law of 1897, which was later consolidated in the Urban Councils Act (Wekwete, 1995). The creation of municipal authorities throughout the territory helped fulfil the second condition. As Wekwete (1995: 21) has observed, the establishment of these authorities 'created favourable conditions for effective town planning' for towns 'that were viewed as European towns'. Thus, the prevailing rules 'were meant to create places 'conducive to European living' – upholding high standards of public health and infrastructure development' (Wekwete, 1995: 21).

The year 1930 witnessed two important actions on the part of the colonial government that significantly influenced the spatial structure of Zimbabwe. One such action was the enactment of the Land Apportionment Act of 1930, which allotted almost the entire central portion of the country's plateau to the White colonists (De Blij, 1964: 147). The second had to do with the adoption of the country's first piece of specifically town planning legislation. This maiden piece of town planning legislation, among other things, gave local authorities power to prepare town planning schemes. In 1945, the colonial state enacted the country's landmark Town and Country Planning Act, tailored after Britain's 1932 Act of the same name.

Town planning

Carole Rakodi is one of those on the forefront of efforts to promote understanding of town planning practice in historical and contemporary perspectives in Zimbabwe. In this regard, her brilliant work (Rakodi, 1995) on the evolution of Harare, an inherited settler colonial city, is especially illuminating. The main square, located in the central business district (CBD) of this city originated as a colonial military settlement in 1890. Currently known as the Africa Unity Square, the site was initially named Fort Salisbury after the British Prime Minister of that time. The British colonial authorities who founded Salisbury, which later became Harare, were bent on giving it a purely British identity. Accordingly, they crafted a town plan adhering to a gridiron pattern aligned to the magnetic north. The area earmarked for development, named the Causeway, was parcelled out into large plots or stands along wide straight streets. Another settlement, linked to the main square by a causeway – hence the name of the initial development – was simultaneously set up to the southwest. This second settlement, named Kopje, had the same design as the main square with the exception of the orientation of its streets. The streets were aligned parallel to the hill upon which the settlement stood.

European colonial authorities in Zimbabwe, like their counterparts elsewhere throughout colonial Africa, had a voracious appetite for land. Land, a major factor of production, was especially valued for its ability to empower those who control it. Accordingly, they rushed to conceive, formulate and implement plans that guaranteed them control over huge parcels of land throughout the new colony. In this regard, the British South Africa Company proceeded with alacrity to subdivide and assign to different societal groups, land in and around the newly developed settlements. Some of the land, 8,150 hectares to be more exact, was designated as a town reserve or commonage (Rakodi, 1995: 45). The term 'commonage' is exceedingly misleading as it gives the erroneous impression that everyone had access to this parcel of land. Not so. Rather, capitalist aims stood prominent among the rationales for creating the commonage. Individuals were charged a fee to use parts of this land for a stipulated duration as pasture, or a source of firewood, building materials or other resources. Commercial reasons were also at the root of the decision to carve out 2,548 plots (stands) from the commonage within Salisbury Township between 1891 and 1894.

In addition, the colonial establishment carved out and transferred on the basis of a special grant, an area at the outskirts of Kopje.

For the colonial state, this huge parcel of land around a fledgling colonial city also served important political, economic and social control functions. For one thing, it permitted the colonial state to control the use of urban land. For another thing, it guaranteed the colonial state access to well-located land for the development of critical colonial government facilities and infrastructure. As Rakodi (1995: 45) noted, the commonage served as the site for several colonial government facilities, including industries, an airfield, a police station, prison and military headquarters, agricultural and veterinary research stations, schools and a sports complex. These developments also went a good way in empowering the settlers while correspondingly disenfranchising members of the indigenous population. Here, it is worth noting that,

> Already by 1900, land prices in the CBD had risen to nearly five times those in the surrounding residential area; throughout the township land values often exceeded the value of buildings on the plots.
>
> (Rakodi, 1995: 48)

To put this in perspective, it is important to note that the settlers had access to funding sources, both in their countries of origin and in the formal sector within the colonies, that were out of the reach of members of the indigenous population.

As a means of boosting the power of members of the settler population over their indigenous counterparts, some of the land in and around the commonage was sold to speculators for token sums of as little as £100 (Rakodi, 1995: 45). There were a lot of other efforts on the part of the colonial establishment to disenfranchise members of the indigenous population. Africans were given no room within the town proper. Rather, they were assigned to the least desirable areas at the outskirts of the town. As in other colonies in sub-Saharan Africa, colonial town planning legislation discouraged indigenous Africans from taking up residence in or around colonial towns. Only employed indigenous Africans were allowed in the town. Thus, the Township Ordinance of 1894 dealt with housing exclusively for employed Africans as opposed to all Africans. The Ordinance endowed the local authority with powers to create and manage housing for Africans engaged in the urban formal sector. Despite colonial government legislation and other efforts to discourage African rural-to-urban migration, the population of urban Africans continued to grow and proliferate. Consequently, the colonial state deemed it necessary to control not only this influx, but also the population of Africans once they were in urban areas. Accordingly, they embarked on crafting a number of social control strategies. Resulting from this was the 1906 decision to develop an African township. This development constituted part of the Native Locations Ordinance of that year. The township, nicknamed 'Ma Tank', but formally known as Harare (present-day Mbare), was developed to the south of Kopje. An advisory board, the African Advisory Board, was created in Mbare in 1937. The name of this maiden board in an exclusively African community is deceitful. The board was anything but exclusively African. Rather, the colonial state exerted as much control over this body as it did in other entities within the colony. To guarantee itself uninhibited control over the African Advisory Board, the colonial state decreed the body's membership to include the following (Rakodi, 1995: 48): two members from the indigenous population appointed by the all-White Salisbury Council; four native Africans, elected by residents of the African community; and two representatives of the European settler population (nominated by the colonial state). Thus, all told, the council had eight members, four (50 per cent) of whom represented the colonial state's interests.

Discussion and conclusion

As intimated earlier, the adoption of the garden city model as the town planning model of choice for Lusaka was intended to showcase Britain's supremacy and creative prowess. Thus, we have some idea of why the model was adopted in Lusaka and in other African countries. What remains unknown, however, is why colonial planners decided to make racial segregation part of the plan. To be sure, in its original form as enunciated by Ebenezer Howard, the garden city model did not spatially segregate people based on their race. Why were colonial authorities in southern Africa preoccupied with strategies to exclude Africans from the city? To adequately address this question, it is necessary to understand the importance of town or urban living in the context of Europe from where the colonial planners originated.

Cities were very dominant in the affairs of Ancient Greece. For instance, cities such as Athens, Sparta, Corinth and Thebes had become very powerful, with each bringing under its control the surrounding rural areas by the sixth century. In more modern times, Western civilization came to identify urbanization as synonymous with modernity. Accordingly, cities came to be viewed as part of a world that considered itself urbanized. Prior to the industrial revolution and for a while thereafter, this view was not based on the fact that the majority of the world lived in cities, but on the fact that the city was seen as the preferred residence of the elite and constituted the main frame of reference for philosophers and other intellectuals. In Ancient Greece, the city was even more powerful as it manifested itself as an independent political community, the polis. This attribute of the ancient European city and especially the intellectual, military and economic power it wielded have continued to fascinate philosophers, political thinkers and sociologists alike from the time of Plato, through Aristotle to Max Weber.

Europeans have historically not only recognized power as the fundamental axis of the city, but have also customarily associated urban residency with power. Thus, at one level, efforts on the part of colonial authorities to exclude Africans from the towns can be seen as a means of consolidating the power of European settlers in the colonies. At another level, such efforts can be viewed as a strategy to ensure that only Europeans benefited from the political, social and economic amenities associated with urban living. Collins (1980) identifies and discusses some of the major steps that were taken to exclude Africans from taking up permanent residence in the new capital. For example, as mentioned above, the original plan as well as the subsequent plans that were drawn up for Lusaka failed to make adequate provision for Africans. Note that the original plan by Adshead provided for 8,000 Europeans and 5,000 Africans despite the fact that the plan was for a new site designed to replace the old capital, which had 7,930 Africans and 1,586 Europeans in 1931 (Collins, 1980: 229). The ratio of Africans to Europeans in this case was 5:1. In Lusaka, at about the same time, there were 1,961 Africans and 470 Europeans – a ratio of 4:1. Therefore, a town plan with a provision for 8,000 Europeans would have logically provided for 40,000 Africans as opposed to the paltry 5,000 as per the original plan. As noted above, the 1952 plan was certainly bolder than previous attempts in its effort to empower the Europeans while disenfranchising the Africans.

There were laws such as South Africa's infamous 'Pass Laws', which were specifically designed to keep indigenous Africans out the cities. Even in territories such as Northern Rhodesia, where there were no formal laws banning Africans from the city, a number of other colonial policies effectively kept the natives out of cities. Examples of such policies include those permitting only employed persons to live in the cities. Laws such as these were also effective in discriminating against women and accentuating gender-based socio-economic disparities. This is particularly because only men were usually offered employment in domestic and other support roles in the towns. The employed men were provided limited space (small plots) in the African zone to construct very tiny huts, which could accommodate only one person. When employers provided employee housing, they made sure that only single rooms in dormitory-type facilities or barracks with communal toilets, kitchen and courtyards were provided. Such facilities were by no means conducive for family and contributed to confining families in the villages. To further ensure that Africans did not take up permanent residence in the city, colonial authorities and private European businesses paid very meagre wages – just enough to suffice for no more than the bare necessities of life. This meant that Africans could never save enough to purchase land or other permanent property in town. Thus, the sources of inequality based on formal education, resource endowment, income, employment and access to the levers of power were reinforced once more with regards to residential location.

John Collins (1980) concludes his piece on the Lusaka plan, or what he refers to elsewhere as 'the myth of the garden city' (see Collins, 1969), by drawing attention to town planning's ineffectiveness as a technical tool. For one thing, town planning was not able to prevent the growth and proliferation of unauthorized development in the town. For another thing, the demand for housing was already outstripping that provided under the Urban African Housing Ordinance of 1948 soon after the ordinance went into effect. However, whatever town planning in colonial southern Africa lost as a technical tool, it more than made up for in its role as a social control instrument. In his discourse on 'the social function of urban planning', Manuel Castells (1978: 71) reminds us that town planning has, and has always had, 'a precise social function which is very closely linked to the social and political interests underlying urban power relations'.

On the surface, the Zambian colonial government's effort to make some provision for urban Africans should not be seen, as Heisler (1971: 125) opines, as 'a case of deliberate investment in urban growth; (and/or) a dramatic instance of far-reaching social change'. While Heisler may be right, it would, however, be naïve to construe the gesture as designed to serve the interest of the Africans. Rather, there is evidence to the effect that any benefits to the indigenous population accruing from the developments undertaken by the colonial authorities were only incidental.

To appreciate my perspective, it helps to understand that the imperative to have power 'over' (Dovey, 1999), to control and to dominate the colonized permeated all aspects of the colonial situation. Having said that, it must be recalled that the post-war era was characterized by a change in thinking about the colonial enterprise as a whole. During this period, there was a general retreat from the blatantly inhumane and oppressive treatment of colonial subjects, especially thanks to the work of social reformers who were increasingly lambasting the brutal and exploitative tendencies of capitalism, colonialism and imperialism. Consequently, colonialists deemed it wise to adopt novel and relatively more humane strategies, which paid some attention to the social conditions of the colonized. This explains, at least in part, colonial policies designed to provide social amenities in African districts of urban centres of settled colonial territories such as the Rhodesias and South Africa. Perhaps more importantly, such policies were in line with the retreat from the more overtly domineering colonial strategies that prevailed during the initial phase of the colonial era towards the more subtle and persuasive strategies that had become common currency during the twilight of that epoch. In contrast to the old strategies that were designed to literally beat the colonial subjects into submission, and to force them to do as the colonial authorities desired, the new strategies sought to win the hearts and minds of these subjects.

The public infrastructure and concomitant facilities that were provided in the urban centres of the settled colonies can therefore be seen in this light. The ultimate objective on the part of the colonial authorities in any case was to ensure power and control 'over' the African. It must be remembered that the policies to provide social amenities in the workers' camps did not, and were never intended to, translate into racial residential desegregation policies. Thus, Africans remained concentrated in specific and well-defined geographic areas – workers' camps, reservations, native homelands or African zones – where they continued to be under effective surveillance and control.

Urban segregation was an adjunct to the national segregationist policies that bolstered cheap migrant labour. Policies that classified native Africans as sojourners in town resulted in effectively preventing Africans from competing for urban jobs and other urban opportunities. Also resulting from such segregationist policies was the fact that African workers were kept dependent solely on the subsistence economies of the reserves, rural areas or so-called 'Black Homelands'. Also, restricted access to urban areas meant that native Africans had to depend exclusively on the less vibrant economies of non-urban areas in order to reproduce themselves. Perhaps more importantly, such restrictions served to guarantee capitalist interest a constant supply of cheap semi-skilled African labour for capitalist interest. The 1920s and 1930s in South Africa were marked by mass slum clearance actions that resulted in the removal of native Africans from urban areas under the Native Urban Areas Act. To be sure, there were other victims of these so-called anti-slum policies, including 'coloureds' and poor Whites. In any case, all the victims were powerless members of society. Thus, town planning legislation and laws were, as argued throughout this book, tools employed by the powerful to continuously oppress and subjugate the powerless.

One would be naïve to ignore the fact that social policies such as those designed to 'stabilize the urban population' were meant primarily to protect the interests of the European mining companies. In fact, Collins (1969: 141) makes this point when he states that:

> The copper mining companies wanted their African workforce ... stabilized in order to raise per capita productivity substantially.

Colonial authorities, however, continued to push for excluding Africans from the cities. One colonial official at the time, the Provincial Commissioner of the region occupied by present-day Copperbelt Province, deplored the rural exodus, which he blamed on 'subsistence poverty and Western education'. In a condescending and paternalistic tone, he once argued that rural Africans do not want any social and cultural transformation but just a chance to make some money near their homes (Collins, 1969). Based on this line of thinking, the Commissioner recommended that, 'the fundamental principle must be to encourage the native to develop his own areas and his own form of government by gradually absorbing ideas of civilized government, as he can understand them' (Collins, 1969: 134).

Finally, no meaningful attempt to understand town planning as a tool of power can be deemed complete without an examination of the land question in colonial Africa. Efforts to dispossess Africans of their ancestral lands cannot be seen in isolation from the power ambitions of the colonial enterprise. For one thing, the control of land was tantamount to controlling an important factor of production. If nothing else, this invariably endowed the colonial authorities in particular and the resident European population in general with economic power. Deborah Pellow (1991: 416) alerts us to the fact that the British colonial authorities, for example, employed land in the colonies 'as a means to their political ends by redefining ownership'. Throughout their colonial possessions in Africa, as noted in the case of the settled colonies discussed in this chapter, such redefinition invariably meant setting aside huge tracts of land as property of the Crown – a euphemism for the colonial state. Within the framework of colonialism and imperialism, control of the means of production translated directly into power.

9 Planning ideology and practice in British East Africa

Introduction

Town planning rose to the status of an important activity of the state throughout the world during the inter-war years. In Africa, planning asserted its prominence during the heydays of colonialism. Concomitant with this development was the crystallization of a set of ideas and propositions that bore the hallmarks of an ideology – the planning ideology. This ideology provides an excellent backdrop against which to evaluate colonial town planning projects. To understand the importance of ideology in this context we must first appreciate the nature and function of ideology and its place in the context of planning or public policy. Ideology provides a philosophic basis and helps us to identify the means and ends of town planning.

Donald Foley (1960) analyzed British town planning – the source of inspiration for town planning in British colonial Africa – at about the same time as the sun was setting on the colonial era. His rigorous analysis revealed that British town planning at the time had the following three major ideological goals (Foley, 1960: 216–17):

- to reconcile competing claims for the use of limited land so as to provide a consistent, balanced and orderly arrangement of land uses;
- to provide a good (or better) physical environment [because] a physical environment of such good quality is essential for the promotion of a healthy and civilized life; and
- to provide the physical basis for better urban community life; [and] to strive toward (a) the provision of low-density residential areas, (b) the fostering of local life, and (c) the control of conurban growth.

I interrogate town and country planning in British colonial East Africa to see the extent to which it was informed by this ideology. I posit that colonial town planning ignored these basic ideological goals of town planning in planning decisions or policies affecting Africans but sought to attain them when the 'planned for' constituted members of the European resident population in the colonies. Rather than a tool for ameliorating living conditions, colonial town planning served as an effective tool for marginalizing Africans.

Furthermore, I posit that the colonial state was interested in bolstering its economic and social power through the systematic domination and exploitation of the colonized territories and people. Therefore, all actions by the colonial state were meant to first and foremost protect its own interests. Thus, I view colonial projects in the area of communication and transportation that helped to launch Africa into the 'modern era' as necessary to facilitate colonial governance and the resource exploitation process and secondarily, to pacify the colonized. The main beneficiary in either case was the colonial state and not Africans. I begin in the next segment by describing urbanization and urban planning practice in colonial East Africa.

Urbanization and urban planning in colonial East Africa

The urban experience of East Africa, although not to the same extent as that of West Africa, pre-dated the European colonial era. Towns such as Kilwa and Mombasa (in present-day Kenya), Zanzibar (in present-day Tanzania), and Sofalla and Mogadishu (in present-day Somalia) boasted significant population sizes prior to this era. However, it is important to note that urbanization on a large scale did not occur in the region until later on during the colonial era. Thus, it is safe to assert that most members of the indigenous population of East Africa were unfamiliar with the urban experience prior to the European colonial epoch. Colonialism, the establishment of colonial administrative centres and cognate activities gave birth to a brand of urbanization never before witnessed in the region. Colonial administrative centres eventually constituted the nucleus for the growth and development of the region's largest townships. The Kenyan capital city of Nairobi originated as a major railway hub as well as a colonial administrative town. Nairobi did not exist as an urban centre before the advent of European colonialism in the region. Its origin as an urban centre can be traced to 1899 when the Uganda railway reached Nairobi, and more especially to 1907 when it was designated as the colonial government capital of the British East African Protectorate. Soon after that, the town began to experience rapid growth as it became the location of choice for business people and activities. The fact that the initial site of the town was on swampy land constituted no more that a minor inconvenience. Although this inconvenience was never completely overcome, colonial authorities on the ground (in Kenya) had made two proposals aimed at dealing with it to their superiors in London. The first proposal was to promulgate sanitary and health legislation specifically designed to protect the well-being of members of the resident European population. The second was to relocate the new colonial capital to drier and more elevated ground. Authorities in London approved of the first proposal but rejected the second.

For many East Africans, as suggested above, the urban experience was novel. This explains, at least partially, the antipathy towards urbanization and concomitant lifestyles on the part of most East Africans. However, it is worthwhile noting that there was a significant difference between male and female perceptions of urban life (Lonsdale, 2002). While East African women considered urban centres as an avenue that could afford them the opportunity to ameliorate their socio-economic status and especially escape from the demands of traditional African society, their male counterparts saw these centres as agents of social disorder, decadence and immorality. East African men were particularly concerned with the negative implications of urbanization for traditional gender relations.

Power and urban space in Kenya

Analyses of urban space and dynamics in Kenya have typically focused on the political and economic capital cities, Nairobi and Mombasa, respectively. Consequently, the smaller, but also important, towns such as Isiolo, Embu, Kisumu, Kakamega and Nyeri have been neglected. Yet, because towns such as these started as colonial administrative centres, they constitute ideal objects of analysis in any meaningful effort to understand how the colonial state employed urban centres or spatial policies to consolidate power in colonial Africa.

Amutabi (2005) has deviated from convention by focalizing on one of these lesser-known urban centres in Kenya, namely Isiolo. Isiolo is located in Kenya's geographic centre, in the midst of historically White-owned farms and ranches, and indigenous nomadic grazing fields. Its importance for the purpose of the present discussion is accentuated by the fact that it affords us an opportunity to appreciate the role of the military and strategic spatial location in reinforcing the power of colonial governments.

Isiolo is a typical colonial town, which, due to its centrality, was often proposed as the capital of colonial Kenya. A colonial capital, Isiolo never was. However, it rose to prominence as an important military outpost of the British imperial power. It served as a bulwark against any possible military or other threat from colonial Kenya's northern frontiers. Perhaps more importantly, it served as the site from which British troops monitored the activities of Emperor Menelik II across Kenya's northern border in Ethiopia. The need to monitor Menelik's activities was amplified by the fact that his troops had defeated the Italian military, which was bent on colonizing Ethiopia. Apart from its strategic role, Isiolo gained prominence as a religious centre. In this regard, Isiolo is unique in that it is the only town in East Africa that was divided almost equally between Muslims and Christians. To appreciate the essence of this in the context of the discourse on colonial power, one must first understand the extent to which European colonial powers went to supplant other religions with (Western) Christianity. For instance, one of the most notable accomplishments of the British colonial empire was its success in destroying the largest Islamic empire in the world, the Ottoman Empire.

Isiolo town served as the base of operations for the colonial forces in the Northern Frontier District (NFD) (Amutabi, 2005). In this regard, Isiolo was the base from which the British launched the military campaigns that rescued Ethiopia from

Mussolini's forces and eventually restored the deposed Haile Selassie to power. In addition to playing an important part in bolstering Western religious power in British colonial Kenya, Isiolo was critical in Britain's efforts to cement its position as a leading economic superpower in the twentieth century. Thus, Isiolo's location in the heart of one of Kenya's most resourceful regions was not by chance. Rather, it was borne of the need on the part of the colonial establishment to exploit the Kenyan hinterlands. Furthermore, Isiolo's unique topography and scenic beauty, complete with magnificent parks, afforded the colonial state an opportunity to offer colonial officials in Kenya and neighbouring colonies, ample recreational facilities. Such facilities were badly needed to entice and retain colonial officials in the colonies.

Race, health and power in colonial Kenya

Racial residential segregation occurred in British and French colonies throughout Africa to almost the same degree. What distinguished French racial spatial segregation policies from those of their British counterparts are the pretexts they employed. On the one hand, the French advanced cultural differences between Europeans and 'others', especially Africans, as a compelling rationale to segregate the races. Witness for instance, the reasons that were advanced for racially segregating Brazzaville, Congo; Antananarivo and Antsirabé, Madagascar; Dakar, Senegal; and Conakry, Guinea. On the other hand, the British were inclined to employ reasons associated with protecting the health of Europeans as justification for promulgating and implementing racial spatial segregation policies. The example of Hill Station, Sierra Leone is illustrative.

The notoriety of the Hill Station project, which was developed exclusively for Europeans on the grounds that it would serve as a 'prophylaxis' against malaria, often gives the false impression that it was the only such project ever implemented in colonial Africa. Although the East and Southern African regions have never been menaced by mosquitoes to the extent that colonial West Africa was, colonial authorities in the region found other creative ways to imagine Africans and other non-Europeans as a health threat to Europeans.

The views of colonial officials in this regard were informed by the pseudo-scientific notion of what some have called 'inherently unhygienic races' (Murunga, 2005: 98). According to this dubious concept, some races, ethnicities and classes of people have habits, mannerisms, cultures and traditions that render them inherently predisposed to perpetual unsanitary and unhygienic living conditions. Within the framework of this racist thinking, Western Europeans were imagined as epitomizing 'cleanliness and beauty' while Africans were viewed as 'filthy, depraved and ugly' (Murunga, 2005: 98).

To protect the European population resident in Africa, it followed that a reasonable physical distance had to be established between them and members of the indigenous African population; and between them and other non-Europeans. In colonial Kenya, this objective became the *raison d'être* for the plethora of laws, ordinances and acts that were designed to exclude indigenous Africans and other non-Europeans from the towns. Yet, except in the case of the bubonic plague that wreaked havoc on Nairobi in 1902, there was never any real or potential health threat that necessitated policies designed to deliberately influence spatial order. Thus, efforts to shape spatial order, particularly when this entailed excluding non-Europeans from the urban areas, as the colonial state constantly did, had no real or distinguishable aims. Policies designed to exclude Africans and other non-Europeans from the towns were part of a more elaborate plan on the part of the colonial state to secure urban privileges exclusively for Europeans.

Subsequent to the outbreak of the bubonic plague in Nairobi, the colonial state was under immense pressure from members of the (European) settler population to enact racial residential segregation laws. By this time, the pseudo-scientific community had managed to convince authorities that 'diseases originated from non-European peoples and spread to Europeans' (Murunga, 2005: 102). By 1907, authorities had been persuaded by arguments advocating a segregated residential pattern for Nairobi. However, before long, a debate on how and where to locate Africans and Indians had emerged which became rancorous. At the same time, Nairobi's location, believed by some to be, in and of itself, unhealthy, had become a cause for consternation. Biomedical knowledge of the time placed a high premium on location, more than any other factor, as a deterrent of disease.

In the meantime, the question of how and where to locate indigenous Africans and other non-Whites, particularly Indians, had been, according to the colonial state, resolved. However, as it turned out, and as we shall see, the measures that were adopted became the source of some of Nairobi's socio-economic problems that outlived the colonial era and still exist today. The colonial state decided that 'African natives', as members of the indigenous population were referred to, were not to be granted permanent residence in Nairobi. Rather, they could only be granted temporary residency, and/or could only enter the town to provide services to members of the resident European population at the latter's request. Soon after that, they were to return to the rural areas, where they belonged. Nairobi was exclusively for 'Whites', and so too were other towns throughout the colonial territory.

As Murunga (2005) noted, the question that remained to be tackled had to do with the town's Indian population. This problem had two prongs. The first prong had to do with where to locate the Indian population. The other was politico-administrative in nature and had to do with the role of Indians in governing Nairobi Township. This problem was both critical and urgent as it dealt with who, between the Europeans and Indians, was more apt to implement colonial government policy in the town in particular and the protectorate in general. The British imperial government in Westminster was interested in a colonial government that was most capable of guaranteeing it the fastest returns on its investments, particularly in ensuring that it could recoup the huge amounts it had invested in the Uganda Railway.

The railway project commanded more attention than any other economic or social activity in colonial Kenya at the time. In fact, all other projects, including the spatial organization of Nairobi, assumed a secondary place vis-à-vis the railway project. The railway authorities were particularly interested in the size and topography of the railway terminal in Nairobi. The terminal had to be large and located on flat land. Accordingly, the Chief Engineer of the project, George Whitehouse, chose a location at the foot of a hill for the railway station and camp on 10 May 1899. This site became the railway headquarters, and for a while, constituted the nucleus of Nairobi Township.

The residential quarters for railway employees were located around the railway headquarters. Low-level employees of Indian origin were housed in large dormitory-style housing units located close to the headquarters. The residential facilities of 'railway subordinates' of both European and Indian extraction were located to the west of the railway headquarters. The railway officers lived in spacious facilities located on a hill to the east, and had a commanding view of the railway headquarters and the vicinity.

Some analysts of the spatial structure of early Nairobi (e.g. Murunga, 2005) have suggested that socio-economic status, rather than class, determined this structure. I tend to disagree. Such an interpretation is flawed on two grounds. First, the absence of members of the indigenous African population is conspicuous. As I noted earlier, Africans were never considered as belonging to the city. Thus, according to the colonial state, the struggle for space and power in Nairobi, or any other (colonial) town in Kenya at the time, was between Indians and Europeans. Second, in comparison to the population of Indian settlers, the European settler population in Nairobi in particular and Kenya in general was rather too thin. As many as 31,983 Indian artisans, clerks and labourers had come to the East African Protectorate (EAP) to work on the railway, of whom 6,724 had decided to remain in the territory once the railway was completed in 1901 (Murunga, 2005: 107). British colonial authorities, with Charles Eliot at the forefront, had hoped to recruit Europeans especially from South Africa to permanently settle in the EAP. However, generous offers of fertile areas in Kenya's highlands, freehold land and cheap labour failed to entice any significant number of Europeans to the region. In fact, in 1901, fewer than 30 persons were present at a meeting that was convened to bring together all European settlers in Nairobi in particular and the EAP in general (Murunga, 2005: 109).

The scantiness of the European population hindered, but did not arrest, efforts on the part of Europeans to politically and socio-economically dominate Nairobi. After all, there was no question that they could always count on the colonial state for support in their quest to emerge as the town's dominant group. Two important resolutions were reached at a meeting of European settlers on 4 January 1902 to facilitate attainment of this goal (Murunga, 2005). The first resolution was to reserve the White highlands exclusively for European settlement and the second called on British colonial authorities to halt further immigration of Indians. Meanwhile, colonial government and private efforts to encourage the immigration of Europeans continued. By May 1904, more than 268 Europeans, most of them from South Africa, had taken up permanent residence in EAP, with more than 100 of them living in or around Nairobi. While this was a paltry number in comparison to the population of Indians in the town, it was sizeable enough to seriously threaten and even usurp other competing interests in the town's scarce resources. The fact that a majority of the European settlers were originating from South Africa where the roots of animosity between Europeans and 'others' (particularly Indians and Africans) run deep did not help. Rather, the new settlers arrived with pent-up prejudice and antagonism against Indians and Africans. Again, I hasten to note that Africans were imagined as non-existent within the political economy of urban centres such as Nairobi.

The presence of Africans in Nairobi pre-dated the colonial era in Kenya. Murunga (2005) draws attention to this phenomenon. Amongst the many African settlements that existed in Nairobi before it became the capital of EAP are Kileleshwa, Maskini, Mombasa and Pangani villages. During the construction of the railway, Indians launched a number of markets to cater to the needs of railway workers. One of these markets, which was located in Nairobi, developed into what became popularly known as the Indian Bazaar. Although Indians constituted a majority of the population in this area, it served as the home for many Africans. However, none of the African residential areas commanded as much importance as Pangani. Pangani was initially developed by Kikuyu widows and comprised housing units of local building materials such as clay and grass. Murunga (2005) mentions another factor that amplified Pangani's importance. This has to do with the fact that the village served as a popular destination for Swahili potters and a favourite location for sojourning caravan traders from hinterland locales such as Congo or other coastal regions. With the establishment of Nairobi as a colonial administrative town, the population of Pangani experienced significant gains. However, its character – comprised completely of buildings of local materials – was increasingly becoming a cause for consternation, especially for colonial government officials. Pangani and cognate native African settlements were viewed as aesthetically unappealing elements of the colonial city's physical environment.

Africans came to the attention of colonial officials and European settlers in Nairobi only as a nuisance and eyesores. Otherwise, they were invisible. The tendency to treat urban Africans as invisible was commonplace throughout colonial Africa. This tendency was given concrete form especially by the practice of excluding them from the urban governance process. For instance, there was no African on the Nairobi Township Committee, which under Sub-Commissioner Ainsworth included three Europeans and two Indians. As Sub-Commissioner, Ainsworth had the powers to nominate 'one colonial official, two railway officials and two leading merchants or other residents of Nairobi to the township committee' (Murunga, 2005: 109). That Ainsworth, who was well-known for his liberal proclivities, could not nominate an African to serve on the all-too-important Township Committee is quite telling. It is a manifestation of the shared desire amongst colonial officials, European settlers and other agents of the colonial establishment to render members of the indigenous population powerless.

Excluding members of the indigenous population from towns such as Nairobi and effectively marginalizing them in the EAP had become accepted practice. This notwithstanding, the committee continued to function as any normal municipal institution would. It was responsible for ensuring the rational development of Nairobi. This was a tall order by any standards as Nairobi had taken off on the wrong foot. The centre of the city was flat and low-lying. While this topography might have served well as a railway terminal, it was poor as a site for residential facilities. Not only did the site prove difficult to drain, it was also unhygienic and unhealthy for human habitation. Inhabitants of Nairobi, including those living on higher ground were becoming increasingly fearful of the threat of disease and pestilence.

Reversing this situation and reassuring residents of Nairobi necessitated an adequate understanding of disease etiology. However, all meaningful efforts to promote such understanding were obfuscated by the racial prejudices of European settlers, especially those on the township committee. European settlers rejected any theory that failed to incriminate non-Europeans, or those they referred to as 'inherently unhygienic people' as the vectors of disease. The European settlers, led by the racist Colonists Association, passionately hated the liberal proclivities of Ainsworth and like-minded colonial government officials. The Association used the argument of 'others' as disease vectors to mount pressure on the colonial government. Its main aim was to have the colonial government promulgate legislation capable of buttressing the power of European settlers to control Nairobi. Such control was necessary as a means of ensuring that Europeans monopolized the economic opportunities that the town offered or could potentially offer.

With the passage of time and the acquiescence and tacit support of the colonial state, the European settlers succeeded in gaining complete control of the township committee in particular and affairs within the EAP in general. With this new-found power, the settlers wasted no time in re-apportioning the territory's resources disproportionately to their advantage.

Colonial authorities employed several strategies to marginalize Indians and especially Africans as a means of reinforcing the power of the European settlers. For instance, there was an overt bias in the provisioning of services. Furthermore, no action was taken to arrest the problem of speculation perpetuated by European settlers. The Indian community was infuriated by this development. Consequently, under the leadership of a prominent member of this community, A.M. Jeevanjee, they embarked on what turned out to be a futile effort to bring some measure of equality in resource allocation in colonial Nairobi in particular and the EAP in general. Jeevanjee's efforts were abortive despite his logical and persuasive invocation of the Royal Charter of 1888 that guaranteed the equitable treatment of all subjects under the Crown.

One factor that continued to work in favour of the resident Asian or Indian population in Nairobi was their increasing population. Between 1904 and 1921, this population rose from 2,000 to 9,000 (Campbell, 2005). The rapidly increasing population of Indians served to secure more social, economic and political power for the Indians. As time went by, the leaders of this group continued to put pressure on the Europeans for more equitable representation in local political forums, particularly the

Nairobi City Council. They also demanded public services in their neighbourhoods commensurate with the proportion of the contribution they made through taxes to the municipal government revenue. The struggle between Europeans and Indians for domination and control of Nairobi, particularly the Nairobi Municipal Council, continued and attained its zenith between 1918 and 1933. When Indians failed to have their concerns addressed by the colonial authorities, they decided in favour of boycotting the Municipal Council and withholding rate payments.

There is no evidence suggesting that the European settlers imagined themselves as 'subjects under the Crown' in the same manner as the Indians and members of the native population. Rather, it would appear that the European settlers envisioned a future in which they were to eventually secure independence from the colonial government and perhaps divest themselves subsequently of the control of metropolitan authorities. What the European settlers had in mind was a model akin to that which had prevailed in South Africa whence most of them originated. The lack of numerical superiority on the part of European settlers prevented this from coming to pass in Kenya. Also, because England was desirous of maintaining Kenya under its Crown, she counteracted any attempt to duplicate the South African model in Kenya (Campbell, 2005).

Segregation and spatial order in colonial Nairobi

Although colonial authorities in London had rejected the proposal to segregate Nairobi, their counterparts on the ground did succeed in ensuring that the races were physically separated. In this regard, members of the resident European population were relocated far away from the overcrowded low-lying areas in and around the railway headquarters. This area contained dormitory-like facilities that served as residential quarters for labourers, traders and other individuals of the lowest socio-economic classes.

Nairobi contained three distinct spatially differentiated neighbourhoods corresponding with the three main ethnic groups which the town comprised. This spatial order was maintained by use of a litany of colonial town planning laws, social control measures and policies. Prominent amongst these policies were those that biased the provisioning of utility and public services in favour of, first and foremost, European, and then, Indian neighbourhoods. As for African neighbourhoods, they were usually without the most basic services. For instance, the Nairobi City Council was spending no more than 2 per cent of its revenue on services in African communities and most of it on services in European settlement areas, as late into the colonial era as the 1930s and 1940s (van Zwanenberg and King, 1975).

Within the framework of colonial town planning and other relevant legislation, Africans were permitted in town only as temporary workers who must exit once their services were no longer required. To be sure, there were no areas throughout Nairobi where Africans were permitted to live independent of their employment (Campbell, 2005; Macharia, 1992). Thus, for all practical purposes, Nairobi was as racially segregated as any town in apartheid South Africa. Like apartheid South Africa, Kenya had 'Pass Laws' for Africans, which were first instituted in 1901; and a Vagrancy Ordinance, which was enacted in 1922. Under 'Pass Laws' members of the indigenous population employed in town were issued an official colonial government document permitting them to be within the town limits. Such individuals were required to be in possession of this document once in town and were to present it to the police on demand. Otherwise they would be penalized for violating the law and subsequently forced out of town. The Vagrancy Ordinance authorized the police to arrest anyone (read African) suspected of loitering or anyone having no proof of active employment. Such individuals were to be punished and returned to their (rural) place of origin. One noteworthy accomplishment of these laws is that they effectively criminalize the presence of Africans in towns such as Nairobi.

Another similarity between colonial Kenya and South Africa is the fact that both had native reserves. Kenya's native reserves were designed to be small and overcrowded. This was a strategy aimed at discouraging any meaningful level of agricultural activity. This effectively transformed members of the native population into wage labourers as opposed to self-supporting farmers (Campbell, 2005). Another policy with an identical objective had to do with excessively taxing real property in the reserves. These policies conspired to drive members of the native population from the reserves and other areas to Nairobi and other towns where they could place their services at the disposal of private and colonial government establishments as well as individual European settlers. Thus, despite efforts to keep Africans out of Nairobi, the town's African population continued to grow and proliferate. In fact, Africans consistently outnumbered European settlers in colonial Nairobi by between 60 and 70 per cent (Campbell, 2005).

By 1906, barely one year before the town was formally designated the colonial capital of Kenya, Nairobi boasted seven small spatially and/or socio-economically distinct areas as follows (Campbell, 2005; White et al., 1948): (1) the railway centre; (2) the Indian bazaar; (3) the European business and administration centre; (4) the railway quarters; (5) the Dhobi or Washerman quarter; (6) the European residential suburbs and coffee estates; and (7) the military area (outside town).

With time, the number and proportion of Africans in Nairobi continued to increase. By the 1920s, colonial authorities could not continue to ignore or exclude the African population of this burgeoning colonial town. Consequently, in 1919, a decision was reached to designate some areas 'native areas', exclusively for members of the indigenous population within the town. In 1928 the colonial government established an institutional body, the Office of Municipal Native Affairs, to cater to residents of the 'native areas'.

The resulting residential pattern of Nairobi was decidedly segregated by the 1940s. The town's European population occupied the best and/or most elevated areas in the city. These areas were located to the west and north of the central business district (CBD). The plots in these areas, including those in Karen, Muthaiga and Westlands, were vast, boasted large gardens, and were surrounded by well-groomed trees and lawns. Members of the Indian or Asian population were allotted residentially zoned areas across the Nairobi River from the bazaar and commercial zone, Ngara and Eastleigh. The most socio-economically well-off members of this group occupied more spacious and aerated plots in the Parklands to the north. Africans occupied the least desirable parts of town, including Nairobi's Eastlands, Pumwani, Shauri Moyo and Karikor, east of the railway yards.

Town planning in Tanzania

Unlike the case of colonial Zambia, which comprised only two major racial groups, Africans and Europeans, colonial authorities in Tanzania, like those in Kenya, had to deal with three groups, the Europeans, Asians and Africans. However, as was the case in colonial Zambia, colonial town planners in Tanzania were preoccupied with addressing the needs of the resident European population. Above all else, these planners understood their first responsibility as contributing to the accomplishment of the goals of the colonial enterprise. In this regard, colonial town planners in Tanzania, like their professional colleagues elsewhere, strived to accomplish the following objectives (Doherty, 1979: 13):

- ensure the efficient functioning of towns as centres for the siphoning of rural surplus to the metropolitan countries;
- bolster the role of towns as centres for the collection and trans-shipment of rural produce;
- ensure the efficient functioning of towns as centres of military and civil control;
- boost the capacity of towns as centres for the distribution of imported commodities;
- facilitate the operation of towns as residential enclaves for the colonial authorities and the resident European population; and
- reinforce the functioning of towns as the base for colonial government administration.

Thus, as was the case in colonial Zambia, Africans were invisible as far as town planning was concerned. Colonial authorities in Tanzania, like those in Zambia, believed that Africans did not belong in towns. This belief, in the case of Tanzania and other colonial East African regions, was articulated in the following statement contained in the East Africa Royal Commission Report of 1955 (quoted in Doherty, 1979: 13):

Centres had to be established where they [Europeans] could live free from the dangers of tropical diseases and from which the surrounding countryside could be administered . . . the town was not a suitable habitat for a permanent African society. The towns have therefore been regarded rather as bases for administration and commercial activities than as centres of civilizing influence, still less of permanent African population.

The foregoing pronouncement makes it abundantly clear that were it not for the European population and the essence of a base for colonial administration, there would be no need for town planning legislation. The presence of Africans in towns was never by design. In fact, Africans had no reason to be in towns unless they were there in the capacity of servants or employees of Europeans. In such a case, they were permitted to either live in servant accommodation on European residential property or in the 'African Quarters' outside the township boundaries where building codes were not applicable.

Two important developments in the town and country planning policy arena occurred in 1925. The first of these had to do with according the practice of racial spatial segregation official status. The second was related to the designation of fifty urban centres as 'townships'. Colonial officials responsible for townships were endowed with the power to establish the external borders of their towns and enact legislation dealing with property and other taxes, construction, health, sanitation and hygiene.

Another noteworthy event in the town planning history of Tanzania occurred in 1948 when the first master plan for its colonial capital, Dar es Salaam, was completed by the London-based town planning consultancy of Sir Alexander Gibbs and Partners. I hasten to note that the Dar es Salaam master plan, like others throughout the British colonial empire at the time, drew its inspiration from the British Town Planning Act of 1932. One year later in 1949, Gibbs and Partners, under the supervisory authority of Harry Ford, and later that of his successor, F. Sylvestor White, completed the plan for Mtwara (Alexander, 1983; Njoh, 1999b). This latter plan is particularly noteworthy because of its preoccupation with achieving ideal conditions for human living leading to the institution of building controls that were more stringent than those articulated in the 1932 British Building Ordinance after which it was modelled (Alexander, 1983).

The Gibbs 1948 plan typified town planning practice as it failed to treat residential differentiation as the derivative of societal politico-economic and social forces that it is. Rather, in typical traditional planning fashion, it viewed such differentiation along racial (as opposed to class) lines as a natural phenomenon. Accordingly, it designated three major types of residential zones: 'high', 'medium' and 'low' density. These designations were euphemisms for residential areas for Africans, Asians, and Europeans. Doherty (1979: 15) notes that despite disclaiming the adoption of racial zoning, the plan recommended 'that each area be occupied by Africans, Asians and Europeans, respectively, in order that provision could be made for "the needs of different races"' (quoting Gibbs and Partners, 1948).

To the extent that the size and location of land constitute instruments of power, it is obvious that the 1948 master plan of Dar es Salaam was designed to reinforce existing power structures in that town. As Doherty (1979: 15) notes, the plan made allowance for densities of 8 to 12 houses per acre (including adjacent roads) in the high density or African districts; 24 to 30 inhabitants per plot in the Asian or medium density areas; and one-acre plots of land per housing unit in the 'European Preserves' or low density areas. In terms of location, the so-called European preserves were set on the best areas of the town, with the next tier of desirable space allocated to Asians. The Africans had the worst parcels of land, particularly in terms of location from the town centre and natural conditions.

Tools of power and social controls in colonial Dar es Salaam

A recent major work by Andrew Burton (2005) undertakes a meticulous and thorough analysis of the major strategies that government authorities employed to consolidate power and regulate the entry and mobility of native Africans in the City of Dar es Salaam during the colonial era. Dar es Salaam, the principal city of the former German colony of Tanganyika, did not come under British colonial control until 1919 subsequent to the outcome of World War I. The town's importance during the colonial era was accentuated by the fact that it served as a military base for the better part of the war and became a civil administrative town from October 1918 until the end of the colonial era. Two years subsequent to this, in 1920, the British colonial authorities created a Township Authority under a Township Ordinance of that year.

One goal of the Township Ordinance was racial spatial segregation, with the important objective of guaranteeing access to the most desirable land exclusively to Europeans, while reserving the second most desirable part of the town for Asians and confining native Africans to the least desirable areas. To attain this goal, Dar es Salaam was divided into three principal zones (Burton, 2005). The first of these zones, Zone I, bordered by Versailles Street to the southwest, the Msimbazi Creek to the north, and the Indian Ocean to the east, was designated as a 'European only' district. It contained the main colonial government administrative offices, the botanical gardens, and European residential facilities. Zone II is where members of the local Asian population resided and operated commercial stores. The area was designated as an area exclusively for buildings of so-called modern and permanent materials. It was designed to have a density greater than that of the European district but a lot less than that of Zone III, discussed below. The area extended from Versailles Street in the northeast, to a green area or a 'Howardian open space', measuring 100 yards (90m) in width and a little more than 1.5km long, to the west. The green was in conformity with Ebenezer Howard's prescription of circumscribing residential areas with a belt of undeveloped land. In this case, the green belt was designed to serve as a buffer to protect the Europeans and Indians from communicable diseases that were believed to originate in African communities. European prejudicial and stereotypical images portrayed African communities as unsanitary and disease-infested. Zone III was designed to hold members of the native population. It was located to the west of the green belt afore-described, and included Kariakoo, which originated as the site for the depot of the British army carrier corps – hence, the appellation 'Kariakoo'

– during World War I. Kariakoo was the population centre and heart of colonial Dar es Salaam. The colonial authorities were a lot more relaxed when it came to enforcing building codes in this zone. Thus, buildings of local materials or so-called non-permanent buildings were allowed in this area, which was designed to have a density far greater than that of the Asian district (Zone II).

The composition of the Dar es Salaam Township Authority deserves some attention. Like the Municipal Committee of Nairobi, this municipal institution had no indigenous Africans in its membership ranks. In fact, more than ten years after its establishment – precisely, as of 1931 – as Andrew Burton (2005) noted, Dar es Salaam's Township Authority or Municipal Council comprised the following representatives of the colonial government: the District Officer, the Senior Health Officer, one official from the Public Works Department, the Municipal Secretary, and two nominated unofficial representatives from both the European and Indian communities.

Excluding Africans from the municipal governance process was certainly not the only instance in which this group was marginalized. Rather, Africans were also marginalized with respect to public service delivery and the distribution of other essential resources. In 1920, the Deputy Director of the colonial government Sanitary Services – by no means an advocate for the rights of Africans – noted that the African neighbourhoods had no playgrounds, no public gardens, no public library, and in fact, nothing to occupy the 'native's leisure' (Burton, 2005). More than a decade later in 1932, the situation remained virtually unchanged, as Andrew Burton (2005: 62) noted that Ilala, an African neighbourhood with a population 1,600 at the time, boasted only one public standpipe, one public toilet, and no refuse collection service, no street lighting and no police patrol. Yet, Africans made significant financial contributions to the colonial government revenue. A perusal of the revenue report for Dar es Salaam in 1930 lends credence to this assertion (see Table 9.1).

The Township Authority was notably active in efforts to control the social, economic and political development of Dar es Salaam. The rules that the Authority enacted were specifically sought to accomplish many interrelated goals in this regard. For instance, some of the rules were designed to maintain order in the town. The

Table 9.1   Revenue sources, Dar es Salaam township, 1930

Item	Revenue source	Amount (£)
1	Non-African land rents	3,037
2	Municipal house tax	5,313
3	House tax	7,767
4	African land rents	1,740
5	African house tax	1,051
6	African hut and poll taxes	3,650
7	Fees from traders in Kariakoo Market and municipal eating house	2,210
8	Pombe market fees	720

Source: Compiled from Burton (2005: 62)

areas covered by these rules included sanitation, building permits, trading licenses, public order, commerce, and offences such as loitering, prostitution, and gambling. An important aspect of the rules had as its objective, regulating the presence and mobility of members of the native population in the town.

The official rationale for efforts on the part of British colonial authorities in Tanganyika to exclude Africans from urban centres such as Dar es Salaam was cynical but strangely couched in paternalistic terminology. For instance, in 1926, the Governor of Tanganyika, Donald Cameron, expressed the need to protect the native from exposure to the ills of urban centres. The native in town, Cameron opined, was not only exposed to several temptations, but he was also very likely to take on evil ways (Burton, 2005). The official stance on this issue was uniformly that once away from his rural setting, and unconstrained by customary demands and norms, the native would be hapless under the glare of bright lights, or as part of the dense, heterogeneous, impersonal and often mean-spirited crowd of urban centres. Urban centres were, as the colonial authorities would like us to believe, turgid with vice and iniquity. Hence, as Orde-Brown, at the time the Labour Commissioner, stated in an official colonial government report of 1927, exposing the natives to urban life would cause irreversible damage to them as a people (Burton, 2005).

It would be naïve at best to attribute any merit to the colonial authorities' apparent concern for the welfare of the African. To be sure, the motives for striving to exclude Africans from urban centres were rooted in factors other than those having anything to do with their welfare. Rather, these efforts had to do with the colonial officials' desire to minimize any possible challenge to colonial order and to preserve pseudo-European environmental standards and quality of life in urban centres in the colonies. Arguably most important of all, colonial officials wanted to keep members of the native population as far away as possible from the lever of socio-economic control and the centre of political power. This was necessary for many reasons. Foremost in this connection was the need to prevent the native from gaining any knowledge of the colonial project and/or apparatus. By knowing little or nothing about the colonialist and his tools, the native was hardly in any position to pose a significant threat to colonial political or economic power. Additionally, the need to exclude Africans from urban centres was prompted by a desire on the part of colonial officials to reserve for members of the resident European population and local agents of the colonial enterprise the positive externalities associated with urban development. Principal amongst these positive externalities was an improved quality of life resulting from better access to social amenities and employment opportunities.

As was the case in neighbouring Kenya, colonial authorities in Tanzania considered native Africans as belonging in the rural areas. The colonial law required that any jobless native African in town be arrested and returned to his/her rural village of origin.

During the second half of 1919, at least 4,000 native Africans in Dar es Salaam were arrested for breaking this law. The Africans were eventually returned to the native areas, where they were supposed to seek gainful employment in the agricultural sector.

Apart from laws prohibiting unemployed Africans in town, the colonial government also enacted a number of other draconian laws with far-reaching implications for members of the indigenous population. One of these laws prohibited hawking, public entertainments and ceremonies of mourning in urban areas. These laws constitute a facsimile of those that obtained in French colonies. This point is critical given the erroneous but popular view that the tendency to discriminate on cultural grounds was exclusively an attribute of French colonialism, while only British colonial authorities were inclined to practise racial discrimination. Section 8 of the Township Regulations stipulated six days as the longest period a native African could stay in town. Section 12 endowed the District Officer (DO) with powers to remove unwanted individuals from the town.

Neighbourhood planning ideology and practice

As the colonial era wore on, the British colonial authorities began re-thinking their approach to colonialism. These authorities were especially concerned with employing strategies capable of helping them realize the important goals of the colonial enterprise without alienating the colonized. The 1940s marked a turning point in British colonialism in Africa. The post-war economic recovery was slow. In her fervent effort to improve the situation, Britain embarked on crafting policies that were bolder than ever before in their articulation of how African colonies and their resources could be used to develop the British economy. At the same time, there was growing disillusionment about colonialism in Africa. Africans were increasingly calling for a move towards independence. British colonial authorities found themselves between a rock and a hard place but recognized the need to do something, especially with assuaging the agitating people of Africa. In the area of urban planning and development, the 1940s and 1950s witnessed more conscious attempts at resource procurement. Particularly, colonial officials on the ground in the colonies were requesting more funds from the metropolis to fund important local projects such as the production of master plans and housing. These efforts yielded dividends as the metropolis began paying attention to social projects. In Kenya, a number of projects, including housing and industrial estates, were funded in Nairobi and other cities such as Mombasa.

Thus, colonial authorities were interested not only in 'ruling' but also in 'winning the hearts and minds' of the colonial subjects. Myers refers to these twin goals of the British colonial enterprise as 'rule', that is domination, and 'goodwill' or legitimation. Garth Myers (1998, 2003) analyzes two neighbourhood development projects, one in Nairobi, Kenya and the other in Zanzibar, Tanzania to demonstrate how the British colonial authorities employed this new strategy in practice. I draw on the cases here especially to show how the manipulation of colonial spatial structures constituted a critical means of social control and domination.

The Nairobi (Pumwani) project

The population of Nairobi witnessed an unprecedented surge in its population between 1920 and 1930. During this decade, which marked the first period in Nairobi's history that Africans constituted the majority, the population of the town increased by almost twofold, from 23,000 to 45,000 (Myers, 2003: 197). While colonial authorities were concerned with the rapid rate of population growth in Nairobi, they were even more bothered by the rapidly increasing number of Africans that were taking up permanent residence in the town. At 26,000, the population of Africans in Nairobi already represented nearly 60 per cent of the total in 1931. The colonial authorities had two choices: (1) discourage rural-to-urban migration or (2) devise strategies to control the urban Africans. In either case, they were amply aware of the need to deal with what they saw as a problem at hand – dealing with the Africans who were already living in town. These developments reminded colonial authorities in Kenya – if such a reminder was ever necessary – that urban planning and political control were inextricably intertwined. As Myers (2003) puts it, these authorities came to realize that space and politics were inseparable.

The authorities recognized the spatial nature of the problem – Africans squatting in areas of town they had no business being – and as they contemplated strategies to deal with what they saw as a nagging and increasingly degenerating problem, they were constantly being reminded of the three ambiguous ideologies of colonial spatial planning – capitalism (colonial towns as theatres of accumulation); state control (rule or domination); and utopian idealism (goodwill or 'winning the hearts and minds of the natives'). In the end, the authorities opted in favour of a 'planned location', Pumwani, where a housing estate was developed for Africans in Nairobi in the 1920s. This was the first project of its kind in the region and, as colonial authorities had planned, it was to be the only such project. History was, however, to prove the authorities wrong as more projects of that kind were later developed in urban areas throughout the country.

The project included streets that were laid out in regular rectangular grids, drains, communal toilets and communal washing blocks. The initial residents were Africans who were forcibly relocated from squatter settlements within the town. The settlements constituted not only what authorities considered an 'eyesore' but were increasingly encroaching on European districts and the Downtown area. Pumwani, designated as a native location and being the only residential district for Africans in the city, constituted the logical repository for those forcibly removed from the squatter settlements. The units in Pumwani were deliberately designed to be small – a strategy, I imagine, that was designed to discourage Africans from accommodating members of their traditionally extended families.

That colonial authorities were successful in actually confining Africans in Nairobi to a specific geographic location was itself a remarkable feat. This is because the city was a locale where the production of space constituted a highly contested exercise despite efforts on the part of the colonial state to control it through meticulous plans (e.g. the 1926 Town Plan of Nairobi).

Zanzibar

Unlike the Pumwani project in Nairobi, the Ng'ambo project in Zanzibar originated as an indigenous settlement comprising Swahili people and Africans. The settlement's history goes as far back as the 1850s. The project under examination here was, however, initiated in 1943. Eric Dutton, a career Secretary who had had extensive experience with the British Colonial Service in Africa, masterminded the project (Myers, 1998, 2003). When he played the lead role in the Pumwani project, he was the Chief Secretary of the Colony of Zanzibar during the post-war era. Dutton began the Ng'ambo project by developing a model neighbourhood, which he christened Holmwood, after Frederick Holmwood, a British anti-slavery crusader. Holmwood died in Zanzibar in the nineteenth century.

Dutton's planning experience for the Ng'ambo project included, amongst others, his work on the Lusaka (Zambia) plan and his role as an assistant to Walton Jameson, a student of Patrick Geddes. Dutton worked with Jameson on the plan for Nairobi in 1926. His role on that project is significant, and as Myers (1998, 2003) notes, says much about his views of the power of planning as a tool of goodwill. The plan, although it never saw the light of day, had, upon Dutton's insistence, included proposed tarred roads lined with flowers and trees and flanked by beautiful buildings including museums, art galleries, shops, theatres, public offices and church buildings. But Dutton also recognized the power and versatility of planning as a tool for ameliorating living conditions for all – an important aim of planning. Thus, he was one of the few colonial officials who did not see planning solely as a tool of domination or a tool to effectuate the colonial objective of 'ruling'. He made a clarion call for more and better-built homes for all in the colonies. For Dutton, therefore, urban planning, and especially the production of model neighbourhoods such as the one he championed in Ng'ambo, Zanzibar, was supposed to be part of efforts to promote goodwill and not simply a means toward domination.

The Ng'ambo (Zanzibar) project was spatially segregated along race and class lines. It contained clearly demarcated neighbourhoods or quarters for different racial and social groups. There were separate areas by law for African working class, Arab-Indian elites and others. It must be noted that this distinction did not exist in the indigenous settlement that authorities had destroyed in order to develop the project. The housing units developed as part of the project were standardized both in shape and size. There was a fixed distinction between the 'inside' and the 'outside'. To put this in perspective, it needs to be recalled that the traditional units the new units were designed to replace were single-storey structures containing three to siz bedrooms. Most of the units which were demolished to make way for the new units had 'outbuildings' with kitchen, toilet and storeroom linked to the main structure by fencing. Each of the old units also had an open courtyard. In sharp contrast, the new project contained, as mentioned earlier, standardized units with regular spacing between homes, party fences separating each line of houses from the row behind them.

Among the many amenities provided as part of the new development were schools, health centres, hospitals, clinics and a civic centre. The civic centre played an important role as a venue for disseminating propaganda materials through media such as the cinema. I hasten to note that hundreds of existing homes were demolished in order to develop the project. To construct the civic centre alone, more than 100 homes had to be destroyed.

Discussion and conclusion

A number of features of the Pumwani (Nairobi) and Ng'ambo (Zanzibar) projects are worth re-examining, particularly because of the light such an exercise can shed on the strategies that colonial authorities employed in their bid to attain important goals of the colonial enterprise. Prominent amongst these goals, especially during the inter-war period, were the following three, which I mentioned above in passing (Myers, 1998, 2003):

- capitalism;
- colonial state control; and
- utopian idealism.

The Pumwani project opened its doors in 1922. The choice of its location was anything but haphazard. Rather, the site was strategic in many respects. First, it maximized the space efficiency of the African urban labour force without posing any health or other dangers to the resident European population. Second, and dovetailing into the colonial preoccupation with the health of Europeans, the facility was located downwind and downstream from the closest European district. Furthermore, it was located no less than a good 20–minute walk from the Downtown area. Third, its design made no attempt at disguising its purpose as a tool of dominance and control. Its natural, psychological and political boundaries were lucidly demarcated and emphatically distinguished it from the surrounding areas, and especially from the rest of the city. It was isolated from the Downtown area across the Nairobi River. Entrance to and exit from the facility were limited and could be blocked with facility and on short notice. Finally, the 'planned location system', which 'enframed' Africans and ensured that they were concentrated in specific well-defined geographic locations such as the facility in question was intended to distinguish between who could be inside the town and who had to remain outside it. Most importantly, as a control mechanism, it ensured that once inside, residents were issued specific and detailed codes of conduct. Issuing and enforcing such codes would have been virtually impossible without first 'enframing' the residents of the facility.

Foremost amongst the important features of the Ng'ambo project is the fact that it sought to introduce racial segregation where people were used to living in inter-racial communities. Why? It is easy to answer this question once we appreciate the fact that Britain, and other colonial powers for that matter, lacked the resources to police or effectively control the colonies. Thus, ordered and segregated spaces reinforced their ability to maintain control in the colonies, but success in the area of social control required more than 'ordered segregated spaces'. It necessitated civic education, psychological domination and propaganda campaigns intended to amplify Europe's grandeur and supremacy. The civic centre in Zanzibar was designed to serve as a forum for such education and propaganda campaigns (e.g. through films). Efforts to immortalize the names of European heroes, as Dutton accomplished when he named the first model neighbourhood after Frederick Holmwood, were also designed to accomplish the same goal. Formal classrooms were also popular venues for aggrandizing Europe's achievements as a means of psychologically dominating Africans. Writing back at the pinnacle of the colonial era in Africa, Ralph Bunche (1936) had observed how the French colonial authorities employed formal classrooms as a stage for extolling the accomplishments of Europeans while discounting or paying no attention to those of Africans. Children in French schools in West Africa, Bunche (1936: 32) observed,

> are taught history, among other things, but the history they recite dates back only to the European occupation of their country, with emphasis upon the glory of the French conquest. The merits in the civilization which their ancestors developed, the brilliant military exploits of their great chieftains, such as Behanzin, are withheld from them.

Another important characteristic of the Ng'ambo project, which had direct implications for spatial control and surveillance, was the alignment of the buildings. The buildings were positioned along wide, well-aligned streets that formed a neat grid pattern. This was necessary to ensure easy access by police, health department and, were the need to arise, military personnel.

The stereotypical view of a planner is that he is an expert who serves in an advisory capacity and does not possess the power to effectuate large-scale change in society. This is because the planner is not endowed with the authority to promulgate laws, exercise the power of eminent domain or enter into contracts. Above all, the planner does not possess the funds necessary for plan implementation. This stereotypical image of the planner does not match the planner in colonial Africa. Here, the planner was not only free, but urged, to use expertise – a critical source of power – to assist colonial governments in their bid to attain important overt and covert goals. Accordingly, urban and regional development policies were enacted and implemented to facilitate attainment of praiseworthy goals such as ensuring sound architectural standards and enhancing the functioning of the built environment. At the same time, plans were also crafted to enable colonial powers to accomplish less popular or contemptuous goals, such as maintaining racial residential segregation, controlling the movement and other activities of members of the indigenous population and bolstering the economic power of the colonial government.

In this chapter I have attempted to demonstrate that planning policies with stated, implied or real goals falling under the latter category constituted part of meticulous and complex strategies by colonialists to assert their perceived social, cultural and technological superiority over Africans. Thus, physical policies were not only tools for objectively designing and regulating the form and function of structures, but also for controlling the activities within these structures in particular and human settlements in general. These policies were above all, used as tools of power by European colonial authorities to effectively dominate, coerce, influence, persuade and control Africans.

The colonial state in British East Africa, and throughout Africa for that matter employed spatial or town planning policy to reinforce its power and control over the colonized territories and peoples. Some clarification of the concept of power is warranted here. Borrowing from Kim Dovey (1999), I use the term power at one level to signify control by one group 'over' another. As I demonstrate here, colonial governments artfully crafted town and country planning policies to enable Europeans to gain inordinate power 'over' Africans. At a second level, I use the concept of power to imply 'the ability to define and control circumstances and events' (Dovey, 1999: 9). This was the genre of power that colonial authorities and governments possessed. It was also the type of power with which planning as an activity and as a profession was endowed. Thus, we can talk of 'planning power' or the 'power of planning'.

The importance of striving to understand the overt and covert objectives of colonial physical policies in Africa cannot be overemphasized. This is because the same policies, or slightly modified versions thereof, continue to guide the growth and development of human settlements throughout the continent today.

10 Mining and plantation company towns

Introduction

Among the many imprints which colonialism left on the landscape of Africa is the company town. Company towns comprise residential structures and related facilities such as convenience stores, canteens, recreational facilities and so on, that are provided for workers of large estates, mining and plantation corporations. These facilities, as Porteous (1970) notes, do not constitute part of the means of production for these corporations. To the extent that this is true, we cannot help pondering why colonial corporations were wont to provide these facilities to their workers. To be sure, colonial corporations developed a considerable number of these facilities. Thus, although often ignored, colonial corporations played a significant role in the housing market of the colonies. Why and how did these corporations get involved in the housing market? The answer to this question can be found by examining the motives of colonial corporations in particular and those of colonialism in general. Colonial corporations, including mining and plantation agriculture companies, were interested in maximizing profits and minimizing expenditure. Company towns or employer-provided housing, which houses employees on the mine sites or on the plantations, made this possible. Perhaps more importantly, by directly housing workers, colonial companies were able to better control their workers. This chapter is intended to explore these issues.

Background

Two parallel developments with implications for town planning occurred as a result of growth in the plantation and mining industries in Africa. The first was the requirement that mining and plantation operators provide housing to their employees. In response, most of the operators embarked on directly constructing workers' camps – or what is commonly known as workers' barracks or hostels. The other development had to do with the decision to relocate members of the native population who were occupying fertile or potentially prime agricultural land. Pedler (1975: 107) notes that, 'between 1938 and 1960, many schemes for the settlement of peasants were undertaken in British tropical Africa'.

Company towns in British colonies

Much research has been conducted on planned worker housing in Europe and North America as part of efforts to promote understanding of the role of state policy in shaping spatial structures and social preferences. However, the company town phenomenon in Africa remains woefully under-researched. The collection of works in Daunton's (1983) *House and Home in the Victorian City: Working Class Housing 1850–1914*, and Daunton (ed., 1990), *Housing the Workers: A Comparative History 1850–1914*, exemplify this genre of research. Although the role of employers in housing supply in Africa is yet to receive the attention it deserves from researchers, the continent lays claim to a long history of employers, including the state, quasi-public and private corporations, actively participating in the housing delivery process. This long and rich history dates back to the colonial era, when the colonial state constructed facilities to house colonial civil servants and required that private employers extend similar benefits to their employees. Efforts in this latter regard led to the production of what came to be widely known as worker housing. This brand of housing has been characterized as 'the commonest built element in the colonial landscape' (Home, 2000: 328). More importantly, worker housing was exceedingly effective in shaping built form and social space in especially British colonies.

To further explicate this claim in particular, and to shed further light on the nature and implications for spatial and social development of worker housing in British colonial Africa in general, I draw extensively, but not exclusively, on the work of Robert K. Home (2000) on worker housing in colonial Natal and Northern Rhodesia and my first-hand knowledge of plantation worker camps in Anglophone Cameroon (formerly British Southern Cameroons).

British colonial Natal and Northern Rhodesia

The most notable, and in fact commonest, form of employer-supplied housing in southern Africa was constructed by, and to house employees of, mining corporations. In southern Africa, mining corporations were prepared to provide such facilities with or without a colonial state mandate obligating them to do so. However, it would be foolhardy if not naïve to assume that the willingness on the part of the corporations to provide this necessary service was driven by a concern for the welfare of the workers. To be sure, this willingness was triggered by a need to fortify their control over, and increase the productivity of, mining and plantation workers. Also, mining corporations and colonial authorities in general found the idea of directly supplying housing to their workers appealing because worker housing served as an effective conduit to transfer to Africa European notions of residential organization, form and household unit. Here, I hasten to draw attention to the fact that European social constructions of the household unit differed sharply from those of Africans. For instance, in designing worker housing in South Africa, the state, mining corporations and plantation companies presumed two specific types of households: 'single men, whose families remained in rural areas and married people, who might or might not have the appropriate legal rights to settle in urban areas' (Home, 2000: 328). These two categories were, for all practical purposes, treated as mutually exclusive. Accordingly, two different types of housing, the barrack or hostel and the single-family, regulated by two different types of state regulations, were developed. These two types of housing came to symbolize alternative approaches to controlling and exploiting labour in the British colonies.

Before progressing further along these lines, a brief history of barracks or hostels as a specialized building type is in order. Influenced by the Utilitarian doctrines of Jeremy Bentham and initially designed to house military personnel, barracks were first introduced in Africa in the nineteenth century (Home, 2000). Concomitant with the growth and proliferation of colonies and advancements in the construction industry subsequent to the Napoleonic Wars, barracks rapidly evolved in both scale and design to become a noteworthy feature of the built environment in colonized territories. In the mid-nineteenth century, many British soldiers became ill and died from tropical diseases. This calamity, amongst other things, occasioned a re-examination of British health policies in the colonies. Resulting from this process were activities geared towards improving conditions in barrack housing, especially with a view to responding to the health consequences of the Industrial Revolution.

Also in the mid-nineteenth century, and more worthy of note for the purpose of the present discussion, barracks were adapted to serve the housing needs of formally employed members of the civilian population. In one of the earliest applications in this regard, barracks were used to accommodate millions of indentured workers from India and China. The need for these workers was accentuated by the fact that slavery, which until then constituted the primary source of labour for colonial plantations and mines, had just been abolished.

The role of the colonial state in promoting worker housing, especially barracks, cannot be overstated. In fact, for half a century, beginning in the 1870s through the 1930s, the colonial state in especially British colonial territories in southern Africa advocated this form of housing for non-White workers. In other regions, such as West Africa, which had an insignificant White settler population, the colonial state enacted policies requiring employers to provide housing for their employees. As mentioned earlier, the labour force in mines and plantations throughout the colonies originated mostly from hinterland regions. In the cocoa and coffee plantations of Ghana, the labourers not only originated in northern interior regions of the country but from neighbouring landlocked countries such as Upper Volta (present-day Burkina Faso), Mali and Niger. In the banana, oil palm and rubber plantations of British Southern Cameroons, the labourers were imported from hinterland regions such as the Bamenda highlands. In South Africa, labourers were imported from neighbouring landlocked countries such as Bechuanaland (now Botswana), Northern Rhodesia (present-day Zambia) and Southern Rhodesia (now Zimbabwe) to work in sugar estates, mines, railways and seaports in South Africa.

South Africa, as Home (2000) notes, served as a testing ground for strategies designed to manage migrant labourers. In this regard, Durban played a crucial role in disseminating the barrack form of housing, which served initially to accommodate indentured Indian labourers working in sugar plantations and the Durban seaport. This housing form was later introduced in Natal and from there it was exported to other colonies within the British Empire. The Natal barrack form was later adopted in the closed mining compounds of Kimberly in the late 1880s and replicated throughout colonial southern and central Africa. As Home (2000) noted, the terminology later evolved from politically incorrect and pejorative terms such as 'barrack' and 'coolies' to the more neutral term 'hostel' in reference to worker housing.

We note that for a long time into the colonial era, employers played a critical role in the housing market. However, the need to minimize expenditures led them to provide hardly more than a dormitory room for workers to retire to in the evening. Conditions in worker housing were, to say the very least, unbearable. Home (2000) noted that Indian indentured workers returning home around 1870, after a decade in worker housing in Natal, recounted endless tales of the inhumane living conditions they had to contend with. Knowledge of these tales led the British colonial administration to request that commissions of inquiry be set up to investigate conditions in worker housing throughout the colonies. The commission assigned to investigate conditions in Natal, known as the Coolie Commission, noted the deplorable state of housing and recommended a number of remedial actions. Prominent in this connection was the recommendation that more women and families be imported as a means of addressing social problems stemming from the dearth of women in workers' communities. Another notable recommendation of the commission had to do with minimum space standards for housing units. Minimum standards of 50 square feet for one adult, and 120 square feet for three men, or one man and one woman with two or less children were prescribed. Adherence to these statutory requirements was supposed to be overseen by central authorities at the Colonial Office in London. This piece of colonial legislation inspired the adoption of standard room sizes of 100 or 120 square feet in the barracks.

Later on in 1887, another commission, the Wragg Commission, also charged with investigating conditions in worker housing, identified three distinguished types of housing (Home, 2000: 336): barracks containing permanent units of concrete walls and corrugated iron sheet roofs (as in the case of housing for the Durban Corporation and also a number of estates in other colonies), barracks containing units of corrugated iron sheets, and barracks containing grass huts. The Wragg Commission, like the Coolie Commission before it, noted the deplorable conditions in worker housing in the colonies. This commission was particularly critical of problems relating to siting, sanitation and overcrowding.

The reports of these commissions led to a number of policy changes such as the minimum space requirements noted above. Paradoxically, policies such as the one that encouraged workers and their families to permanently or semi-permanently live in the barracks and other workers' residential areas, created social problems of their own. For instance, the White residents of Durban were especially disdainful of, and voiced their opposition against, any effort to have African natives live permanently in the urban areas. This opposition led to the promulgation of blatantly racist pieces of legislation, such as that of 1869, which sought to punish 'idle and disorderly vagrants' within the Colony of Natal. This piece of legislation was also responsible for creating 'vagrant houses'. These facilities, which could easily pass for jails, were set up to harbour unemployed Africans in the urban areas.

In the context of colonial housing policy in Africa, South Africa is arguably best known as the point of origin for state-sanctioned actions geared towards racially and/or socio-economically segregating residential areas. In this way, the present discussion cannot be deemed exhaustive without mention of actions on the part of the colonial government in South Africa to discourage native Africans from settling permanently in urban areas. Under the notorious Durban system, the colonial state formulated and implemented policies designed to generate tax revenues from the sale of beer. The funds from this source were used to defray the cost of worker housing and social amenities for Africans. This effectively freed White rate payers of any financial obligation. It is important to note that the Durban system later served as the model for urban control throughout British colonial Africa (Home, 2000).

This type of housing possessed a number of unique features. The first is that they were designed to serve only single men. The second is that they were meant to provide not permanent, but rather, temporary accommodation for workers. This was in concert with British colonial location policy that had set aside towns for Europeans while relegating native Africans to rural areas. It followed, as King (in Cherry, 1980: 208) noted, that no African was allowed in town unless he was there to serve a European. Even then, there was a bias in favour of male, as opposed to female, workers.

A third distinctive feature of barracks was their close proximity to the workplace (mines, plantations, etc.). In most cases, these units were set in the heart of the workplace as in the case of plantation worker housing. This feature is inextricably tied to the colonialists' need to control and dominate the colonized. Perhaps more importantly, the feature was based on the belief that the productivity of workers depended on the extent to which the workers were controlled and supervised. Accordingly, barracks or hostels came to symbolize a housing strategy whose main objective was to control labour in the colonies.

A fourth unique characteristic of barracks and/or hostels relates to their size and shape. A vivid picture of these two attributes as they relate to colonial southern Africa has been painted by Robert Home (2000: 328–9). Barrack and/or hostel units are typically long, single-storey structures. In a few cases, especially in urban areas, they may rise to two or more storeys. The internal space of such a unit is often arranged as a single or double row of standard sized rooms, each measuring 3m × 3m. A few measured 3m × 4.5m. The walls were usually of sawn timber, stone, brick or concrete blocks. The typical roofing material for these structures was corrugated aluminium sheets (zinc), while the floors were of either plank or beaten earth. The units had no ceilings, which meant that their interiors attained oven-heat levels under the excruciatingly hot temperatures typical of the tropics. Each building was furnished with a veranda or corridor that ran its entire length. The units were all provided with shuttered opening for windows. Bed spaces were usually formed out of rough concrete cast in situ. Kitchen, washing and toilet facilities were respectively of the communal genre and were usually located in separate detached facilities.

The buildings were usually poorly finished and woefully devoid of aesthetic appeal. Together, the buildings were drab, repetitive and bore a striking resemblance to gigantic 'match boxes' juxtaposed around a barren courtyard. This confirms a central hypothesis of this book, namely that private companies contributed immensely to shaping the structure of the built environment in colonial Africa. By extension, therefore, private companies such as mining and plantation agricultural corporations contributed to developments in municipal government and town planning during the colonial era on the continent.

Railways and urban municipal governance

The contribution captioned 'Urban Local Authorities' by Alan Greenwood and John Howell to the collection on *Administration in Zambia* edited by William Tordoff (1980) provides essential material that sheds light on how the colonial state and private companies conspired to shape the urban landscape in British colonial Africa.

Zambia, at the time Northern Rhodesia, is one of the British colonial territories in which private companies were very active in infrastructure development, municipal and regional administration. In 1889, the British imperial government granted a Royal Charter to a private entity, the British South Africa Company (BSA Co.) to extend the main north–south rail line northwards across the River Zambezi. In the course of executing this task, the engineers created sidings, about ten miles apart, along the railway line. Many of these sidings eventually became the site for new human settlements. Initially, the settlements served exclusively as homes for railway workers. Eventually, the settlements developed into small, medium and large towns in need of municipal governments. The Charter assigned the responsibility for municipal governance to the BSA Company. The BSA Company was required to, amongst other things, promote 'good government' by formulating and implementing appropriate urban development regulations. During the course of the ensuing five years (1889–94), the BSA Company introduced the notion of local government and concomitantly established a Village Management Board (VMB), whose main responsibility was to formulate and implement urban development regulations. Resulting from this exercise was a set of regulatory measures, most of which had to do with environmental health, streets and buildings. The VMBs remained operational until 1924 when the British Government subsumed Northern Rhodesia (present-day Zambia) as a protectorate under its colonial empire. Concomitant with the extension of protectorate status was the establishment of a plethora of colonial government institutions, including the Office of Governor, legislative and executive councils, and so on, in Northern Rhodesia. One of the earliest and best-known achievements of the new colonial government was the enactment of two major ordinances, namely the Municipal Corporations Ordinance (1927) and the Townships Ordinance (1928). Resulting from the former were Livingstone (1928) and Ndola, the administrative centre of the Copperbelt area (1932), Northern Rhodesia's first two, and for more than two decades only, municipal corporations.

The institutional reform initiatives that produced these ordinances and consequently established municipal corporations in Zambia can be better appreciated in light of the colonial state's efforts to consolidate power and effectuate social control in that colony. The doctrine of 'indirect rule', a well-known cost-effective social and political control strategy in British colonial Africa, was introduced in Zambia in 1924. This strategy found utility in the rural areas, while the 1927 and 1928 Ordinances gave urban municipal councils wide discretionary powers to control urban-based social, political and economic activities. For instance, as Greenwood and Howell (1980: 164) noted,

> The Municipal Corporations Ordinance allowed councils to establish markets, parks, slaughterhouses, sewerage systems, refuse disposal services, and water and electricity supplies.

The creation of specific areas designated for each of the foregoing activities went a long way in facilitating the colonial state's efforts to monitor, tax and effectuate control over transactions in the public sphere. In this regard, the councils were specifically charged with the responsibility of implementing colonial state laws relating to the ownership or possession of firearms, trespassing, burglary, prostitution and other social transgressions. To help fund these and other colonial state activities, each municipal council was permitted to levy a tax on all real property and land improvements within its jurisdiction.

Mining and mine townships

The growth and proliferation of mining activities particularly in British colonial southern Africa, affected not only the spatial structure, but also posed a unique challenge to municipal governance in the region. The challenge was unique because the mining areas fell outside the administrative jurisdiction of established Municipal Corporations and Townships Ordinances. Yet, as Greenwood and Howell (1980) noted in the case of Zambia, mining companies were required, under colonial government legislation, to provide housing for their employees. This housing and the attendant services required a novel and effective municipal governance structure. In Zambia, colonial government authorities responded to this inescapable need by enacting, in 1933, the Mine Township Ordinance (Greenwood and Howell, 1980). This ordinance resulted in the creation of a municipal governance structure that bore a striking resemblance to those of municipal corporations or townships. For instance, like municipalities, mine townships had boards. Mine Township Boards were endowed with powers to maintain and implement colonial state laws relating to hygiene and public health, and social and economic development. Particularly, Mine Township Boards were required to preserve good order and facilitate attainment of the broader objectives of the colonial project by ensuring the welfare of mine employees. This latter was necessary to guarantee the reproduction of labour.

Plantation housing

The case of British Southern Cameroons

To fully understand plantation worker housing in colonial Africa, it is vital to examine the origins of colonial plantation agriculture. The case of British Southern Cameroons is particularly interesting because of the territory's checkered colonial history. The Germans were the first European powers to establish colonial control over the territory comprising present-day Cameroon. As far back as 1882, Bismarck, the German Chancellor at the time, had contemplated extending imperial protection to the territory. It was, however, not until two years later on 12 July 1884 that Nachtigal, a representative of the German government, signed the treaty that sealed the formal annexation of the territory – what at the time Germans called Kamerun. Elsewhere (Njoh, 2003: 76), I observed that,

> Apart from a desire on the part of the German colonial state to protect commercial, hence capitalist interests in the territory, the signing of the treaty was predicated on one other important consideration, namely the plantation agricultural potential of the volcanic soils at the foot of Mount Cameroon.

To meet its objectives in this regards, and subsequent to signing the treaty, the Germans moved speedily to convert almost all the land at the foot of the mountain into German Crown land. Most of this land was subsequently transferred to private German farmers, who proceeded to establish plantations thereupon. Authorities on the ground in the colonial territory were specifically instructed to acquire as much land as possible. In fact, an official letter dated 6 May 1884 from Adolf Woerman, a high-level official in the German imperial government, contained the following instructions to the colonial authorities in Kamerun: 'by all means, get the cession of very extensive lands as private property – especially those suitable for plantations' (quoted in Njoh, 2003: 76). Furthermore, the letter underscored the importance of converting most of the 'native' lands to German imperial government land.

Of particular importance for the purpose of the present discussion is the fact that efforts to dispossess the natives of their land comprised a number of perfidious and repugnant schemes. Paramount amongst these schemes is the one that was concocted by von Puttkamer, Governor of Kamerun at the time. Von Puttkamer recommended that the native population, namely the Bakweri, be re-located to small reservation enclaves, or what they called 'native reserves'. According to one account (AUF website), von Puttkamer's scheme succeeded in 'concentrating the Bakweri into inaccessible, disease infested and inhospitable Native Reserves'. Accordingly, 'hundreds of thousands of Bakweri were forcefully displaced from their homes and herded off onto strange and unfriendly patches of lands around the plantations' (AUF website). While it is highly unlikely that the number of indigenes forced into the 'native reservations' was actually in the 'hundreds of thousands' – as the Bakweri have always been a small group – there is no doubt that the policy resulted in freeing up inordinate amounts of land for the Germans. According to the colonial governor, the move was effective in paving the path for German farmers interested in carrying out plantation agriculture in the territory. All told, the Germans confiscated approximately 400 square miles of the most cultivatable land at the foot of Mount Cameroon, and more than 200,000 acres of the fertile lands throughout Victoria Division (present-day Fako Division).

In 1885, barely one year after the treaty annexing Kamerun was signed, plantation agriculture was formally established in the territory. Two major German agricultural firms, namely Woerman and Jantzen und Thormalen, constituted the first plantation companies in the territory. The success of these companies depended largely on their ability to recruit and retain workers. With the immediate native population, the Bakweri, already alienated by the draconian land confiscation strategies of the German colonial authorities, the companies were compelled to venture into the hinterland to recruit workers. It was, however, not enough to simply recruit and transport workers to coastal plantations. The plantation operators needed to ensure retention of the workers. It is effectively the need to address this latter concern that led to efforts to embark on the construction of housing for plantation workers. As time went by, the plantations grew and began encroaching on the native reserves. This, and especially the fact that more people were increasingly immigrating from the hinterland, led to problems of housing shortages in the coastal region.

How the German imperial government opted to deal with the growing problem of landlessness resulting from the proliferation of plantation agricultural activities in Tiko is worthy of note. Located at the foot of Mount Cameroon and on the coast of the Atlantic Ocean in present-day Cameroon, Tiko has grown to become a cosmopolitan town. Prior to the colonial era, Tiko was known as Keka. It emerged as an important agricultural town as far back as 1892. Earlier that year, German colonial authorities had determined that Tiko was suitable for plantation agriculture (Njoh, 2002: 409). This led the authorities to craft plans designed to procure as much of the land as possible for purposes of agricultural plantation development. An initial step in this connection entailed conducting a census of the area. Conducted in 1908, the census revealed that Tiko contained 50 male adults. Three years later in 1911, the German colonial government embarked on actions designed to actually execute its perfidious plan to place under its control every centimetre of land in the region. One of the first actions in this regard included allotting 300 hectares to the adult male inhabitants of Tiko on the basis of 6 hectares per person or household. The rest of the land in the region was declared 'unoccupied' and converted into German Crown Land. This land was in turn placed at the disposal of German plantation corporations. A number of private German plantations, including the African Fruit Company and Holforth Company, took advantage of the new opportunities and embarked on establishing plantations in the area. By 1912, the agricultural plantation corporations had planted bananas on as much as 2,000 hectares of land in the area. Bananas, a cash crop, had been introduced in the territory only five years earlier in 1907.

A number of consequential changes occurred subsequent to World War I. Before the outbreak of the war, as stated above, Germany controlled the entire Kamerun. Most of the land around Mount Cameroon resided in the hands of German companies and individuals involved in large-scale plantation agriculture. By some accounts, as much as 264,000 acres of land in Victoria Division (now Fako Division) and Kumba Division (now Meme Division and Ndian Division) were controlled by German farmers and held as German Crown Land (Njoh, 2003: 82). Once the war came to an end, the vanquished Germans were obligated to relinquish their claims to all the territory they occupied throughout Africa. The lands throughout Kamerun, like others elsewhere in erstwhile German colonies, were mandated by the League of Nations to the Allied powers. Kamerun was divided into two unequal parts of one-fifth and four-fifths, with the smaller portion of the territory being placed under the auspices of Britain. Britain decided, for reasons of administrative efficiency, to administer the territory through Nigeria, which was already an established British colony next-door.

The British imperial power was interested in the plantation left behind by the departing German colonial authorities only to the extent that they could find private companies and/or individuals in Britain or other Allied countries prepared and willing to take over their management and operation. As it turned out, they had no luck in this connection. Initial efforts to dispose of the plantations consisted mainly of an auction that was held in London in October 1922. The auction failed to register any significant positive results, perhaps because only entities from Allied countries were eligible to bid. At the same time, the need to dispose of the plantations, which had become a burden to the British colonial authorities, grew increasingly urgent. In November 1924, two years after the first unsuccessful attempt to sell the plantations, British colonial authorities decided to organize another auction. This second attempt differed significantly from the previous effort, particularly because it accepted bids from German business entities. The organizers of the auction were right in assuming that this change could increase the chances for success. In the end, most of the plantations were sold to their former owners. Thus, after World War I, German plantation companies continued to operate in Allied-controlled British Southern Cameroons.

One of the first actions with implications for housing in particular, and spatial development in general, taken by the British colonial administration was to commission a study of living conditions in the plantations and adjoining areas. Among the many revelations of the study was the fact that 34 Bakweri villages were confined in 'native reserves' that were engulfed by plantations belonging to West African Plantations Victoria (WAPV). Another important revelation of the study was recorded in a report to the League of Nations in 1922. Speaking of living conditions of the Bakweri subsequent to the establishment of agricultural plantations in the area, the report stated thus (AUF website),

> uprooted from the homes of their forebears, settled willy-nilly on strange soil, deprived of their old-time hunting grounds, and fishing rights, the Bakweri have retained but a small sense of tribal unity or cohesion.

The colonial government's acknowledgement of the appalling conditions in and around the plantations notwithstanding, no effort was made to curb the excesses of the plantation companies, which were bent on minimizing overhead costs and maximizing profits. One way by which this objective was attained was to provide workers with only the basic minimum social services, including housing. Also, the plantation companies continued to do everything to limit the activities of the native population exclusively to the 'native reserves' even when members of this population had numerically outgrown space within the reserves.

Occasionally, population pressures caused some members of the native population to relocate to areas beyond the 'native reservations'. For their part, plantation companies branded anyone living beyond the limits of reserves a 'squatter' and moved swiftly to evict such an individual. For instance, in 1926 the WAPV issued eviction notices to a group of individuals from the native (Bakweri) population living on what the company alleged to be its parcel of land.

Thus, by the time World War II broke out in 1939, the Germans were paradoxically in control of the agricultural plantations in British Southern Cameroons. At the end of the war in 1945, colonial authorities had made a number of consequential resolutions. Prominent in this regard is the decision forbidding the return of the plantations to German entities, be they private or public. Thus, for the remainder of the colonial epoch in the territory, all the plantations were transformed into the property of the British colonial state and vested in the Governor. A colonial government ordinance, Ordinance Number 39 of 1946, established the Cameroons Development Corporation (CDC) to take over control and operation of all ex-German plantations. The CDC formally assumed this responsibility on 1 January 1947.

Plantation workers' housing in British Southern Cameroons

Plantation operators in British Southern Cameroon, like their counterparts elsewhere in colonial Africa, found the idea of directly housing their workers appealing. As mentioned earlier, this idea gained the favour of plantation operators particularly because it served as a viable element in efforts to subjugate and dominate plantation workers. If nothing else, such housing ensured that employees remained under the watchful eyes of their employers not only during working hours but around the clock. Workers' camps came complete with facilities such as company stores, First Aid Post or dispensaries, recreational grounds, clubhouses (for senior staff), schools and central hospitals. This effectively nullified the need for workers to travel beyond the limits of the camps.

Plantation workers' camps bore a striking resemblance to military barracks in form and function. Workers were awoken by the loud sound of a bell at 5:00 am. Another sound of the bell called workers to assemble for roll call and be hauled to the fields or plantations in tippers, cargo trucks and farm-tractor-drawn trailers at 5:30 am. Work began on the fields at 6:00 am and ended at 5:30 pm (with a brief thirty–minute break at noon) every weekday and from 5:30 am to noon every Saturday.

The Cameroons Development Corporation (CDC) operated five categories of worker housing, corresponding with the following categories of workers:

- labourer housing, comprising multi-units of one room, one kitchen with communal toilet facilities;
- clerical staff and senior labourer housing, comprising single, duplex, triplex and sometimes multi-units of one bedroom, one living room, one kitchen and communal toilet facilities;
- intermediate staff housing, comprising self-contained duplex units of one bedroom;
- junior staff housing, comprising modestly furnished self-contained two-bedroom bungalows, each of which was equipped with a small garden; and
- senior staff housing, comprising well-furnished three and sometimes four-bedroom bungalows, each of which was equipped with a bar, large kitchen, a two-car garage, servants quarters, a large garden and an orchard as well as lawns that were catered for by company labourers.

The present discussion of plantation workers' housing is limited to the first and second categories. However, it is noteworthy that the senior staff housing, which was always located in isolated areas that were far-removed from areas housing other classes of employees, was almost exclusively for European employees of the corporation. The clubhouses mentioned earlier constituted part of the senior staff quarters. The intermediate and junior staff quarters were designed to house educated native (usually graduates of secondary grammar and technical schools) employees.

Plantation camps were peculiar for many reasons. For example, in contrast to the assorted housing units in the surrounding environment, housing units in plantation camps were not only of identical design, but were also constructed of modern materials such as cement blocks (for the walls), steel (for the door and window shutters and frames) and aluminium sheets (for the roofs). The camps in some cases assumed the name of the native area in which they were located. Mondoni, Esuke, Moliwe and Bota exemplify camps in this category. In a number of cases, the camps were named after the plantation in which they were located (e.g. Middle Farms). Some of the camps were named after the construction company which built them (e.g. Upper Costains and Middle Costains, named after the British construction company, Costains). The names of some of the camps reflect very little or no creativity on the part of the christeners. Foremost in this regard are the camps that were simply assigned a number for a name (e.g. Camp I, Camp II, Camp III, and so on).

Conclusion

Although company towns in Africa do not qualify as what Foucault (1977) characterized as 'the Great Confinement' (Markus, 1993), they certainly constitute tools of 'spatial coercion' (Dovey, 1999). By 'the Great Confinement', Foucault was referring to structures designed as part of a system to confine those that authorities considered a threat to social order. Although company towns were not designed for this purpose, they certainly had as a primary objective 'making people work', which was also an important objective of the system Foucault had in mind when he coined the phrase. As I noted above, the lives of residents in workers' barracks in colonial Africa were regimented in every sense of that word. They were always awoken by the sound of a bell in the morning to go for roll call and then either marched or freighted in trucks to work. At the end of the workday, they were transported back to the camp, which was often a considerable distance from their villages or regions of origin. The workers' barracks contained single-rooms for men without room for their families – akin to life in a prison. Thus, while there were no whips, no chains and no compulsion involved, workers' camps were exceedingly successful in manipulating workers to do as the employers desired. In essence, the camps simply coerced the workers to work.

11 Planning, public health and spatial structures

Introduction

In Europe, the professions of town planning and public health emerged in response to a common problem – the health consequences of the industrial revolution. Efforts in both professions to wrestle with cholera and other epidemics in Europe from 1830 to 1880 is further testament to their shared goals. During this period, planning focused intensely on functionality and hierarchical ordering of land use through zoning. The overriding goal here was to regulate the type of contact occurring between people and land use activities. The European colonial era began in Africa just about when urban planners were becoming increasingly conscious of the health implications of urban development. However, the health challenges faced by planners and public health authorities on the continent were unique and bore little if any resemblance to what their counterparts in Europe were used to. In Africa, the urgent need to extract profit – an important objective of the colonial enterprise – necessitated the subjection of Africans to dangerous conditions as porters, cultivators, miners, and so on, for extended periods, in regions far removed from their families and kin. This, amongst other things, exposed Africans to new diseases and environments. Similarly, Europeans who were present in Africa as members of the colonial civil service, soldiers, traders, missionaries and/or explorers were exposed to health, environmental and other problems previously unknown to them. Paradoxically, the health and cognate authorities of the time appeared oblivious in several instances to the stark contrast between public health problems in Africa and those that characterized Europe at the time. Otherwise, it is difficult to explain the tendency on the part of these authorities to transfer without alteration, to Africa, health protection strategies (e.g. building codes) that had been crafted for use in Europe. However, I would be remiss if I failed to mention that colonial authorities, especially in Britain, went to great lengths to craft health protection policies specifically tailored to conditions that were prevalent in the tropics at the time. These policies, a number of which are discussed in greater detail below, were based on the findings of research at academic institutions such as the Liverpool and London Schools of Tropical Medicine. These institutions had been created to specifically work towards curtailing the toll on Europeans exposed to the insalubrious conditions characteristic of tropical colonies.

There is hardly any paucity of knowledge on the process by which the transfer of planning knowledge from Europe to Africa occurred (see e.g. Njoh, 2002; Chokor, 1993; Simon, 1992; King, 1990, 1976; Kanyeihamba, 1980; Abu-Lughod, 1965). Also, there is a growing body of literature on the implications for development of employing European town planning schemes in Africa (see e.g. Njoh, 1999b, 2003; King, 1990). However, with a few exceptions (e.g. Frenkel and Western, 1988; Curtin, 1985), little has been done to determine the impact of these policies on power relations between colonial authorities and members of the indigenous population in the colonized territories. Far less has been done to explore the impact of the policies on spatial structures in colonial and post-colonial Africa. This chapter seeks to contribute to efforts aimed at redressing this deficiency in the literature. It does so by examining a number of very specific health or sanitary planning schemes in colonial Africa. One objective of this exercise is to demonstrate that these schemes were only a pretext for implementing policies whose less publicized aim was to facilitate the consolidation and perpetuation of European colonial power in Africa. Another objective is to show the impact of these schemes on spatial structures in Africa.

Public health and town planning in historical perspectives

Public health and town planning have been characterized as 'blood cousins, with common ancestry in the sanitary movement of the 1840s' (Hebbert, 1999: 433, citing Ashworth, 1954; Peterson, 1979). From their birth in the 1800s, town planning and public health, as professions, have always had shared goals. What came to be known as the new town planning movement was inspired in the early twentieth century by the need to protect public health. In Britain, this movement was articulated with the creation of the Ministry of Health in 1919. This ministerial body combined under a single administrative unit, medical care, personal health services, sanitation, public health and town planning.

Public health emerged to especially redress the real and potential health problems of a world that was becoming increasingly dominated by *laissez-faire* capitalism. Prominent amongst the pioneers of the movement to re-insert public health in the public, as opposed to the private, domain was Edwin Chadwick. Chadwick employed statistics on urban morbidity and mortality to persuasively argue against relegating public health to the private domain – a trend that was becoming increasingly commonplace as part of the liberal tendency to individualize the pursuit of wealth. Chadwick and his colleagues further deployed relevant statistics to demonstrate that unsanitary conditions anywhere constituted a threat to healthy conditions everywhere. These public health pioneers were particularly alarmed by the increasingly deplorable living conditions of the inner city poor in the rapidly industrializing city of London and to some extent, cognate cities in Europe as a whole. As Michael Hebbert notes, the health pioneers drew inspiration from established medical theories, such as pythogenic theory or what, at the time, was known in the United States as 'filth theory' (Hebbert, 1999). According to this theory, a common cause of disease in human populations is the gas that is given up by decomposing organic matter. Thus, illness is seen as a function of the air humans breathe. Therefore, to prevent illnesses, it was necessary to construct buildings with ample ventilation, afforded by large windows, flues and ventilation bricks. Additionally, all windows must open into the exterior of the building. Apart from their interest in the form and structure of buildings, public health pioneers also strived to effectuate change on the design of urban layouts. In this connection, they were particularly interested in altering the morphological relationship between streets, blocks and dwelling units (Hebbert, 1999).

To better appreciate the concerns of these pioneers, it is important to understand that concomitant with the industrial revolution had been a growth and proliferation of the demand for housing in European cities. The urgent need to respond to this demand led members of the property-owning class to subdivide the few units they owned in the urban centres. Additionally, some members of this new proletariat resorted to 'infilling' back gardens and courtyards as well as 'developing dense courtyards around short alleyways off the main thoroughfare' (Hebbert, 1999: 435). The buoyant real estate market of the 1830s acted as a further incentive for developers to disregard building regulations, and in some cases, actually build across streets, thereby effectively blocking light from reaching adjacent property.

The solution to this growing problematic resided not in the health domain proper but fell under the purview of town planning. Accordingly, town planners and public health officials working under the auspices of local governments embarked on rather ambitious programmes and projects to make streets more open. This endeavour led to a ban against 'dead-end' streets, and the opening up of both ends of all streets. The aim of efforts in this connection was to permit the uninterrupted circulation of fresh air. These efforts had their basis in empirical epidemiological evidence, which incriminated closed streets as a leading cause of death in human settlements regardless of their density (Hebbert, 1999: 435, citing Parliamentary Papers, 1884: 62, 1845: 50).

Before the English health pioneers of the 1840s, there had been Roman engineers, such as Vitruvus, who, centuries earlier, had underscored the importance of street alignment for ventilation. Additionally, there were others such as Christopher Wren, who recommended, subsequent to the Great Fire of London, 1666, that the crooked medieval streets of the City of London be straightened. By some estimates, the implementation of this recommendation alone led to a one-third reduction in the death rate of the City of London (Lewis, 1952).

Although hard pavements were later to constitute a significant aspect of town planning schemes in colonial Africa, it needs to be stressed that by the onset of the European colonial era on the continent, the street-based sanitary paradigm was no longer in vogue even in Britain, where it originated. By this time, the notion that hard pavements were associated with good health had been replaced by the view of good health as a function of a more natural environment, requiring the planting of trees, shrubs, flowerbeds and grass. At the forefront of the movement to reunite urbanites with the natural environment was Ebenezer Howard, whose famous Garden City Manifesto promised to 'countrify' the City of London (Hebbert, 1999). No discussion of this movement can be deemed complete without mention of the Metropolitan Public Gardens Association, whose chairman, the Earl of Meath, was an ardent advocate for playgrounds, parks and gardens in the cities. In fact, some of his critics, such as Lord Rosebery, believed that given the opportunity, he would not have hesitated to raze London and create a large garden in its stead (Hebbert, 1999, citing Aalen, 1992). In a way, this is exactly what Howard's famous Garden City Manifesto promised to do. Although this never came to pass, the 'greening' of human settlements became an axiomatic aspect of town planning in Britain in particular and Western Europe in general. One characteristic of this new health-conscious town planning, which pre-dated the advent of the European colonial era, but was never acknowledged by colonial town planners in Africa, is the grouping of dwelling units around green spaces to constitute what are commonly referred to as compounds. Michael Hebbert (1999: 439) describes how such configurations became fashionable in Britain in the following words:

> The building line which had regimented nineteenth-century street development was relaxed to allow informal grouping around greenspace.

As noted at the beginning of this chapter, when the colonial era began, colonial town planners wasted no time in introducing duplicates of these policies in Africa. It is understandable that colonial town planners were wont to introduce only policies with which they were intimately familiar. However, at a more critical level, one cannot but ponder why, as was the case in Europe, building and spatial development regulations were not employed as a tool for protecting the health of the public at large. Rather, as we shall see, these policies were selectively applied, with the beneficiary population in most cases being the Europeans. This is not to say that town planning policies designed to promote public health were never implemented in non-European districts. After all, sanitation received credit for eradicating the scourge of disease in Europe and especially Britain, in the late-nineteenth century. The sanitary reform movements and efforts to eradicate the epidemics of smallpox and cholera in Britain at the time provided inspiration for identical efforts to save the colonies from diseases. This notwithstanding, it is important to acknowledge the fact that even when sanitation sought to improve health conditions for the general public, the ultimate beneficiaries were the European residents in general and the colonial enterprise in particular. Thus, we contend that the policies were designed to serve important goals of the colonial enterprise. Prominent in this regard is the goal to dominate and control the colonial subjects.

Colonial public health policies with spatial dimensions

The European colonial period began in Africa barely one decade following the emergence of town planning and public health as disciplines with one of their avowed purposes being to combat the health consequences of industrialization and the concomitant urbanization. The science of sanitation held that 'by managing the environment and restructuring space using scientific principles, it is possible to banish disease' (Yeoh, 2003: 86). Accordingly, the protection of public health was central to town planning in colonial Africa. It is therefore not surprising that health concerns constituted the official rationale for most town planning schemes that were implemented by colonial authorities in the region. A good many of these schemes had significant spatial implications. The most prominent of these schemes can be conveniently discussed under the following different but overlapping headings: (1) anti-malarial schemes; (2) sanitation and general hygiene schemes; and (3) plague-combating schemes.

Anti-malarial planning schemes

One of the deadliest threats to humans, especially Europeans, in Africa during the colonial era was malaria. It was not until the twilight of the nineteenth century before it was discovered that malaria in humans is caused by four species of a protozoan parasite of the genus *Plasmodium* – *P. falciparum*, *P. vivax*, *P. malariae* and *P. ovale*. It is worth noting that while all these species are dangerous and capable of causing severe debilitating illnesses, only the first, *P. falciparum*, is sufficiently virulent to be deadly (Desowitz, 1981). To the extent that the carrier of this species, the anopheles mosquito, is indigenous to the sub-Saharan African region, living in this region effectively amounted to playing Russian roulette with one's life. Once the anopheles mosquito was incriminated as the vector of the malaria-causing parasite, colonial authorities immediately embarked on crafting and implementing a number of wide-ranging and arguably dubious health-promoting policies with spatial implications. Prominent amongst these policies were the following: the location of European living areas on hilltops or hill stations; nocturnal separation of the races in particular and racial residential segregation in general; maximum ventilation of European housing units; and the elimination of mosquito-breeding places, such as standing water, and bushes.

From the early- to mid-nineteenth century, conventional wisdom suggested that particular locations, soils, temperatures and rainfalls were all determinants of health conditions. In other words, the health status of a place was considered a function of its location (on the hill or in a valley); the characteristics of the soil of the place (loose versus hard soil, dry versus wet soil); the temperature of the place (hot or cold); and the extent or degree of rainfall at the place (heavy or light). This belief is one of a number of rationales that were advanced in defence of the selection of higher ground, especially hilltops, as the location of choice for European residential and colonial administrative facilities. In fact, stipulations to the effect that housing for military personnel and Europeans in, especially, colonial Africa, India, and the West Indies be located on higher ground and/or placed on stilts and elevated to ten to fifteen feet above the ground were rooted in this belief (Curtin, 1985). On the one hand, higher altitudes, it was believed for centuries, translated to cooler weather, which was in turn associated with good health. On the other hand, lower elevation was associated with warm or hot weather, which in turn translated into putrefaction and hence disease.

The British colonial hill station in Freetown, Sierra Leone came to epitomize the hill station concept in Africa. Before delving into the specific attributes of Freetown's hill station project, it will help tremendously to appreciate the fact that this project drew its inspiration from an identical project that had been implemented earlier on by the British colonial authorities in India. Between 1820 and the 1880s, as many as 80 hill stations were constructed at elevations between 4,000 and 8,000 feet throughout India (Kenny, 1997: 655, 657). Unlike the case of Freetown, most discussions regarding the preferable location of colonial government administrative facilities in India focused on climate as opposed to disease. However, both were ultimately concerned with the health of Europeans resident in the colonies. Thus, the choice of the hilltops and plateaus was premised on the assumption that Europeans would enjoy better health in these locations. To be sure, the case for hill stations in India was premised on a number of other factors. For instance, Sir John Lawrence, the first Viceroy named after the 1857 rebellion, contended that the cooler climate of hilltops and plateaus would significantly increase productivity – an advantage that could not be ignored given what he characterized as the growing workloads of the British imperial government in India at the time (Kenny, 1997). Other factors that were given serious thought in the selection of sites for administrative facilities in British colonial India can be summarized under the following five broad categories (Kenny, 1997). First, the site had to be elevated enough to afford a clear view of the surrounding areas. Second, the site was supposed to be easily accessible. Third, it had to possess enough space for, and be readily adaptable to military activities. Fourth, the site had to be out of the reach of an attacking foe and be easily defensible. Finally, it had to be within quick reach of the chief productive energies of all provinces under its jurisdiction.

Apart from the hill station project, there were a number of other aspects of British colonial health policies in India that were transplanted to Africa. Particularly noteworthy in this connection are the sanitation reform measures that were instituted in India and later transplanted to colonial Africa. The best known of these measures are those that were adopted in 1863 to address health problems created by the Sepoy Mutiny of 1857 and the Crimean War (Curtin, 1985). One aspect of these reforms that was later transferred to colonial Africa has to do with the establishment of the cantonment system (1870s and 1880s), which entailed the construction of permanent military camps in locations far removed from the native areas as a means of protecting the health of European soldiers resident in the colonies. Colonial authorities argued that such locations were necessary to isolate British military personnel from 'noxious odours of native habitation' (Curtin, 1985: 595). The same argument was advanced in defence of the decision to locate European residential areas far away from native districts. Apart from their isolated locations, these units possessed another noteworthy feature that distinguished them from native housing, namely excessive ventilation.

The requirement that European housing units be generously ventilated was predicated on theories that linked the spread of contagious diseases to unventilated environments. However, such theories, like a number of others before them (see above), were later found to be inaccurate, especially as the nature of germs became amply understood. In this regard, the efforts of Louis Pasteur and Robert Koch, to reveal that some bacteria can invade and live on an organism as a parasite before causing disease, deserve special attention.

New germ theories such as the foregoing prepared the stage for a lot of noteworthy works, which significantly influenced health and spatial policies in tropical Africa. Perhaps the most prominent development in this regard is Carlos Finlay's discovery in 1881 that mosquitoes were the vector for yellow fever. In this regard, the mosquitoes carried the yellow fever parasite from person to person. Philip Curtin (1985: 597) draws attention to a number of other major works that served to bolster Finlay's theory. Worth noting in this connection is the discovery by Alfonse Laveran of malaria parasites in the blood of malaria patients and evidence corroborating this theory from France, Italy, England and the United States. In England, particularly at the Liverpool School of Tropical Medicine, Ronald Ross and his colleagues had concluded that the anopheles mosquito carried plasmodia, the malaria parasite, which passes through one stage of development within the mosquito and another within the human host.

In 1899, Ross and a number of his colleagues were dispatched to Sierra Leone, a bastion for malaria, to conduct studies ascertaining that the anopheles mosquito was indeed the vector for malaria in Africa. Ross and his colleagues conducted two malaria control experiments in Sierra Leone, one in 1899 and another in 1900. In addition to establishing with certainty the link between the anopheles mosquito and malaria, Ross and his colleagues also determined that the anopheles mosquito did most of its biting and infecting at night and not during the day. Therefore, as a public health strategy, only nocturnal segregation of the European from the indigenous population was necessary. In practice, the scientists argued, it was possible for Europeans and members of the indigenous population to work together as long as they were spatially separated at night. Thus, Europeans could work and visit indigenous areas of the town during the day and return to their homes in the European districts at night. Similarly, servants, gardeners and others could work in the European districts during the day and return to the indigenous settlements at night. As I discuss below, these recommendations appear fastidious at best as they conveniently fail to acknowledge the fact that some workers, such as night watchmen, because of the nature of their jobs, had to spend the night in the European districts. Soon after Ross and his colleagues reported their findings and recommendations, Joseph Chamberlain, the Colonial Secretary at the time, adopted racial residential segregation as official policy in all of Britain's sub-Saharan African colonies.

Among his many recommendations, Ross had opined that the best way to deal with the malaria problem in Africa was to adopt the cantonment policy, which, in his opinion, had been successfully used in British colonial India. Accordingly, he recommended that housing for Europeans be located at least two kilometres from indigenous settlements. This was based on two main, seemingly contradictory, assumptions. First, it was believed that the African anopheles mosquito preferred the blood of Africans as opposed to that of Europeans. Hence, the mosquito would have a propensity for flying within African settlements regardless of the distance they are capable of traversing. Second, scientific knowledge of the time suggested that, factoring in the possibility of being assisted by the wind, the anopheles mosquito could not traverse a distance in excess of two kilometres. These two assumptions, as it turned out, were erroneous. One more erroneous assumption with implications for spatial organization in general and town planning laws in particular is that malaria emanated from the soil. A little later on, as germ theory advanced, it was believed that African adults possessed some type of immunity against malaria. This conclusion was derived from a number of studies revealing that blood samples from adults in Africa rarely contained actual plasmodia. On the contrary, the blood of children manifesting clinical symptoms contained the parasites. Therefore, the malariologists of that time concluded, African children and not adults were the primary source of malarial infection. However, this and identical theories regarding the source of malaria were later to be debunked by works identifying the anopheles mosquito as the disease's vector.

As a public health strategy, it was not enough, colonial authorities believed, to simply isolate European residential units from indigenous settlements. Medical scientists such as Robert Koch, who had had extensive experience in Asia and had conducted a number of studies, some on malaria and blackwater fever in Africa in 1897–8, recommended the prophylactic use of quinine. Others, such as S.R. Christophers and J.W.W. Stephens of the Liverpool School of Tropical Medicine considered Koch's recommendation not feasible and therefore mistaken. They further criticized any suggestions to the effect that the vector of the malaria itself, namely the anopheles mosquito, be attacked. Instead, they recommended that every effort be directed at singling out and protecting the Europeans. Removal of the 'susceptible Europeans' from the midst of malaria was only one of the many possible strategies rooted in recommendations such as these. Based on the erroneous belief that African children were the prime source of malarial infection, Europeans were strongly advised against being in the vicinity of native children from zero to five years of age (Christophers and Stephens, 1900).

The foregoing instructions were rather swiftly adopted by colonial officials on the ground in the colonies albeit to significantly different degrees. In Sierra Leone, the colonial government moved rapidly to incorporate the instructions into its spatial planning schemes, with the most conspicuous manifestations of actions in this connection being the development of Hill Station. Work on Hill Station in Freetown, Sierra Leone was initiated in 1902 and by 1904, a considerable number of units, including the Governor's residence, were ready for occupation. The community was developed along the lines of identical developments, also named hill stations, in British colonial India.

The land for the project was confiscated from some members of the native population. Developed as an exclusively European residential community, Hill Station overlooks, and is connected to, Freetown by a narrow gauge mountain railway (Njoh, 1999b; Frenkel and Western, 1988). Hill Station is four miles removed from the main city, Freetown, and only 700 feet above sea level – a far cry from the 4,000–5,000 feet altitude recommended to protect the health of Europeans in the colonies. A number of peculiar features of the units in the community are worth mentioning. The units were built to face north and supported by columns several feet above ground level, while the ground beneath the buildings was covered with cement. The orientation was designed to take advantage of the air/wind pattern thus permitting maximum ventilation and air circulation within the units, while raising the structure and cementing the ground beneath was believed to be a strategy for preventing 'malarial poisons' from rising from the soil and percolating into the building. This recommendation was based on archaic, anachronistic and erroneous theories that viewed the soil as the source of malaria. A strip of land a quarter of a mile wide, and cleared of all shrubbery, was left vacant to provide a shield around Hill Station. Outside this strip of land was a zone one mile wide containing tall vegetation but in which no housing units were authorized.

Once isolated, the Europeans' residential units needed to be further protected from the mosquito and other vectors of diseases. In this regard, several measures were recommended. The first was to screen the residential units of Europeans as a means of keeping the mosquitoes out. The second was to use electric fans, which according to Ross, who opposed the use of screens primarily because they compromised efforts to maximize ventilation, served a dual purpose – keeping the body cool and driving off the mosquitoes. The third was to destroy all mosquito breeding grounds in and around Hill Station. However, this strategy turned out to be more problematic than the colonial authorities had anticipated. The most important reason for this is the fact that the authorities were not quite conversant with the *Anopheles gambiae* and the *Anopheles funestus*, which are arguably the most dangerous of the malaria vectors in West Africa. The *A. gambiae* and the *A. funestus*, as scientific knowledge was to later reveal, could breed not only during the rainy season, in swamps or low places, but also in spots as small as depressions caused by footprints as long as they could hold water for a considerable duration. This characteristic of the *A. gambiae* and the *A. funestus* made them difficult to control and distinguished them from the Caribbean Anopheles and the *Aedes egyptae* with which the authorities were familiar. The *A. egyptae*, the carrier of the yellow fever parasite, had proven to be less problematic to control particularly because its flight range was extremely short and also because it bred in built-up areas.

The ideas of Ross, especially his staunch and unwavering opposition to the prophylactic use of quinine and the screening of European residential units, appeared to have carried the day as they found their way into British colonial government health policy directives. For example, as of May 1900, the Colonial Office in London began distributing pamphlets that were prepared at the Liverpool School of Tropical Medicine instructing colonial officials on the ground in tropical Africa to adopt strategies to eliminate the anopheles mosquito, protect Europeans against mosquito bites (not through the screening of European residential units) and spatially segregate European residential districts.

Although colonial officials on the ground were swift in adhering to these instructions, their strategies varied significantly in practice. In making this observation, Curtin (1985) draws attention to five specific colonies in British West Africa, namely Gambia, Sierra Leone, the Gold Coast, and Northern and Southern Nigeria. In Sierra Leone, as already noted, the colonial government had decided in favour of protecting the health of members of the resident European population by segregating the races. Initially, against vehement opposition from the natives, colonial authorities had proceeded to confiscate native lands at the highest elevation and construct a 'European Only' residential area that was far-removed from the main city, Freetown. In voicing their opposition to this project, members of the native population in Freetown, which had a Black mayor at the time, argued that the horrendous amounts of money and other scarce resources that went into developing the project would have been better spent on improving public infrastructure and other facilities in the city. The opposition of the natives fell on deaf ears and the authorities moved to implement what they contended was segregation on sanitary grounds. As time went on, a number of other suburban projects were developed and segregated on grounds that had nothing to do with health.

In Gambia, racial residential segregation for health or any other reason for that matter was practised at a very minimal scale, entailing no more than the segregation of a few streets in the capital, Bathurst, during World War I. Efforts to combat malaria tapped the ideas of Koch by providing quinine free of charge to schoolchildren. This was not necessarily because the colonial authorities on the ground in Gambia were negatively predisposed to the idea of segregation. Rather, it is especially because of the scant resident European population in that colony. One account places the number of Europeans in the entire colony at one point at fewer than 100, with the capital city, Bathurst, containing as few as twenty-two European residences (Curtin, 1985: 601). Also, members of the native population in the capital city were as economically well-off as their European counterparts. Thus, it is likely that any attempts at racial residential segregation would have met with more fierce resistance than that which the British colonial authorities had encountered with the Hill Station project in Freetown, Sierra Leone.

Perhaps most importantly, efforts to racially segregate the upscale part of Bathurst, where Europeans and wealthy Africans lived, would have entailed the prohibitively costly wholesale reconfiguration, rebuilding and redesigning of the entire area. For mainly these reasons, medical authorities deemed it wise abandoning any plan that would have racially segregated the city for health or any other reason. One such plan that was called off specifically because of a lack of funds, was designed to develop a segregated community for Europeans on the thirty-foot cliffs at Cape Saint Mary, at the point where the Gambia River enters the Atlantic Ocean, some seven and a half miles below the main city, Bathurst (Curtin, 1985: 601). Rather, the authorities opted for strategies that entailed as little spatial segregation of the races as possible. One notable policy in this connection was that which called for the screening of servants' housing units but not those of their European masters. The aim here was to ensure that the ventilation of units housing Europeans was not compromised by screens while at the same time preventing them from being bitten by infected mosquitoes from the servants' quarters.

In Accra, Ghana, where the history of urbanization preceded the arrival of European colonial rule, and where, similar to the case of Bathurst, Gambia, there were many wealthy Africans, racial residential segregation encountered significant opposition. In fact, members of the native population were well organized and constituted a political force to reckon with. In this regard, they are on record for successfully challenging and causing the colonial government to rescind a number of potentially adverse bills, including a proposed lands bill in 1898. Unable to proceed with ostensibly racial residential segregation policies on health pretexts, the colonial government in Accra moved to enact and implement other town planning policies geared towards protecting public health. One prominent activity in this connection was the mass demolition for health reasons of so-called dilapidated buildings that was frequently undertaken in Accra and other urban areas in the colony. Another was the attempt to eradicate mosquitoes in urban areas by eliminating mosquito breeding grounds. Finally, there were a few, albeit half-hearted efforts to segregate the residential areas of government officials in Accra as well as other urban locales throughout the colony. If these efforts were half-hearted, it is mainly because colonial officials in Ghana, particularly the Governor at the time (especially during World War I), Sir Hugh Clifford, were worried that any attempt at complete and compulsory segregation could have had negative repercussions for race relations.

The reluctance to implement racial residential segregation policy, on the part of officials on the ground – itself a function of their intimate knowledge of the forces that prevailed in Ghana at the time – was not echoed by authorities at the Colonial Office in London. These authorities insisted on segregation as an official policy throughout all British colonies. Accordingly, they moved in 1912 to draw up a plan whose goal was to complete the racial segregation of all towns in these colonies within a ten-year span (Curtin, 1985: 602). Although they were not quite successful in their bid to segregate the older towns of Ghana such as Accra and Kumasi, they achieved considerable success in this regard with the newer ones. Curtin (1985) speculates that the relative ease of shaping the spatial pattern of new towns as opposed to existing ones, is one reason why, despite the odds, colonial authorities were able to implement a racially segregated town plan for Tamale, which at the time was the new capital of the Northern Territories of the Gold Coast. As a site for European colonial residential and administrative facilities, Tamale shared a lot of characteristics with sites that were typically selected for colonial government business. It was located on a plateau, a considerable distance away from the nearest native settlement and surrounded by an open space. Although Tamale provided the officials a clean slate to work with, they nevertheless had to wrestle with a number of seemingly intractable problems. Prominent in this connection was the problem of protecting the members of the European population not only from the general population but also from the Africans who worked side-by-side with the Europeans. The most pragmatic solution was to isolate the entire colonial government staff from the native population at large and then segregate the European from the African staff. The proposition turned out to be expensive and served to bolster the economic case against segregation efforts.

Sanitation and general hygiene schemes

Colonial government actions constituting what I will discuss here under the broad heading of sanitation and hygiene schemes include, but are not limited to, the following:

- the destruction of so-called squalid and dilapidated buildings;
- the enactment and implementation of health and related building codes;
- the enactment and implementation of zoning and cognate ordinances;
- efforts to prevent noise pollution; and
- the crafting and implementation of ordinances disallowing or prohibiting African traditional structures (e.g. earth/thatch units) from urban areas.

Apart from Gambia, the Gold Coast (present-day Ghana) and Sierra Leone, Britain controlled two other colonies in West Africa before World War I. These two colonies, Northern Nigeria and Southern Nigeria, were later merged to constitute the colony of Nigeria in 1914. As part of efforts on the part of colonial authorities to make colonial territories in Africa a healthier place for Europeans to live and work, they initiated a policy that ensured the assignment of officials with medical backgrounds to the territories. Governor William MacGregor, who served at one point in the colonial Southern Nigeria, exemplifies officials in this category.

Governor MacGregor was keenly aware of medical findings and reports on malaria and other diseases that were known to threaten the health of Europeans in the region. He was also patently aware of, but questioned, the recommendations of authorities in the Colonial Office in London regarding what needed to be done to achieve the goal of a healthier tropical Africa for Europeans. He was particularly troubled by the recommendation that parts of existing cities such as Lagos be demolished to create sanitary cordons as a means of protecting the health of Europeans. In his opinion, such a move possessed all the ingredients for eliciting vehement and possibly violent opposition from members of the indigenous population. Furthermore, he believed, the strategy had a slim, if any, chance of succeeding. MacGregor was right, especially in view of the fact that the Lagos government fiercely opposed efforts to implement a sanitary segregation policy that had sought to convert seven acres of urban land along the Lagos racecourse into a segregated European residential area. The natives, supported by a number of other organized groups such as the Aborigines Protection Society, were successful in thwarting the colonial government's effort to create an exclusively European residential district on what was, for all practical purposes, land confiscated from members of the native population.

A number of the colonial public health actions were designed to avert or combat the effect of plagues that were commonplace at the time. Here, I hasten to mention quarantine and identical ordinances that were designed to isolate infected populations; the mass relocation of members of the indigenous populations who were infected, could potentially be infected or were simply viewed as threats to the health of Europeans. For instance, between September and October 1914, 2,900 Africans were expelled from Dakar. Similarly, in Douala, the Germans initiated a mass relocation scheme to move all natives from the area around the sea to hinterland areas en masse from Mombasa and Nairobi, respectively to hinterland areas. Finally, there was the large-scale elimination through the burning of infected African villages or African sections of urban centres.

Governor MacGregor was steadfastly convinced that sanitary segregation was not a viable strategy for combating health threats to Europeans in tropical Africa. To have any chance for success, he believed, efforts to improve the health conditions of Europeans in this region must be directed at attacking all threatening and potentially threatening diseases at their sources. In the case of malaria he recommended thus: if it could be concretely established that Africans were the reservoir for the parasites causing this life-threatening disease, it follows that eradicating it would entail focusing attention on Africans themselves. If anything, sanitary segregation could serve as no more than a temporary measure to control the spread of the disease.

Therefore, Governor MacGregor broke ranks with most of his contemporaries in other colonies when it came to adopting public health strategies. In this connection, he instituted prophylactic measures such as the requirement that all colonial government officials take quinine, the gratis provision of quinine to everyone, including Africans, resident in Lagos and its suburbs, the screening of all European residential units, offices and workplaces, and regular campaign programmes to educate the public on methods to free their surroundings of mosquitoes.

Unlike Governor MacGregor, the governor of the colony of Northern Nigeria, Sir Frederick Lugard, subscribed to theories advocating racial residential segregation as a viable strategy for protecting the health of Europeans in tropical Africa. Incidentally, Lugard had the entire scantily developed territory of Northern Nigeria to test the workability of the Colonial Office's recommendations regarding the accomplishment of public health goals through spatial organization in tropical Africa. Lugard's first action in this regard was to replicate the cantonment system, a well-known attribute of British colonialism in India. This entailed relocating the administrative headquarters of Northern Nigeria from Lokoja to a new isolated site one mile away. Apart from adopting the cantonment system, Lugard adhered stringently to Ross's directives regarding the physical segregation of the races. In this case, he issued edicts requiring the segregation of all district headquarters, including residential units or 'rest houses' that served to accommodate exclusively European colonial government officials on tour away from the administrative headquarters. As a requirement, each of these units was located at least 400 yards – presumably a distance that could not be traversed by an anopheles mosquito – away from the closest residence of a member of the indigenous population. Ironically, members of the native population who worked as domestic servants were allowed to live in servants' quarters in the White residential areas. Some have explained this irony as resulting from a desire on the part of Europeans 'to be segregated but not inconvenienced' (Curtin, 1985: 605). Lugard was also drawn to theories that linked health to environmental conditions as well as to physical activity. Accordingly, he sought to adopt construction policies based on antiquated scientific knowledge, such as raising buildings on piers as a means of protecting them from having direct contact with tropical Africa's contaminated soil. Additionally and perhaps most importantly, he did set aside colonial government funds to provide or subsidize the provision of tennis courts, polo clubs, golf courses and other recreational facilities. The aim was to encourage exercise through sporting activities amongst Europeans in the continent as a means of improving their health. Lugard also subscribed to the notion of providing European housing units with large verandahs and plentiful ventilation as well as the idea of protecting the units from the direct rays of the sun.

Lugard's administration was bolder in its enactment and implementation of policies designed to accomplish health objectives through the spatial segregation of the races than most others in the region. In this regard, the administration's chief authority on public health, Dr M. Cameron, the Senior Sanitary Officer (for Northern Nigeria), proposed the enforcement of sanitary segregation laws in the commercial areas as well. In practice, this meant that only Europeans were to own stores in these areas. In addition, no servants were to pass the night in the commercial districts. Lugard's town planning and health policies resulted in a unique urban spatial structure in Northern Nigeria. A notable feature of this structure was the division into four distinct districts of each urban area, born of European town planning efforts in the colony. The four districts were as follows (Curtin, 1985: 605): the colonial administrative and European residential district, located at least 400 yards in the windward direction of all other areas; the commercial/industrial zone, located by the railway/station; the African clerks and high-ranking artisans' quarters; and the strangers' quarters (or in Hausa, *Sabon Gari*), where native labourers and other less privileged members of the population lived. In the older urban settings, such as Zaria and Kano, the *Sabon Garis* served as the residential areas for immigrants and not necessarily the underprivileged members of society, although this group could more likely be found in this than any other part of town.

As time went by, protecting the health of Europeans through racial residential segregation increasingly gained ground as official policy throughout Northern Nigeria. At the same time the policy was gaining more and more endorsement from members of the colonial medical community. In fact, this community is on record for approving the insertion in the *West African Pocket Book* – an informational manual for Europeans in West Africa – of a passage claiming that racial segregation constitutes one of the most viable strategies for protecting Europeans against tropical diseases. In 1914, seven years after this, Lugard became Governor-General of Nigeria, which at this time had become a single colony. He immediately proceeded to make racial residential segregation the official government policy of colonial Nigeria. He was very forceful in this regard to the extent of making it, under the Township Ordinance of 1917, a crime punishable by a fine or imprisonment for any European to live in a non-European district.

The British were by no means the only colonial authorities who employed town planning schemes as a strategy for promoting good health. Rather, this strategy had become commonplace during the heydays of European colonialism in Africa. Here, in contrast to other colonized regions such as India, colonial authorities had become more specific in prescribing the spatial attributes, such as the altitudes and linear distances from indigenous settlements, that were necessary to make European residential areas in the colonies healthy. However, opinion varied widely with respect to the exact altitude and distances that were necessary to attain this objective. For instance, while in some circles it was believed that an altitude of 400 feet was sufficient, in others, the recommended altitude was 3,000–5,000 feet (Curtin, 1985: 595). In tropical Africa, altitudes of 5,000 feet were considered sufficient for safety once the anopheles mosquito had been identified as the vector for malaria. This is because 5,000 feet was considered to be above the range of the mosquito. The decision of German colonial authorities to locate the administrative capital of colonial Cameroon (Kamerun) on the slopes of Mount Cameroon, with a peak of more than 13,000 feet, was rooted in this belief.

Although the Germans were initially persuaded by theories advocating prophylactic measures such as the mass distribution of quinine as a means of protecting Europeans against tropical diseases such as malaria, they later subscribed to the notion of sanitary segregation. In leaning towards sanitary segregation, a good number of German medical authorities argued that prophylactic measures such as mass use of quinine were both impractical and unfeasible. One reason for this was, these authorities argued, the fact that Africans were incapable of practising proper mosquito control. Thus, they insisted on absolute segregation, which in some cases entailed the mass relocation of members of the native population to make room for 'White Only' settlements. This was the case in Douala, where German colonial officials, after reaching the rather dubious and baseless conclusion that as much as 72 per cent of the native population along the city's seafront area were infested with the malaria parasite, decided in favour of relocating all 20,000 of the native residents of this area to an inland location (Curtin, 1985: 606).

This case stands out in the annals of European colonial history for two main reasons. First, the decision was indefensible on all logical fronts. Consequently, members of the native population, European missionary and other philanthropic organizations in the colony vehemently opposed it. Also, and paradoxically, members of the German colonial medical community who had advanced the notion of sanitary segregation went on record to assert that the decision made no sense on medical grounds. The opposition notwithstanding, the German colonial government in Cameroon (or Kamerun as per the Germans), backed by their superiors in Berlin, pushed forward with the decision. The case is also noteworthy because of the ruthless manner in which the German colonial government reacted to the indigenous leadership's opposition to its indefensible decision. Some details on the nature of the opposition and said reaction are in order.

The native leadership of Douala sought to oppose what it saw as the German colonial government's unjust decisions in much the same way that leaders of the native population in British colonies such as Ghana, Gambia and Nigeria had done. Accordingly, German-educated King Rudolf Manga Bell, the indigenous leader of Douala, who had incidentally gained German approval, decided in favour of petitioning the colonial government's decision. When the local colonial government ignored his petition, he proceeded, with the assistance of a German lawyer, to present his case, or more appropriately, the Douala people's case, to the *Kolonialamt* in Berlin and onward to the *Reichstag*. Upon noticing King Bell's persistence, the German colonial government in Kamerun decided to withdraw its recognition of him as the official leader of the people of Douala – in effect removing him from his post as the recognized official leader of Douala. For his part, King Bell decided to seek the support of other European powers in his bid to reclaim the ancestral lands of the Douala people that had been unjustly confiscated by the German colonial authorities. This move on King Bell's part was made in summer 1914, or the eve of World War I – a period that was marked by bitter tensions and rivalries amongst Europeans. Once the war was started, the Germans proceeded immediately to arrest King Bell and his secretary, Mr Ngoso Din, on the ridiculous and perfidious charge of treason. Both were tried, found guilty and executed by the German colonial government. The tragic conclusion to this tale cannot but make one ponder the extent to which confiscating the seafront land of the Douala people was simply a strategy to protect the health of the town's European residents. Similar attempts at mass relocation in other parts of colonial Africa suggest that such policies sought to accomplish much more than health goals. For instance, at one time during the heyday of British colonialism in East Africa, when the European population on Mombasa island was only a mere 148 in comparison to 27,000 natives, a colonial medical officer had suggested that all natives be relocated to a location far-removed from the island (Curtin, 1985: 611).

Efforts to promote public health, especially with respect to protecting the health of Europeans in French colonial Africa, were informed by knowledge gleaned from the British colonial medical experience and experiments, especially those relating to mosquito/malaria control in the region. In fact, as far back as 1903, as Curtin (1985: 610) notes, 'the standard French text of tropical hygiene had picked up the recent works of British antimalarial segregationists like Christopher and Stephens and presented them as the teachings of "science"'.

Plague-combating schemes

Mosquitoes and malaria were certainly not the only problems of concern to health authorities in colonial Africa. Other health problems included, but were by no means limited to, smallpox, whooping cough, tuberculosis and plagues such as the infamous bubonic plague that was visited upon one or more parts of the continent at one point or another between 1898 and 1914. The strategies designed to deal with contagious diseases and plagues such as this by French colonial authorities are worthy of note particularly because of their spatial implications. Apart from their inclination towards older ideas about controlling such diseases through quarantine, especially by creating *les cordons sanitaires*, the French simply reversed the procedures to control malaria, which advocated the removal of Europeans from native areas, by devising strategies requiring that infected natives be removed from European towns.

French architecture and urban planning made the task of distinguishing European from native towns quite easy. The French, perhaps more so than other Europeans, are well known for their efforts to create replicas of French towns in their colonial territories. The ancient city of Saint-Louis (part of present-day Dakar), Senegal, was designed to take the form of an eighteenth-century French town, complete with a central place, a gridiron street pattern and European-style buildings. Although from the onset, Saint-Louis, which began having African mayors as far back as the eighteenth century, was never racially segregated, the newer city of Dakar developed during a period of heightened racism in colonial Africa was. French colonial authorities did everything possible, without portraying themselves as blatantly racist, to exclude members of the native population from Dakar.

In this regard, and under the pretext of protecting public health, they designated the most desirable section of the city as a 'hygienic village'. No traditional African structure, including all buildings of earth and thatch, was permitted in this section of the city. Under the same pretext, a zone containing no man-made structure – a green area or *cordon sanitaire* – encircled the highest point in the city or the *plateau*, which contained the residential units of Europeans. Elsewhere in francophone Africa, green areas or *les cordons sanitaires* were also used as a means to protect the health of the resident European population during the colonial era. For instance, in the Belgian Congo (present-day Democratic Republic of Congo, formerly Zaire), Kalina, the European district, was separated from the rest of Leopoldville (now, Kinshasa) by a *cordon sanitaire* comprising a golf course, a botanical garden and a zoo. Members of the native population, with the exception of domestic servants, were not permitted in Kalina from 9:00 pm to 6:00 am and could only be allowed in with special passes under exceptional circumstances such as emergencies. Also, no Europeans were permitted in the native areas during these hours.

In 1914, when the bubonic plague was visited upon the city of Dakar, the French colonial government immediately ordered that all traditional housing units as well as all the units in which any plague victim lived around European residential areas be burned down as a means of protecting the health of Europeans in the city

(Berque, 1958; Stren, 1972; Curtin, 1985). Additionally, the government ordered mass relocation of the remainder of the native population to a new African town on the periphery of the city. The new town was christened Medina after identical towns in North Africa. All accounted for, some 38,000 Africans were relocated in the process.

Members of the native population were, similiar to their counterparts in Douala, Accra, Bathurst, Freetown and Lagos, opposed to any form of relocation, let alone mass relocation. However, their opposition was tempered by the fact that the policy was sold as one designed to protect their own health. It is important to note that in 1914, Dakar and a number of other communes in Senegal were successful in electing their own native representatives to the National Assembly in Paris. With the presence of Africans in the French National Assembly, it became increasingly difficult for French authorities to enact any blatantly racist policies on health or any other pretexts. Thus, they resorted to policies that discriminated on the basis of culture as opposed to race. Hence, while a distinct European town continued to exist, its distinguishing features were in terms of architectural style as opposed to its racial composition. In fact, it was possible for anyone to live in a European town as long as s/he was prepared to abide by European standards of architecture and social behaviour.

Health, sanitation, power and control in the colonies

The thread connecting health and sanitation to power and control in colonial Africa can be appreciated from at least three different but overlapping perspectives. First, it is important to understand that colonial authorities derived power from their expertise in the science of health and sanitation. Second, it is necessary to understand the power and control implications of locating European residential facilities on hilltops. Finally, it must be understood that improved health meant commercial and economic gains for colonial authorities.

Power implications of expertise in health and sanitation

Advances in the areas of bacteriology and parasitology that had been made in Europe in the late-nineteenth century, constituted, in and of themselves, a potent source of power for Europeans. Thus, when the colonial era began in Africa at about the same time, European planners, medical and consanguine professionals were confident that they could control and/or conquer any disease and epidemic by simply applying the relevant Western scientific principles and techniques. The ability of sanitary sciences to improve living conditions resulted in ameliorating the status of public health officials and urban planners. Almost immediately, these professionals became what Michel Foucault has alluded to as the frontline experts on spatial order, particularly because of their ability to deal with spatial concerns. These spatial concerns included, but were not limited to conditions of local climate and soil; the coexistence of human beings; the coexistence of human beings with other objects and things; and questions relating to the propagation of disease (Yeoh, 2003). These questions, and particularly others dealing with the location and juxtaposition of 'locally undesirable' land use activities such as slaughterhouses and cemeteries as well as questions relating to population density came under the orbit of (sanitary) sciences, hence requiring scientific intervention.

This unwavering confidence in the majesty and supremacy of Western science and technology endowed European sanitary and other colonial officials with a genre of power, which Foucault eloquently described in his power/knowledge (*pouvoir/savoir*) treatise. Foucault carefully weaves a single thread linking knowledge, science, statistics and anecdotes, and demonstrates their relationship to power. Also, in a similar fashion, Francis Bacon must have coined his now famous phrase, 'knowledge is power', to emphasize the all-too-important link between knowledge and power. It is important to note that planning in the colonial territories commanded a degree of respect that would, by today's standards, be deemed unusual for a profession that some, such as Charles Hoch (1994), have characterized as 'marginal'. Thus, in colonial planning practice, the line between craft, that is the 'competent application of skilled inquiry and composition to the creation of a useful product' and rhetoric, the judgments professionals make (Hoch, 1994: 322), was effectively blurred. Accordingly, the elements of craft in colonial urban planning frequently, if not always, defined the rhetoric. This meant, amongst other things, that colonial urban planners and cognate professionals, thanks to their expertise, were given enormous powers to influence spatial order as they deemed fit or as was necessary to facilitate the accomplishment of the goals and objectives of the colonial enterprise. It is unlikely that this would have been possible without the authoritarian nature of colonialism. In democratic settings, urban planners are far less powerful and their craft tends to be frequently defined by rhetoric. One reason for this, Hoch (1994: 322) explains, is because the planning craft 'does not enjoy substantial institutional legitimacy and support' in such settings, where the craft often proves vulnerable in the face of powerful local institutions. While local institutions were not absent from the colonial scene in Africa, they were certainly not powerful.

Also worthy of note with respect to efforts on the part of colonial urban planners and health officials to facilitate the process of consolidating power in the colonial territories was the supplanting of indigenous African health practices with Western varieties; and also efforts designed to institutionalize Western health practices. In the first instance, the practice on the part of colonial health officials was to disparage African traditional systems of managing health and disease as they proceeded to institute European varieties in their stead. In the second instance, these officials vigorously strived to clad their, sometimes dubious, health policies in institutional garbs thereby endowing the policies with what Mannheim (1985) alludes to as canalized power. Such power 'is vested in institutions and produces orderly patterns of human interaction subject to norms and codes and rules' (p. 48). One of the best-known strategies for institutionalizing colonial hygiene/health and cognate policies was to accord them the power of law. Thus, violating or defaulting any hygiene/health regulations was tantamount to violating a law. In a good number of cases, health and hygiene laws that were already in force in Europe were simply transplanted to the colonies. This was the case with the French health, hygiene and aesthetic law of 1943 that was transplanted verbatim to colonial Niger. To better understand the thrust of this discourse, it is necessary to appreciate the fact that the institutionalization of any public activity is an established means for consolidating state power.

In his power/knowledge treatise, Foucault paints a lucid picture depicting the importance of institutionalization as an element of power especially in matters of public health. During the Middle Ages, power was necessary to effectuate war and maintain peace. Here, the state's power was bolstered by its monopolization of arms, and of the right to arbitrate lawsuits and punish crimes. By the end of the Middle Ages, power was required to exercise two additional functions – those of maintaining order and organizing wealth. In the eighteenth century, and up to the late nineteenth century, when the European colonial era began in Africa, power assumed an additional function, that of 'the disposition of society as a milieu of physical well-being, health and optimum longevity' (Foucault, 1982: 170). Foucault is quick to note that 'the exercise of these three latter functions – order, enrichment and health – is assured less through a single apparatus than by an ensemble of multiple regulations and institutions' (p. 170). In the eighteenth century, these regulations and institutions went under the generic appellation 'police', meaning the totality of mechanisms designed to serve or ensure order, the properly channelled growth of wealth and the conditions of the preservation of health in general.

The claim to knowledge of health and hygiene led colonial authorities in Africa to adopt measures designed to control all aspects of urban life. Accordingly, the powers of planners and health officials were significantly bolstered. Attempts to reinforce the powers of these officials assumed several forms and effectively contributed to an inordinate expansion of the state apparatus. This expansion constituted the exercise of a form of power similar to what Foucault calls 'pastoral power' (Foucault, 1982). Pastoral power, as Foucault explains, focuses on salvation, particularly with respect to reforming people's health or habits and the use of 'individualizing techniques' (Yeoh, 2003). As Brenda Yeoh argues, with respect to colonial Singapore, while each institution might have been assigned a unique function, they shared the use of common disciplinary forms to control the activities of the colonized body and the space it inhabited. This effectively facilitated the attainment of social order and economic advancement – both of which constituted important objectives of the colonial enterprise.

A critical examination of colonial policies whose avowed aim was to protect public health and consanguine public interests in the colonies is revealing. Colonial urban planners used the pretext of protecting the health, safety and welfare of the public to craft spatial policies whose actual purpose was to buttress the power of the colonial state and facilitate efforts to effectuate social control in the colonies. Projects designed to facilitate attainment of the goal of maintaining racial segregation, but masquerading as schemes to combat malarial infection, exemplify this tendency. The need to mask the true objectives of these projects was accentuated in French colonies particularly because the French populace at home avowedly disapproved of any attempts at racial segregation in the colonies. Thus, in colonial Madagascar, Wright (1991) notes that colonial planners disguised the 1928 law requiring that buildings in certain districts be constructed exclusively of European building materials as a policy designed to promote a healthy, liveable and aesthetically pleasing environment as opposed to a policy intended to achieve the goal of racial segregation. Earlier on in 1924, in an interview to the newspaper, *Tribune de Madagascar*, Georges Cassaigne, an architect from France's prestigious *Ecole des Beaux Arts*, used the cloak of the powers conferred on him by his expertise and professional affiliation to defend the law in an attempt to shroud what was obviously a racist policy in scientific and technical garbs.

The relentless efforts on the part of colonial authorities to promote racial segregation as a viable strategy to promote health, had far-reaching implications for power and social control. To appreciate these implications, it is necessary to note that racial segregation policies invariably guaranteed Europeans access to larger and better-located parcels of land, while members of the indigenous population were cramped into the least desirable parcels. If we consider space a repository of social power, it follows that its reorganization, which colonial planners effectively carried out, translates into a reorganization of the framework for expressing this power (Cooper, 2000: 92, citing Foucault, 1975). By establishing exclusively European districts, colonial authorities found it easier to neglect areas housing members of the native population. Consequently, these areas, which had very little in the way of modern amenities, often stood in stark contrast to the European districts, which boasted an excess of such amenities. It has been suggested that ethnic segregation uses visibility as an effective means of oppression (Cooper, 2000). To the extent that this is true, we contend that racial residential segregation policies not only accentuated the power and dominance of Europeans over Africans, it also effectively oppressed them.

For the record, European colonial authorities did equip some, if only very few, areas in the native districts with modern amenities and infrastructure. However, it would be naïve to suggest that the provision of basic services such as access roads, water and electricity was meant to bring some level of equality between the races. In my opinion, the provision of basic services in selected areas of the native districts was only one of many strategies employed by Europeans to gain and/or maintain political control in the colonial territories. In this case, colonial authorities used the provision of public infrastructure as an instrument for broadcasting power. Additionally, and more importantly, the access roads developed as part of this process constituted an indispensable element in efforts to maintain formal authority in the colonies, particularly because they permitted the movement of 'essential' colonial government officials, such as tax collectors, sanitary inspectors, civil administrators, and elements of the security, police and military forces.

Economic implications of sanitation and health policies

It is hardly surprising that colonial authorities in Africa were concerned with, amongst other things, the problems of morbidity and mortality in the native population. This concern was in line with the goal of minimizing costs and maximizing profits in the colonies. The spread of diseases and the concomitant loss of lives would not only have debilitated the native population, but also crippled commerce and trade in the colonies. Large and healthy populations were necessary to provide the labour force necessary for territorial defence and economic productivity in the colonies. Such populations were also necessary for energizing commerce and trade, which were critical ingredients in the recipe for colonial and imperial power. Thus the impetus for promoting sanitation, hygiene and ultimately improved health amongst members of the native populations in colonial Africa can be better understood as part of a meticulous plan on the part of colonial authorities to ensure the survival, growth and development of the colonial enterprise. It is worth noting that sanitized environments had resulted in a significant reduction in morbidity and mortality rates, which in turn led to economic prosperity in Europe. It is therefore conceivable that efforts to promote sanitized environments in Africa constituted attempts on the part of European colonial authorities to achieve similar results in colonial Africa.

12 The political economy of urban planning in colonial Africa

Introduction

Critics view the colonial enterprise as reprehensible, morally repugnant and essentially evil. Some (e.g. Conklin, 1998) have gone so far as to brand it 'state sanctioned violence'. Some of the egregious excesses of colonialism, such as the forcible 'pacification' of natives who resisted colonization, are well established. In its most subtle form, colonialism entailed coercive practices that conflicted sharply with basic human rights and democratic values. In both principle and practice colonized people were considered subjects as opposed to citizens and were assigned duties but never given any rights. Paradoxically, as Conklin (1998) suggests, colonial powers appeared oblivious to the fact that their activities in the conquered or colonized territories were in contradiction of their own democratic values. Perhaps more ironic is the exceeding degree of faith that these powers had in the moral legitimacy of the colonial enterprise.

Colonial powers (e.g. French policymakers during the Third Republic) defended the colonial enterprise as part of a universal mission to civilize the 'inferior races' – or the *mission civilisatrice*. From this vantage point, the colonial venture in Africa was meant to liberate Africans from all forms of oppression. Thus, urban planning and cognate activities that sought to institute spatial order can be considered part of this liberating and/or civilizing mission. What is of much intellectual curiosity is not the fact that ubiquitous and empirically unverifiable reasons have been advanced to rationalize colonial planning schemes that sought to replace indigenous spatial and physical structures with European varieties. Rather, it is the fact that few (see e.g. King, 1980, 1990; Yeoh, 2003; Dovey, 1999; Home, 1997; Anyumba, 1995; Markus, 1993; Simon, 1992; Ross and Telcamp, 1985; Abu-Lughod, 1980) have paused to critically explore the 'actual' motives of colonial town planning projects in Africa and other erstwhile colonized regions. However, a lot more ground needs to be covered in order to promote understanding of the 'real' aims of the many urban planning schemes that were conceived, formulated and implemented in colonized territories in Africa in particular and the world in general.

The 'actual' aims of colonial urban planning policies in Africa can be better understood within the broader context of well-known, if only debatable reasons for

Europe's colonization of the continent. Few of those who actively participated in the colonial enterprise were as succinct in their characterization of the goals of this enterprise as King Leopold II of Belgium. He is said to have stated in an unpublished manuscript he had prepared prior to ascending to the throne that:

> I should be happy to see Belgians trading with and in colonies in general but I think the country must also, in its own interests, possess territories overseas. I see in this a means of giving us a more important place in the world, of opening up fresh careers for our fellow citizens, of supplying ourselves with a new financial structure which might, as in Java, yield a surplus and give an opportunity for investing capital in places where our own laws hold sway, and much more advantageously than in the metal industry or even railways, which yield between 3 and 3.5 per cent.
>
> (quoted in Brunschwig, 1964: 31)

Eminent Africanist Ali Mazrui (1969) has argued that Europeans colonized Africa to foster the attainment of three important goals, namely the acquisition of scientific knowledge, the establishment of presumed European racial superiority, and the bolstering of Europe's grandeur and economic prowess. For the purpose of the discussion in this book, the colonization of Africa constituted part of a grand scheme by Europeans in particular and Westerners as a whole to consolidate their power and control of the rest of the world in intellectual, cultural, ideological and economic terms. The purpose of this concluding chapter is to show how British and French colonial urban planning policies in Africa constituted part of this grand scheme.

The acquisition of scientific knowledge

Discussions of knowledge acquisition as an objective of the conquest of Africa by Europeans are often restricted to geographical knowledge. Here, the works of early explorers, such as Vasco da Gamma, Prince Henry the Navigator, Samuel Baker, Joseph Thompson, David Livingstone, Richard Burton, John Speke and others who undertook expeditions to 'discover' or gain a better appreciation of what Europeans knew as no more than the 'Dark Continent', come to mind. The emphasis on geographical knowledge is certainly not surprising given that those, such as Prince Henry the Navigator, who were willing and able to fund such expeditions in those days exclusively favoured the collection of geographical data. The bias in favour of geographical data notwithstanding, it would be naïve to conclude that no other form of knowledge was ever acquired in the process. The annals of colonialism are replete with knowledge on the African experience that was acquired by anthropologists, Christian missionaries, doctors and other scientists working for the colonial civil service, religious organizations, philanthropic agencies and other private entities.

The experiences of colonial officials involved in spatial planning and sanitation served as invaluable inputs in many scientific endeavours. For instance, the work of

Dr Ronald Ross and others who participated in the mosquito control and eradication projects in Sierra Leone (1899–1900) contributed in no small way to contemporary knowledge on malaria. In fact, inspiration for the creation of the Schools of Tropical Medicine at the University of Liverpool and the University of London was drawn, at least in part, from the need to make life in the tropical colonies more liveable, especially for Europeans. Another important development that drew inspiration from the experience of colonial town planners was the creation of an institute dedicated to the study of tropical architecture at the Architectural Association, which was later moved to University College London as the Development Planning Unit (DPU).

Apart from the aforementioned activities, there were a number of other developments of scientific significance that resulted from the experience of colonial planners. Although these planners were hasty in their efforts to supplant indigenous African solutions to planning and related problems with European varieties, they sooner rather than later came to the realization that conditions prevalent on the continent rendered European solutions untenable. This was perhaps more true in building construction than in other areas of urban planning. As the colonial era progressed, it became increasingly evident that building construction in warm or tropical climates differed markedly from that which obtains in the cooler climates of Europe with which colonial planners and engineers were familiar. This difference was conspicuous in three respects (Stevens, 1955: 2). First, buildings in the tropics needed to possess a thermostatic capacity to make the inside cool when it is hot outside and warm inside during the periods of the year when outside temperatures are low. Also, there is a need for abundant ventilation in the humid climate of the tropics. Efforts to insulate buildings in such regions encounter enormous difficulties. Second, while there is little or no risk of damage from frost attack, there is the threat from mould and fungal growth, rotting and insect attack, which buildings in the tropics face. Finally, there is the problem of scarce financial resources – a problem that is not prevalent in Europe. One can conveniently add to this list, the shortage of technicians skilled in so-called modern building craft.

Colonial authorities were fully aware of these problems and had embarked, in some limited fashion earlier in the colonial era, on efforts to acquire the scientific knowledge necessary to resolve the problem. These efforts were multiplied during the post-World War II era. Before then, the efforts were sporadic and had been limited to the creation of building industries in South Africa, Southern Rhodesia (present-day Zimbabwe), Northern Rhodesia (present-day Zambia) and Kenya. Outside Africa, a number of building research centres had been established by British colonial authorities in Hong Kong, Singapore, India and Ceylon (present-day Sri Lanka). During the War II, colonial urban planners in Africa had encountered serious problems securing building materials from the colonial master nations. This accentuated the need to develop local substitutes. Efforts in this connection began during the war and continued thereafter. One such effort, which specifically involves the East African Industrial Research Board (EAIRB) deserves mention in this respect. The EAIRB operated laboratories in Nairobi during the early 1940s. The purpose of this board was to create 'secondary industries essential to East Africa's war effort' (Stevens, 1955: 3). Apart from the fact that this board was a colonial creation designed to promote the acquisition of scientific knowledge relating to tropical building construction, I must note that one of its founding members was a former director of the United Kingdom Building Research Station. Prominent amongst the products of the research endeavours of this Board were a technical pamphlet on the local manufacture of bricks, tiles, lime, paints and distemper and facilities for testing clays and limestones.

Although no similar institution existed in West Africa during the immediate post-World War II era or before then, it is worth noting that the Town Engineer in Kumasi, the Gold Coast (present-day Ghana) was actively involved in experiments in the use of cement-stabilized lateritic earths for block-making as far back as 1944. In 1948, British colonial authorities recommended the creation of a regional building research organization to address scientific and technical questions regarding construction works in British West Africa. Subsequently, a grant was made to defray the preliminary cost of this endeavour by the Colonial Development and Welfare Research Fund. The organization's first director was appointed in 1952 and operated from its headquarters in Accra. Civil engineers with extensive experience in West Africa assisted the director. These officers acted as liaisons between the colonial territories and the Central Building Laboratory in the metropolitan country.

Another related development of significance was a study commissioned by the British Ministry of Supply and a number of other government departments. The study, published in 1951 under the caption 'The weathering and durability of building materials under tropical conditions' in the Proceedings of the Building Research Congress, London, was designed to promote understanding of the deterioration of materials in tropical climates. Yet another development that was supported by colonial authorities seeking to promote understanding of building construction science and technology in Africa was the establishment of a building control investigation unit in 1942 by the South African Government Building Controller. The unit was assigned the special task of collaborating with the Civil Engineering Department of the University of Witwatersrand, and the Public Works Department to test the economic and structural viability of timber as a building material.

To be sure, the British were not the only colonial authorities with research institutions established to acquire knowledge on urban planning and related matters in Africa. The French colonial authorities also set up similar institutes such as the Bureau Central d'Etudes pour les Equipements d'Outre-mer attached to the Secretariat des Missions d'Urbanisme et d'Habitat, which was in charge of research on tropical housing. In addition, scientific institutions such as the Laboratoire des Ponts et Chaussées and the Centre du Bois Tropical, working under the auspices of l'Agence Coopération et Aménagement based in France, were involved in tropical spatial planning and building material research. The Belgian colonial authorities, for their part, operated the Office des Cités Africaines in Congo (which became known as Zaire and is now the Democratic Republic of Congo or DRC).

Apart from their work on tropical housing and building materials, colonial urban planners also made significant contributions to the development of spatial planning practice and theory. As I have argued elsewhere (Njoh, 1999b), colonial urban planners saw in the colonized territories of Africa, an opportunity to test newly acquired planning theories and techniques. To better appreciate this line of thought, it is necessary to understand that urban planning as a professional discipline emerged at about the same time as European powers were initiating their colonial ventures in the sub-Saharan African region. Accordingly, the vast territories that were acquired in the region were considered timely and served as a testing ground for the lofty planning projects that had been proposed by European urban architects and others interested in spatial order at the time.

Here, the schemes that were espoused by thinkers such as Patrick Geddes and Ebenezer Howard come to mind. The works of Kropotkin and earlier utopian writers such as Thomas Spence and James Buckingham Silk influenced Ebenezer Howard, who came to be known as the father of the Garden City movement. Howard's ideas of what an ideal city should look like are articulated in his treatise, *Garden Cities of Tomorrow*. These ideas are largely rooted in the ancient Greek notion of a natural limit to the growth of human settlement. It is this notion that constituted Howard's proposal of what he branded a Garden City, which, he argued, constituted a better, more environmentally sound and rational strategy for dealing with problems engendered by the purposeless mass congestion problems of the large human settlements that were growing and proliferating in Europe at the time. The city Howard had in mind would, to a large extent, be self-sufficient and contain a limited number of inhabitants within a geographically small area that would be encapsulated by a permanent greenbelt or agricultural land.

Howard's ideas were radical and had never been tested. Perhaps more importantly for the purpose of the present discussion, fully testing them in Europe was impractical particularly because of space constraints. Accordingly, planners and others involved in spatial organization considered the vast lands in the newly conquered colonies ideally suited for testing the feasibility of ideas such as those articulated by Howard. Efforts to accord the ideas of Howard concrete form around the world abound. With regards to colonial Africa, the activities of two ardent proponents of the Garden City model are worth recounting here. These proponents are S.D. Adshead and Albert Thompson. Adshead was a professor of Town Planning at London University and past President of the Town Planning Institute in 1931 when, as a consultant, he was assigned the task of developing a plan for Northern Rhodesia's (present-day Zambia) capital city, Lusaka. He seized the occasion to produce a plan that adhered religiously to the principles and structure enunciated in Howard's Garden City model. Albert Thompson was an architect trained in the famous architectural practice of Raymond Unwin and Barry Parker. He started his professional practice in Britain in 1914 and was actively involved in the planning of Letchworth and of Hampstead Garden Suburb before proceeding to Africa in 1920. His earliest assignments on the continent included designing the Pinelands Garden Suburb of Cape Town and the Durban North Estate, both in South Africa. Later on in his practice in colonial Africa, Thompson played leading roles in the design of a housing estate in Yaba (Lagos), Nigeria (1926), and in the re-planning of a number of other Nigerian towns, including Warri, Sapele, Benin and Onitsha.

Maxwell Fry, the first Town Planning Adviser to the Resident Minister of British West Africa (1943–45), eloquently stated the role of the vast colonial territories of Africa as being essential venues for testing European town planning ideas. In an address he gave at a meeting he had with the Royal Empire Society on 26 June 1946, he stated thus (Fry, 1946: 201):

> We have always felt that we wanted to study village planning but we never had time to do it properly. In West Africa we felt there was a really grand opportunity … So we met things as we went along – and in fact a book on village planning has now gone to the publisher. It is the fruit of our experience over two years.

The importance of the knowledge that was generated thanks to the work of professional urban planners such as Fry, Thompson and Reade and related professionals (e.g. those involved in health and building research) in colonial Africa can be appreciated on a number of different levels. At a very basic level, research and cognate activities such as those alluded to above constituted the source of vital information on standards, costs and design that colonial authorities exchanged amongst themselves and with other Western countries, including public, private for-profit and non-profit entities therein, with an interest in Africa (see King, 1980). To the extent that knowledge can be translated into power in the sense articulated by Francis Bacon (as in 'knowledge is power'), and to some extent as espoused by Michel Foucault (as in *pouvoir/savoir*), it is safe to argue that the acquisition of knowledge occasioned by colonial activities (including research) in the urban planning arena went a good way in buttressing the prestige and politico-economic status of European colonial powers such as the British and the French who were privileged to colonize tropical Africa vis-à-vis their Western counterparts who never had this privilege.

Colonial planning schemes as cultural projects

Anthony King (e.g. 1980), the doyen of colonial urban planning studies, has eloquently characterized the history of town and country planning in Britain in the industrial and post-industrial era as being culture-specific. This characterization holds equally true for the history of urban planning in Europe as a whole – it possesses unique cultural attributes rooted in historical experience, geography and the ideological beliefs of Europeans. Thus, the products of urban planning – particularly the resultant human settlements – must be seen not merely as streets, buildings and other physical structures but as artifacts bearing traces of the cultural values, economic system (particularly the mode of production), history and geography of their specific environmental context.

Why therefore did colonial authorities deem the wholesale transfer of European planning models to Africa apropos? What objectives were these authorities trying to achieve? A more important question for the purpose of this discussion is as follows: did the need to attain certain (political, ideological or economic) goals necessitate different urban planning policies and schemes? As I demonstrate below, this question must be answered in the affirmative. There is hardly any question that the production of spatial form involves conflicting socio-political forces (Low, 1995; Harvey, 1985). To the extent that this assertion is accurate, any spatio-physical structure reflects the view of the strongest of these forces. In colonial Africa, the strongest force was the colonial state. In more general terms, as Low (1995: 748) sees it, 'the design of urban space reflects the political agency of the state'. From this vantage point, architecture and urban planning can be, and are often, used as tools of domination by one group or entity over others. In colonial Africa, European colonial authorities aptly employed this tool to dominate and pacify members of the indigenous population. Urban planning served yet another important function in colonial Africa; it was instrumental in the colonizer's efforts to watch and control the movement of the colonized (see Rabinow, 1989; Foucault, 1975). In this case, urban planning, in Foucaultian terms, was used as a tool for territorial governance. The need for governments to think of the territories under their jurisdiction along the lines of the model of the city was already widely recognized in Europe by the beginning of the seventeenth century (Foucault, 2000). Thus, cities served as templates for the form of governance and spatial order that was to apply to the entire territory. Accordingly, it was believed that 'a state will be well organized when a system of policing as tight and efficient as that of the cities extends over the entire territory' (Foucault, 2000: 351). Here, it is necessary to shed some light on the concept of 'policing' alluded to by Foucault. It is certainly not the notion often conjured in common parlance – as in uniformed officers of law and order. Rather, policing in the Foucaultian – and, in fact, seventeenth century European – sense signifies a programme of governmental rationality comprising a system designed to control the conduct of people and other societal elements – e.g. traffic, social intercourse – to the point of self-sustenance without the need for intervention. This notion of spatial and territorial order – one that ensured the colonial state control over the cities in particular and any given colonial territory in general – was central to the thinking of European urban planners in colonial Africa. Thus, colonial physical space was ordered to afford the colonial state total and inordinate control over the capital city, other cities and the colonial territory as a whole, in that order.

Furthermore, it must be noted that British town planning dominated by the Garden City movement during the first half of the twentieth century was context-specific as it was intended to counter the health and other problems created by the industrial city of the nineteenth century. This place-specific fact appeared to have eluded colonial authorities as they worked indefatigably to ensure the exportation of European urban planning models to the colonized territories of Africa. However, it would appear that accusing these authorities of inattention to the cultural and ideological factors at the root of European urban planning models is misleading. Rather, it seems more apropos to view colonial urban planners as proficient not only as organizers of space but also, and above all, as agents of the colonial enterprise. In this case, their activities must be viewed as constituting part of the efforts that were designed to attain the colonial objective of 'universalizing' European culture.

This objective is in line with the so-called civilizing mission of the colonial enterprise. It can also be seen as a manifestation of the belief on the part of colonialists that European culture was inherently superior to all other cultures. Accordingly, colonialists considered it their duty to spread this culture throughout the world. This belief, what has come to be known as Euro-centricity, was therefore at the root of efforts to export European planning models to Africa during the colonial era. The specific and immediate ideological objective of this exercise was to universalize European middle-class environmental standards. In this connection, conscious efforts (e.g. via specified standards in building codes) were made to discourage the use of local materials in favour of European varieties. This caused several problems which can best be appreciated by re-examining the notion of ideology, particularly in terms of what Althusser (1971) and Therborn (1980) have called the 'subjection-qualification' dialectic (Oliga, 1996). On the one hand, subjection refers to the individual's (or subject's) 'subjugation to a particular force or social order that favors or disfavors certain values and beliefs' (Oliga, 1996: 172). In colonial Africa, the values and beliefs of the natives in relation to the production of housing and spatial form were discounted in favour of those of European origin. On the other hand, qualification has to do with training subjects to carry out activities necessary for the system's survival. Thus, the ruled unquestioningly accept the rulers' ideologies as dominant. In the French colonies, those members of the indigenous population who exhibited a propensity to quickly accept or master these ideologies were labelled 'les évolués' and given the privilege to live in residential areas that were equipped with modern amenities. Their counterparts who refused or were slow to adopt these ideologies were labelled 'les indigènes' and given access only to the most undesirable locales with few, if any, modern amenities. It is therefore hardly any wonder that in colonial Africa it became fashionable and a status symbol to live and act like Europeans. In spatio-physical terms, this meant adopting spatial structures and using building materials imported from Europe. Yet the production of space and housing is something Africans have done for centuries pre-dating the colonial era.

European economic power and the colonial state

Colonial urban planning and the concomitant Euro-centric notion of modernity succeeded in irreversibly changing the taste and consumption habits of Africans in favour of goods and services originating in Europe. Before throwing more light on this subject, it is necessary to take a moment to reflect on the concept of modernity or modernization and its implications for the development aspirations of peripheral economies. For colonial urban planners in Africa, modernization meant the replacement of indigenous land tenure and management systems, construction materials and transportation facilities with European varieties.

In effect, as Gwendolyn Wright (1991: 8) notes, this constituted a 'shift from a local to international capitalism, from production based on self-sufficiency and exchange to a system that responds only to distant consumer markets'. Colonial urban planners can therefore be said to have contributed significantly to attainment of one crucial goal of the colonial enterprise – that of expanding the market for European products. Colonies were supposed to be not only a source of raw materials for European manufacturing plants and industries, but also a captive market for European manufactured goods. More importantly, state action was required to actualize this and cognate goals. Colonial urban planning policies can therefore be seen as constituting part of this action. This line of thinking obviously oversimplifies an otherwise complex politico-economic situation. However, it does well to draw attention to the dependent economic relationship between the metropolitan and peripheral countries – in other words, the colonizing and colonized countries. In this relationship, the colonized are relegated to the role of raw material producers while the colonizers assume of the role of processing the raw materials for consumption in the metropolis and shipping the surplus to be sold at exorbitant prices in the colonies. This relationship can only be characterized as exploitative. Equally exploitative were policies such as those that were designed to regulate building activities that ostensibly favour materials produced in Europe or other Western regions. To be sure, a number of activities designed to understand the nature and utility of local building materials in Africa were initiated towards the end of the colonial era. However, it is important to note that key roles in these initiatives belonged to Europeans and not Africans.

Thus, those who stood to derive the most economic gains from the urban planning schemes designed to control the dependent or colonially driven urbanization that was occurring in colonial Africa were Europeans. The following commentary on the need for British town planners in Nigeria by Colonel J.W. Henderson, a member of the British colonial administration in 1958, lends credence to the foregoing assertion:

> With Nigeria on the threshold of independence, rapid development in its Federal capital of Lagos is taking place, and planning in Lagos today is faced with practically every problem that the United Kingdom Planner has faced in a gradual sense over the last 50 years ...Opportunity abounds for experienced officers from the United Kingdom, and also for younger planning officers to gain wide experience in a remarkably short time, where responsibility is readily available beyond what he can ever hope to obtain at present in the United Kingdom.
>
> (Henderson, 1958: 115)

The European roots of urban planning legislation on the African continent is one reason why most urban development projects on the continent continue to be contracted out to European consulting firms. It is unlikely that such economic opportunities for Europeans would have existed without the wholesale adoption of European urban planning laws occasioned by the continent's colonial experience.

The British and French colonial authorities guaranteed economic gains and opportunities for Europeans through the land reform measures they instituted in Africa. An important objective of the measures was to effectively transform land, a previously communally-controlled entity, into a commodity. In practice, this facilitated the buying, selling, transferring and alienation of land. The African land tenure system differs sharply and, in fact, conflicts with the Euro-centric system, particularly on account of the fact that it does not treat land as a commodity. More worthy of note is the fact that African customary laws recognize only groups of people or communities, and certainly not individuals, as the entities that may control or 'own' land. For Africans, land is seen as belonging to the ancestors, living and unborn members of any given community (see Meek, 1949). Essentially, therefore, under the African land tenure system, everyone has access to land. In contrast, the Euro-centric model places land exclusively at the disposal of those with the economic and/or political power.

The need on the part of Europeans to transform the traditional land tenure system was driven by many factors, the most important of which are economic in nature. Before discussing the economic benefits that colonial authorities derived from their actions in the land policy field, it is helpful to take a moment and examine some of the official reasons that were advanced for these actions. Colonial authorities contended that the African land tenure system, particularly because it assigned ownership and/ or control over land to groups as opposed to individuals, presented innumerable obstacles to economic development. More specifically, the African traditional land tenure system was incriminated for fragmenting land ownership patterns, increasing the cost of land, failing to guarantee security of tenure, stifling transferability and alienation of land ownership rights, and failing to enable the use of land as collateral for bank loans (see Njoh, 1998; Barrows and Roth, 1990; Feder and Noronha, 1987; Feeney, 1982; Tomasugi, 1980; Baron, 1978). A closer examination of these reasons reveals them as not persuasive. Hence, I contend that they were advanced to mask the economic motives of the colonial establishment. Consider the claim that traditional land tenure systems constitute a source of high land costs. Colonial authorities made no effort to empirically validate this claim. In fact, post-colonial research on this subject has revealed that land tenure and land supply are not related in any statistically significant fashion. This suggests that land costs cannot possibly be a function of the land tenure system. It has been shown that land supply problems are as serious in cities such as Karachi and Delhi, where much land is concentrated in public hands, as in Bangkok, Manila and Seoul, where land is predominantly privately owned (Brennan, 1993).

The claim that traditional land tenure systems do not guarantee security of ownership or entitlement also appears hollow. In traditional Africa, communal control over land meant communal ownership. Thus, one is guaranteed access, hence security, to land by simply belonging to a family or community. Also, whole families or communities, and not individuals, are responsible for defending their rights of entitlement to any given tract of land. Given that there is strength in numbers, it follows that groups are in a better position to articulate and defend their rights of entitlement to any piece of property than individuals. Equally indefensible is the claim that the African traditional land tenure system renders transferability of land ownership rights impossible. In traditional Africa, there was a very effective mechanism for transferring land or other property rights before the advent of European colonialism. Property could change hands through inheritance, outright transfers between kinship groups or through allocation by a chief or community leader. Finally, the claim that the African traditional land tenure system does not permit the use of land as collateral for bank or other loans is also problematic. Here, the clash of cultures is evident. While the Euro-centric model attributes an economic value to land, the African traditional model attaches importance to the land's use value. Thus, traditional Africans were known to use not land but landed property, such as oil palm trees, wine palm trees, cola nut trees and cognate cash crops, as collateral for loans. In practice, the borrower was required to transfer the rights to use these crops for any purpose to the lender until the debt was repaid.

If the African traditional land tenure system was as functional as the foregoing passage suggests, why were European colonial authorities bent on supplanting it with Euro-centric varieties? As I have already stated, the rationale for colonial land reform initiatives in Africa can be better understood within the broader context of the power and economic motives of colonialism and imperialism. There is no question that colonial powers in Africa were preoccupied with the control of land as a factor of production and perhaps more importantly as a source of political power. Jeffrey Herbst (2000) explains the colonial powers' infatuation with land as a function of Europe's history of scrambling for scarce land. Here, it is important to note the importance of land or territorial control as a means of articulating state authority. Herbst (2000: 36) underscores the value of land as a basis for state power in the following words:

> The focus on control of land as the basis of state authority is not surprising in Europe where, due to population densities, land was in short supply. Indeed, an assumption that land was scarce, and therefore control of territory was an important indication of power, underlies much of Weber's own analysis. Similarly, control of territory is the basis of international understanding of state authority since states in Europe fought about land.

This explains actions that were designed to endow the colonial state with huge parcels of land on the part of colonial land management authorities and planners. For instance, colonial authorities promulgated laws making all so-called vacant and unoccupied lands within the colonies property of the chief executive or monarch in the colonial master nation: thus, the Crown Lands, that were later converted into state lands during the post-colonial era. Citizens claiming any entitlements to occupied lands were required to formalize their claims by registering the land and securing the necessary land ownership certification.

The implications for colonial and imperial power of the aforementioned requirements were far-reaching. First, it must be understood that requiring the formalization of land entitlements and rights invariably reinforced the colonial state's ability to keep track of all transactions in land. Furthermore, this was a necessary element in the colonial powers' efforts to control their colonial territories. Also, the fact that formalizing land entitlements and land ownership rights entailed the payment of substantial sums of money into the colonial state treasury cannot be ignored. To the extent that this is true, it is easy to appreciate the fact that the land tenure reform measures effectively guaranteed the colonial state a dependable source of revenue. The revenues in this connection were materialized through the fees applicants for land certificates paid and the taxes levied on professionals such as land surveyors, architects and building contractors in the land policy field. Further revenue was also generated through direct taxes on land and landed property. To put this in perspective, it must be understood that one of the most nagging problems that colonial authorities faced, especially during the twilight of the colonial era in Africa, had to do with defraying the daunting cost of colonialism. Accordingly, the importance of revenue generation was accentuated.

This discussion will be deemed incomplete without mention of the enormous opportunities that were created for European farmers in particular and Europeans in general by the land tenure reform measures that were introduced in Africa by colonial powers. Immediately after instituting the reform measures, the colonial state proceeded with alacrity to transfer free of charge or at token prices the most fertile and/or ideally situated parcels of land to Europeans for use as agricultural or residential land. This was the case in British colonial Southern and East Africa and in German Kamerun (Cameroon). The ongoing land problematic in Zimbabwe has its roots in policies of the genre being alluded to here.

I have already discussed the practice of providing housing for plantation workers in barracks located on the plantations. Let me revisit the issue briefly here in order to demonstrate the interconnectedness of micro- and macro-colonial policies. On the surface, one may view policies to house workers as evidence of a concern for the welfare of the workers on the part of the employers. However, upon closer examination, it is revealed that these policies constitute part of the colonial enterprise's preoccupation with control and domination. From this vantage point, workers' camps or barracks were necessary to control the activities of workers twenty-four hours a day, seven days a week. As a means of advancing the economic motives of colonialism and imperialism, workers' housing was necessary to maintain a dependable workforce conveniently located in close proximity to places of work so as to reduce waste resulting from long work-related journeys, thereby maximizing productivity. The activities that were introduced in these barracks can also be seen in the same light. In fact, one reason for the sporting and related activities that were introduced by the Commonwealth Development Corporation (CDC) workers' camps in British Southern Cameroons was to inculcate in the workers a sense of discipline – an important determinant of productivity (Njoh, 2003; Kwo, 1984).

Conclusion

This chapter has demonstrated that colonial urban planning cannot be meaningfully discussed without due regard to the broader objectives of the colonial enterprise. This is particularly because colonial urban planners were neither working in isolation nor for themselves. Rather, they were working with other colonial authorities and on orders from their superiors in the colonial master nations. Thus, whether known or unbeknownst to these planners, the plans and other projects they produced constituted part of a larger scheme to realize the goals and objectives of the colonial enterprise. I have identified and discussed three of those objectives in this final chapter. In doing so, I have paid particular attention to the specific role of urban planning/planners in the process.

Therefore, colonial urban planning can no longer be seen to have assumed the stereotypical role of juxtaposing land use activities in a manner designed to facilitate spatial order. Rather, it must be recognized as a tool that immensely helped the colonial enterprise achieve its avowed or unofficial goals of acquiring knowledge; promoting and spreading European culture, ideology and worldview; and bolstering the politico-economic power of the colonial state.

Bibliography

Abu-Lughod, J.L. (1965) 'Tale of Two Cities: The Origins of Modern Cairo', *Comparative Studies in Society and History*, 7, 429–57.

Abu-Lughod, J.L. (1980) *Rabat: Urban Apartheid in Morocco*. Princeton, NJ: Princeton University Press.

Aka, E.O. (1993) 'Town and Country Planning and Administration in Nigeria', *The International Journal of Public Sector Management*, 6 (3), 47–64.

Alexander, L. (1983) 'European Planning Ideology in Tanzania', *Habitat International*, 7 (1/2), 17–36.

Allen, B. (1999) 'Power/Knowledge' in Racevskis, K. (ed.), *Critical Essays on Michel Foucault*. New York: G.K. Hall & Co.

AlSayyad, N. (1992) *Forms of Dominance: On the Architecture and Urbanism of the Colonial Enterprise*. Aldershot: Avebury.

Althusser, L. (1971) *Lenin and Philosophy and other Essays*. London: New Left Books.

Amutabi, M. N. (2005) 'Captured and Steeped in Colonial Dynamics and Legacy: The Case of Isiolo Town in Kenya' in Salm, S.J. and Falola, T. (eds), *African Urban Spaces in Historical Perspective*. Rochester, NY: Rochester University Press.

Anyumba, G. (1995) *Kisumu Town: History of the Built Form, Planning and Environment, 1890–1990*. Delft: Delft University Press.

AUF (African Unification Front) (nd) 'Cameroon: A Case Study' web-based material from: http://www.africanfront.com/conflict7.php.

Azevedo, M. (1981) 'The Human Price of Development: The Brazzaville Railroad and the Sara of Chad', *African Studies Review*, 24 (1), 1–19.

Balandier, G. (1952) 'Approche Sociologique des "Brazzaville Noires": Etude Preliminaire', *Africa: Journal of the International African Institute*, 22 (1), 23–34.

Barber, W.J. (1967) 'Urbanization and Economic Growth: The Cases of Two White Settler Territories' in Miner, H. (ed.), *The City in Modern Africa*. New York: Praeger.

Barnett, D. and Njama, K. (1966) *Mau Mau from Within: An Analysis of Kenya's Peasant Revolt*. New York: Monthly Review.

Baron, D. (1978) *Land Reform in Sub-Saharan Africa: An Annotated Bibliography*. Washington, DC: US Agency for International Development, Office of Rural Development.

Barrows, R. and Roth, M. (1990) 'Land Tenure and Investment in African Agriculture: Theory and Evidence', *Journal of Modern African Studies*, 28, 265–97.

Berman, B.J. (1984) 'Structure and Process in the Bureaucratic States of Colonial Africa', *Development and Change*, 15, 23–41.

Berman, B.J. (1993) 'The Concept of "Articulation" and the Political Economy of Colonialism', *Canadian Journal of African Studies*, 18 (2), 407–14.

Berman, B.J. (1997) 'The Perils of Bula Matari: Constraint and Power in the Colonial State', *Canadian Journal of African Studies*, 31 (3), 556–70.

Berman, B.J. (1998) 'Ethnicity and the African State: The Politics of Uncivil Nationalism', *African Affairs*, 97 (388), 305–41.

Berman, B. and Lonsdale, J. (1992) 'Crises of Accumulation, Coercion and the Colonial State: The Development of the Labour Control System, 1919–29' in B. Berman and J. Lonsdale (eds), *Unhappy Valley: Conflict in Kenya and Africa*. London: James Currey.

Berque, J. (1958) 'Medinas, Villeneuves et Bidonvilles', *Cahiers de Tunisie*, 6, 5–42.

Brennan, E.M. (1993) 'Urban Land and Housing Issues Facing the Third World' in J.D. Kasarda and A.M. Parnell (eds), *Third World Cities: Problems, Policies and Prospects*. Newbury Park: Sage.

Brode, H. (1977) *British and German East Africa: Their Economic and Commercial Relations*. New York: Arno Press.

Brunschwig, H. (1964) *French Colonialism 1871–1914: Myths and Realities*. New York: Frederick Praeger.

Bryce, J. (1898) *Impressions of South Africa*. New York and London: Macmillan & Co.

Bunche, R. (1936) 'French and British Imperialism in West Africa', *The Journal of Negro History*, 21 (1), 31–46.

Burgess, R. (1985) 'The Limits of State Self-Help Housing Programmes', *Development and Change*, 16, 217–312.

Burton, A. (2002) *The Urban Experience in Eastern Africa c. 1750 2000*. Nairobi: British Institute in Eastern Africa.

Burton, A. (2005) *African Underclass: Urbanisation, Crime and Colonial Order in Dar es Salaam*. Oxford: James Currey/Athens, OH: Ohio University Press.

Campbell, E.H. (2005) 'Formalizing the Informal Economy: Somali Refugee and Migrant Trade Networks in Nairobi', *Global Migration Perspectives*, 47, Global Commission on International Migration. http://www.gcim.org/attachements/GMP%20No%2047.pdf.

Canel, P., Delis, P. and Girard, C. (1990) *Construire la Ville Africaine: Chroniques du Citadin Promoteur*. Paris: Karthala.

Castells, M. (1978) *City, Class and Power* (trans. E. Lebas). New York: St. Martin's Press.

CEDA (1994) *Géographie*. Paris: Hatier.

Çelik, Z. (1997) *Urban Forms and Colonial Confrontations: Algiers under French Rule*. Berkeley, CA and London: University of California Press.

Cell, J.W. (1986) 'Anglo-Indian Medical Theory and the Origins of Segregation in West Africa', *The American Historical Review*, 91 (2), 307–35.

Cherry, G.E. (1980) *Shaping the World*. New York: St. Martins Press.

Chokor, B.A. (1993) 'External European Influences and Indigenous Social Values in Urban Development Planning in the Third World: The Case of Ibadan, Nigeria', *Planning Perspective*, 8, 283–306.

Christophers, S.R. and Stephens, J.W.W. (1900) 'Destruction of Anopheles in Lagos' in Royal Society, *Reports of the Malaria Committee of the Royal Society*. London: HMSO.

CIDI (1995) 'L'urbanisation en Afrique: le défi d'une croissance sans précédent', *Express* (6) Paris: Centre d'Information sur le Développement International.

Collier, P. and Lal, D. (1986) *Labour and Poverty in Kenya 1900–1980*. Oxford: Clarendon Press.

Collins, J. (1969) 'Lusaka: the Myth of the Garden City', *Zambian Urban Studies*, 2, 1–32.

Bibliography

Collins, J. (1980) 'Lusaka: Urban Planning in a British Colony, 1931–1964' in Gordon E. Cherry (ed.), *Shaping the World*. New York: St. Martins Press.

Conklin, A.L. (1998) 'Colonialism and Human Rights, A Contradiction in Terms? The Case of France and West Africa, 1895–1914', *The American Historical Review*, 103 (2), 419–42.

Cooper, N. (2000) 'Urban Planning and Architecture in Colonial Indochina', *French Cultural Studies*, 11 (1), 75–99.

Coquery-Vidrovitch, C. (1993) *Histoire des Villes d'Afrique Noire: des Origines à la Colonisation*. Paris: A. Michel.

Coquery-Vidrovitch, C. (1996) *L'Afrique Occidentale au temps de français: colonisateurs et colonisés (c. 1860–1960)*. Paris: La Découverte.

Coquery-Vidrovitch, C. and Goerg, O. (1996) *La Ville Européenne Outre Mers, un Modèle Conquérant? XVᵉ–XXᵉ Siecles*. Paris/Montréal: l'Harmattan.

Cowan, G.L. (1959) *Local Government in West Africa*. New York: Columbia University Press.

Curtin, P.D. (1985) 'Medical Knowledge and Urban Planning in Tropical Africa', *The American Historical Review*, 90 (3), 594–613.

Dahl, R.A. (1961) 'The Concept of Power' in Ulmer, S.S. (ed.), *Introductory Readings in Political Behavior*. Chicago, IL: University of Chicago Press.

Daunton, M.J. (1983) *House and Home in the Victorian City: Working Class Housing 1850–1914*. London: E. Arnold.

Daunton, M.J. (1990) *Housing the Workers: A Comparative Perspective*. Leicester: Leicester University Press.

Davidson, B. (1968) *Africa in History*. New York: Macmillan.

De Blij, H.J. (1964) *A Geography of Subsaharan Africa*. Chicago, IL: Rand McNally & Company.

Debussman, R. (1996) 'Introduction' in Debusmann, R. and Arnold, S. (eds), *Land Law and Land Ownership in Africa: Case Studies from Colonial and Contemporary Cameroon and Tanzania*. Bayreuth: Eckhard Breitinger, University of Bayreuth.

DeLancey, M.W. (1978) 'Health and Disease on the Plantations of Cameroon, 1884–1939' in Hartwig, G.W. and Patterson, K.D. (eds), *Disease in African History: An Introductory Survey and Case Studies*. Durham, NC: Duke University Press.

Desowitz, R.S. (1981) *New Guinea Tapeworms and Jewish Grandmothers: Tales of Parasites and People*. New York: W.W. Norton.

DHS (Demographic and Health Survey) (1999) *Niger: Enquête démographique et de santé 1998*. Calverton, MD: Macro International.

Doherty, J. (1979) 'Ideology and Town Planning: The Tanzanian Experience', *Antipode*, 11 (3), 12–23.

Dovey, K. (1999) *Framing Places: Mediating Power in Built Form*. New York and London: Routledge.

Dulucq, S. and Goerg, O. (1989) *Les Investissements Publics dans les Villes Africaines (1930–1985): Habitat et transports*. Paris: l'Harmattan.

Edelman, M. (1964) *The Symbolical Uses of Politics*. Urbana, IL: University of Illinois. Press.

Elleh, N. (2002) *Architecture and Power in Africa*. Westport, CT: Praeger/Greenwood.

Fanon, F. (1963) *The Wretched of the Earth*. New York: Grove Press.

Fathy, H. (1973) *Architecture for the Poor*. Chicago, IL: University of Chicago Press.

Faubion, J.D. (ed.) (2000) *Power: Essential Works of Foucault 1954–1984 (Volume 3)* (trans. R. Hurley *et al.*). New York: The New Press.

Feder, G. and R. Noronha (1987) 'Land Rights Systems and Agricultural Development in Sub-Saharan Africa', *Research Observer*, 2, 142–71.

Feeney, D. (1982) *The Political Economy of Productivity: Thai Agricultural Development 1880–1875*. Vancouver: University of British Columbia.

Fieldhouse, D.K. (1981) *Colonialism 1870–1945: An Introduction*. New York: St. Martins Press.

Fischler, R. (1995) 'Strategy and History in Professional Practice: Planning as World Making' in Liggett, H. and Perry, D.C. (eds), *Spatial Practices: Critical Exploration in Social/Spatial Theory*. Thousand Oaks, CA: Sage Publications.

Fisiy, F. C. (1992) *Power and Privilege in the Administration of Law: Land Law Reforms and Social Differentiation in Cameroon*. Leiden: African Studies Centre.

Flint J.E. (1966) *Nigeria and Ghana*, Englewood Cliffs, NJ: Prentice Hall.

Foley, D.L. (1960) 'British Town Planning: One Ideology or Three?', *The British Journal of Sociology*, 11 (3), 211–31.

Fonge, F.P. (1997) *Modernization Without Development in Africa: Patterns of Change and Continuity in Post-Independence Cameroonian Public Service*. Trenton, NJ: Africa World Press.

Forester, J. (1989) *Planning in the Face of Power*. Los Angeles, CA: University of California Press.

Foucault, M. (1975) *Suiveiller et Punir: Naissance de la Prison*. Paris: Gallimard.

Foucault, M. (1977) *Discipline and Punish: The Birth of the Prison* (trans. Alan Sheridan). New York: Vintage.

Foucault, M. (1980a) *Power/Knowledge: Selected Interviews and Other Writings 1972–1977* (ed. Colin Gordon, trans. Colin Gordon *et al.*). New York: Pantheon Books.

Foucault, M. (1980b) 'The Politics of Health in the Eighteenth Century' in Colin Gordon (ed.), *Michel Foucault, Selected Interviews and Other Writings, 1972–1977*. Brighton: Harvester Press.

Foucault, M. (1982) *Beyond Structuralism and Hermeneutics*. Brighton: Harvester Press.

Foucault, M. (2000) 'The Subject and Power', *Essential Works of Foucault 1954–1984, vol. 3*. London: Penguin.

Franqueville, A. (1984) *Yaoundé: Construire une capitale*. Paris: OSTROM.

Frenkel, S. and Western, J. (1988) 'Pretext or Prophylaxis? Racial Segregation and Malarial Mosquitos in a British Tropical Colony: Sierra Leone', *Annals of the Association of American Geographers*, 78, 211–28.

Freund, B. (1998) *The Making of Contemporary Africa: the Development of African Society Since 1800*. Boulder, CO: Lynne Rienner.

Freund, B. (2001) 'Contrasts in Urban Segregation: A Tale of Two African Cities, Durban (South Africa) and Abidjan (Côte d'Ivoire)', *Journal of Southern African Studies*, 27 (3), 527–46.

Friedrich, C.J. (1963) *Man and His Government*. New York: Oxford University Press.

Fry, E. M. (1946) 'Town Planning in West Africa', *African Affairs*, 45 (181), 197–204.

Fyfe, C. (1968) 'The Foundation of Freetown' in Fyfe, C. and Jones, E. (eds), *Freetown: A Symposium*. Oxford: Oxford University Press, pp. 1–23.

Gapyisi, E. (1989) *Le défi urbain en Afrique*. Paris: l'Harmattan.

Gerth, H. and Mills, C.W. (1964) *Character and Social Structure: The Psychology of Social Institutions*. New York: Harcourt Brace & World, Inc.

Gibbs & Partners (1948) *Tanganyika Territory: A Plan for Dar es Salaam*. Unpublished Document.

Goerg, O. (1986) *Commerce et colonisation en Guinée 1850 –1913*. Paris: l'Harmattan.

Bibliography

Goerg, O. (1998) 'From Hill Station (Freetown) to Downtown Conakry (First Ward): Comparing French and British Approaches to Segregation in Colonial Cities at the Beginning of the Twentieth Century', *Canadian Journal of African Studies*, 32 (1), 1–31.

Gordon, E. (1950) 'A Land Use Map of Kuntaur in the Gambia', *The Geographical Journal*, 116 (4/6), 216–17.

Gray, A. (1904) 'West Africa', *Journal of the Society of Comparative Legislation* (New Ser.), 5 (2), 399–407.

Gray, C. and Ngolet, F. (1999) 'Lambaréné, Okoume and the Transformation of Labor along the Middle Ogooue (Gabon), 1870–1945', *The Journal of African History*, 40 (1), 87–107.

Gray, G. (1970) *Rhodesia: A Human Geography*. London: University of London Press.

Greenwood, A. and Howell, J. (1980) 'Urban Local Authorities' in Tordoff, W. (ed.) *Administration in Zambia*. Madison, WI: University of Wisconsin Press/Manchester: Manchester University Press.

Griffiths, I.L. (1995) *The African Inheritance*. London and New York: Routledge.

Gugler, J. and Flanagan, W.G. (1978) *Urbanization and Social Change in West Africa*. Cambridge: Cambridge University Press.

Harvey, D. (1985) *The Urbanization of Capital: Theory of Capitalist Urbanization*. Washington, DC: Johns Hopkins University Press.

Hebbert, M. (1999) 'A City in Good Shape: Town Planning and Public Health', *Town Planning Review*, 70 (4), 433–53.

Heisler, H. (1971) 'The Creation of a Stabilized Urban Society: A Turning Point in the Development of Northern Rhodesia', *African Affairs*, 70 (279), 125–45.

Henderson, J.W. (1958) 'Lagos, Nigeria: The Work of the Lagos Executive Development Board', *Journal of the Town Planning Institute*, 44, 114–18.

Herbst, J. (2000) *States and Power in Africa: Comparative Lessons in Authority and Control*. Princeton, NJ: Princeton University Press.

Hill, M.F. (1957) *Permanent Way: The Story of the Kenya and Uganda Railway*. Nairobi: East African Railways and Harbours.

Hillier, B. and Hanson, J. (1984) *The Social Logic of Space*. New York: Cambridge University Press.

Hoch, C. (1984) 'Pragmaticism, Planning and Power', *Journal of Planning Education and Research*, 4 (2), 86–95.

Hoch, C. (1994) *What Planners Do: Power, Politics and Persuasion*. Chicago, IL and Washington, DC: American Planning Association.

Home, R.K. (1974) 'The Influence of Colonial Government Upon Urbanisation in Nigeria'. Unpublished PhD thesis, University of London.

Home, R.K. (1983) 'Town Planning, Segregation and Indirect Rule in Colonial Nigeria', *Third World Planning Review*, 5 (2), 165–175.

Home, R.K. (1990) 'Town Planning and Garden Cities in the British Colonial Empire 1910–1940', *Planning Perspectives*, 5, 23–37.

Home, R.K. (1997) *Of Planting and Planning: The Making of British Colonial Cities*. London: E & FN Spon.

Home, R.K. (2000) 'From Barrack Compounds to the Single-Family House: Planning Worker Housing in Colonial Natal and Northern Rhodesia', *Planning Perspectives*, 15, 327–47.

Hull, R.W. (1976) *African Cities and Towns before the European Conquest*. London and New York: W.W. Norton & Co.

Huxley, E. (1969) *Settlers of Kenya*. London: Longmans, Green and Co.

Jarosz, L. (1992) 'Constructing the Dark Continent: Metaphor as Geographic Representation of Africa', *Geografiska Annaler. Series B, Human Geography*, 74 (2), 105–15.

Jarrett, H.R. (1948) 'Population and Settlement in the Gambia', *Geographical Review*, 8 (4), 633–6.

Kanyeihamba, G.W. (1980) 'The Impact of Received Law on Planning and Development in Anglophone Africa', *International Journal of Urban and Regional Research*, 4, 239–66.

Katzenellenbogen, S.E. (1975) 'The Miner's Frontier, Transport and General Economic Development' in Duignan, P. and Gann, L.H. (eds), *Colonialism in Africa, Vol. IV: The Economics of Colonialism*. Cambridge: Cambridge University Press.

Kay, G. (1970) *Rhodesia: A Human Geography*. London: University of London Press.

Kenny, J.T. (1997) 'Claiming the High Ground: Theories of Imperial Authority and the British Hill Stations in India', *Political Geography*, 16 (8), 655–73.

Khapoya, V.B. (1998) *The African Experience: An Introduction* (2nd edn). Upper Saddle River, NJ: Prentice Hall.

King, A.D. (1976) *Colonial Urban Development: Culture, Social Power and Environment*. London: Routledge and Kegan Paul.

King, A.D. (1980) 'Exporting Planning: The Colonial and Neo-Colonial Experience' in Cherry, G. (ed.), *Shaping an Urban World*. New York: St. Martin's Press.

King, A.D. (1990) *Urbanism, Colonialism, and the World Economy: Cultural and Spatial Foundations of the World Urban System*. London and New York: Routledge.

Ki-Zerbo, J. (1978) *Histoire de l'Afrique Noire: D'Hier à Demain*. Paris: Hatier.

Knights, D. and Willmott, H. (1985) 'Power and Identity in Theory and Practice', *Sociological Review*, 33 (1), 32–46.

Konadu-Agyemang, K. (2001) *The Political Economy of Housing and Urban Development in Africa: Ghana's Experience from Colonial Times to 1998*. Westport, CT: Praeger.

Kwo, M. (1984) 'Community Education and Community Development in Cameroon: The British Colonial Experience, 1922–1961', *Community Development Journal*, 19 (4), 204–13.

Labor Law Talk Forum (nd) 'House Arrest.' http://www.dictionary.laborlawtalk.com/House_arrest.

Lasswell, H.D. and Kaplan, A. (1950) *Power and Society: A Framework for Political Inquiry*. New Haven, CT: Yale University Press.

Lastarria-Cornhiel, S. (1997) 'Impact of Privatization on Gender and Property Rights in Africa', *World Development*, 25, 1317–33.

Le Vine, V. (1964) *The Cameroon Federal Republic*. Ithaca, NY and London: Cornell University Press.

Lefebvre, H. (1974) *The Production of Space* (trans. D. Nicholson-Smith). Oxford: Blackwell.

Lewis, M.D. (1962) 'One Hundred Million Frenchmen: The Assimilationist Theory in French Colonial Policy', *Comparative Studies in Society and History*, 4 (2), 129–53.

Lewis, R.A. (1952) *Edwin Chadwick and the Public Health Movement 1832–1854*. London: Longmans.

Lipton, M. (1977) *Why Poor People Stay Poor: The Urban Bias in World Development*. Cambridge, MA: Harvard University Press.

Lonsdale, J. (2002) 'Town Life in Colonial Kenya' in Burton, A. (ed.), *The Urban Experience in Eastern Africa c. 1750–2000*. Nairobi: British Institute in Eastern Africa.

Low, S.M. (1995) 'Indigenous Architecture and the Spanish American Plaza in Mesoamerica and the Caribbean', *American Anthropologist*, New Series, 97 (4), 748–62.

Lugard, F. (1922) *The Dual Mandate in British Tropical Africa*. London: Blackwood.

Lukes, S. (1974) *Power: A Radical View*. London: Macmillan.

Mabogunje, A.L. (1981) *The Development Process: A Spatial Perspective*. New York: Holmes & Meier.

Macharia, K. (1992) 'Slum Clearance and the Informal Economy in Nairobi', *The Journal of Modern African Studies*, 30 (2), 221–36.

Mamdani, M. (1996) *Citizen and Subject: Contemporary Africa and the Legacy of Late Colonialism*. Princeton, NJ: Princeton University Press.

Mannheim, K. (1950) *Freedom, Power and Democratic Planning*. New York: Oxford University Press.

Mannheim, K. (1985) *Ideology and Utopia, An Introduction to the Sociology of Knowledge*. New York: Harcourt Brace & Co.

Markus, T.A. (1993) *Building and Power: Freedom and Control in the Origin of Modern Building Types*. New York and London: Routledge.

Martin, P.M. (1995) *Leisure and Society in Colonial Brazzaville*. Cambridge: Cambridge University Press.

Massigli, R. (1957) 'New Conceptions of French Policy in Tropical Africa', *International Affairs*, 33 (4), 403–15.

Mazrui, A.A. (1969) 'European Exploration and Africa's Self-Discovery', *The Journal of Modern African Studies*, 7 (4), 661–6.

Mazrui, A.A. (1983) 'Francophone Nations and English-Speaking States: Imperial Ethnicity and African Political Formation' in Rothchild, D. and Olorunsula, A. (eds), *State Versus Ethnic Claim: African Policy Dilemma*. Boulder, CO: Westview.

Mazrui, A.A. (1986) *The Africans: A Triple Heritage*. Boston, MA and Toronto: Little, Brown & Company.

Meek, C.K. (1949) *Land Law and Custom in the Colonies* (2nd edn). Oxford, London and New York: Oxford University Press.

Meek, C.K. (1957) *Land Tenure and Land Administration in Nigeria and the Cameroons*. London: HM Stationery Office.

Miliband, R. (1969) *The State in Capitalist Society: An Analysis of the Western System of Power*. New York: Basic Books.

Mills, C.W. (1956) *The Power Elite*. New York: Oxford University Press.

Murunga, G.R. (2005) '"Inherently Unhygienic Race": Plague and the Origins of Settler Dominance in Nairobi, 1899–1907' in Salm, S.J. and Falola, T. (eds), *African Urban Spaces in Historical Perspective*. Rochester, NY: Rochester University Press.

Myers, G.A. (1998) 'Intellectual of Empire: Eric Dutton and Hegemony in British Africa', *Annals of the Association of American Geographers*, 88 (1), 1–27.

Myers, G.A. (2003) 'Designing Power: Forms and Purposes of Colonial Model Neighborhoods in British Africa', *Habitat International*, 27, 193–204.

Njoh, A.J. (1995) 'Building and Urban Land Use Controls in Developing Countries: A Critical Appraisal of the Kumba (Cameroon) Zoning Ordinance', *Third World Planning Review*, 17, 337–56.

Njoh, A.J. (1998) 'The Political Economy of Urban Land Reforms in a Post-Colonial State', *International Journal of Urban and Regional Research*, 22, 408–23.

Njoh, A.J. (1999a) 'The State, Urban Development Policy and Society in Cameroon', *Cities*, 16 (2), 111–22.

Njoh, A.J. (1999b) *Urban Planning, Housing and Spatial Structures in Sub-Saharan Africa: Nature, Impact and Development Implications of Exogenous Forces*. Aldershot: Ashgate.

Njoh, A.J. (2000) 'Continuity and change in Cameroonian Land Policy', *Planning Perspectives*, 15 (3), 241–65.

Njoh, A.J. (2002) 'Development Implications of Colonial Land and Human Settlement Schemes in Cameroon', *Habitat International*, 26, 399–415.

Njoh, A.J. (2003) *Planning in Contemporary Africa: The State, Town Planning and Society in Cameroon.* Aldershot: Ashgate.

Njoh, A.J. (2004) 'The Experience and Legacy of French Colonial Urban Planning in Sub-Saharan Africa', *Planning Perspectives*, 19, 435–54.

Nye, Jr., J. (1963) 'Tanganyika's Self-Help', *Transition*, 11, 35–9.

Oliga, J.C. (1996) *Power, Ideology, and Control.* New York and London: Plenum Press.

Olu-Wright, R.J. (1968) 'The Physical Growth of Freetown' in Fyfe, C. and Jones, E. (eds), *Freetown: A Symposium.* Oxford: Oxford University Press, pp. 24–37.

Omotola, J.A. (1991) 'Planning Law in Nigeria', *Third World Planning Review*, 13 (4), 381–98.

Parnell, S. (1993) 'Creating Racial Privilege: The Origins of South African Public Health and Town Planning Legislation', *Journal of Southern African Studies*, 19 (3), 471–88.

Parnell, S. and Mabin, A. (1995) 'Rethinking Urban South Africa', *Journal of Southern African Studies*, 21 (1), 39–61.

Partridge, P.H. (1963) 'Some Notes on the Concept of Power', *Political Studies*, 11, 107–125.

Pedler, F. (1975) 'British Planning and Private Enterprise in Colonial Africa' in Duignan, P. and Gann, L.H. (eds), *Colonialism in Africa, Vol. IV: The Economics of Colonialism.* Cambridge: Cambridge University Press.

Peemans, J.-P. (1975) 'Capital Accumulation in the Congo under Colonialism: The Role of the State' in Duignan, P. and Gann, L.H. (eds), *Colonialism in Africa, Vol. IV: The Economics of Colonialism.* Cambridge: Cambridge University Press.

Pellow, D. (1991) 'The Power of Space in the Evolution of an Accra Zongo', *Ethnohistory*, 38 (4), 414–50.

Perlstein, M. (1943) 'L'enseignement en Afrique Equatoriale Française', *Africa: Journal of the International African Institute*, 14 (3), 130–5.

Peterson, J. (1968) 'The Enlightenment and the Founding of Freetown: An Interpretation of Sierra Leone History, 1787–1816' in Fyfe, C. and Jones, E. (eds), *Freetown: A Symposium.* Oxford: Oxford University Press.

Peterson, J. (1979) 'The Impact of Sanitary Reform Upon American Urban Planning', *Journal of Social History*, 13, 84–9.

Phillips, A. (1989) *The Enigma of Colonialism: British Policy in West Africa.* London: James Currey/Bloomington and Indianapolis, IN: Indiana University Press.

Polèse, M. (1997) 'Urbanisation et Développement', *Express sur le Développement.* (No. 4) Centre d'Information sur le Développement International/Agence Canadienne de Développement International (ACDI).

Porteous, J.D. (1970) 'The Nature of the Company Town', *Transactions of the Institute of British Geographers*, (51), 127–42.

Poulantzas, N. (1973) *Political Power and Social Classes.* London: New Left Books.

Rabinow, P. (1989) *French Modern: Norms and Forms of the Social Environment.* Chicago, IL: University of Chicago Press.

Rakodi, C. (1995) *Harare, Inheriting a Settler-Colonial City: Change or Continuity?* New York: John Wiley & Sons.

Ranger, T. (1979) 'White Presence and Power in Africa', *Journal of African History*, 20 (4), 463–9.

Reese, J.G. (1952) 'Housing in a Gambian Village', *African Affairs*, 51 (204), 230–7.

Republic of Cameroon (nd) *Land Tenure and State Lands.* Yaoundé: National Printing Press.

Riddell, J.R. (1970) *Spatial Dynamics of Modernization in Sierra Leone.* Evanston, IL: Northwestern University Press.

Riddell, J.C. (1988) 'Dynamics of Land Tenure and Spontaneous Changes in African Agrarian System' in FAO (ed.), *Land Reform: Land Settlement and Cooperatives.* Rome: Food and Agricultural Organization.

Robinson, K. (1956) 'A Survey of the Background Material for the Study of Government in French Tropical Africa', *The American Political Science Review*, 50 (1), 179–98.

Robinson, R. (1964) 'Introduction' in H. Brunshwig (ed.), *French Colonialism 1871–1914: Myths and Realities.* New York: Praeger.

Robson, K. and Cooper, D. (1989) 'Power and Management Control' in Chua, W.F., Lowe, E.A. and Puxty, A.G. (eds), *Critical Perspectives in Management Control.* London: Macmillan.

Ross, R. and Telcamp, G.J. (1985) *Colonial Cities: Essays on Urbanism in a Colonial Context.* Leiden: Leiden University Press.

Salm, S.J. and Falola, T. (2005) *African Urban Spaces in Historical Perspective.* Rochester, NY: Rochester University Press.

Schaffer, D. (1982) *Garden Cities for America: The Radburn Experience.* Philadelphia, PA: Temple University Press.

Schön, D.A. (1983) *The Reflective Practitioner: How Professionals Think in Action.* New York: Basic Books.

Shively, W.P. (2001) *Power and Choice: An Introduction to Political Science.* Boston, MA: McGraw-Hill.

Simon, D. (1992) *Cities, Capital and Development: African Cities in the World Economy.* London: Belhaven Press.

Sinou, A. (1993) *Comptoirs et Villes Coloniales du Sénégal: Saint Louis, Gorée, Dakar.* Paris: Karthala/l'ORSTOM.

Sinou, A. (1995) *Le Comptoir de Ouidah: Une Ville Africaine Singulière.* Paris: Karthala.

Sinou, A., Poinsot, J. and Sternadel, J. (1989) *Les Villes d'Afrique Noire: Politiques et Opérations d'Urbanisme et d'Habitat entre 1650 et 1960.* Paris: Ministère de la Coopération et du Développement.

Souillou, J. (1989) *Douala: Un Siècle en Images.* Paris: L'Harmattan.

Southorn, T. (1944), 'The Gambia: Background for Progress', *Journal of the Royal African Society*, 43 (170), 10–15.

Stark, D. (nd) 'Urbanisation and Cultural Assimilation in British and French West Africa 1900–60.' Unpublished electronic paper, from http://www.Donaldstark.co.uk/baguette.html (retrieved, Sept. 9, 2005).

Stevens, R.M. (1955) 'Planning Legislation', *Colonial Building Notes*, 31, 1–15.

Strassman, P.W. (1986) 'Types of Neighbourhood and Home-Based Enterprises: Evidence from Lima, Peru', *Urban Studies*, 23, 485–500.

Stren, R. (1972) 'Urban Policy in Africa: A Political Analysis', *African Studies Review*, 15 (3), 489–516.

Stren, R.E. and White, R.R. with Coquery, M. (1993) *Villes Africaines en Crise: Gérer la Croissance Urbaine au Sud du Sahara.* Paris: l'Harmattan.

Therborn, G. (1980) *The Ideology of Power and the Power of Ideology.* London: Verso/New Left Books.

Tipple, A.G. (1987) *The Development of Housing Policy in Kumasi, Ghana 1901–1981.* Newcastle Upon Tyne: Centre for Architectural Research and Development Overseas.

Tomasugi, T. (1980) *A Structural Analysis of Thai Economic History: A Case Study of a Northern Chao Phraya Delta Village.* Tokyo: Institute for Developing Economics.

Tordoff, W. (1980) *Administration in Zambia*. Madison, WI: University of Wisconsin Press/ Manchester: Manchester University Press.

Tordoff, W. (1984) *Government and Politics in Africa*. London: Macmillan.

Turner, J.F.C. (1972) 'Housing as a Verb' in Turner, J.F.C. and Fichter, R. (eds), *Freedom to Build: Dweller Control of the Housing Process*. New York: Macmillan.

Uganda Railway (1908) *The Uganda Railway: British East Africa, from Mombasa to Lake Victoria Nyanza and by Steamer Round the Great Lake*. London: Waterlow and Sons.

United Nations (1981) *Building Codes and Regulations in Developing Countries*, Report of the Proceedings of the United Nations Seminar of Experts on Building Codes and Regulations in Developing Countries held in Talbert and Stockholm, Sweden, 17–24 March 1980. Nairobi: United Nations Centre for Human Settlement (UNCHS).

USLC (nd) 'Country Studies Chad/French-and-Colonial Administration', http://www.country-studies.com.

Van Zwanenberg, R. and King, A. (1975) *Colonial Capitalism and Labour in Kenya, 1919–1939*. Nairobi: East African Literature Bureau.

Vassal, G. (1932) 'French Equatorial Africa', *Journal of Royal African Society*, 31 (123), 167–72.

Venard, J.-L. (1986) *Intervention Française dans le Secteur Urbain en Afrique Noire Francophone*. Paris: Economica.

Weber, M. (1991) 'Structures of Power' in Gerth, H.H. and Mills, C.M. (eds), *From Max Weber: Essays in Sociology*. London and New York: Routledge.

Weinstein, B. (1970) 'Felix Eboue and the Chiefs: Perceptions of Power in Early Oubangui-Chari', *The Journal of African History*, 11 (1), 107–26.

Wekwete, K. (1995) 'Planning Law in Sub-Saharan Africa: A Focus on the Experiences in Southern and Eastern Africa', *Habitat International*, 19, 13–28.

White, L.W.T., Silberman, L. and Anderson, P.R. (1948) *Nairobi: Master Plan for a Colonial Capital*. London: HM Stationery Office.

Willis, J. (1995) '"Men on the Spot", Labor, and the Colonial State in British East Africa: The Mombassa Water Supply, 1911–1917', *International Journal of African Historical Studies*, 28 (1), 25–48.

Winters, C. (1982) 'Urban Morphogenesis in Francophone Black Africa', *Geographical Review*, 72 (2), 139–54.

Wright, G. (1987) 'Tradition in the Service of Modernity: Architecture and Urbanism in French Colonial Policy, 1900–1930', *The Journal of Modern History*, 59 (2), 291–316.

Wright, G. (1991) *The Politics of Design in French Colonial Urbanism*. Chicago, IL: University of Chicago Press.

Yeoh, B. (2003) *Contested Space in Colonial Singapore: Power Relations and the Urban Built Environment*. Singapore: Singapore University Press.

Young, C. (1994) *The African Colonial State in Comparative Perspective*. New Haven, CT and London: Yale University Press.

Yudelman, M. (1975) 'Imperialism and the Transfer of Agricultural Techniques' in Duignan, P. and Gann, L.H. (eds), *Colonialism in Africa, Vol. IV: The Economics of Colonialism*. Cambridge: Cambridge University Press.

Index